WARSHIPS OF
THE USSR AND RUSSIA
1945–1995

WARSHIPS OF THE USSR AND RUSSIA 1945–1995

A. S. Pavlov

Translator: Gregory Tokar

Editor (English-language edition): Norman Friedman

Naval Institute Press

Annapolis, Maryland

Library of Congress Cataloging-in-Publication Data

Pavlov, A.S.
[Voennye korabli SSSR i Rossii, 1945–1995. English]
Warships of the USSR and Russia, 1945–1995 / A.S. Pavlov ;
translator, Gregory Tokar ; editor (English language edition),
Norman Friedman.
     p.   cm.
 Includes index.
 ISBN 1-55750-671-X
 1. Soviet Union. Voenno-Morskoĭ Flot—Lists of vessels.
2. Russia (Federation). Voenno-Morskoĭ Flot—Lists of vessels.
3. Warships—Soviet Union. 4. Warships—Russia (Federation)
I. Friedman, Norman, 1946– . II. Title.
VA573.A2813 1997
 359.8'3'0947—dc21   96-30077

Printed in the United States of America on acid-free paper ∞

04 03 02 01 00 99 98 97   9 8 7 6 5 4 3 2
First printing

Contents

Part I.

Ships of Prewar Design

{Note: All class names are NATO classes except for those in *italic* which are unique to this Navy.}

Part II.

Ships of Postwar Design

Part III

Transports and Cargo Vessels

Project / Class Name

Author's Introduction

Until very recently, the great majority of Russians interested in navies could not obtain accurate data, either on their own fleet or even on foreign fleets. This gap was partially filled by the first edition of this handbook (published in Yakutsk in 1991), describing the Soviet fleet of 1990–91. It relied heavily on the famous *Jane's Fighting Ships,* with all its errors and omissions. Even so, the small printing of 3000 copies was soon gone, sold both to enthusiasts and to naval personnel. A second edition (4000 copies) included data and corrections down to late 1991 or early 1992, i.e., up to the time of the breakup of the Soviet Union and of its fleet. It included numerous suggestions and corrections from readers. After this edition sold out (in a year), a third was planned, but because so few ships had been added to the fleet and so many had been stricken, the author decided instead to produce a complete record of the period 1946–1995, excluding war prizes, civilian vessels taken over only temporarily, or Lend-Lease ships. Thus this handbook naturally includes many ships already stricken. This is the first book of its kind. Unfortunately it was prepared and completed by an enthusiast without access to complete official data. Professionals probably will find mistakes and omissions, but the author hopes that readers will continue to help him, so that corrections can be made in a future edition.

Most of the drawings were made by the author and are published here for the first time. Technical and combat characteristics of ships were taken from open domestic and foreign sources. Numbers of projects of ships come from the open press. Technical descriptions cannot of course be entirely accurate, so anyone using them should be aware of this source.

Even so, the data in this handbook should be useful to many: to naval enthusiasts, to naval personnel and cadets, to modelers, and to those who are simply interested in the equipment and glorious history of our country.

The author would like to thank all (about 550 people) who assisted in the preparation of this edition.

This edition closed for publication in August 1994. [Ed.: Corrections from a revised Russian edition have been included.]

A. S. Pavlov
677000 Yakutsk, 43 Kurashova St., Apt 212

Author's Notes

This handbook is in three sections: (i) Ships built and completed from prewar and wartime projects, including those launched and completed (to modified designs) after December 1945. Not included are prizes, reparations, and ships never completed. (ii) Ships of postwar projects of all types specially built for the navy (known as Naval Forces until 10 Mar. '53). (iii) Civilian-type ships and vessels included in the navy list except for ships used only for single assignments.

Ships and vessels are arranged by ranks and classes in each section. Names of ships and projects are arranged in alphabetical order and by increasing numbers. If possible, ships are listed in order of completion. Unrealized projects and ships not launched (e.g. carrier *Ulyanovsk*, projected nuclear destroyer project *Anchar*) are not included.

Editor's Introduction

This is a remarkable book. It is our first full glimpse of the huge navy the Soviet Union built up after World War II. Although much was known in the West about major warships, in many cases the numbers built, and even many of the names, of those ships were unknown outside the Soviet Navy. Names of major equipment were unknown to the point that they were called mainly by official NATO nicknames. Nor was there much knowledge of the Project numbers under which Soviet warships were designed, built, and known within the Soviet Union. In a few cases, particularly major river combatants, ships were entirely unknown in the West. Now Mr. Pavlov has very largely solved those problems to present a full and detailed picture of the ships built in the Soviet Union, their origins and their equipment.

The author, Alexander Sergeevich Pavlov, is a naval architect at the Lena Amalgamated River Shipping Line. For his first edition, he not only wrote and produced drawings, but he also typeset and made up the book, stitching together the sheets to produce the bound copies published. His second edition was about twice the size of the first; in effect this book is his third edition, extending back to include the post–World War II history of the Soviet fleet.

To some extent, Pavlov's books can be considered the culmination of efforts by a large circle of Russian ship enthusiasts, who during the Soviet period could never publish and had no legal access to information. Nevertheless, they accumulated handwritten notes, and now they are publishing a variety of magazines and books. Most prominent among the magazines in recent years has been *Gangut,* which published the first full history of the first class of Russian nuclear submarines, Project 627. A Russian magazine compared Pavlov himself to Fred T. Jane, who also started as an enthusiast, and who also did his own research and made his own sketches for his first edition in 1897.

While this book was being compiled, the official Russian press began to print histories of individual ship types, in the magazines *Morskoi Sbornik* (roughly equivalent to the *Proceedings* of the U.S. Naval Institute) and *Sudostroenie* (the official shipbuilding journal, perhaps broadly comparable to *Naval Engineers Journal).* Some accounts have also appeared in the official English/Russian-language magazine *Military Parade,* which describes Russian equipment. As the 300th anniversary of the Russian Navy (1996) approached, books on the navy began to appear. Perhaps the most prominent is Vice Admiral V. N. Burov's, *Otechestvennoe Veonnoe Korablestroenie v Tret'em Stoletii svoi Istorii (National Naval Shipbuilding in the Third Century of its History),* published by Sudostroeniye Press in St. Petersburg in 1995. In addition, S. S. Berezhnoi, who has published complete fleet lists of the Soviet Navy up through 1945, has also published an account (with names, dates, and fates) of destroyers and larger post–1945 ships. A remarkable new book by E. A. Shitikov, V. N. Krasnov, and V. V. Balabin, *Korabl-Stroenie V SSSR V God' Velikoi Otechestvennoi Voyeniy (Naval Shipbuilding in the USSR During the Years of the Great Patriotic War)* describes wartime and immediate postwar programs in considerable detail, providing information on some projects closely related to ships Pavlov de-

Table 1: Central Design Bureaus (TsKBs)

TsKB-1   Small craft (e.g., torpedo boats) at Nikolaev (Yard 445).

TsKB-4   The prewar battleship design office. It did not survive the war, and the battleship project was transferred to TsKB-17.

TsKB-5   Small combatants, including missile boats and missile systems; merged with Almaz (TsKB-19) by about 1973. This may also have been designated Special KB-5 (OKB-5) as an NKVD (predecessor of the KGB) design bureau; as such it developed Project 183. TsKB-5 was at Yard 5 at Leningrad, at which Lend-Lease torpedo boats were assembled.

TsKB-16   (Malakhit): hived off from TsKB-17 to develop heavy cruisers postwar, then assigned to submarine design.

TsKB-17   (Nevskiy PKB): the main prewar cruiser-destroyer design office; later responsible for carriers.

TsKB-18   (Rubin): the sole submarine design office until after World War II.

TsKB-19   (Almaz): small combatants; also developed postwar riverine craft and air-cushion vehicles.

TsKB-32   Small combatants, merged with TsKB-50 in 1942.

TsKB-36   Mines and sweeps, joined with remains of TsKB-39 as NII-400 in 1946.

TsKB-39   Torpedoes, split in 1943 into OKB-182 and OKB-175.

TsKB-50   Small combatants; merged with TsKB-32 in 1942. Later revived as a minesweeper design office (Western PKB); absorbed TsKB-363 from Leningrad. It also designed some amphibious ships.

TsKB-51   River craft.

TsKB-52   Electronics.

TsKB-53   (Northern PKB): destroyer and frigate design office. This organization designed the Kirov class.

TsKB-112 (Lazurit): originally KB-112, the local design office of the Krasnoe Sormovo submarine yard at Gorkiy (now Nizhniy Novgorod), later a major submarine design office.

TsKB-143 Walter and then nuclear submarine design (Peregudov design bureau), later merged into TsKB-16, now Malakhit.

TsKB-820 Design office for Kaliningrad, created about 1950; frigate designs from Project 50 onwards (Project 50 was developed by the Leningrad office of this TsKB, but most designers were later transferred to Kaliningrad).

scribes. Finally, Aleksandr Shirokorad has published a number of remarkable historical articles on Soviet-era ships and weapons, including an account of the cruisers planned for the 1956–65 program.

I have inserted some notes from these books and articles, and I have used Mr. Berezhnoi's dates for the larger vessels. I have also indicated Western lists of transfers abroad when they conflict with Pavlov's data. The reader should not consider these corrections, since in many cases precise information about transfers probably was not easily available to Westerners. In some cases, Pavlov's data may indicate unsuccessful plans. Except for dates, I have indicated all insertions by Ed.: and by square brackets.

Some notes on Soviet design practice and overall shipbuilding policy seem to be in order.

Pavlov mentions several stages in the origins of ships. One is the decree by the Council of Ministers authorizing construction. Another is the issue of a set of tactical-technical requirements (a TTZ). Others are the completion of the sketch project (design), and the technical project (design). Council of Ministers decrees seem to have begun only after Stalin's death.

Ships began as elements of larger programs developed by the navy and other government agencies. Planning had to begin well before any orders were placed, because in a planned command economy provision had to be made for timely orders for all materials and subsystems, and probably even for transportation. Major subsystems could come from all over the Soviet Union; indeed, the attempt seems to have been made to distribute production facilities so as to help bind the Union together (with disastrous consequences for shipbuilding once the Union came apart in 1991). For example, production of large marine gas turbines was centralized in Ukraine.

Development by the main naval staff began with an operational-tactical requirement (OTZ), a set of desired capabilities. A higher naval institute (NII) within the navy developed sketch plans to test the feasibility of the OTZ. At times, particularly immediately after World War II, the main design bureaus (TsKBs) might help produce such feasibility studies. The results were fed back into the main naval staff, which then produced the tactical-technical requirement (TTZ) to which the ship was actually developed. At this stage the main naval staff had in hand a rough sketch design, which might or might not form the basis for the actual design. The shipbuilding ministry became involved at this point, probably in part because it had to work out the material consequences of various alternative TTZs.

Detailed design was the province of the design bureaus (KBs, most of them central KBs or TsKBs). They developed the sketch design and then the technical design from which the ship was built. In some cases, such as that of the *Moskva* class, considerable changes were made during the design process. Too, in some cases (such as that of the *Victor* class, Project 671), the TsKB could sell the navy something quite different from that envisaged by the NII and the main staff. However, it should be emphasized that it was the naval staff and the NII, not the design bureaus, which generally developed basic designs. In a very few cases, TsKBs were called upon to offer competitive solutions to a TTZ, but much more often a TTZ would be associated with a single specialist TsKB.

Several TsKBs are now called PKBs, planning and design bureaus.

The main design bureaus (current names in parentheses) are listed in Table 1.

At the end of World War II, the decision was made to continue the ambitious prewar building program. That entailed rebuilding the shattered naval industry. A special naval commission was formed to discuss the lessons of World War II, and to develop a ten-year

Table 2: Stalin's Ten-Year Plan (1946–55)

Key:
    (1) Initial navy program proposal
    (2) Reduced navy program proposal
    (3) Ten-Year Plan (ships to be completed by 1 January 1956)
    (4) Ships actually completed during 1946–55

	(1)	(2)	(3)	(4)
Battleships	9	4	0	0
Heavy Cruisers	12	10	4	0
Cruisers	30	30	0	0
Light Cruisers	60	54	30	19
Large Carriers	9	6	0	0
Small Carriers	6	6	0	0
Seagoing Monitors	18	12	18	0
Large Destroyers	144	132	0	0
Destroyers	222	226	188	85
Seagoing Gunboats	42	38	36	0
SKR	546	558	177	48
Large ASW Craft (BO)	327	345	345	157
Large Submarines	168	168	40	6
Medium Submarines	204	204	204	151
Small Submarines	117	123	123	66
Fleet Minesweepers	110	110	30	0
Base Minesweepers	237	237	400	about 150
Roadstead Minesweepers	297	330	306	over 100
Small ASW Craft (MO)	564	600	600	86
Torpedo Boats (TK)	738	828	828	about 730
Landing Craft	476	135	195	1

Table 3: Performance of the Ten-Year Plan, 1946–55

	1946–50	1951–55
Light Cruisers	8 (5)	22 (14)
Destroyers	46 (38)	142 (47)
SKR	23 (2)	154 (46)
Base Minesweepers	35 (60)	(no data)
Roadstead Minesweepers	82 (65)	(no data)
Large Submarines	17 (0)	23 (6)
Medium Submarines	23 (2)	181 (149)
Small Submarines	105 (33)	18 (33)
Torpedo Boats	418 (280)	(no data)

Numbers in parentheses are actual versus planned figures. Planned figures are presumably those projected when the plan was approved in 1945.

program, 1946–55. Note that it spanned two conventional Five-Year Plans. The second half was more speculative than the first, involving designs to be developed during the first half of the plan and open to some revision depending on how they developed.

Stalin's plan was to have been followed by a second ten-year program, 1956–65, but in 1955 Khrushchev seems to have decided to suspend the plan so as to concentrate on new technologies, such as missile-armed nuclear submarines. He is known to have stopped the 1956–60 Five-Year Plan, causing considerable disruption within Soviet industry, largely in order to redirect the Soviet military industrial machine toward a greater emphasis on missiles and nuclear weapons (in what he called the "revolution in military affairs"). Khrushchev then instituted a Seven-Year Plan, 1959–65. Probably it was associated with a shipbuilding plan running through 1970, with some flexibility in the second period, 1966–70. A 1971–80 plan was approved in September 1969, and presumably a 1981–90 plan was approved some time in 1979.

According to Burov, the postwar ten-year plan envisaged first the completion of warships suspended during World War II to corrected ("K" suffix) designs; they are described in the first part of this book: Project 68K cruisers *(Chapaev),* Project 30K destroyers *(Ognevoi* class), Project 29K small escorts *(Bird* class), and Project 73K minesweepers, among others. Presumably the first half of the planning period also included designs, such as the Project 68bis *(Sverdlov* class) cruiser and the Project 30bis destroyer, based on earlier types. This group also included the Project 254 (T 43) minesweeper, designed in 1944, which was urgently needed to clear wartime minefields.

The second half of the plan period would have seen the construction of new types of ships developed during the first half: Project 24 battleships, Project 82 heavy cruisers, Project 65 light cruisers (soon superseded by Project 68bis, the *Sverdlov* class, because there was insufficient capacity to develop a wholly new design), Project 41 destroyers *(Talinn,* soon superseded by *Kotlin),* Project 42 escorts *(Kola* class, superseded by Project 50, the *Riga* class), Project 611 large submarines *(Zulu* class), Project 612 small submarines (superseded by Project 615, the *Quebec* class), Project 613 medium submarines *(Whiskey* class), Project 201 small sub-chasers (SO 1 class), Project 183 large torpedo boats (P 6 class), Project 184 small torpedo boats, Project 190 large armored river gunboats, Project 145 short-range landing ships (not built), Project 185 long-range landing ships (not built), Project 311 large river monitors (not built), Project 303 small river monitors (not built), Project 259 fleet minesweepers (not built), Project 264 seagoing minesweepers (T 58), and Project 265 *(Sasha)* roadstead minesweepers.

A recent Russian article summarizes the ten-year plan. See Table 2. Note that it does not include ships to be laid down during the second five-year period (1951–55) to be completed after 1 January 1956. Delays in construction pushed much of the plan out beyond 1955. Table 3 gives some details of planned versus actual construction during the two five-year plans embraced by the ten-year plan.

According to a recent account of Soviet carrier programs (by a senior naval constructor), the ten-year plan concentrated on cruisers (four heavy and thirty light) but also included a battleship, to be built at Severodvinsk (Molotovsk). During 1953–56 additional ships would have been laid down, two more battleships, three heavy, and seven light cruisers. The 1953–56 figure may include the ex-German heavy cruiser *Petropavlovsk* (ex-*Lutzow*), completion of which (to a drastically modified design) was apparently envisaged under Project 83 (later 83R); this project was dropped about the time of Stalin's death, although the hull was not scrapped until about 1958.

The destroyer target was apparently cut from about 250 to about 200. Russian writers have mentioned a target of 188 destroyers, corresponding to completion of the 10 Project 30K ships and construction of 68 Project 30bis during the first plan period, followed by 110 Project 41 destroyers during the second plan period.

In 1945 the naval staff wanted totals of 168 large, 204 medium, and 123 small submarines. At that time no more than one large submarine was under construction (she was broken up on the slip in 1949), together with seven S-class medium submarines. Eventually sixty-five small submarines (M-class) were laid down, some of them never being completed. Stalin cut the large submarine program to forty units, on the ground that it would interfere with surface ship construction. These figures suggest that planned construction of entirely new designs amounted to 39 large, 197 medium, and 58 small submarines (designs for each were prepared about 1946). Presumably numbers were readjusted before large-scale production began under the 1951–55 Five-Year Plan, since in the end more medium submarines (Project 613) and somewhat fewer large (Project 611) and small (Project 615) submarines were built. Note that about 1948 a Russian admiral reportedly spoke of a plan to build 1200 submarines within the next two decades. The 1945 proposal amounted to 495 units, and it seems plausible that at the time Gorkiy was being expanded to the point at which 600 or 700 submarines might have been built during a second ten-year plan (1956–65). In fact, of course, these numbers were never approached, partly because of the shift to much larger and more expensive types.

The first half of the plan period included two experimental submarines, Projects 615 *(Quebec)* and 617 *(Whale)*. The former was apparently promising enough to lead to immediate construction during the second half of the ten-year program. On the other hand, the alternative technology represented by Project 617 clearly was not mature enough for the 1951–55 period, although follow-on construction seems to have been planned for the following period.

The naval staff apparently also wanted a variety of specialized submarines, which Stalin rejected on the ground that work on them would overload the design offices. Apparently they were revived after Stalin died.

Although a torpedo-tube mine, PLT-3, was accepted for service in 1944, at the end of the war the main naval staff was still interested in minelayers; its proposed postwar program included 1200-ton minelayers, to carry 126 mines, with an endurance of up to 25,000 nm. This idea was dropped, apparently in the interest of producing large numbers of submarines, but it was revived on 20 September 1956 with the approval of a TTZ for a large submarine minelayer, Project 632, to carry 80 to 100 mines of the new PLT-6 type, planting 10 to 15 at a time at a speed of 3 to 10 kts. The minelayer could also carry 100 special assault troops or aviation fuel. A sketch design was approved in February 1958. This submarine would have displaced 3200 tons. A nuclear version, Project 632M (using a 6000 HP O-153 powerplant), was also considered. However, neither version was included in the 1959–65 program approved in December 1958. Almost in parallel with Project 632, TsKB-16 developed a large transport submarine, Project 648, intended to resupply attack and missile submarines at sea; it would have carried ten reload P-5/P-6 (SS-N-3) missiles or forty spare 53 cm torpedoes (or 120 wounded troops) as well as 20–40 cm torpedoes, all in addition to its own armament (four 53 cm torpedoes in tubes, plus four 40 cm torpedoes in tubes and another eighteen in racks. The TTZ was issued in May 1957. The sketch design was approved on 10 July 1958, and a minelaying function (eighty-four to ninety-six mines, depending on type) added due to the cancellation of Project 632. Project 611 and 613 submarines and a Project 30 destroyer were assigned for the necessary experimental work; they were refitted for the purpose at Severodvinsk, emerging from that yard in 1960 to begin trials at sea. The approved design called for a 6950 ton ship (with a full load of 1000 t of diesel fuel or 500 t of avgas and 490 t of oil), 102 × 12.8 m, capable of diving to 300 m, with a maximum submerged speed of 12.5 kts (14 kts surfaced). Work on Project 648 began at Severodvinsk early in 1961. It went very slowly, because the yard management saw little point in expending much effort on a single rather complex submarine, and every effort was made

to shift the order to another yard. As in the case of Project 632, a parallel nuclear-powered Project 648M (using two O-153s) had been considered and rejected. Meanwhile work began on nuclear-powered transport/minelayer (Project 664) and support (Project 717) submarines, both using the more powerful nuclear plants developed for attack submarines, as well as the new generation of sensors. Both were ultimately abortive. Meanwhile, presumably in view of how much better these new designs were likely to be, Project 648 was canceled on 21 June 1961.

The secondary transport role may be traceable to wartime interest, culminating in a huge abortive Project 621, work on which began in 1948; it was to have been capable of carrying ten T-34 tanks and three fighter aircraft.

Stalin's plan was not entirely rigid, as the notes above on designs superseding others suggest. Too, there seem to have been major changes about 1951, i.e., at the break between the two Five-Year Plans the shipbuilding plan spanned. That was also when Admiral N. G. Kuznetzov, the prewar architect of Stalin's shipbuilding plan, was, in effect, brought back from exile in the Far East. Admiral Kuznetzov's return coincides roughly with the decision to abandon battleship construction and with the decisions to substitute smaller ships for the relatively large Project 41 destroyer and Project 42 escort.

Upon Stalin's death in 1953 the three Project 82 cruisers laid down in 1951–52 were all stopped. They appear in this book only in the form of a hulk launched to clear a slip.

Attempts to include carriers in the 1946–55 program failed, the leadership (presumably Stalin) arguing that possession of offshore coastal areas such as Sakhalin provided airfields which could dominate inshore areas. Burov reports that Admiral Gorshkov, later the architect of the Soviet missile fleet, suggested that the five Project 68 cruiser hulls (Chapaev class) be completed as light carriers, building from a design prepared in 1939 (details of which have recently been published, as Project 71). Carriers were formally rejected in January 1947, with the proviso that the question would be reopened for the second ten-year plan. Apparently some sort of sketch plan for a large carrier was under development by 1950, since at that time the Tupolev aircraft design office was asked to develop a carrier strike aircraft, initially a development of the big land-based Tu-14. Later a twin-turboprop Tu-91 was designed and built. Accounts of the Tupolev design bureau indicate that large carrier-based aircraft were abandoned with Stalin's death, the Tu-91 being reordered as a shore-based naval strike bomber, then canceled by Khrushchev when a naval officer artlessly said that it had the firepower of a cruiser (Khrushchev just having canceled the Soviet cruiser program). No details of the Stalin-era large carrier have emerged. In fact in March 1955 the Council of Ministers ordered construction of two light carriers (Project 85). This ship would have displaced 27,000/35,000 tons and would have carried twenty-two MiG-15 fighters. According to Shirokorad, the final approved form of the 1956–65 program included five Project 85 carriers, to be built at Severodvinsk in 1961–65.

Work was already underway on adapting missiles to warships. Burov mentions a 1949 TsKB-18 submarine project, P-2, to design a submarine to carry twelve R-1 (modified V-2) ballistic missiles. Although P-2 was never built, clearly it led to further interest. There was also a 1949 project, P-4 (later Project 624), a version of Project 611 ("Zulu") to carry up to nine Lavochkin pulse-jet cruise missiles (presumably comparable to the German V-1). There was also interest in a T-15 strategic torpedo, a 1.5 m diameter weapon (which was the original payload of the Project 627 nuclear submarine). Work on this weapon apparently began about 1952; about 1953 came the first proposal to adapt the V-2 successor, Scud (R-11), to a submarine.

At about the same time, work was proceeding on a variety of anti-ship missiles, designed to be launched by aircraft and from shore positions (it is not clear to what extent shipboard launching was contemplated). Major projects were the KS (NATO AS-1 and SSC-1), Shchuka (NATO SS-N-1), 10 KhN, a navalized V-1 derivative, and Shtorm, a turbojet cruise missile (about 80 km range). Of these weapons, KS was adopted for aircraft and coast defense, but a cruiser-borne version was rejected after 1956 tests. Shtorm (1948–53) seems not to have been adopted in its original form, but an offshoot designed as an engine test bed (LM-15) seems to have introduced the wing planform later adopted for P-15 (NATO SS-N-2 *Styx*). The designer, M. R. Bisnovat, lost his design bureau in 1953, his staff going to the favored Mikoyan (MiG) bureau. That staff included Berezhniak, the developer of the KS missile, who soon proposed P-15 as a patrol boat weapon. V. N. Chelomey, who worked on 10 KhN, had his design bureau closed (due to political preference for Beria's son and for Mikoyan) in 1953, found a place in a navy NII and developed P-5 (NATO SS-N-3 *Shaddock*) and its successors. Shchuka was developed directly into the weapon of the Project 57bis *(Krupny)* destroyer.

On 26 January 1954 the Council of Ministers approved a plan (Project Volna) to place long-range cruise and ballistic missiles on board submarines. The immediate fruits of this project were a modified army Scud missile (R-11FM), which was test-fired by a Project 611 submarine *(Zulu),* and a pair of cruise missiles, Chelomey's P-5 (SS-N-3 *Shaddock*), which was test-fired by a Project 613 *(Whiskey)* class submarine, and Beriev's larger P-10, which was test-fired by a Project 611 submarine *(Zulu).* It seems likely that plans originally called for new submarines to carry both series of weapons operationally.

There was also interest in adapting existing anti-ship weapons for surface ships. Probably it was formalized at about this time, since Russian accounts date the origin of P-15 to 1955. Plans initially called for new types of ships to carry both Shchuka (Project 57bis) and P-15 (Project 205 *Osa*). Shchuka was test-fired by a converted Project 56 *(Kotlin)* destroyer, and P-15 by a converted torpedo boat (Project 183).

According to Shirokorad, the abortive 1956–65 program included a variety of cruisers, most of them intended to fire missiles:

> • Project 84 cruisers, armed with 180 mm SM-48 ballistics, like the *Kirov* class MK-3-180 (97.5 kg shell, range 36.2 km) but with a high rate of fire (10 rpgpm), to train nearly twice as fast (20 versus 12 deg/sec), with maximum elevation 76° (i.e., DP).

Almost all *Sverdlov* hulls were to be refitted with missiles:

> • Project 67 ("light cruiser with close-range missile armament"), four ships to be completed under a 30 December 1954 decree, with conversions of already-completed ships to follow: all 152 mm turrets removed, replaced by a pair of rotating stabilized SM-58 launchers 12 m long, with armored boxes (5–10 mm) at their rear ends for a pair of missiles. Magazine loads: nine missiles forward, six aft, total nineteen KSS missiles (3.5 t each). On the first four ships to be handed over in 1959, four 100 mm twin SM-5-1 mounts would be retained. Later units

would have four new 100 mm automatic SM-62 twin mounts. All would have 6 × 4 57 mm ZiF-75 mounts. The lead unit, *Admiral Nakhimov,* was used for KSS trials. They failed, but KSS was adopted as the S-2 Sopka coast defense missile. The cruiser project was canceled by a decree of 4 July 1957, and *Nakhimov* was stricken on 28 July 1960 and broken up.

• Project 63 ("light cruiser with long-range missile armament") was a *Sverdlov* class hull with a nuclear powerplant and new missiles. Design work began in September 1955. Plans were to build seven ships in 1961–64 at Leningrad and Nikolaev. The main armament was to be a 400 km range inertially guided P-40 missile, which could be used against both moving ships (i.e., was both extremely fast and nuclear-armed) and shore targets. The corresponding FCS was Tenzor. These ships would have three or four SM-69 launchers (eighteen or twenty-four missiles) for their P-40s, and two defensive SAM systems, the new long-range M-3 and the short-range M-1 (NATO SAN-1). The M-3 system employed two twin stabilized SM-68 launchers and twenty V-800 missiles (2–25 km ceiling, range 55 km). The M-1 system comprised four twin ZiF-101 launchers (sixty-four V-600 missiles) and two Yatagan (NATO Peel Group) fire control systems. These ships would also have four twin 76 mm ZiF-67 mounts with Turel' FCS. As it happened, neither P-40 nor M-3 ever entered service.

• Project 64: five *Sverdlov* class cruisers to be rebuilt 1960–61 with a pair of SM-77 launchers (for P-6 and P-7 [SS-N-3] missiles) replacing the 152 mm turrets. These appear to have been quadruple launchers similar to the SM-70 type later employed on "Kynda" class cruises. The long-range SAM battery comprised two SM-68 launchers for long-range M-3 missiles with twenty V-800s. In the event M-3 was not ready in time, the ships would be equipped with M-2bis (NATO SAN-2, a version of SA-2) with two SM-64-1 launchers and twenty V-755 missiles. The M-3 system used a pair of Fregat FCS radars; M-2bis used Korvet. The short-range missile battery comprised four ZiF-101 launchers (sixty-four V-600 missiles) for the M-1 system, with four Yatagan FCS. Gun armament consisted of four twin ZiF-67 76 mm with two Turel' FCS.

• Project 70 anti-aircraft cruiser, developed under a 13 August 1955 decree, added M-2 (NATO SA-N-2) missiles to a *Sverdlov*. In the final version, one 152 mm turret was deleted, together with two 100 mm mounts, and the light AA battery would be reduced to four quadruple 57 mm ZiF-75 guns. The missile battery comprised three stabilized SM-64 with forty-four V-750 missiles and two Korvet FCS. Work on this project was stopped by a 10 August 1957 decree, only the conversion of the experimental *Dzerzhinski* (Project 70Eh) being allowed to continue. She had only a single SM-64 launcher with ten missiles and a Korvet-Sevan FCS. On its first trial, the system shot down a drone Il-28 bomber at an altitude of 10 km. However, the V-750 missile used liquid fuel, which had to be loaded before launch and removed if the missile was not used.

In addition, the plan called for five Project 81 fleet air defense ships to have been built at Yard 194 and placed in service in 1960–61. They would have been armed with the M-3 missile system (SM-68 launcher, forty V-800 missiles). This project was canceled by decree of 5 July 1957.

No account of the submarines or of the smaller combatants abortive 1956–65 plan has appeared, but clearly the program would have included the *November* class nuclear submarines (Project 627), *Golf* class missile submarines (Project 629), improved versions of the two main conventional submarines (Projects 633 and 641, *Romeo* and *Foxtrot*), *Krupnys,* and *Osas.* Planned experimental ships included a prototype gas turbine sub-chaser, Project 159 *(Petya).* The choice of a cruise missile submarine was probably held over pending a choice between the two alternative submarine-launched cruise missiles.

In October 1955 Khrushchev held a meeting at Sevastopol at which the future shape of the navy was discussed. According to his memoirs, Khrushchev had just seen demonstrations of the new anti-ship missiles; he doubted that surface fleets had much of a future. Instead, he wanted the navy built around missile-carrying land-based bombers (at that time, Tu-16 *Badgers*) and submarines. He also wanted seagoing ASW craft armed with rocket ASW weapons, presumably to counter the expected threat of Western missile submarines. Khrushchev also argued that destroyers needed both improved AAW and improved ASW weapons. Supporting Khrushchev, his Minister of Defense, Marshal Zhukov, argued for an emphasis on submarines. New surface ships should be designed to support the submarine fleet and to cooperate with ground forces: preference should go to fast missile cruisers, destroyers armed with short-range missiles, patrol combatants, submarine hunters, and minesweepers.

Khrushchev canceled the new carrier project. All work stopped in December 1955. According to his memoirs, Khrushchev also canceled four cruisers at this time. Burov observes that Khrushchev killed off remaining *Sverdlov* construction, which would be consistent with a decision not to build large missile ships.

As a consequence of the October 1955 meeting, the Council of Ministers issued new directives for warship design on 17 and 25 August 1956. Warships ordered at this time included the Project 658 *(Hotel)* and Project 659 *(Echo I)* class nuclear strategic ballistic- and cruise-missile submarines, the Project 58 *(Kynda)* class missile cruisers, and the Project 61 *(Kashin)* class destroyers. At about the same time Khrushchev approved a proposal to expand the submarine missile program. There was probably also a proposal to expand the anti-ship missile program. Both probably entailed building production versions of the existing ships used to test new missiles, such as Project 611 and 613 submarines, Project 56 destroyers, and Project 183 torpedo boats.

By this time long-range submarine-launched missiles seem to have enjoyed the highest priority. In August 1956 the Council of Ministers approved a seven-year plan to develop both new submarine weapons (including second-generation ballistic and cruise missiles) and new powerplants (including the new liquid-metal reactor). The new ballistic missiles were D-2 (NATO SS-N-4), to replace D-1 (Scud), and D-3. Like D-1, D-2 was surface launched from a platform raised to the top of the submarine's sail. Yangel's alternative D-3 offered greater range (1000 km) and launch from within the tube. It was, however, considerably more massive than D-2. The parallel long-range strategic cruise missile was Ilyushin's P-20 (Mach 3, 3500 km range, 30 t in a 4.6 × 25 m canister). Malakhit designed submarines to carry both D-3 (Project 639) and P-20 (Projects P-627A, for one missile, and 653, for two side by side).

By 1957 the new shipbuilding plan was being written. Presumably it spanned Khrushchev's Seven-Year Plan (1959–65) and the succeeding Five-Year Plan (1966–70). Decisions made at this time seem to have included production of the prototype gas-turbine sub-chaser (Project 159) and, somewhat later, construction of the *Moskva* class carriers (Project 1123) and of diesel cruise missile submarines (Project 651 *Juliett*).

In 1960 progress was reviewed and projects weeded out. The big strategic cruise missile, P-20, was dropped in favor of ballistic weapons, and the D-3 ballistic missile was also dropped. At this time, too, the decision was made to abandon work on closed-cycle submarine powerplants.

The plan period ended in 1970 with a massive fleet exercise, Okean, which demonstrated oceanic capabilities using a new generation of central control exercised from the shore. Okean may also have shown that some lower-level control was needed, since true flagships such as the *Kirov* and *Kiev* classes were developed in its wake.

Khrushchev fell in 1964, partly because of the problems he had caused Soviet industry (his successor, Leonid Brezhnev, was the Communist Party official in charge of military industry). Khrushchev's aversion to large combatants seems to have been reversed after his downfall. It also became possible once more to consider using fixed-wing aircraft at sea. This period saw the origin of the *Kiev* concept.

The 1965–70 Plan included the new-generation Project 667A *(Yankee)* class ballistic missile submarine, which had to be able to break out of Soviet waters in order to get within firing range of targets in North America. New types of long-range ASW ships (Project 1134A and 1134B, *Kresta II* and *Kara*) were built.

By 1968 work was under way on a 1971–80 Plan, which was officially adopted on 1 September 1969. It was at this time, apparently, that the decision was made to build submarine-launched strategic missiles with such long ranges that their carriers could remain within Soviet-protected waters ("bastions") throughout a war. Bastion defense, usually described as maintaining the combat stability of the submarines, became a vital naval mission.

Greater emphasis was to be placed on open-ocean ASW. This plan included the development of long-range surveillance systems, presumably comparable in theory (though, as it turned out, not in range) to the U.S. SOSUS system. Presumably the Tu-142 Bear maritime patrol aircraft was developed under this plan.

As in the past, interest in attacking U.S. carrier battle groups continued.

Burov seems to imply that the most important element of the plan was the decision to move forces further out from the Soviet Union. Thus this planning period saw the construction of two classes of much larger combatants, Projects 1143 (*Kiev* class) and 1144 (*Kirov* class).

Burov also specifically mentions interest in naval forces to support assaults and ground troops. A recent Russian account of the design of the Project 956 *Sovremennyy* class destroyer indicates that it began life as a shore bombardment ship.

Burov associates the 1969–80 plan period specifically with increased interest in reducing ship signatures. Major research programs were conducted in 1970–75 to study not only acoustic signatures, but also pressure (hydrodynamic) and electromagnetic signatures. The new submarines designed at this time (Projects 945 and 971, *Sierra* and *Akula*) were expected to take advantage of the new silencing technology (e.g., sound isolation and acoustic coverings).

There is little evidence of the planned 1981–90 shipbuilding program. The only major warship clearly included was the carrier *Kuznetzov* (Project 1143.5), which a Russian article indicates was approved in 1978. The new frigate *Neustrashimmyy* (Project 1154) seems to have been designed during the first half of the plan period for construction during the second. This plan probably also included the surface-effect missile boat *Dergach* (Project 1239). Whatever new submarines were conceived for construction during this period were not laid down due to the sudden collapse of Soviet fortunes; Project 885

(*Severodvinsk*) was presumably planned for earlier construction, and was probably the sole survivor of a series of projects. Other warships associated with this planning period may have been the nuclear carrier *Ulyanovsk* and a nuclear destroyer, code-named Anchar. Neither is described in this book, and indeed no very complete descriptions of these projects seem to exist.

For assistance in obtaining and translating recent Russian publications, the editor would like to thank the translator, Gregory Tokar, and also Steven J. Zaloga, Christopher C. Wright, A. D. Baker III, and Stuart Slade.

Author's Notes on Weapon Systems

Because books on Russian gun and missile systems have already appeared, data on these systems are not provided here. The list below indicates which weapons are associated with which radars. [Ed.: NATO designators are in square brackets]

Strategic Ballistic Missile Systems

- System D-9RM (rocket RSM-54, NATO SS-N-23 Skiff): weight 40 t, length 14 m, range 4500 nm (8300 km), 7 RVs. For Project 667BDRM.
- System D-19 (rocket RSM-52/3R-65, NATO SS-N-20 Sturgeon): weight 60 t, length 14.7 m, range 4500 nm (8300 km), 10 RVs. For Project 941.
- System D-11 (rocket RSM-45, NATO SS-N-17 Snipe): weight 30 t, length 13.5 m, range 4000 nm (7300 km). Single warhead. For Project 667AM.
- System D-9R (rocket RSM-50/R-29R, NATO SS-N-18 Stingray): weight 34 t, length 13.6 m, range 3500 nm (6500 km). 3 RVs. For Project 667BDR.
- System D-9U (rocket RSM-40/R-29U, NATO SS-N-8 Sawfly): weight 30 t, length 13 m, range 4910 nm (9100 km). 2 RVs. For Project 667BD.
- System D-9 (rocket RSM-40/R-29, NATO SS-N-8 Sawfly): weight 28 t, length 13 m, range 4210 nm (7800 km). Single warhead. For Project 667B.
- System D-7 (rocket RSM-25, NATO SS-N-6 Serb): weight 18.9 t, length 9.9 m, range 1600 nm (3000 km). 2 RVs. For Project 667A.
- System D-5 (rocket 4K-18, NATO SS-NX-13): length 10 m, range 1000 km. Tested on Project 605 (Golf).[Ed.: According to a recent article, SS-N-6 was D-5/R-27; SS-NX-13 was D-5K/R-27K, the suffix indicating a corrected course. This article identified D-7/RT-15 as an unsuccessful solid-fuel alternative to SS-N-6, for which the "Yankee" (Project 667) submarine was originally designed. D-7 in turn was a replacement for an earlier D-6, started under a June 1960 decree and stopped a year later. RT-15 was launched from a modified Project 613 submarine and then from a Project 629B submarine in 1963; the project was stopped in mid-1964.]
- System D-4 (rocket R-21/4K-55, NATO SS-N-5 Serb), length 12.9 m, range 750 nm (1400 km). Single warhead. For Projects 658M, 629A.
- System D-2 (rocket R-13/4K-50, NATO SS-N-4 Sark), length 11.8 m, range 350 nm (650 km). Single warhead. For Projects 658, 629.
- System D-1 (rocket R-11FM, NATO Scud-A), length 10.4 m, range 55 nm (150 km). Single warhead. For Project AB-611.

Ship-launched Cruise Missile Systems

- Oniks: for nuclear submarine *Severodvinsk.* However, in the third edition this missile is associated with the Garpun [Plank Shave] radar.
- P-1000 (SS-N-27): control system Argon.
- 82-R Vikhr (SUWN-1): rocket torpedo. Radar system Sprut.
- 3M-24 Uran (SS-N-25): missile for surface and air launch.
- 3M-25 Meteor(SS-N-24): for submarine "Andromeda."
- 3M-80 Moskit (SS-N-22): launched from surface ships and aircraft; uses Mustang [Band Stand] radar system.
- RK-55 Granat (SS-N-21): launched from submarines and aircraft.
- P-700 Granit (SS-N-19): launched from submarines and surface ships.
- P-500 Bazalt (SS-N-12): ship and submarine launched. The associated radar is SU-Argon [Front Door/Front Piece]. The successor system is Vulkan (no NATO designator).
- P-120 Malakhit (SS-N-9): ship and submarine launched.
- P-20M Ametist (SS-N-7): submarine launched.
- P-5D (SS-N-3C): submarine launched, using Sever radar.

- P-35 Progress-M (SS-N-3B): surface ship launched, using Binom [Scoop Pair] radar.
- P-6 Progress (SS-N-3A): surface launched from a submarine, using Argument radar.
- P-15 Termit (SS-N-2A/C): from surface craft, using Rangout radar.
- P-15U (SS-N-2B): from surface craft, using Monolit [Band Stand] radar.
- KSShch Shchuka (SS-N-1): from surface ships.

AA Missile Systems:

System	Radar System
Volna [SA-N-1]	Yatagan [Peel Group]
Shtorm [SA-N-3]	Grom [Head Lights]
Osa [SA-N-4]	Osa [Pop Group]
Fort [SA-N-6]	Volna [Top Dome]
Uragan [SA-N-7]	Orekh [Front Dome]
Kinzhal [SA-N-9]	Podkat [Cross Swords]
Yozh [SA-N-7 successor]	Podberiozovik

ASW Systems:

Rastrub [SS-N-14C]	Sprut [Eye Bowl]
Metel' [SS-N-14]	Drakon [Eye Bowl]

Gun Systems:

MK-5 [6 in. cruiser gun]	Zalp [Top Bow]
AK-130 [current twin 130 mm]	MR-218 Lev [Kite Screech]
AK-100 [current single 100 mm]	MR-218 Lev [Kite Screech]

[Ed.: According to other Russian sources, Lev is MR-145/MR-184.]

AK-726 [twin 76 mm]	MR-105 Turel' [Owl Screech]
AK-725 [twin 57 mm]	MR-103 Bars [Muff Cob]
AK-176 and AK-630	MR-123 Vympel [Bass Tilt]
V-11 [twin 37 mm]	Redan [Fire Iron] or Zarya [Post Lamp]
AK-230 [twin 30 mm]	MR-104 Rys [Drum Tilt]

Major Torpedo Types:
- VA-111 Shkval is intended to attack submarines with speeds of up to 50 kts operating down to 400 m. Caliber is 533 mm, length 8.2 m. Range 6 nm, speed about 200 kts.
- 53-65K: 533 mm oxygen torpedo, length 7.95 m, range 9 nm at 45 kts.
- SET-65: 533 mm electric torpedo, length 7.8 m, range 8 nm at 40 kts.
- SAET-60M: 533 mm anti-ship torpedo, length 7.8 m, range/speed 8 nm/35 kts or 7 nm/42 kts.
- 65-76: 65 cm steam-gas anti-ship torpedo, length 11 m, range 27 nm at 50 kts.
- 53-61: steam-gas antisubmarine torpedo, 400 mm caliber.
[Ed: This is probably a misprint, since 53-61 must be a 533 mm weapon.]
- SET-73: electric antisubmarine torpedo, 400 mm caliber.

Anti-Submarine Missiles
- 86-R (SS-N-16): launched from submarines, 650 mm caliber tubes.
- 81-R Viyuga (SS-N-15): rocket-torpedo launched from submarines. [Ed.: Uses 53-cm tubes.]
- 85-R (85-RU) Metel'/Rastrub (SS-N-14): ship-launched, uses Drakon guidance radar.

Editor's Notes

Generators: TG indicates a turbogenerator, DG a diesel generator; the number is the rating in kilowatts. These are NOT designations.

Endurance *in days* indicates stores endurance.

Unless otherwise noted, single dates are dates of completion. Multiple dates are dates laid down (l.d.), launched (lch), completed. Break-up dates are dates ships were sent to the breakers; hulls may have survived beyond these dates.

Dimensions are in meters; displacement is in metric tons. *BU* refers to "broken up." For *submarines,* displacement is surfaced/submerged. Diving depth is maximum/working. The figure in parentheses after the beam is overall depth from keel to top of sail. The designation *Fr* refers to frame. Decomm stands for decommissioned.

Part I
Ships of Prewar Design

Project: 23

Class Name: SOVIETSKIY SOYUZ

Names:

	laid down	launched	completed
SOVETSKIY SOYUZ	15 July '38	16 June '49	– – –
SOVETSKIY UKRAINA	31 Oct. '38	– – –	
SOVETSKIY ROSSIA	21 Dec. '39	– – –	

Builders: Baltic Yard, Leningrad; 61 Kommunar Yard, Nikolaev; and Severodvinsk.

Displacement: 59,150/65,150

Dimensions: 269.4 × 38.9 × 10.4

Armament: 3×3 406.4 mm (B-37, 900 shells), 6×2 152.4 mm (B-38, 1800 rounds), 2×4 100 mm (B-54, 2400 rounds), 8×4 37 mm (46-K, 25,600 rounds); 4×KOR-2 aircraft in hangar, 1 catapult, 200 mines

Armor: Belt at waterline 420 mm (ends 375 mm), deck of citadel (stern to bow bulkheads) 100 mm, bulkheads 400 mm (closing belt). Turrets and conning tower 425 mm. Underwater protection (Pugliese system) 8.1 m deep.

Machinery: 6 boilers, 3 geared steam turbines, 3 shafts, 201,000 HP (forced: 231,000 HP for 2 hours) = 26 kts; 4 TG, 4 DG generators; 5580 nm/14 kts, 5530 t oil fuel

Complement: 1664 (112 officers, 266 petty officers, 1281 sailors)

Electronics: Radar: Redut-KM; Radio: Uragan-M; Receivers: Burya, Groza; Sonar: Mars

Chief constructor B. G. Chilikin. Technical project (design) approved 13 May '39. Of 6 planned ships of this type, 3 were canceled on 19 Oct. '40. All work on the remaining 3 was stopped on 10 July '41, and they were stricken on 10 Sept. '41. Armor of the battleship *Sovetskiy Soyuz* was used to build fortifications around Leningrad. The prototype main-caliber gun was in action 23 Aug. '41–10 June '44 on the Nevskiy, Kolpinskiy, and Karelskiy fronts around Leningrad. After being launched to clear the slip, the hull was used until 1956 as a target for missile tests. The other hulls were dismantled on their slips.

[Ed.: *Sov. Ukraina* was captured by the Germans and blown up on the slip when they evacuated Nikolaev. The hull of *Sovetsky Rossia* survived the war in the construction building at Severodvinsk, but work was never resumed.

According to Shitikov et al., an OTZ for a new type of battleship, Project 24, was issued in 1941. Armament would have comprised 9 06 mm in 3 triple turrets, 6 twin 152 mm, and 16 100 mm, with 4–6 KOR-2 seaplanes. Speed would have been 30 kts, and endurance 10,000 nm. By June '44 the OTZ had been revised to show 24 130 mm dual-purpose guns rather than the earlier mixed secondary battery, plus 48 45 mm guns. Further revision in 1945 gave a displacement of 75,000 tons, a maximum speed of 30 kts (24 kts cruising speed, 18 kts economical speed), a range of 8000 nm, and the armament above (with 48–60 45 mm anti-aircraft guns). The ship would have been protected against 406 mm shellfire, and against 1000 kg bombs dropped from 5000 m. She would have had 2 catapults and 6 aircraft. Later the anti-aircraft battery was increased by 130 25 mm guns. The OTZ was formally issued in December 1945, and a TTZ (reflecting a feasibility study) was issued only in 1950, shortly before the project died altogether.]

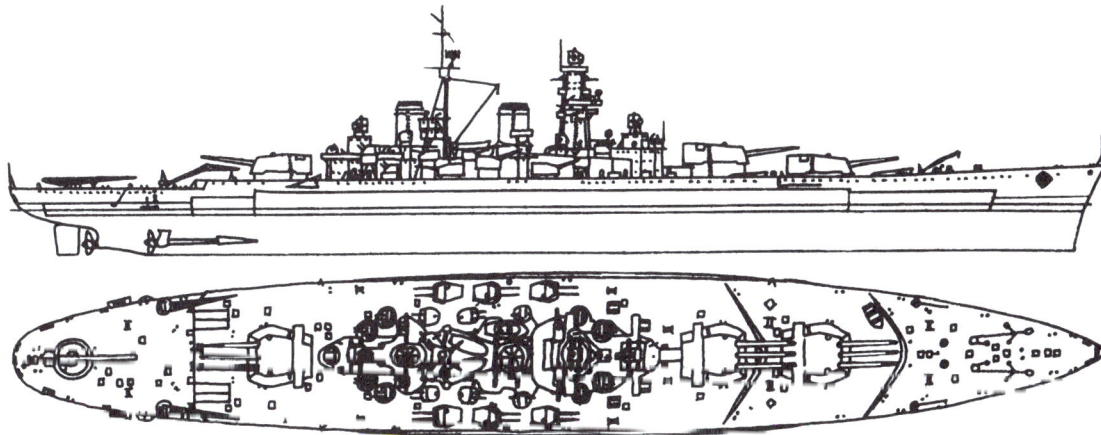

Project: 68-K

Class Name: CHAPAEV

Names:

	laid down	launched	completed	stricken
CHAPAEV	8 Oct. '39 Black Sea	28 Aug. '41	16 May '50	Apr. '63
CHKALOV	31 Aug. '39 Black Sea	25 Oct. '47	5 Nov. '50 (renamed *Komsomolets* 29 Oct. '58)	Oct. '75
ZHELEZNIAKOV	31 Oct. '39	25 June '41	19 Apr. '50	
FRUNZE	29 Aug. '39 Black Sea	31 Dec. '40	19 Dec. '50	28 Feb. '60
KUIYBYSHEV	31 Aug. '39 Black Sea	31 Jan. '41	20 Apr. '50	16 Apr. '65

Displacement: 11,864/13,420

Dimensions: 199.2 × 18.73 × 6.93

Armament: 4×3 152.4 mm (MK-5, 2100 rounds), 4×2 100 mm (B-54, 2400 rounds), 16×2 37 mm (V-11, 14,400 rounds), 2×3 533 mm TT, 60 mines (KB or AGSB or RM-1) or 48 KDM-1000

Armor: Waterline 150 mm amidships, ends 35 mm; bulkheads 120 mm forward, 100 mm aft, deck 50-40 mm. Gunhouses and conning towers 175-100 mm 175 mm. Total armor weight 2993 t. Underwater protection 3.5 m deep.

Machinery: 6 boilers (KV-68: 106 t steam/hr, 26 atm, 325°C), 2 steam turbines, 2 shafts, 110,000 HP = 33.5 kts; 4 TG and 2 DG-250 generators; 5500 nm/17.3 kts, 1445 nm/33 kts; 2500 t fuel. Endurance 30 days.

Complement: 1184

Electronics: Radars: Kliver (air search), Don (navigation); Sonar: Tamir

Chief designer A. N. Maslov. Riveted hulls. Laid down at

Frunze (V. V. Kostrichenko)

Chkalov (A. N. Sokolov)

Zheleznyakov (A. N. Sokolov)

Komsomoletz (Pavlov collection)

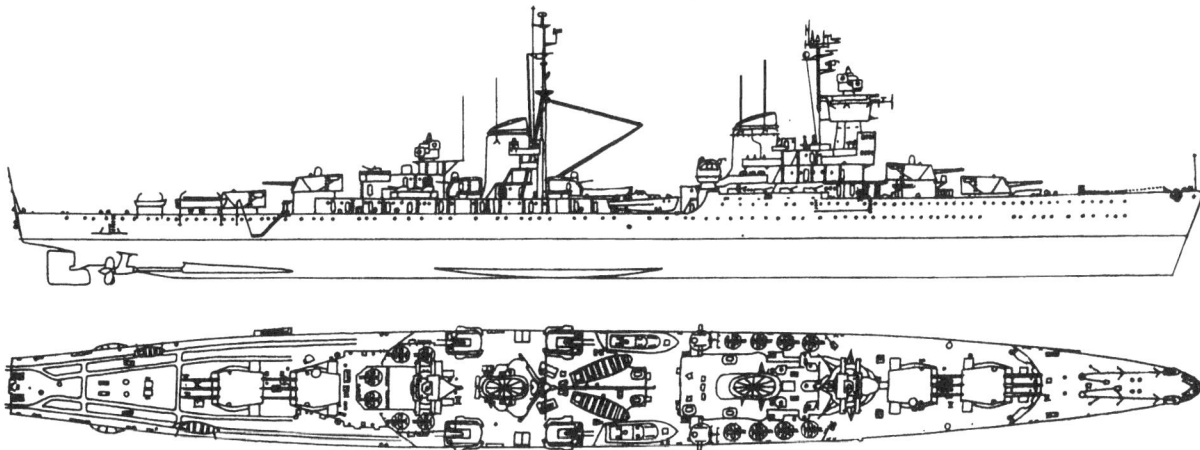

Baltic Yard, Leningrad: *Chapaev, Chkalov, Dzerzhinskiy, Lenin;* at Marti Yard, Nikolaev: *Frunze;* at Admiralty Yard, Leningrad: *Zheleznyakov, Ordzhonikidze* (blown up 23 Aug. '41), *Avrora;* at 61 Kommunar Yard, Nikolaev: *Kuiybyshev* (completed at Marti Yard), *Sverdlov* (destroyed), *Kotovskiy,* *Parkhomenko, Shchors.* Planned for construction at Komsomolsk-on-Amur: *Lazo. Chapaev* and *Chkalov* in Baltic, *Frunze* and *Kuiybyshev* in Black Sea Fleet. Rerated training cruisers 18 Apr. '58. *Chapaev* renamed PKZ-25 20 Oct. '60.

Project: 30-K

Class Name: OGNEVOIY

Names:

laid down   *launched*   *completed*

OTLICHNYY

  2 Dec. '39   7 May '47   30 Oct. '48   30 Oct. '48
to TsL-69 14 Mar. '60, to PKZ-43 6 Apr. '62, str 1966

OBRAZTSOVYY

  2 Dec. '39   30 July '47   29 Dec. '49   29 Sept. '49
to TsL-41 20 Aug. '59, str 20 June '71

OTVAZHNYY

  30 July '40   2 Jan. '48   2 Mar. '50   16 Apr. '50
str 1966

ODARENNYY

  30 Dec. '39   27 Dec. '48   28 June '50   6 Aug. '50
to UTS-86 18 Apr. '58, str 1965

OZORNOIY

  20 Nov. '39   25 Dec. '40   9 Jan. '49   9 Jan. '49
to Bulgaria '50 *(G. Dimitrov)*

VNUSHITELNIY

  16 Dec. '40   14 May '47   29 Dec. '47   29 Dec. '47
to TsL-32 18 Apr. '50, to UTS-90 14 May '59, str 1960

V'NOSLIVIY

  29 Oct. '40   17 Nov. '47   5 Dec. '48   5 Dec. '48
to TsL-51, str 30 Aug. '60

VLASTNIY

  29 Oct '40   15 June '48   27 Dec. '48   27 Dec. '48
to TsL-48 20 Feb. '59, str 30 Aug. '60

OSMOTRITELNYY

  5 May '40   24 Aug. '47   29 Sept. '47   29 Sept. '47
to TsL-30 1958, to PKZ-151 12 Sept. '58, str 1966

OKHOTNIY

  25 June '40   19 July '47   29 Sept. '47   29 Sept. '47
Renamed *Stalin* 17 Dec. '46

Displacement: 2125/2860

Dimensions: 117 × 11 × 4.25

Armament: 2×2 130 mm (B-2LM, 600 rounds),
1×2 85 mm (92-K, 600 rounds), 6×1 37 mm (70-K, 6300
rounds), 2×3 533 mm TT (TTA-53-30K), 52 KB-KRAB
or 60 M-26 mines, 2 depth charge throwers (BMB-1, 22
depth charges)

Machinery: 4 water-tube boilers (KV-30: 27 atm, super-
heat temperature 350°C), 2 steam turbines, 2 shafts,
54,000 HP = 36.5 kts, 3500 nm/15.5 kts, 2950 nm/16.9 kts;
2 DG-50 generators; 778 t fuel, endurance 10 days

Complement: 301 (20 officers)

Electronics: Radar: Gyuis-1b, Ryf-1; Navigational radar:
Rim-1; AA fire control radar: Vympel-2; Sonar: Tamir-5N

    Chief designer A. M. Yunovidov (TsKB-53). When ships
were fitted with degaussing coils, 60 t of ballast had to be
added to correct stability. Hulls were partially riveted and
partially welded. Lead ship *Ognevoiy* (Project 30) was completed 5 Apr. '45, became TsL-2 27 Dec. '55. Built at Leningrad (Zhdanov), *Obraztsovyy* completed at the Baltic Yard,
Otvazhnyy and *Odarennyy* completed at the Marti Yard
(Leningrad), *Osmotritelniy* and *Okhotniy* built in Severodvinsk, *Ozornoiy* in Nikolaev (Yard 445), *Vnushitelniy* and
the remainder built in Komsomolsk. *Otmenniy, Obuchenniy,
Otchayannyy, Obshitelniy* captured by the German Army on
the slip at Nikolaev. Not completed: *Ognenniy, Ozhesto-
chenniy, Ostriy, Oslepitelniy, Ostorozhniy, Otchetlivniy.*

Project: 1190

NATO Class Name: None

Names:

laid down   launched   completed

SIVASH
    18 Apr. '39   20 Aug. '40   31 Oct. '46
    l.d. as *Serishev,* renamed 25 Sept. '40

Displacement: 1704/2400

Dimensions: 88.03 × 11.1 × 2.8

Armament: 3×2 130 mm (B-28, 1800 rounds),
2×2 76.2 mm (39-K, 1200 rounds), 2×2 45 mm (41-K,
12,050 rounds), 5×2 12.7 mm (M-26, 41,100 rounds),
29 KB mines (as overload)

Armor: Waterline 77 mm (ends 35.5 mm), deck of citadel
40 mm, deck at ends 25 mm, bulkheads 25 mm, gunhouses
and conning tower 50-100 mm, machine gun turrets 10 mm

Machinery: 4 diesels (38KR-8), 4 shafts, 3200 HP =
15.14 kts, 167 t oil, 17,000 km/10 kts. Endurance 10 days.

Complement: 242 (14 officers, 49 petty officers, 179 sailors)

Designed by TsKB-19, flagship monitor for lower part
of Amur River and Tartar Straits. Built in Gorkiy and transferred in sections to Amur, assembled in Khabarovsk and
completed and armed in Komsomolsk. Sisters: *Khasan* completed 1942, *Perekop* completed 1944. *Sivash* was disarmed
in 1958, used to test combat systems of Amur River monitors. She was renamed PKZ-22 5 Oct. '66, transferred to
Kamchatka 1971, and beached in a storm in the fall of 1974.

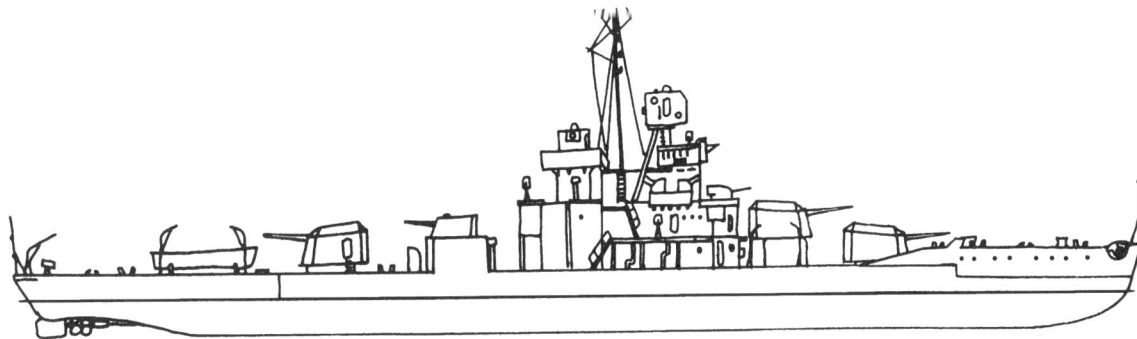

Sivash (N. F. Sungorkin)

Project: 29-K

NATO Class Name: BIRDS

Names:

	completed
ALBATROS	1 Feb. '46
BUREVESTNIK	14 Feb. '47

originally named *Chaika* and renamed Sept. '40

KORSHUN	3 May '47
ZORKIY	21 Feb. '50

originally named *Voron*, renamed 1940

OREL	20 Feb. '51

Displacement: 912/1073

Dimensions: 85.7 × 8.4 × 2.61

Armament: 3×1 100 mm (B-34, 750 rounds), 4×2 12.7 mm (DShK-2, 16,000 rounds; replaced 1946 by 2×1 37 mm 70-K), 1×3 450 mm TT (TTA-45-29K), 20 large depth charges (BGB), 40 small depth charges (MGB), 24 KB-KRAB mines (as overload could carry smoke generators)

Machinery: 2 boilers, 2 steam turbines, 2 shafts, 23,000 HP = 34 kts, 3000 nm/15 kts, 1200 nm/24 kts, 110 t oil, endurance 5 days.

Complement: 112 (7 officers, 8 petty officers, 97 sailors)

Electronics: Sonar: Tamir-5

Chief constructor Ya. A. Koperzhinskiy *(TsKB-32)*. Technical project (design) approved 15 Feb. '39. A total of 19 units of 29 were laid down. The lead ship, *Yastreb* (Project 29), was completed 23 Feb. '45. *Albatros* and *Burvestnik* were built at Komsomolsk, the remainder in Leningrad (Yard 190). Uncompleted units: laid down at Yard 198, *Tigr, Leopard, Ris', Yaguar, Kuguar, Pantera;* and at Yard 199 Komsomolsk, *Fregat,* and *Orlan. Orel* became OS-27 18 Aug. '58 and PKZ-17 Mar. '64, to the breakers Sept. '65. *Korshun* became OS-28 in 1958, to the breakers Jan. '64. *Zorkiy* became UTS-9 Nov. '56, str Feb. '75. *Albatros* became UTS-82 Mar. '58, to the breakers Feb. '61. *Burevestnik* became UTS-48 May '57, to the breakers Jan. '58. *Zorkiy* went to the Kiev DOSAAF in 1990.

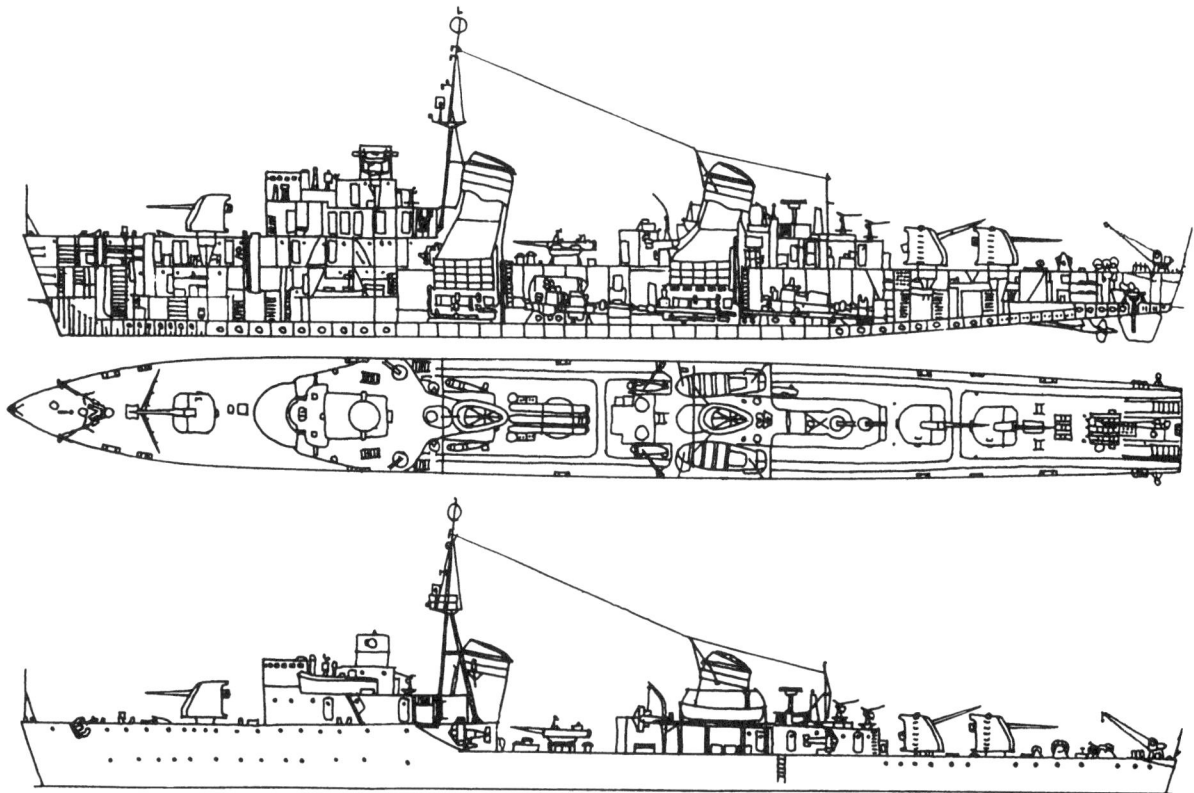

Project: IX-bis

NATO Class Name: (S-class)

Names

	completed
S-21	27 Apr. '46
S-22	15 July '46
S-23	10 Aug. '47
S-24	19 Dec. '47
S-25	29 Mar. '48
S-26	21 Dec. '48
S-35	18 Feb. '48

Displacement: 866.1/1107.8

Dimensions: 77.8 × 6.4 × 4.1 (pressure hull diameter 4.6 m, thickness 18 mm)

Diving Depth: 100/80; diving time 65 sec

Armament: 6 533 mm TT (4 bow, 2 stern; 12 torpedoes, including 6 in racks), 1 100 mm (B-24 PL, with 200 rounds), 1 45 mm (21-K, with 500 rounds); all guns removed 1957

Machinery: 2 diesels (1-D), 4000 HP; 2 electric motors (PG-100), 1080 HP, 2 shafts, 19.5/8.8 kts; surfaced 2700 nm/19.5 kts, 9500 nm/10 kts; submerged 8.8 nm/8.8 kts, 135 nm/3 kts; 40.2 t fuel; 2 batteries (62 cells each, type 46 SU); 1 DG-75 generator. Submerged endurance 72 hr; endurance at sea 30 days.

Complement: 45 (8 officers, 16 petty officers, 21 seamen)

Electronics: Passive sonar: Mars-12; Underwater communications: Sirius; Radios: Okun', Shchuka, Ryejd; Radio receivers: Dozor, Myetel'; Gyrocompass: Kurs-2.

Design was prepared in 1934 in cooperation with a Dutch firm [Ed: Original says "Holland," but it seems more likely that this refers to the Dutch cover firm used by the Germans at this time than to Electric Boat in the United States.] Working plans were developed by TsKBS-2 (B. M. Malinin, C. G. Turkov, and others). The formal decision to build Series IX and IX-bis boats was taken on 4 Aug. '34. Starting from S-21, pressure hulls were welded. There were 7 compartments.

Boats were built at Gorkiy (Krasnoye Sormovo) and Leningrad (Sudomekh) between 1936 (S-1) and 1946. A total of 27 boats were completed; another 9 were dismantled incomplete. Project 97 was developed from Series IX-bis and a model built, but it was never produced.

Four boats, including S-52 and S-53, were transferred to China in 1954. Soviet S-class submarines were stricken 1961–65.

Note that Shch-411 and -412 were commissioned in July–Aug. '46 in Leningrad with conning towers like that of Series IX-bis.

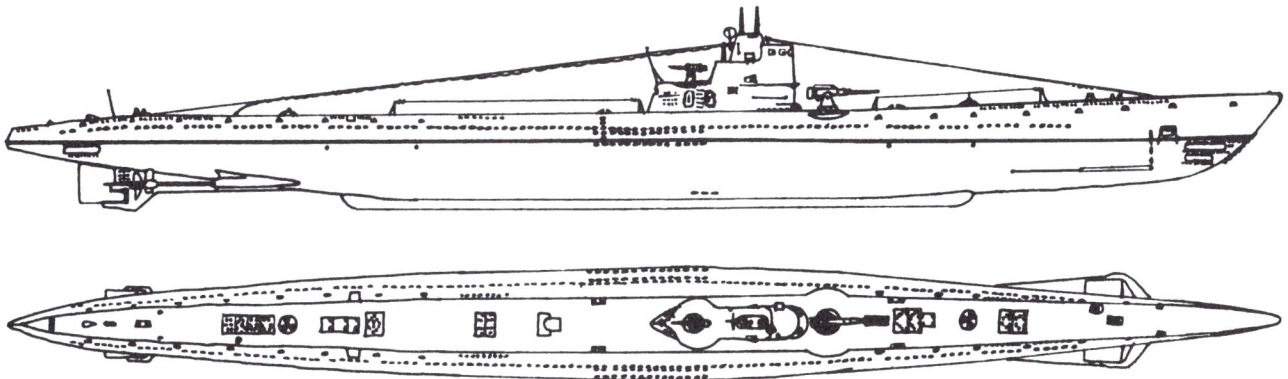

S-56 (A. S. Pavlov)

Project: 96 (Series XV)

NATO Class Name: (M-class)

Names:

	laid down	launched	completed
M-204			
	31 Oct. '40	17 July '46	25 June '47

completed 1947:

M-205

M-206

M-214

M-215

M-216

completed 1948:

M-234

M-235

M-236

M-237

M-238

completed 1949:

M-239

M-240

M-241

M-242

M-243

M-244

M-245

M-246

M-247

M-248

M-249

completed 1950:

M-250

M-251

M-252

M-253

M-270–276

completed 1951:

M-277

M-278–284

completed 1952:

M-285

M-291

completed 1953:

M-292

M-293

M-294   3 Mar. '53

Displacement: 280/353

Dimensions: 49.5 × 4.4 × 2.84

Diving Depth: 70/60

Armament: 4 533 mm TT (4 bow, 4 torpedoes), 1 45 mm (21-K, 200 rounds, removed 1957), 2 7.62 mm machine guns

Machinery: 2 diesels (11-D), 1200 HP; 2 electric motors (PG-17), 436 HP, 15.5/7.9 kts; battery: 60 cells in 2 groups (type MS); 24 t fuel oil; surfaced 965 nm/15.5 kts and 4500 nm/8 kts, submerged 9.7 nm/7.9 kts and 85 nm/2.9 kts. Endurance 15 days; time submerged 48 hr.

Complement: 28

Electronics: Gyrocompass: Kurs-3

Designed by chief engineer F. F. Polushkin. This 1-hull submarine was built in six sections. Boats were built in Leningrad (Sudomekh) and at Gorkiy (Sormovo); all Gorkiy boats except M-214 were assembled in Astrakhan and Severodvinsk. The prototype, M-200 Myest', was completed in 1943 (and sunk Oct. '56 by collision in Tallin Bay). A total of 4 were completed before 1946; M-235 was the last of the class laid down prewar. One incomplete boat, M-219, was used as a floating tank.

Transfers: Bulgaria (3 in 1947–48), China 4 in 1954–55), Egypt (2 in 1957–59), Poland (6: 1 on 18 June, 1 on 25 Sept. '54, 1 on 27 May '55 and 3 on 18 Oct. '54), Romania (4 in 1954–57).

M-273, M-281–284, M-286–289, 292 (Pacific) were broken up in 1968.

M-241 and M-242 (N. F. Starikov)

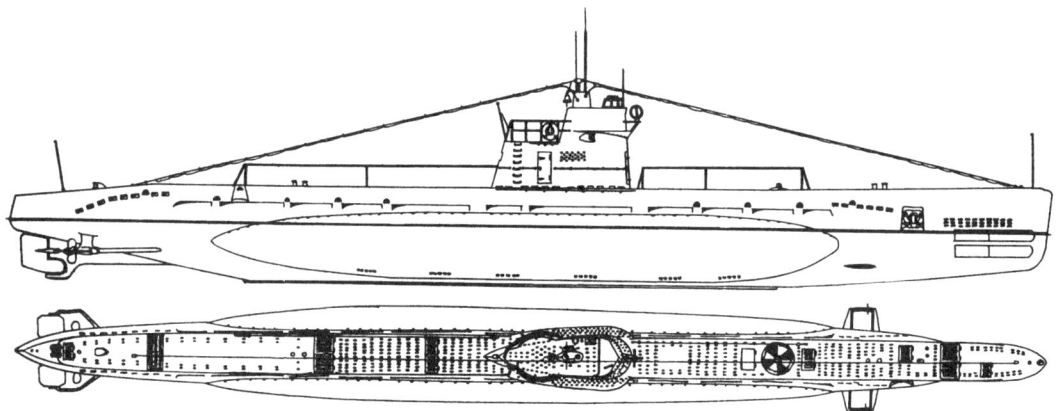

Project: 52

Class Name: PURGA

Names:

PURGA

Displacement: 3165/3819

Dimensions: 95.28 × 15.18 × 5.7

Armament: 4×1 100 mm (B-34 USM-A, 1094 rounds), 6×2 37 mm (V-11M, 14,000 rounds; 2 V-11M later removed), 4 depth charge throwers (BMB-2, 12 charges plus 12 on tracks aft), 30 mines (KB).

Machinery: 6 diesels (37-D), 3 shafts, 12,000 HP = 17.5 kts (9 kts on center shaft only), 12,588 nm/10.2 kts, 3467 nm/17.5 kts; 700 t fuel, 98.4 t potable water, 23.3 t boiler feed water. Endurance 35 days

Complement: 219 (peace)/284 (war)

Electronics: Radar: Ryf; Navigation radar: Rym-1; IFF: Nikel-Khrom; Sonar: Tamir-5; Radios: P-670, 671, 673; Gyrocompass: Kurs-3. [Ed: Navigation radar may mean Loran.]

This coast guard frigate with icebreaker hull was designed by TsKB-32 in 1937, then redesigned by TsKB-15 in 1946–47. She could penetrate 30–40 cm thick ice with snow cover, or a maximum thickness of 50–70 cm. The ship was laid down 17 Dec. '38 at Leningrad (Yard 196), and stopped in 1941. Work resumed in 1951 (Yard 194) and the ship was completed 31 Mar. '57. She was transferred to the Pacific via the Northern Seaway. The ship was stricken 16 Apr. '90.

Purga (V. N. Muratov)

Project: 122-B

NATO Class Name: KRONSTADT

Names:

BO-143–179

BO-181–202

BO-245–255

BO-266–297*

BO-348

BO-357

BO-364

BO-424–471*

BO-531–539

Displacement: 210/320

Dimensions: 52.24 × 6.2 × 2.2

Armament: 1 85 mm (90-K, 240 rounds), 2×1 37 mm (70-K, 1200 rounds), 3×2 12.7 mm (2M-1, 3000 rounds), 2 depth charge throwers (BMB-1; 20 BGB depth charges, 16 MGB-20 depth charges), 18 mines (KB); last series (*) had 2×5 RBU-1200 instead of BMBs.

Armor: 10 mm on waterline, 8 mm on deckhouse (also given as 13 mm)

Machinery: 3 diesels (9-D; first series had 960 HP General Motors diesels), 3 shafts, 3300 HP = 18.7 kts; 3000 nm/8.5 kts, 399 nm/18.5 kts; 2 DG-18 generators. Endurance 10 days.

Complement: 49

Electronics: Radar (air and navigational): Neptun; Sonar: Tamir.

Designed by TsKB-51 Vympel (Gorkiy) in 1948 on the basis of the prewar Project 122 sub-chaser, as ordered by the General Direction Committee of the Navy; chief constructor was N. G. Loshchinskiy. This design had an aluminum deckhouse. Units were built in Zelenodolsk and Severodvinsk in 1946–55. All were redesignated small anti-submarine ship (MPK) from 1966. BO-180 was not completed.

Fates: BO-172 was renamed BRN-47 1961; BO-173 became BRN-48; BO-191 was transferred to the MGU; BO-197 was transferred to the Moscow Junior Sailors' Club (KUM); BO-199 and BO-277 were transferred to the Leningrad KUM; BO-248 and BO-249 were transferred to SNKh of Rostov; BO-252 (BRN-1), BO-253 (BRN-2), BO-254 (BRN-3), BO-272, BO-283 were transferred to the Black Sea Steamship Co. (TChMP); BO-274 was transferred to the Kiev DOSAAF on 14 May '60; BO-275 (renamed KTs-275) and BO-276 were transferred 6 Feb. '61 to the Ukrainian Ministry of Geology. The rest were renamed for transfer to various organizations. New names were *Polyarnyi, Zarya, Ural, Yunyi Sevastopolyets, Kryetchyet* (PC-8, stricken in the Caspian 1972).

Transfers: Albania (4 in 1958), Bulgaria (2 in 1957), China (10 in July 1955, 14 built under license), Cuba (18 in 1962–68), Indonesia (14 in 1962), Poland (4 on 27 May '55 and 4 on 15 Sept. '57), Romania (3 in 1960).

[Ed.: According to Western sources Cuba received 6 units.]

BO-276 (A. N. Sokolov)

Project: 73-K

Class Name: POLUKHIN

Names:

		completed
T-251	PAVEL KHOKHRYAKOV	25 Nov. '49
T-252	ALEXANDER PETROV	8 Dec. '49
T-253	KARL ZYEDIN	18 Sept. '48
T-255	ADRIAN ZESIMOV	15 Feb. '50
T-256	VLADIMIR TREFOLEV	27 Dec. '47
T-257	TIMOFEI ULYANTSEV	4 Jan. '49
T-258	MIKHAIL MARTYNEV	12 Aug. '48
T-259	FYODOR MITROFANOV	7 Nov. '47
T-260	LUHKA PANKOV	23 Feb. '48
T-261	PAVLIN VINOGRADOV	Sept. '49
T-262	STEPAN GRYADUHSHKO	Sept. '49
T-263	SEMYON PYELIKHOV	Sept. '49
T-451	IVAN BORISOV	Sept. '48
T-452	SERGEI SHUVALOV	Apr. '48
T-454	TIMOFEI SLADKOV	Apr. '48

Displacement: 698/858

Dimensions: 78 × 8.2 × 2.47

Armament: 2×1 85 mm (90-K, 600 rounds), 4×1 37 mm (70-K, 2400 rounds), 4 DShK 12.7 mm machine guns, 2 depth charge throwers (BMB-1, 20 depth charges), 2 bottom sweeps (PT), 1 sea sweep (MT-2), magnetic sweep (TEM 1), 2 acoustic sweeps (BAT-2)

Machinery: 2 diesels (General Motors), 3200 HP = 16 kts (12.5 kts towing contact sweep), 3700 nm/16 kts. Endurance 15 days.

Complement: 119

Electronics: Radar: Ryf-1, Sonar: Tamir-5

Designed by chief engineer K. P. Narykov (TsKB-32). Laid down as *Vladimir Polukhin* class (Project 59) turbine minesweepers, but completed with diesels. Hull was riveted, with degausser RV-5. T-250–263 were built in Leningrad (Petrozavod) and T-451–455 in Sevastopol. All were reclassified in 1956. T-251 became the test boat *Kyefal* (broken up 1972). T-252 became the salvage ship *Agatan* (TsL-13 from 1957, broken up 1959). T-256 became training ship UTS-2 (broken up 1988). T-257 became test ship *Losos* (broken up 1964). T-258 became BRN-22 (to TsL-14 1957, broken up

T-259 (Pavlov collection)

13

1959). T-259 became OS-12, then UTS-74 in 1959, then broken up in 1960. T-270 *Paltus* was broken up in 1964. T-261 became OS-11, then PKZ-171 in 1970, and was broken up in 1972. T-262 became BRN-24, then TsL-68 in 1956, and was broken up in 1958. T-263 became OS-2 and was broken up in 1977. T-450 *Pavel Golovin* was beached by a storm near Tuapse in 1952. T-451 became EMTShch-13, then BRN-17 in May '56, and was broken up in 1958. T-452 (EMTShch-11) became BRN-16 and was broken up in 1958. T-453 *Semen Roshal'* was never completed. T-454 (EMTShch-12 and then BRN-18) was broken up in 1964. T-455 *Nikolaj Markin* was dismantled before completion. T-456 *Boris Zhemchuzhin* was never laid down.

Ivan Borisov (V. P. Zablotskij)

Project: 253-LP and 255

NATO Class Name: T-301

Names:

T-229

T-330

T-301–313

T-314–316

T-328

T-340 350

T-364–369

T-392–400

T-436–458

T-480

T-481

T-494–500

T-528–533

T-651–655

T-726–731

T-741–746

T-313 was *Shakhin;* T-500 was *Evgeniy Nikonov.*
103 units.

Displacement: 147.8/164

Dimensions: 38 × 5.7 × 1.58

Armament: 2×1 45 mm (21-KM, 3000 rounds),
2×2 12.7 mm machine guns (originally Colt Browning, later
DShK), 12 mines (KB), 12 depth bombs (MGB). Sweeps:

paravane sweep (MT-3), magnetic sweep (PEMT-4),
acoustic sweep (BAT). Contact sweep designed by Shultz
(OTSh-1).

Armor: 8 mm deckhouse.

Machinery: 3 diesels (Superior), 690 HP = 12.5 kts (9.3 kts
towing contact sweep), 2400 nm/7.1 kts on 10.1 t fuel;
3 DG-15 generators. Endurance 5 days.

Complement: 35

Electronics: Sonar: Tamir.

Designed by chief engineer S. A. Basilevskiy. This class
had a simple welded hull, for easy production. A total of
92 were built in 1943–46 (Project 253-L) at Leningrad
(Baltic, Zhdanov, Petrozavod yards), followed by an improved design (255-K) built at Rybinsk in 1947–52, powered by domestically built ZD-12 diesels (chief engineer
A. G. Sokolov). Sweeps were updated: bottom contact
sweep OPT, contact sweep MT-3, magnetic sweep PEMT-4,
2 acoustic sweeps BAT-2.

Nikonov was handed over to the Togliatti DOSAAF in
1955. In 1969 she was used for seismic studies on the water
reservoir at Rybinsk. *Shakhin (Sokol)* was handed over to
the Baku DOSAAF. One unit became the diving boat VM-
70. Two became the training ships *Kronstadt* and *Sevastopol.*
The first series was broken up in Riga in 1956.

Transfers: Albania (6 in 1960), Egypt (2 in 1959), Poland
(T-225, T-228, T-231, T-241, T-243, T-244, T-246, T-465,
T-467 transferred Apr. '46, all war-built).

[Ed.: According to Shitikov et al., the TTZ for this design
was issued in Apr. '42. The ship was designed by TsKB-51,
whose design was approved on 26 Feb. '43.]

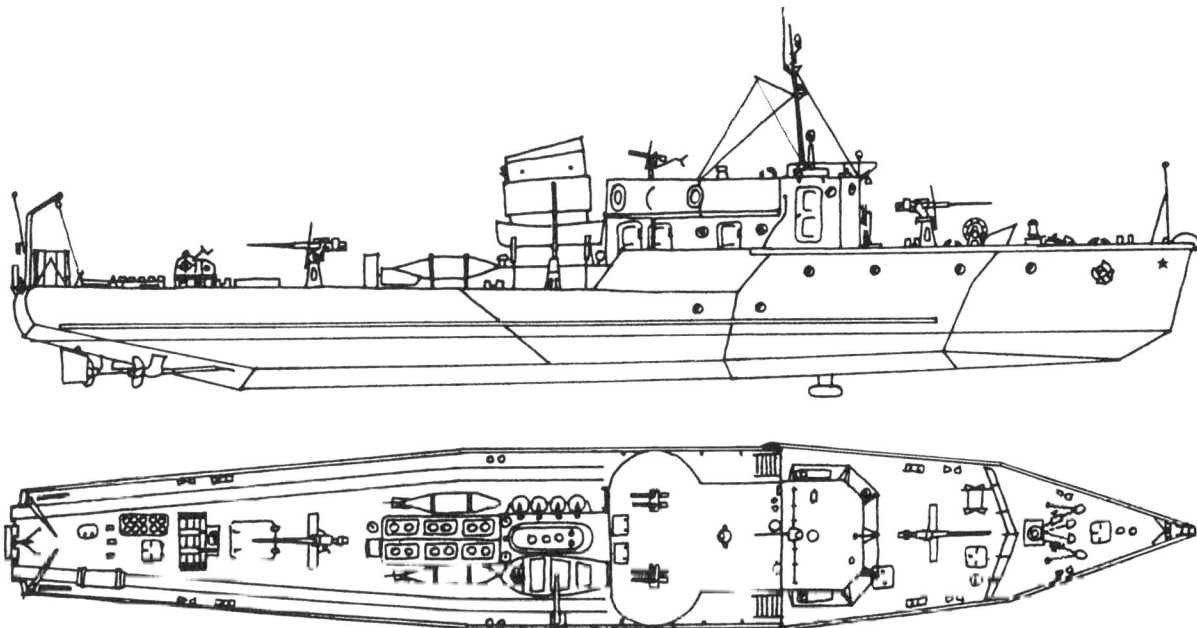

Project: 53-U and 58

Class Name: FUGAS

Names:

		completed
T-220		
T-221	DMITRIY L'ISOV	1946

Displacement: 425/550

Dimensions: 62 × 7.2 × 1.98

Armament: 1×45 mm (21-K, 1500 rounds), 3×1 37 mm (70-K, 1800 rounds), 2×1 12.7 mm DShK machine guns, 2 depth charge throwers (BMB-1, 20 charges), 46 mine shields or 20 mines (KB); sweeps: Shultz OTSh-1 type, paravane sweep, bottom sweep (OPT)

Machinery: 2 diesels (42-BMRN by Kolomensky works), 2 shafts, 2800 HP = 18 kts (14.4 kts with contact sweep), 58 t oil fuel, 3300 nm/18 kts

Complement: 66 (including 8 officers)

Built at Sevastopol (Morzavod, Yard 201). These *Tral* class base (district) minesweepers were laid down before World War II; forty were built before 1946. T-414 and T-415 were scrapped on the slip.

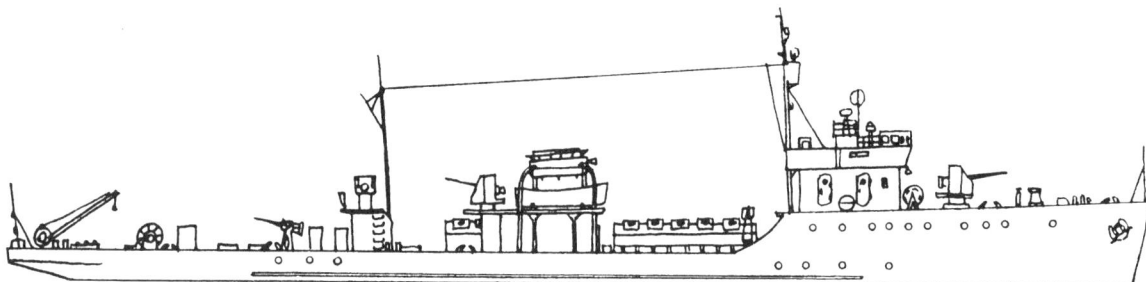

Project: 186

NATO Class Name: None

Names:
BK-529–559
  Twenty-nine units

Displacement: 156/163.5

Dimensions: 38.5 × 5.56 × 1.55

Armament: 2×1 85 mm (200 rounds), 1 37 mm (70-K, 1200 rounds), 2×2 12.7 mm DShK

Armor: 30 mm waterline amidships, 13 mm ends; deck 20 mm amidships, 8 mm at ends

Machinery: 2 diesels, 2 shafts, 1000 HP = 14.1 kts, 750 nm/13 kts, 600 nm/14 kts

Complement: 42

Seaworthy river gunboats built at Leningrad (Admiralty and Sudomekh); eight (beginning with BK-521, laid down 31 Aug. '44 and completed 18 Aug. '45) were built prior to Jan. '46. Hulls were assembled from three welded sub-assemblies. Units operated in the Baltic Fleet. In 1960, five were equipped with Zarnitsa radars.

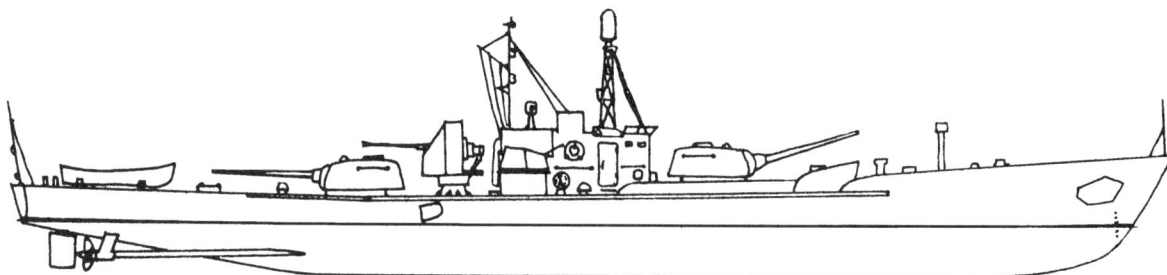

Project: 1125

NATO Class Name: None

Names:

BK-153

BK-155

BK-157

BK-187–199

BK-335–339

BK-425–430

BK-435–459

Fifty-one units

Displacement: 26.5/29.3

Dimensions: 22.65 × 3.55 × 0.56

Armament: 1 76.2 mm (D-11/F-34) in standard T-34 tank turret with 7.62 mm machine gun (77 and 4725 rounds, respectively), 3×1 12.7 mm DShK in DShKBM-2B turrets

Armor: Turrets: 45 mm face, 40 mm sides and 16 mm roof; hull sides and deckhouse 10 mm, deck 4 mm

Machinery: 1 gasoline engine (GAM-34b non-reversing), 850 HP = 18 kts, 250 nm/15 kts, 180 nm/18 kts; 2.2 t fuel. Endurance 2 days.

Complement: 10

Designed by chief engineer Yu. A. Benua (TsKB-19). Lead boat (BK-1) was completed in 1943 at Zelenodolsk; others were built at Astrakhan. A total of 151 were completed by Dec. '45, and construction continued through Dec. '47. Units could be transported by railroad. From 1965 they were classified as artillery cutters (AK). They were stricken in 1966–69.

There were also two Project 1124 boats laid down 1943 in Novosibirsk: BK-344 (placed in preservation in June 1946, transferred to Bulgaria in 1951) and BK-346 (assigned to the Dnepr River flotilla on 9 July '46 and to the Danube flotilla in Apr. '51). Characteristics: 43.8 t, 25.3 m length, 2 76.2 mm guns, 2 12.7 mm machine guns.

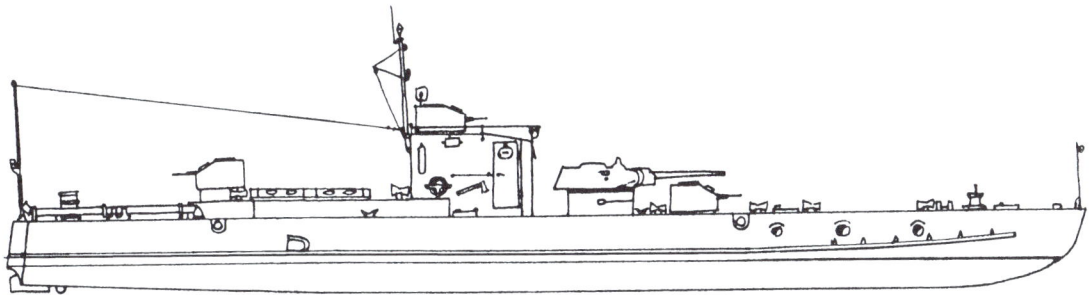

BK-1125 (N. F. Sungorkin)

Project: OD-200 bis

NATO Class Name: MO-V

Names:

MO-269–300

MO-310

MO-471–474

MO-641–663

MO-691

MO-692

MO-694

    Sixty-three units

Displacement: 41.6/48.2

Dimensions: 23.4 × 4 × 1.75

Armament: 1 37 mm (70-K, 500 rounds), 2×1 12.7 mm DShK (4000 rounds), 4 BGB (large depth charges), 8 MGB (small depth charges)

Machinery: 2 diesels (M-50), 2000 HP = 29 kts, 470 nm/29 kts, 1500 nm/8 kts; 6 t fuel; DG-3.6 generator. Endurance 5 days.

Complement: 16

Electronics: Sonar: Tamir-10

    Designed by chief engineer L. L. Yermash (TsKB-32). These wooden boats were built in Leningrad and at Sosnovski; eighty-eight were completed in 1943–46, and construction ended in 1948.

    Transfers: Bulgaria (MO-471–474 in 1947) and Poland (Eleven war-built units on 5 Apr. '46). Reclassifications: MO-289–291 to OK-45, OK-43, OK-44; MO-659 to DZ-14; MO-661–662 to SK-298–299. MO-283–292 were transferred to DOSAAF. Four were transferred to the Border Guards.

Project: TD-200 and TD-200 bis*

NATO Class Name: P-2

Names:

TK-16–20

TK-31

TK-32

TK-36

TK-37

TK-40

TK-42

TK-47

TK-49–54

TK-74–78

TK-86

TK-91

TK-92

TK-96

TK-121

TK-126

TK-134

TK-149

TK-169

TK-170

TK-180–187

TK-202–220

TK-255–266

TK-421–449

TK-701–720

TK-839–845

TK-890–939

TK-1090–1106

    167 units

Displacement: 40.8/46.8 (48.2*)

Dimensions: 23.7 × 4.7 × 1.6

Armament: 2×1 533 mm TT, 2×2 12.7 mm

Machinery: 3 M-50 diesels, 3000 HP = 38 kts, 600 nm/25 kts, 1000 nm/8 kts; 1 5.6 kW diesel generator. Endurance 6 days.

Complement: 11

    Designed by chief engineer L. L. Yermash (TsKB-32), developed from the prewar OD-200 sub-chaser design. These wooden boats were built in Leningrad (Yard 5) in 1946–52 (prototype was completed in Apr. '46). Radar was installed on forty-six units: Zarnitsa search radar, Fakel IFF interrogator, and Khrom transponder.

    [Ed.: Western sources reported that many of these boats were transferred to China.]

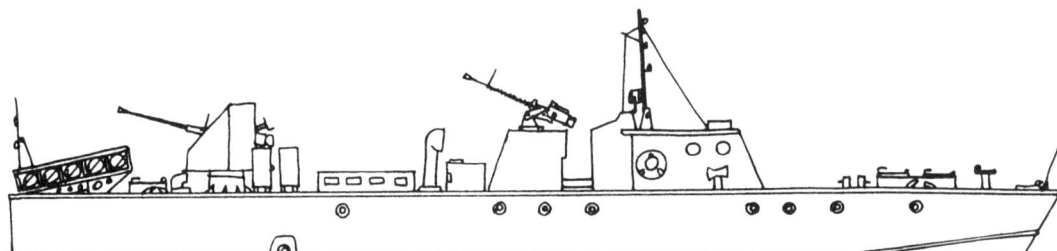

Project: 123 bis, M-123 bis*, 123K (KOMSOMOLETS)

NATO Class Name: P-4

Names:

TK-1–6

TK-8–12

TK-21–30

TK-46

TK-95

TK-188–191

TK-271–301

TK-317–320

TK-327–332

TK-337–350

TK-352–380

TK-386–420

TK-460–471

TK-482–512

TK-551–558

TK-574

TK-575

TK-597

TK-599

TK-601–606

TK-607   KOMSOMOLETS KAZAKHSTANA

TK-608   PIONER KAZAKHSTANA

TK-609

TK-637–660*

TK-667–670*

TK-677–700*

TK-721–740

TK-751–771*

TK-809–838*

TK-940–957

TK-972

TK-980–995

  349 units

Displacement: 21.7*, 22.6/25

Dimensions: 18.7 × 3.4 × 1

Armament: 2×1 450 mm TT, 4 12.7 mm or 1×2 14.5 mm DShK*, 6 MGB-20 depth charges

Armor: 7 mm deckhouse

Machinery: 2 Packard gasoline engines or 2 diesels (M-50) in echelon*, 2 shafts, 2000 HP = 42 kts (up to 45 kts*), 410 nm/30 kts

Complement: 12

Electronics: Radar: Zarnitsa

Chief engineers: F. P. Livyentsev (KB of Tyumyensky works No. 639) and V. M. Burlakov* (TsKB-19). The hulls were of Duralumin, with four bulkheads. Boats could be transported by railroad. The prototype, TK-351, was completed 25 Oct. '40, and a total of 31 boats were completed prior to 1946. Postwar construction: 89 in Tyumen 1946–55, 255 in Feodosiya (Yard 831) beginning in Nov. '49. In 1947, TK-981 was fitted with experimental hydrofoils, achieving over 60 kts. Another eight units (including TK-290, 289, 551, and 557) were fitted with forward hydrofoils in 1956 (chief engineer R. E. Alekseeyev), achieving 47 kts.

From 1965, TK-4, 5, and 10 (Pacific) were reclassified as patrol boats (AK), with 2×2 14.5 mm (2M-7) instead of TT; AK-4 and -5 were stricken in 1978. TK-691 was handed over to the aircraft works in Taganrog in 1954. TK-413–415, 505, and 605 served in the Caspian. TAK-6, TAK-9, TAK-21, TAK-22, TAK-30, TAK-293, and TAK-295 (Pacific) were target boats.

Transfers: Albania (5), Benin (2 in 1979), Bulgaria (8), China (55), Cuba (18), North Korea (40), Romania (10 in 1957, including TK-983, TK-986–989), Somalia (6), Syria (12), Vietnam (TK-287, TK-294, TK-296–299, TK-317, TK-319, TK-320, TK-552, TK-553, TK-556 in 1961), Zaire (3).

[Ed.: According to Western sources, transfers were as follows: Albania (6 in 1956, plus 6 from China in 1965), Bangladesh (4 from China in 1965), Benin (2 from North Korea in 1979), Bulgaria (8 in 1956), China (70, including home-built units), Cuba (12 in 1962–64), Cyprus (6 in 1964–65), Egypt (4 from Syria in 1970), Korea (12 in 1952–53 plus at least fifteen built locally), Romania (12), Somalia (4 in 1972), Syria (17 in 1958–60), Tanzania (4 in 1972-73), North Yemen (1 in 1969, 3 in 1970–71), South Yemen (4 in 1978).]

Memorials: TK-725 on Sapun Mount in Sevastopol, TK-288 in Vladivostok, TK-456 in Petropavlovsk-Kamchatskiy.

TK-123 bis (A. N. Sokolov)

Project: TM-200, TM-200 bis

NATO Class Name: None

Names:

TK-455–459

TK-708–711

TK-741–750

Displacement: 40.7/46.8

Dimensions: 24.8 × 4 × 1.7

Armament: 2×1 533 mm TT, 3 12.7 mm DShK machine guns (4500 rounds), 4 BGB depth charges or 8 MGB-20 depth charges; DA-7 smoke maker

Armor: 10 mm deckhouse

Machinery: 3 Packard gasoline engines, 3600 HP = 38 kts, 325 nm/33 kts, 850 nm/7 kts; 5 t fuel. Endurance 6 days.

Complement: 11

   Chief designer L. L. Yermash (TsKB-32). The prototype, TK-450, was built in Rybinsk, and five units were completed prior to 1946. Boats originally served in the Baltic, but from Jan. '48 they operated in the Black Sea. They were stricken in 1951–53 due to excessive hull corrosion.

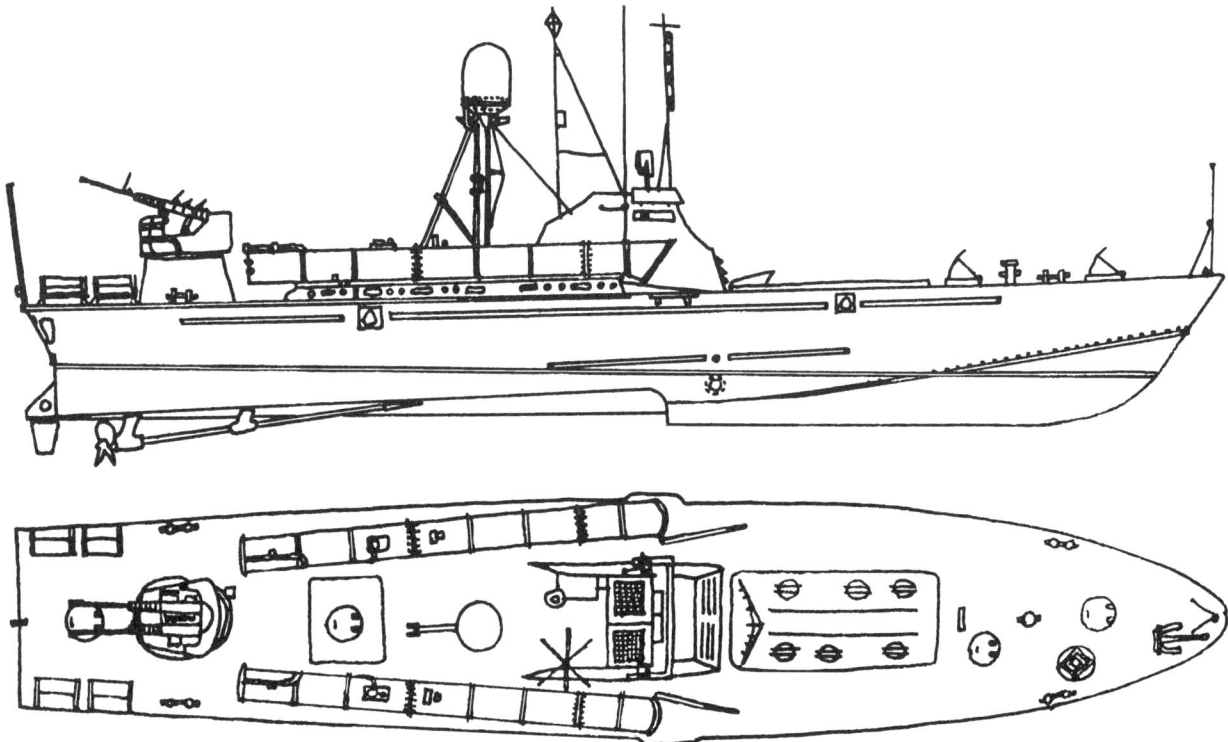

Part II
Ships of Postwar Design

Project: 941 (AKULA)

NATO Class Name: TYPHOON

Names:

All built at Severodvinsk

	laid down	launched	completed
TK-208	3 Mar. '77	23 Sept. '80	12 Dec. '81
TK-202	1 Oct. '80	26 Apr. '82	28 Dec. '83
TK-12	27 Apr. '82	17 Dec. '83	27 Dec. '84
TK-13	5 Jan. '84	21 Feb. '85	29 Dec. '85
TK-17	24 Feb. '85	Aug. '86	6 Nov. '87
TK-20	6 Jan. '87	July '88	Sept. '89

Displacement: 24,500/33,800

Dimensions: 175 × 22.8 × 11.5

Diving Depth: – – –

Armament: 20 missiles (rocket RSM-52, complex D-19), 8 AA missiles (Igla-1), 4 533 mm TT (torpedoes 53-65K, SET-65, SAET-60M), 2 650 mm TT (torpedoes 65–76)

Machinery: 2×190 MW pressurized-water reactors (OK-650), 2 steam turbines, 2 shafts, 100,000 HP = 16/27 kts; 4 3200 kW turbo-generators, 2 diesel generators (DG-750); 2 creep motors (260 HP each)

Complement: 150 (50 officers, 80 petty officers)

Electronics: Sonar: Skat; Radar: Albatros; ESM: Nakat-M; Navigation System Tobo Responder: Kremniy-2; Satellite navigation system: Simfonia; Satellite communications system: Tsunami; Radio system: Molniya

Classified as Heavy Cruisers of 1st Rank. Chief designer: S. N. Kovalev (TsKB-18 Rubin). The Technical Assignment for this submarine was approved in Dec. '72. Reactors are analogous to those of current nuclear icebreakers. Machinery is in two completely separate installations. Built in nine-

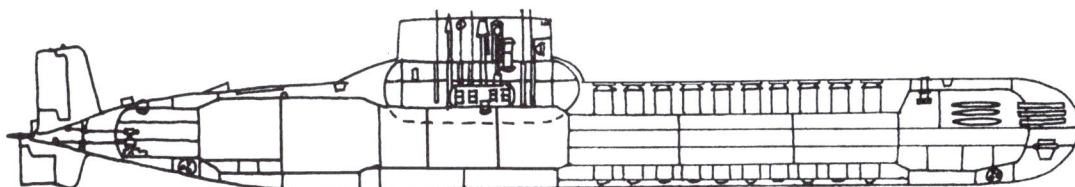

TK-202 (U. A. Pakhomov)

Typhoon class (U.S. Naval Institute Photographic Collection)

teen sections, in two separate pressure hulls (7.2 m in diameter) and three separate sections: torpedo, central, and steering. Missile launchers are between the pressure hulls. At the base of the conning tower are rescue chambers. Silencing is by double-cascade rubber cord cushioning. All units are in the Northern Fleet, based at Nyerpichya Cove. TK-208 began modernization in 1992. A seventh unit was broken up on the slip.

Typhoon class (M.O.D. U.K.)

Project: 667BDRM (DELF'IN)

NATO Class Name: DELTA-4

Names:

	laid down	launched	completed
K-51	23 Feb. '81	Jan. '85	Feb. '86
K-84	Nov. '84	Dec. '85	Feb. '86
K-64	Nov. '85	Dec. '86	Feb. '88
K-114	Dec. '86	Sept. '87	Jan. '89
K-117	Sept. '87	Sept. '88	Mar. '90
K-18	Sept. '88	Nov. '89	Sept. '91
K-407	Nov. '89	Jan. '91	20 Feb. '92

Displacement: 10,210/12,000

Dimensions: 167 × 12.2 × 8.8

Diving Depth: – – –

Armament: 16 missiles (rocket RSM-54, complex D-9RM), 4 533 mm TT (12 torpedoes and rocket-torpedoes)

Machinery: 2 VM-4SG reactors, 2 steam turbines, 2 shafts (quieter propellers), 60,000 HP = 14/24 kts. Endurance 90 days.

Complement: 130

Electronics: Sonar: Skat-2, includes a towed array; Navigational system: Tobol-M; Communications system: Tsunami and Molniya

Built in Severodvinsk. Construction was ordered 10 Dec. '75. Chief designer was S. N. Kovalev. The navigational system uses both astrocorrection and bottom transponders (beacons). Missiles are launched from 55 m depth, in sea states up to 6–7, at 6 kts; all missiles are fired in a single salvo. Compared to previous sonars, Skat has a much more powerful transmitter and a more streamlined ribless (cellular) plastic sonar dome. An escape chamber is installed abaft the missile section. All are in the Northern Fleet, based at Olyenia Cove.

K-64 (U. A. Pakhomov)

Project: 667BDR (KAL'MAR)

NATO Class Name: DELTA-3

Names:

	laid down	launched	completed
K-441	1975	1976	Dec. '76
K-424		1977	
K-449		1977	
K-455		1978	
K-490		1978	
K-407		1978	
K-44		1979	
K-496		1979	
K-506		1979	
K-211		1980	
K-223		1980	
K-180		1980	
K-433		1981	
K-129		1981	

All built at Severodvinsk. Until Apr. '92, K-441 was named 26 Syezda KPSS.

Displacement: 8940/10,600

Dimensions: 155 × 11.7 × 8.7

Diving Depth: ———

Armament: 16 missiles (rocket RSM-50, complex D-9R), 4 533 mm TT, 2 406 mm TT (18 torpedoes)

Machinery: 2 reactors, 2 steam turbines, 2 shafts, 60,000 SHP = 14/25 kts. Endurance 90 days.

Complement: 130

Electronics: Sonar: Rubikon, Radar navigation system: Tobol M-2 (radar Albatros); Navigational System: Tsiklon, using astrocorrection (2 day period) and bottom sonar beacons

Chief designer: S. M. Koralyov. This class, which carries three versions of its missile, carried the first Soviet sea-based missiles with MIRVed warheads. The hull is built in eleven compartments. Height from keel to top of sail is 17.7 m. These submarines have maneuvering propellers (taxi-up devices). They are being removed from service under the START treaty. Basing: five in Northern Fleet (three in Yagelnaya Cove, two in Olyenya Cove) and nine in Pacific Fleet (Rybachij).

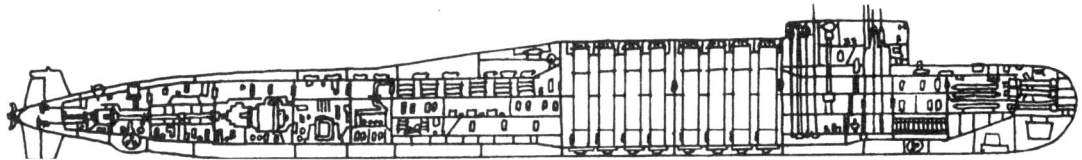

Delta-3 class (U.S. Naval Institute Photographic Collection)

Project: 667BD (MURENA-M)

NATO Class Name: DELTA-2

Names:

	laid down	launched	completed
K-182	Apr. '73	Jan. '75	20 Sept. '75

named *Shestidesyatiletie Velikogo Oktyabrya*
4 Nov. '77–'91

	laid down	launched	completed
K-92	'73	'75	17 Dec. '75
K-193	'74	'75	30 Dec. '75
K-421	'74	'75	30 Dec. '75

All built in Severodvinsk.

Displacement: 9350/10,500

Dimensions: $155 \times 11.7 \times 8.6$

Diving Depth: 550/390

Armament: 16 missiles (rocket RSM-40/R-29U, complex D-9U), 4 533 mm TT, 2 406 mm TT (18 torpedoes)

Machinery: 2 reactors (VM type), 2 steam turbines in separate compartments (echelon arrangement), 2 shafts, 55,000 HP = 14/25 kts

Complement: 126

Electronics: Sonar system: Rubikon; Navigational system: Tobol-667BD; Space communications system: Molniya (antenna Sintez)

Chief designer: S. N. Kovalev. Compartments, fore to aft: (i) torpedo, (ii) batteries and officers' quarters, (iii) central command post, (iv) and (v) missiles, (vi) diesel generators (2 DG-460), (vii) reactors, (viii) and (ix) turbines, (x) electrical compartment. This class has a television observation system. These submarines are being withdrawn under the START treaty. All are in the Northern Fleet (based at Yagyelnaya Cove).

Project: 667B (MURENA)

NATO Class Name: DELTA-1

Names:

	laid down	launched	completed
Severodvinsk:			
K-279	'71	Jan. '72	22 Dec. '72
K-447		1973	
K-450		1973	
K-385		1974	
K-457		1974	
K-453		1974	
K-460		1975	
K-472		1975	
K-475		1975	
K-171		1976	
Komsomolsk:			
K-366		1974	
K-417		1974	
K-477		1975	
K-497		1975	
K-500		1976	
K-512		1976	

28 Oct. '88–'91 named *70 Let Vlksm*

	laid down	launched	completed
K-523		1977	
K-530		1977	

Displacement: 7800/10,000

Dimensions: $139 \times 11.7 \times 8.4$

Delta-1 class (U.S. Naval Institute Photographic Collection)

Delta-1 class (M.O.D. U.K.)

Diving Depth: 550/390

Armament: 12 missiles (rocket RSM-40, complex D-9), 4 533 mm (12 torpedoes), 2 406 mm (8 torpedoes)

Machinery: 2 reactors (VM-4 type), 2 steam turbines (OK-700 with GTZA-635 gearing), 2 shafts, 52,000 HP = 16/26 kts; 2 creep motors, 260 HP each; TMV-32 (3000 kW) turbo generators

Complement: 120

Electronics: Sonar: Kerch; Radar navigation system: Tobol; Satellite navigational system: Tsiklon-B; Automated communications system: Molniya-1; have a central computer system (not named)

Chief designer S. N. Kovalev (TsKB-18). Average time between refuelings is about 5 years. Fire a full salvo of missiles while submerged at 5 kts, in sea states up to 6. These submarines are being withdrawn under the START treaty. Basing: Northern Fleet (9 in Ostrovnoj), Pacific Fleet (6 in Pavlovskiy, 3 in Rybachiy). K-171 passed through four oceans en route to the Pacific Fleet, 1976. K-279 went to the breakers in 1992 at Severodvinsk.

Delta-1 class (M.O.D. U.K.)

Project: 667

NATO Class Name: YANKEE

Names:

Severodvinsk:

	laid down	launched	completed
K-137 LENINETS	9 Nov. '64	28 Aug. '66	5 Nov. '67
K-140			30 Dec. '67
K-26			3 Sept. '68
K-32			26 Oct. '68
K-216			27 Dec. '68
K-207			30 Dec. '68
K-210			6 Aug. '69
K-249			27 Sept. '69
K-253*			28 Oct. '69
K-395*			5 Dec. '69
K-408*			25 Dec. '69
K-411			31 Aug. '70
K-418			22 Sept. '70
K-420			29 Oct. '70
K-423*			13 Nov. '71
K-426			22 Dec. '70
K-415*			30 Dec. '71
K-403			20 Aug. '71
K-245			16 Dec. '71
K-214			31 Dec. '71
K-219			31 Dec. '71
K-228			31 Dec. '72
K-241			23 Dec. '71
K-444			9 Dec. '72

Komsomolsk:

	completed
K 399*	24 Dec. '69
K-434	21 Oct. '70
K-236*	27 Dec. '70
K-389	1970
K-252	1971
K-258	1971
K-446	1971
K-451*	1971
K-436	1972
K-430	1972

Severodvinsk units were Project Navaga; Komsomolsk units were Project Nalim.

K-137 *Leninets* (U. A. Pakhomov)

Andromeda (S. P. Bukan')

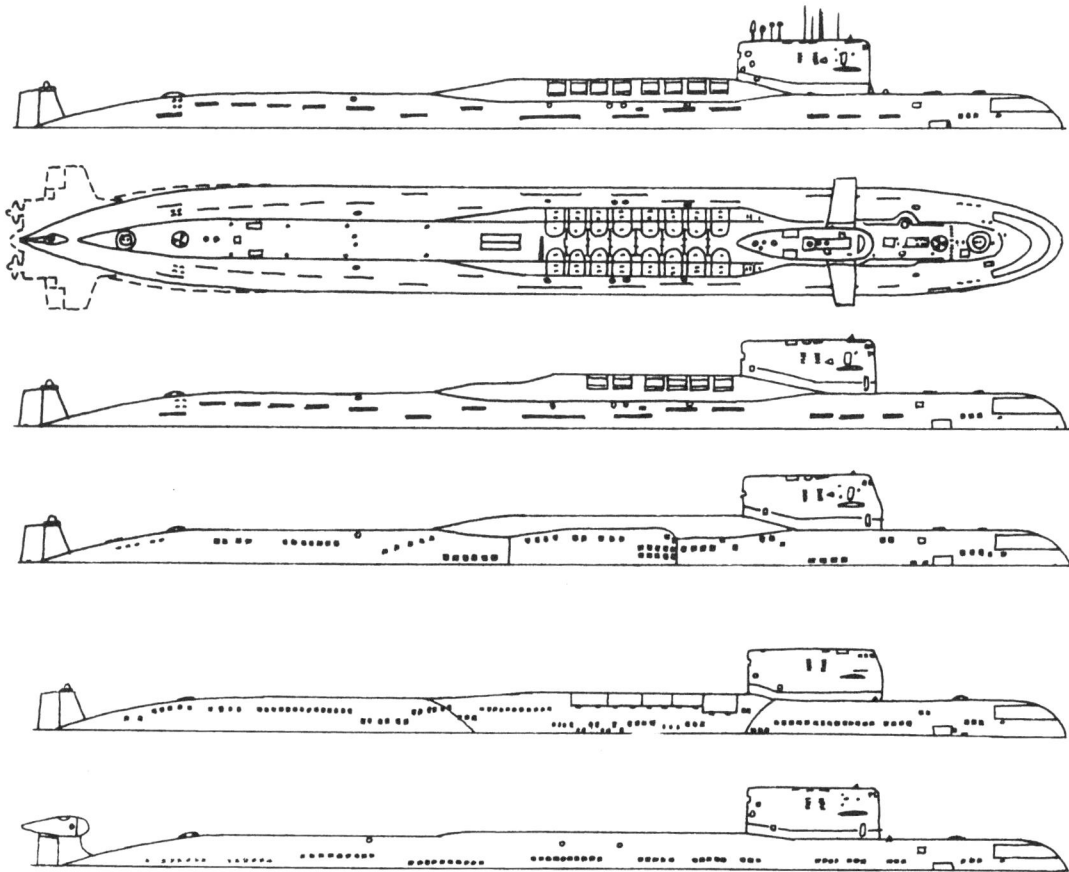

Displacement: 7766/9300

Dimensions: 129.8 × 11.7 × 8.7

Diving Depth: 450/380

Armament: 16 missiles (rocket RSM-25, complex D-7), 4 533 mm (12 torpedoes, types 53-65K and SET-65), 2 406 mm (8 torpedoes, type SET-73). Torpedoes can be launched at 250 m depth.

Machinery: 2 reactors (VM-4/2, 89.2 MW each), 2 steam turbines (OK-700, TZA-635 gearing) en echelon (2 independent power units), 2 shafts, 52,000 HP — 16 26 kts; 2 creep motors (PG-153: 225 kW each); 2 batteries (112×48-SM cells each); 2 DG-460 diesel generators. Endurance 70 days.

Complement: 120

Electronics: Sonar: MGK-100 Kerch; Radar: Albatros; ESM: Zaliv-P; IFF: Khrom-KM; Navigational System: Tobol-667A; Gyrocompass: Mayak

Chief designer S. N. Kovalev. The technical project for this class was approved in 1964. There are 10 compartments. K-219, K-228, K-241, K-245, K-430, K-436, K-44, K-446, and K-451 were completed to Project 667AU.

K-140 was modified in Severodvinsk 1977–80 (Project 667AM) to fire 12 solid-fuel RSM-45 (SS-N-17) missiles (system D-11, by *Arsenal* factory). The missiles were destroyed by firing in 1989 and the submarine stricken in 1990. In 1982–91 seven units were rebuilt under Project 667AT *Grusha* (Chief Designer O. Ya. Margolin: NATO Yankee-Notch). The missiles were removed and 2×4 533 mm TT were fitted in the side to launch torpedoes and cruise missiles (56 torpedoes). Of this project, K-236, K-399, K-408, and K-415 served in the Pacific; the rest were in the Northern Fleet. K-420 was rebuilt in 1979–80 to fire twelve Meteorit (3M-25, NATO SS-N-24) cruise missiles from angled launchers outside the pressure hull (Project 667M Andromeda). K-403 was modified 1978–80 under Project 09774 Akson (NATO Yankee-Pod) as a Large Nuclear Submarine for Special Duties (1st Rank): missiles were removed and replaced by electronics; a towed array was added in a streamlined pod. The submarine was renamed KS-403. Another is being modified to this configuration. K-411 became KS-411, a midget-submarine carrier (Project 09780, NATO Yankee-Stretch).

K-219 was sunk 6 Oct. '86 after a fire off the U.S. coast. K-137 was broken up in 1992. Under the strategic arms limitation treaties, units of this class were withdrawn from service, their hulls (less their missile sections) preserved for further modification: 2 in 1979, 2 in Jan. '80, 1 in Jan. '81, 2 in Jan. '82, 1 in Nov. '82, 1 in June '83, 1 in Jan. '84, 2 in Apr. '85, 2 in Mar. '86, 2 in 1987, the rest in 1988–89. Northern Fleet units had been based at Yagyelnaya Cove, Pacific Fleet units at Rybachij and Pavlovskij.

Project: 658, 658M*, 701**

NATO Class Name: HOTEL

Names:

	laid down	launched	completed
K-19	17 Oct. '58	8 Aug. '59	12 Nov. '60
K-33			6 June '61
K-55			12 Aug. '62
K-40			28 Dec. '62
K-16			15 June '63
K-145			19 Dec. '63
K-149			12 Feb. '64

named *Ukrainskiy Komsomolets* in 1969

| K-178 | | | Dec. '62 |

All built in Severodvinsk.

Displacement: 4030/5000

Dimensions: 114.1 × 9.2 × 7.31; 127 × 9.2 × 7.1**

Diving Depth: 300/250

Armament: 3 missiles (6**), 4 533 mm, 2 406 mm (stern) (12 SET-65 and 53-65k in racks and for 53-61 in tubes)

Machinery: 2 reactors (VM-A, 140 MW each), 2 geared turbines (60-DM), 2 shafts, 39,200 HP = 21–26 kts; 2 creep motors (PG-116, 450 HP each). 2 diesel generators (400 kW M-820s, operating at 400 Hz, 380 V; AC is inverted to DC). 2 batteries (112×28 SM-1 cells each). 31,000 nm/26 kts, 28,000 nm/24 kts (80 percent power). Endurance 50 days.

Complement: 128

Electronics: Sonar: MG-200 Arktika, passive sonar MG-10; ESM: Nakat; IFF: Khrom-K; Navigational system: Pluton-658

Chief designer S. N. Kovalev. Built by Soviet Ministry order 26 Aug. '56. These were double-hull submarines with 10 compartments. Initially they were armed with R-13FM (system D-2) surface-launched missiles (time after surfacing to launch the third missile was 12 minutes). In 1965–70 they were rearmed with submerged-launch R-21 missiles (D-4 system). In 1966 K-145** was rearmed with R-29 (D-9 system) missiles in Severodvinsk (under supervision of chief designer N. F. Shul'zhenko). K-40 became a communications ship (KS-40) in 1977. K-55 and K-178 (Pacific) were rebuilt as torpedo submarines (Project 658T) in Bol'shoi Kamyen'.

K-19 suffered a main reactor breakdown on 4 July '61, and her reactor section was removed and replaced in 1962–64; she was stricken in 1991. Northern Fleet units were stricken in 1988–90.

[Ed.: A recent article in *Morskoi Sbornik* recounts the design of an unsuccessful alternative to this submarine, Malakhit's Project 639, which was intended to carry the D-3 (R-15) missile, which was substantially larger than the D-2. To keep the Project 627 *(November)* inner hull, the designers tried to stow the missiles horizontally, raising them to the vertical to fire. An alternative was magazine stowage, using a horizontal tube to fire. Some young designers proposed a two-row arrangement of missile tubes, in which the inner hull diameter would be reduced to 10 m. In the end, Malakhit decided to repeat the first-generation arrange-

Hotel class
(Royal Navy)

ment, with vertical tubes passing through the sail. Stability on the surface was achieved by widening the hull. The preliminary design was completed in Nov. '57; the submarine could be propelled by either lead-bismuth or light-water reactor. For the first time in their history Malakhit adopted AC power, since the required load could not have been met by DC. To protect against shock, missiles would have been stowed unfuelled. This project died when D-3 was canceled. Characteristics: $114.1 \times 11.4 \times 8.0$ m = approx 6000 t, $2 \times 35,000$ HP LMR = 25–26 kts, or $2 \times 25,000$ HP PWR = 22.5–23.5 kts.]

K-33 (A. N. Sokolov)

Project: 629

NATO Class Name: GOLF

Names:

	renamed	
Severodvinsk:		
B-92	K-96	20 Jan. '60
B-40	K-72	then K-372 in 1974
B-41	K-79	
B-42	K-83	then K-183 in 1974
B-121	K-102	
B-125	K-167	
B-45	K-88	
B-61	K-93	
B-15	K-113	
K-118		
K-36	K-106	
K-91		
K-110		
K-153	BS-153	
K-142		
Komsomolsk-na-Amur:		
B-93	K-126	
B-103	K-129	
B-109	K-136	
B-113	K-139	
K-75	B-575	
K-99		
K-163		

Displacement: 2820/3553

Dimensions: $98.9 \times 8.2 \times 8$

Diving Depth: 300/250

Armament: 3 missile tubes (SM-60) firing R-13 rockets; complex D-2; 6 533 mm TT (4 bow, 2 stern; 6 torpedoes in tubes). Torpedoes could be launched at 80 m depth at any speed.

Machinery: 3 diesels (37-D), 6000 HP, 3 electric motors (2700 HP PG-102 on center shaft, 1350 HP PG-101s on wing shafts, total 5400 HP) = 15.5/12.5 kts. Range: under snorkel (RPD), with extra fuel, 16,000 nm/7 kts or 14,000 nm/7.5 kts; surfaced, 5000 nm/15.5 kts or 27,000 nm/8.5 kts. Diesel generator DG-120. Battery: 120-STs (4 groups, 112 cells each). Endurance 70 days.

Complement: 59 (10 officers)

Electronics: Sonar: Arktika, MG-15; Underwater communications system: Svyet-M; Radar: Albatros; ESM: Nakat; IFF: Khrom; Navigational system: Pluton-629

Chief designer N. N. Isanin (TsKB-16 Malakhit). Construction ordered 1955, completed 1959–62. Double-hulled submarines with 8 compartments: (i) torpedo room; (ii) batteries (two groups), officers' mess, sonar; (iii) TsP, navigational and gyro system; (iv) missile section and air conditioning; (v) batteries, galley, sick bay, petty officers' cabins; (vi) diesels; (vii) electric motors and switchboard; (viii) torpedo room and crews' quarters. Originally designed to launch missiles on the surface (at up to 15 kts in sea states up to 4–5; first missile 4 min after surfacing, then at 4 min intervals). Modernized to fire R-21 (system D-4) submerged-launch missiles under Project 629A (NATO Golf II) under an order dated 2 July '62. They (except for K-136 in the Pacific, stricken 1980) also received a new navigational system, Sigma-629A. Beginning in 1968 they received a towed communications antenna, Paravan. One of the modified submarines, K-129 (reconstruction completed 22 June '67), sank 8 Mar. '68 and was stricken 30 Aug. '68; in 1974 it was partly raised by the Americans.

K-142 was rebuilt (Project 629B) to test submerged launches, with two launchers. In 1967 three launchers were installed in Project 629A. K-102 was rebuilt in Severodvinsk beginning in Nov. '68 under Project 605 (chief designer V. V. Borisov) to test the 4K18 missile (D-5 system, four launchers). K-118 was rebuilt Dec. '76 under Project 601 (chief designer V. V. Borisov), lengthened to 117.6 m, with six launchers for the D-9 system (NATO Golf III). K-153 was rebuilt in 1978 on the Black Sea under Project 619 (chief designer Yu. N. Kormilitsin, TsKB-18; NATO Golf V) with a single D-19 launcher. She was renamed BS-153 in 1991, and was broken up in 1992. K-83, K-107, and K-96 were transferred from the Northern to the Pacific Fleet in 1973–79 and were rebuilt in Dal'zavod as radio relay submarines (Project 629R, chief designer V. V. Borisov). Missiles and stern torpedo tubes were removed. K-107 was returned to the Northern Fleet. K-113 was transferred to the Pacific for reconstruction as a minelayer (Project 629E) at Dal'zavod; she was stricken in 1974.

Transfers: K-36 and K-91 to Pacific, stricken 1980. K-372, K-79, K-93, K-96, K-142, and K-183 to Baltic, all out of service 1991.

Three were ordered by China. The first, built in Komsomolsk, was towed to China without missiles. The second was shipped in sections. The third was separate parts, for assembly in Shanghai. One Chinese submarine of this type was sunk.

[Ed.: According to a recent Russian account, on 9 Jan. '59 the Soviet Council of Ministers ordered that all technical documents on both Project 629 and the R-11FM (naval Scud) missile be handed over to the Chinese; TsKB-16 was named lead organization for construction in China. As the Sino-Soviet split deepened, all Soviet specialists were ordered home in Aug. '60. By that time much of the material for the lead ship had already been delivered to China, and that submarine was completed.

According to this account, although Project 629 was conceived as a platform for the R-13 missile, delays in the missile project led to a decision to deliver submarines laid down in 1957 with R-11FMs, the new missiles being installed during yard periods. Several improvements were made in 1958–60: beginning with Yard 811, new communications and ESM gear, and beginning with Yard 815, a new passive sonar, MG-10. Earlier ships were fitted with this equipment during overhauls.

These submarines were designed to launch their missiles when surfaced. Trials with models of the R-11FM missile showed that a missile could be launched submerged, and the Project 611 submarine B-67 was converted for tests in 1960. It was already clear that something better than the short-range R-11FM was needed; a 20 Mar. '58 governmental resolution ordered development of a new underwater-launch missile. A sixteenth ship of this class (Project 629bis) was ordered to test the two alternative submerged-launch

K-36 (A. N. Sokolov)

BS-153 (V. V. Kostrichenko)

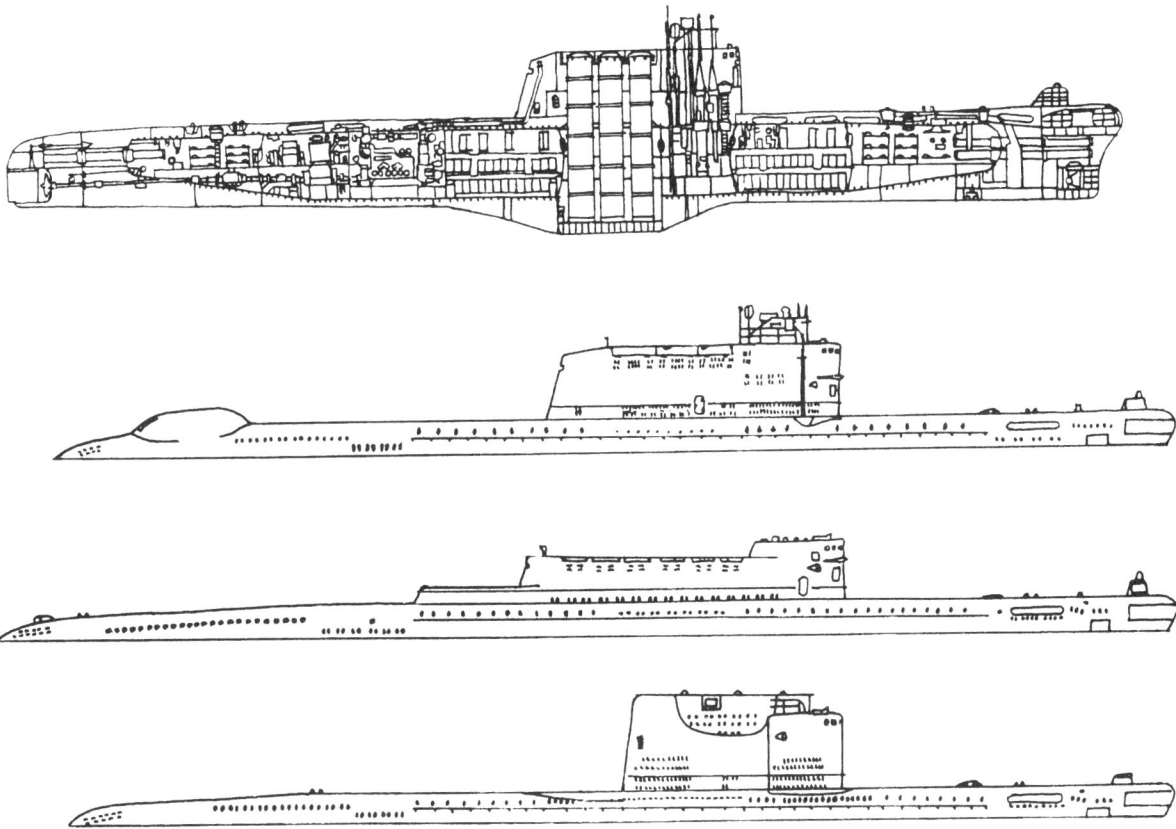

weapons, a liquid-fuelled one developed by the Makeev OKB and a solid-fuel one developed by a team led by P. A. Tiurin. This project also embraced the first Soviet solid-state shipboard computer for missile fire control (chief constructor O. A. Beliaev). The submarine emerged with two operational missile tubes, the third being left empty. The solid-fuel rocket never saw trials, the liquid-fuel alter-native being adopted. Project 629A required a new naviga-tional system (Sigma-629A in place of Pluton 629).

The first Project 629A submarine (with the new missiles) was K-88, delivered to Severodvinsk for reconstruction in Aug. '64, but work began only in 1965; she emerged for dock trials between 14 and 20 Nov. '66, and ran builders' trials beginning 22 Nov. '66. She was accepted for service on 28 Dec. '66. Fourteen units were rebuilt. By that time the class was already obsolescent, as nuclear submarines with longer-range weapons were much more attractive. At the end of 1967, then, the naval leadership established TTZs to modify Project 629 submarines to test two new types of ballistic missile: Project 605, to test the 4K18 (SS-NX-13) missile intended to attack warships at sea; and Project 601, to test six 4K75 ballistic missiles (SS-N-6).

Project 605 required a lengthened hull. The design was submitted in Dec. '69 and approved early in 1970. K-102, modified at Severodvinsk, was launched in 1973.

Project 601 (K-118) required much more, including a new navigational system (MOST-U-601), a new radio-sextant (Samum), a new log (LA-1), a new antenna (Zu-

batka), and new and more powerful storage batteries.

The naval staff also badly needed some means of ensuring reliable communications with deployed units; the Soviet Union lacked an overseas network of HF relay stations. Design work began late in 1971; Rubin (TsKB-16) presented a sketch design early in 1972, and it was accepted on 20 June '72. Four submarines (B-42, K-107, K-61, and K-113) were assigned for conversion to Project 629R (retransmission). Work took nearly three years, the prototype, K-61, being delivered to the yard at Vladivostok on 23 Jan. '74 and emerging (as BS-167) in Dec. '76; BS-107 (K-107) and BS-83 (B-42) were delivered in 1977 and 1978. Work on K-113 was canceled.]

Project: 949 (GRANIT) and 949A (ANTEIY)

NATO Class Name: OSCAR 1 and 2

Names:

Project 949:

K-525 (named *Minskiy Komomolets* 30 Dec. '80–91, then *Arkhangelsk*)

K-206 MURMANSK

New names for Project 949A:

		completed
K-173	TAMBOV	
K-410	SMOLENSK	
K-442		1991
K-456	KASATKA	1991
K-266	OREL	

named *Severodvinsk* prior to 1991; lch 22 Mar. '92, completed 1992

K-186	OMSK	

lch 8 Mar. '93, completed 15 Dec. '93

K-141	KURSK	20 Jan. '95
TOMSK		1996

All built in Severodvinsk, beginning 1978.

Displacement: 12,500/17,000 (949A: 13,400/18,000)

Dimensions: 143 × 18.2 × 9 (949A: 154 × 18.2 × 9)

Diving Depth: – – –

Armament: 24 missiles (Granit system), 4 533 mm TT, 2 650 mm TT (total 28 torpedoes)

Machinery: 2 reactors (OK-650B, 190 MW each), 2 steam

Oscar-2 class (M.O.D. U.K.)

K-148 (S. P. Bukan')

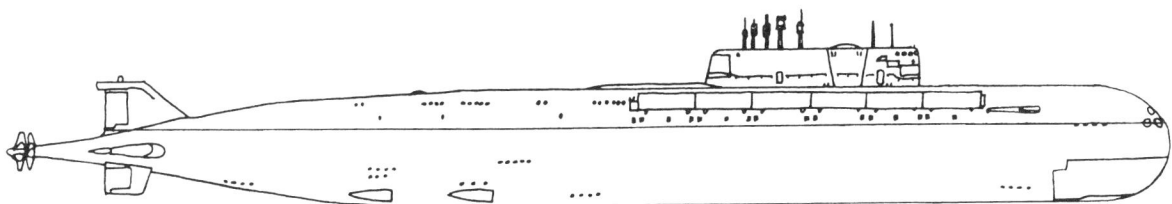

Oscar class (Friedman collection)

turbines (OK-9), 2 shafts, 98,000 HP = 30 kts (28 kts in 949A), 4 turbogenerators (3200 kW each), 2 diesel generators (DG-190). 2 taxi-up devices. Propellers have "stream direction device."

Complement: 130

Electronics: Sonar: MGK-540, Skat-3; Radar: Tobol; Navigational system: Medveditsa-949M; Communications system: Tsunami

The technical assignment (staff requirement) was stated in 1969. Chief designer: P. P. Pustyntsev (from 1977, E. L. Bazanov). Missiles are located outside the pressure hull. Unit machinery, largely duplicating that of Project 941 (Typhoon). These submarines are rated as nuclear submerged cruisers (1st Rank). All in Northern Fleet except K-132, K-173, K-442, K-456 (Pacific).

Project: 885 (YASEN)

NATO Class Name: GRANAY

Names:

SVERODVINSK   laid down 22 Jan. '93

Displacement: 5900/8600

Dimensions: 111 × 12 × 8.4

Diving Depth: – – –

Armament: 4 533 mm, 20 650 mm missile tubes (Oniks missile) [Ed: number of missile tubes may actually indicate number of missiles]

Machinery: One reactor, one geared steam turbine, 1 shaft, 43,000 HP = 19/31 kts

Complement: 50 (22 officers)

Electronics: Sonar: Ayaks; Navigational system: Medveditsa-M; Towed communications antenna: Paravan

Designed by TsKB-18. Building in Severodvinsk. Rated as Nuclear Submerged Cruiser (1st Rank). There is a safety chamber for the whole crew and this submarine has two taxi-up devices.

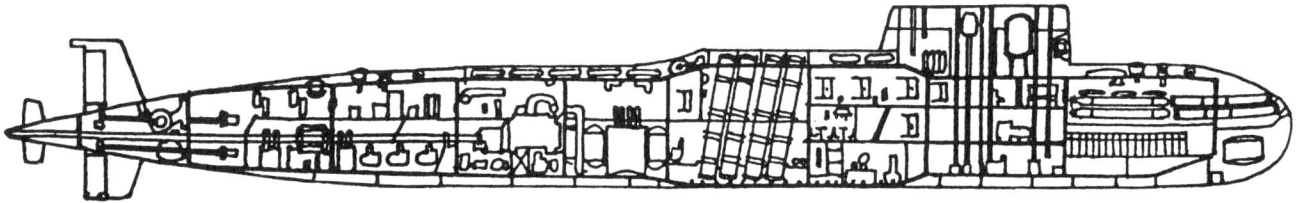

Project: 661 (ANCHAR)

NATO Class Name: PAPA

Names:

K-162   laid down 28 Dec. '63, lch 21 Dec. '68, completed 31 Dec. '69

Built in Severodvinsk.

Displacement: 5197/7000

Dimensions: 106.92 × 11.5 × 8.2

Diving Depth: 550/400

Armament: 10 missiles (Ametyst system), 4 533 mm TT (8 torpedoes); torpedoes could be launched down to 200 m.

Machinery: 2 reactors (177.4 MW each), 2 steam turbines, 2 shafts, 80,000 HP = 25/45 kts; 3000 kW turbogenerators; 2 silver-zinc batteries (152 cells each). Endurance 70 days.

Complement: 82

Electronics: Sonar: Rubin; Torpedo FCS: Ladoga; Navigational system: Sigma-661.

Ordered built 28 Aug. '58. Chief designer N. N. Isanin (later N. F. Shul'zhenko, TsKB-16). Broke the world underwater speed record on trials [Ed: 44.7 kts, which is still the record]. Titanium pressure hull with nine compartments: (i) and (ii) (figure-8) torpedo room and battery; (iii) quarters and batteries; (iv) command center and quarters; (v) reactors; (vi) turbines; (vii) turbo-generators, main switchboard; (viii) auxiliaries (refrigerators, compressors); (ix) electric motors and steering equipment. Distance between shafts, 5 m. All missiles could be launched in two salvoes with three minute interval between salvoes. This submarine served in the Northern Fleet, being placed in reserve in 1988.

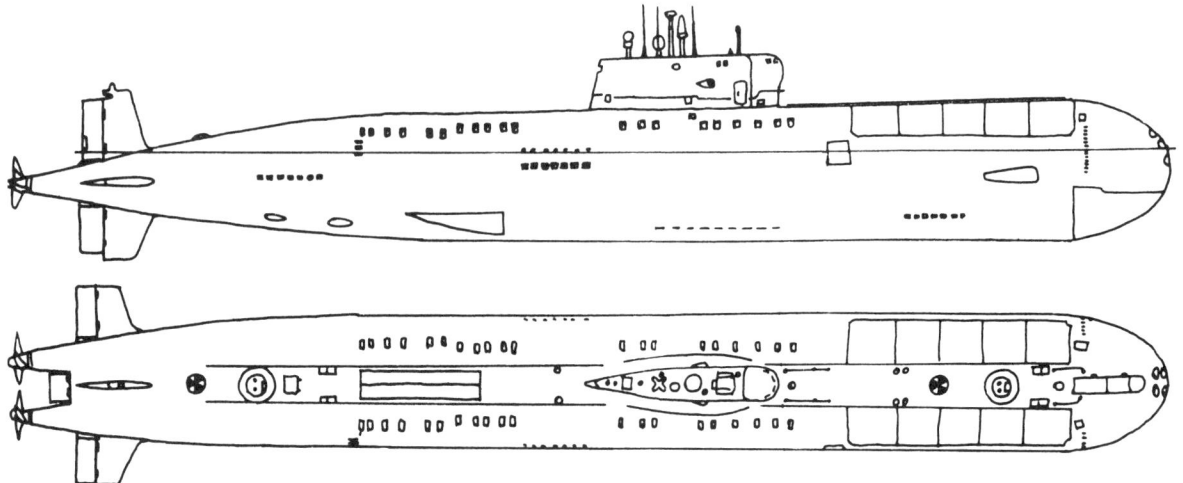

Papa class (U.S. Navy)

K-28 (A. F. Kuznyetsov)

[Ed: According to the published design history of this submarine, she was part of a program to develop a new fast submarine, new types of powerplants, and other new submarine systems. They included the new Rubin sonar. The concept design and TTZ were approved early in 1960. No further units were ordered because of the excessive noise level at high speed, tactical shortcomings of the missile system, and because of the inadequate service lifetimes of the primary equipment. Building time was considered too lengthy, which probably means that the submarine was too costly in resource terms. The TTZ apparently called for a speed of 38 kts, and the submarine was rated at 42 kts.]

Project: 670A (SKAT)

NATO Class Name: CHARLIE-1

Names:

	completed
K-43	
K-87	renamed K-212 in 1972
K-25	
K-121	
K-313	
K-308	20 Sept. '70
K-320	15 Sept. '71
K-303	
K-325	
K-429	
K-201	26 Dec. '72

All built at Gorkiy 1967–72.

Displacement: 3574/4980

Dimensions: 94.3 × 9.9 × 7.5

Diving Depth: 350/270

Armament: 8 missiles (complex Ametyst), 4 533 mm TT (12 torpedoes), 2 406 mm TT (4 torpedoes)

Machinery: 1 reactor (VM-4, 89.2 MW), 1 steam turbine (OK-350), 1 shaft, 18,800 HP = 12/26 kts, 1 DG-500 diesel generator, 2 autonomous turbogenerators (TM-88, 2000 kW each), 2 groups of battery cells (224 cells)

Complement: 100

Electronics: Sonar: Kerch, MG-14, MG-24; Radar: Topol; ESM: Zaliv-P; IFF: Nikhrom-M; Navigational system: Sigma-670A

The technical project for this design was approved in 1961 and completed in 1963. Chief designer was V. P. Vorob'ev (TsKB-112). Missiles could be fired submerged at 5 kts in sea states 4–5.

K-43 was the unit leased to India Jan. '88–Jan. '91 as Chakra (as Project 06709). K-320 was damaged on the slip during reactor hydraulic tests, 18 Jan. '70. K-429 sank off Kamchatka Peninsula 24 June '83 and then again on 13 Sept. '85; stricken 1987.

All units served in the Pacific Fleet. K-201 and K-320 were placed in reserve 1994.

[Ed: According to an account of Project 671 in *Morskoy Sbornik,* this submarine was conceived as a small torpedo submarine for mass production (which probably accounts for the use of a single reactor), then redesigned as a missile shooter. According to another recent Russian account, the TTZ was issued in May '60. To save weight, the conning tower and fairwater are aluminum, and the sonar domes are titanium alloy. This class has a floating radio buoy to receive commands and target designation data (as well as satellite navigation data) without coming to periscope depth. The forepart of the hull, between the external missile tubes, has a figure eight section extending aft about 21 meters.]

Charlie-1 class (U.S. Navy)

Project: 670M (SKAT-M)

NATO Class Name: CHARLIE-2

Names:

K-452*   named *Berkut* 1989

K-458

K-479

K-503

K-508

K-209

All built in Gorkiy 1973–80

Displacement: 4372/5500

Dimensions: 104.9 × 9.9 × 7.8

Diving Depth: [Ed: 320/250 m, according to a recent Russian publication]

Armament: 8 missiles, Malakhit system (Vulkan*), 4 533 mm TT (12 torpedoes), 2 406 mm TT (4 torpedoes) [Ed: According to a recent Russian publication, these submarines have 2 650 mm and 4 533 mm TT, with a total of 14 weapons, including SS-N-15 (81-R) ASW missiles]

Machinery: 2 reactors (VM-4, 75 MW each), 1 steam turbine (OK-300), 1 shaft, 18,800 HP = 15/24 kts

Complement: 98

Electronics: Sonar: Skat-M (after modernization under Project 06704, MGK-400 Rubin); Radar: Albatros; ESM: Zaliv-P; Navigational system: Sigma-670

[Ed: According to a recent Russian publication, these submarines have a Brest combat direction system and Usta-670 and Tantal-670 missile/torpedo fire control systems (one is probably for Charlie I, the other for Charlie II). Compared to Project 670, this class is lengthened by a compartment to provide a more elaborate missile fire control system.]

Chief designer V. P. Vorob'ev (TsKB-112 Lazurit). All in Northern Fleet, currently being modernized to carry the Vulkan missile system. [Ed: According to the recent Russian publication mentioned above, B-452 (Project P-670) carries the Oniks missile; the corresponding fire control system is Ladoga-P-670.]

Project: 675, 657M, 675MKB*

NATO Class Name: ECHO-2

Names:

K-1

K-7   renamed K-127 in 1968

K-10

K-22   *Krasnogvardeets*

K-23

K-28   renamed K-428

K-31   renamed K-431 29 Apr. '69

K-34   *Kefal'*, renamed K-134

K-35

K-47

K-48

K-56   accepted 9 Sept. '66 in Pacific

K-57   renamed K-557

K-74

K-86

K-90

K-94

K-104   renamed K-144

K-108

K-116

K-125

K-128

K-131

K-135

K-160

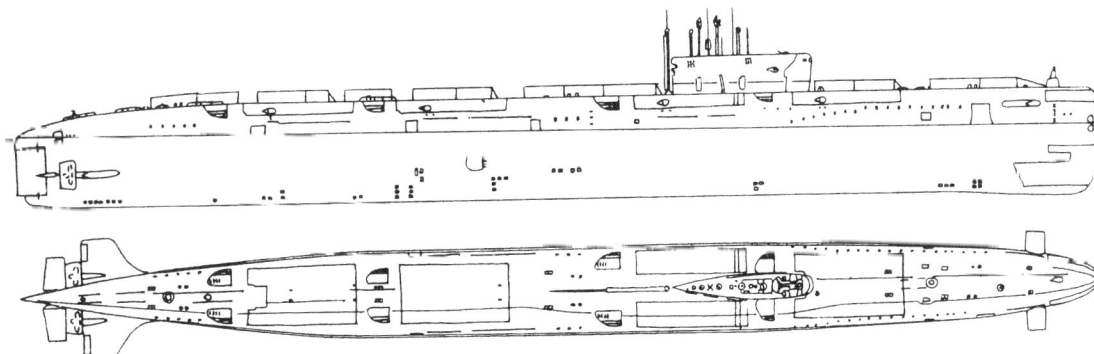

Echo-2 class (U.S. Navy)

K-172

K-175

K-184

K-199

Total twenty-nine units.

Builders: Komsomolsk (beginning with K-10) and Severodvinsk (beginning with K-166) in 1961–67.

Displacement: 4500/5760

Dimensions: 115.4 × 9.3 × 7.1

Diving Depth: 300/240

Armament: 8 missiles (P-6, with capability to use P-5; later carried P-500 Bazalt), 4 533 mm TT (bow), 2 406 mm (stern). Maximum torpedo launch depth: 100 m (bow), 250 m (stern).

Machinery: 2 reactors (VM-A, 70 MW each), 2 steam turbines (60-D1), 2 shafts, 39,000 HP = 15/23 kts (could be forced to 29 kts); 2 DG-400 (M-820) generators; 2 creep motors (PG-116, 450 HP each). Reactor endurance 3600 hr (presumably at full power). Endurance 60 days.

Complement: 137 (22 officers, 25 petty officers, 90 seamen)

Electronics: Sonar: Kerch, MG-10, MG-23, MG-29; Radar: Albatros; Radar for missile control: Argument (on turntable at forward end of sail); Radar receiver for target direction and control: Uspekh; ESM: Nakat; IFF: Nikhrom-M; Short-wave radio transmitter: Iva; Navigational system: Sila N-675; Gyrocompass: Mayak; Gyroazimuth Sila GA; Log: LP-2; Astronavigational system: Lira-11; Radio direction-finder: ARP-53; Sounder: NEL-6; Echo-icemeter: EL-1.

Chief designer P. P. Pustyntsev. Time from surfacing to first missile launch, 20 min. Missiles were originally P-5D for shore targets and P-6 for ship targets. The double hull

was covered in rubber. Pressure hull diameter was 7 m. There were ten compartments: (i) torpedo room; (ii) batteries, quarters, and officers' mess; (iii) radar transmitter and missile fire control; (iv) command center; (v) diesel generator and condenser; (vi) reactors; (vii) turbines; (viii) electric motors; (ix) quarters, galley, sick bay, refrigerators; (x) torpedo room, provisions, steering gear. Project 675K and 675MK had Kasatka-B (satellite targeting) system installed. Project 675MKV carried the Vulkan P-1000 missile with Argon-675 fire control system. K-86 was converted into a frogman carrier.

[Ed.: According to Burov, this design (a modified version of Project 659) was modified twice. The first revision, completed in June '59, added a new sonar and anechoic (rubber) coating. The second (Sept. '60) added an additional pair of missiles as well as improved sonar and communications equipment. Missiles could be launched in sea state 4–5 at a speed of 8–10 kts. Burov seems to imply that this design was ordered in parallel with that of Project 659, under the same Aug. '56 directive. If, however, the 670 block of project numbers was used only in 1959, then it must be of later conception. According to another recent Russian publication, K-1 (1987), K-22 (1993), and K-35 (1991) were converted to 675MK; conversion of K-10 and K-34 was canceled for lack of funds. Project 675K (K-48) was a mid-life upgrade in which batteries were replaced and compartments were rearranged.]

K-56 collided with research vessel *Berg* 13 June '73 and suffered twenty-seven killed. In 1978 K-116 suffered reactor damage. In 1980 K-10 collided with a Chinese submarine (she was scrapped in 1982). K-431 exploded in Chazhma Bay during reactor refueling on 10 Aug. '1985.

Project: 659 and 659T*

NATO Class Name: ECHO-1

Names:

K-45

l.d. 28 Dec. '57, lch 12 May '59, in service 18 Sept. '60, operational June '61

	completed
K-59	10 Dec. '61
K-66	10 Dec. '61
K-122	13 Apr. '62
K-151	Dec. '62

All built at Komsomolsk and all converted to attack submarines under Project 659T.

Displacement: 3731/4920

Dimensions: 111.2 × 9.2 × 7.6

Diving Depth: 300/240

Armament: 6 missiles (P-5D), 4 533 mm TT (bow), 4 406 mm (stern) (20 SET-65 or 12 53-61). Torpedo launch depth: 100 m (bow), 240 m (stern).

Machinery: 2 reactors (VM-A, 70 MW each), 2 steam turbines with 2-stage gearing, 2 shafts, 35,000 HP = 21–29 kts, 31,000 nm/26 kts; 2 creep motors (PG-116, 450 HP each); 2 DG-400 (DC diesel generators); 2 batteries, 112 cells each. Endurance 50 days. Maximum submerged time 1500 hrs.

Complement: 120

Electronics: Sonar: Arktika (MG-200), passive sonar MG-15, sonar intercept receiver MG-13; Radar: Prizma; Missile guidance radar (in forward part of sail, removed when missiles were removed): Sever; ESM: Nakat-M; IFF: Khrom-KM; Navigational system: Pluton-659; Gyrocompass: Mayak; Log: LG-8; Echo-icemeter: EL-1

Built under order of 26 Aug. '56 to attack shore targets. Chief designer P. P. Pustyntsev, then N. A. Klimov. All missiles removed Aug. '65–1969 at Bol'shoi Kamyen' under SALT treaty; submarines converted to torpedo type (Project 659T, chief designer O. Ya. Margolin). Pressure hull diameter was 6.8 m. These double-hull submarines had nine compartments. All served in the Pacific.

After a 1980 accident, K-66 was placed in reserve. K-122 was stricken after a 21 Aug. '83 fire that killed fourteen.

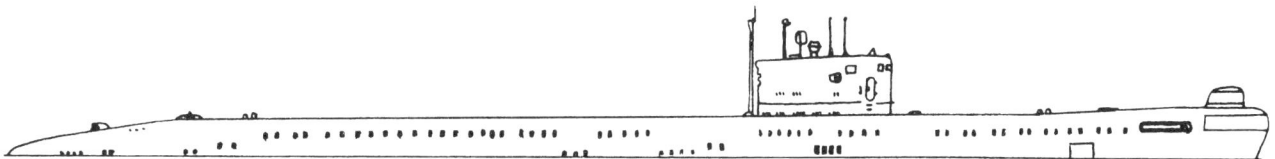

K-45 (V. E. Koryenyev)

Project: 971 (SHCHUKA-B)

NATO Class Name: AKULA

Names:

Komsomolsk:

		laid down	launched	completed
K-284		6 Oct. '82	30 Dec. '84	
K-263	DELFIN		15 Jul. '84	1985
K-322	KASHALOT			1986
K-391	KIT			1987
K-331	NARVAL			1989
K-419	MORZH			1992
K-267	DRAKON		15 July '94	1995
	NERPA			1995

Severodvinsk:

			laid down	launched	completed
K-480	BARS		1989		Dec. '89
K-317	PANTERA			Nov. '86	May '90
	in service 30 Dec. '90				
K-461	VOLK	1986		11 June '91	27 Jan. '92
K-328	LEOPARD				
		Oct. '88		6 Oct. '92	15 Jan. '93
K-157	TIGR	1989		10 July '93	5 Jan. '94
	GEPARD			1995	
	VEPR'	1991		10 Dec. '94	

Displacement: 5700/7900

Dimensions: 108 × 13.5 × 9.6

Diving Depth: 550/450

Armament: 4 533 mm TT (Shkval, RK-55, torpedoes SAET-60M, 53-65K), 4 650 mm TT (torpedo 65-76)

Machinery: 1 reactor (OK-650B), 1 steam turbine, 1 shaft, 43,000 HP = 20/35 kts; has taxi-up device

Complement: 62 (including 31 officers)

Electronics: Sonar: MGK-503 Skat; Communications system: Molniya-M (satellite and towed antenna); Navigational system: Myedvyeditsa-971

Technical characteristics were approved in 1972. Chief designer G. N. Tchyernyshov (TsKB-16 Malakhit). There are 8 compartments, and the escape chamber is large enough for the whole crew. This is the quietest of all Russian submarines. Construction of units in Komsomolsk stopped in 1993, the tenth unit being scrapped on the slip. Submarines serve in the Pacific and Northern Fleets (Zapadnaya Litza).

[Ed.: According to Burov, this design was developed (decision July '76) specifically to increase building capacity of submarines equivalent to the *Sierra* (945) class; the only difference was to have been a steel rather than titanium hull. The technical design was approved on 13 Sept. '77, but had to be reworked in 1978–80 to accomodate Tomahawk-like cruise missiles and to overcome inferiority in sonar. The weapon system was redesigned to fire both torpedoes and cruise missiles; reloads were to be missiles rather than torpedoes. Cruise missiles required their own fire control system. The technical design envisaged a new sonar system with a large bow array and enlarged flank arrays, with digital processing. Compared to the *Victor* class system, detection range was tripled, and time for TMA reduced. This design employed two-stage silencing: units of machinery were rafted on sound-isolated foundations, which in turn were sound-isolated from the submarine hull. Adopting steel rather than titanium (as in the *Sierra* design) cost displacement; since power was not increased, this submarine is 2 kts slower than a *Sierra*.]

Akula class (U.S. Naval Institute Photographic Collection)

Akula class (Royal Navy)

Volk (Pavlov collection)

Project: 685 (PLAVNIK)

NATO Class Name: MIKE

Names:

		laid down	launched	completed
K-278	KOMSOMOLETS			
		22 Apr. '78	3 June '83	20 Oct. '83

Named Oct. '88
Built in Severodvinsk.

Displacement: 5750/7810

Dimensions: $117.5 \times 10.7 \times 8$

Diving Depth: 1000/1250

Armament: 6 533 mm TT (bow) for RK-55 (2), Shkval (2), torpedo SAET-60M(2) plus 6 rockets or 10 torpedoes

Machinery: 1 pressurized-water reactor (OK-650B-5, 190 MW), 1 geared turbine, 43,000 HP = 14/30.6 kts; 2 creep motors (300 kW each); 2 turbogenerators (2000 kW each), 1 diesel generator (500 kW); 1 battery (112 cells).

Complement: 57 (29 officers, 26 petty officers, 2 rated men); increased to 64 in 1986

Electronics: Sonar: Skat; Radar: Chibis; ESM: Bukhta; Communications system: Molniya; Satellite communications system: Sintez; Short and ultra-short-wave (presumably HF and UHF) transmitters: Anis and Korn; Navigational system: Myedvyeditsa-685. The central computer complex was called Omnibus.

The technical assignment (staff requirement) for this deep-diving large torpedo submarine was issued in 1966, and the technical project approved 16 Dec. '74. Chief designer was N. A. Klimov (Yu. N. Kormilitsyn from 1977 on). The hull was built of titanium (48-T alloy). There were seven compartments: (i) torpedo room, batteries, special underwater communications; (ii) quarters, officers' mess, provisions, galley; (iii) command center, computer complex, diesel generators; (iv) reactors; (v) main switchboard, pumps; (vi) geared turbine; (vii) electric motors, steering gear, pumps. The design included an escape chamber capable of bringing the entire crew up from a depth of 1500 m.

The submarine ran tests from Aug. '84 through July '88. On 7 Apr. '89 she sank 180 km southwest of Medvyezhiy Island in the Norwegian Sea with two nuclear missiles on board; forty-two were killed. Since she cannot be salvaged, there is interest in preserving the submarine on the bottom.

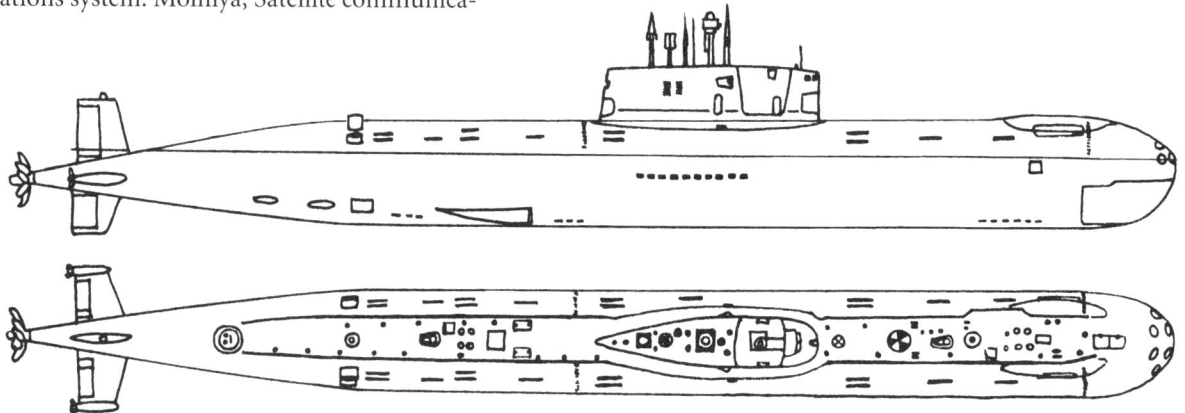

K-278 (S. P. Bukan')

Project: 945 (BARRACUDA), 945A* (KONDOR)

NATO Class Name: SIERRA

Names:

All built at Gorkiy (Krasnoye Sormovo) and completed in Severodvinsk.

		laid down	launched	completed
K-239	KARP	Aug. '83	Apr. '83	1987
K-276	KRAB	5 Aug. '82	29 Jul. '83	21 Sept. '84
K-534	ZUBATKA	June '86	June '88	28 Dec. '90
K-336	OKUN'*	May '90	June '92	1993

Displacement: 5200/6800* (5300/7100)

Dimensions: 107, 112.7* × 11.2 × 8.5

Diving Depth: 800/70 [Ed.: According to Burov, limiting depth was 50% greater than that of the previous (671) class.]

Armament: 4 533 mm TT, 4 650 mm TT (total 40 83-R rocket-torpedoes, 65-76 torpedoes, and Shkval missiles); can carry 42 mines instead of torpedoes and missiles in racks.

Machinery: 1 reactor, 1 steam turbine, 1 propeller with improved silencing; 43,000 HP = 18/35 kts (powerplant similar to that of Project 971)

[Ed: According to Burov, the plant has 4 steam generators and 2 SSTGs; the emergency powerplant comprised 2 750 kW diesel generators with fuel for 10 days. Two 370 kW electric motors, each with its own propeller, could drive the submarine at 5 kts.]

Complement: 60 (31 officers, 28 petty officers)

Electronics: Sonar: MGK-503 Skat; Communications: Tsunami and Molniya-M (towed communications antenna Paravan)

Technical assignment approved by CinC Mar. '72. Chief designer was N. E. Kvasha (TsKB-112 Lazurit). There are six compartments (seven in 945A), the hull is titanium alloy, and there is a surfacing escape chamber. Rated as Large Submarines of 1st Rank. All are in the Northern Fleet. The fifth unit, which would have been Project 945B (Mars), was broken up incomplete on the slip in 1993.

[Ed.: According to Burov, compared with the *Victor* class, these submarines had twice as many reloads; ASW missile range increased by a factor of three and torpedo range by a factor of 1.5, presumably due to adoption of 65 cm tubes to fire SS-N-16 missiles and 65 cm wake-following torpedoes; time to fire the first salvo was halved. This class had a new sonar with better than twice the range of its predecessors (an improvement achieved in part due to much better silencing). The new design was needed because it was impossible to modify the existing *Victor* (671) design to accomodate the new detection, targeting, navigation, and command data systems, and also to provide the required improvements in speed and diving depth. Minimum navigational error was reduced by a factor of five, communications range was doubled, and radio signals could be received at three times the previous depth. This class apparently introduced an emergency ballast-blowing system employing solid-fuel to blow two tanks. It also had a rescue chamber large enough to accomodate the whole crew. The new submarine had to be small enough to be built at the *Krasnoe Sormovo* yard in Gorkiy. To do that, size had to be cut; adopting titanium alloy saved 25–30 percent in hull weight, hence a considerable savings in overall size.]

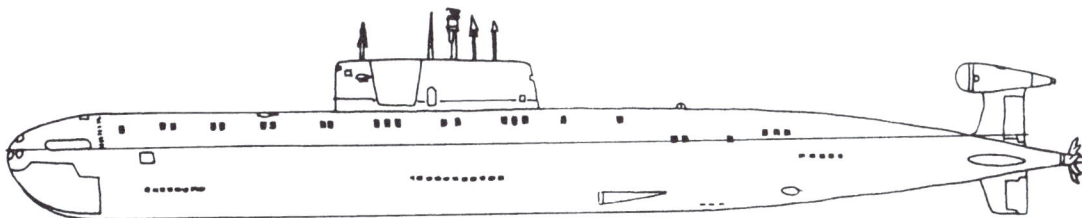

Project: 645

NATO Class Name: NOVEMBER

Names:

	laid down	*launched*	*completed*
K-27	15 June '58	Apr. '62	30 Oct. '63

Built in Severodvinsk

Displacement: 3420/4380

Dimensions: 109.8 × 8.3 × 5.85

Diving Depth: 300/270

Armament: 8 533 mm TT (12 torpedoes: 53-57 and SET-65). Torpedoes could be launched down to 100 m at any speed.

Machinery: 2 liquid-metal (lead-bismuth) reactors (VT-1, 146 MW, producing steam at 97 tons/hr), 2 steam turbines, 2 shafts, 35,000 HP = 14.7/30.2 kts; 2 creep motors (PG-116, 450 HP each); 35,400 nm/30.2 kts. Endurance 50 days.

Complement: 105

Electronics: Sonar: Arktika-M, MG-10, MG-13; Mine-locating sonar: Luch; Radar: RLK-101; ESM: Nakat-M; IFF: Khrom-KM; Navigational system: Pluton-645

Ordered built 22 Oct. '55; chief designer V. N. Peregudov (A. K. Nazarov after 1956). Double-hull of low-magnetic steel, with nine compartments: (i) torpedo room with quick-loading device; (ii) batteries and quarters; (iii) command center; (iv) reactors [Ed.: side by side rather than in tandem, as on Project 627]; (v) turbo-generators, diesel generators, refrigerators, auxiliaries; (vi) turbines, engine control room; (vii) electric motors; (viii) quarters and refrigerators; (ix) quarters, steering gear. This was very nearly a repeat Project 627 (*November*) with a new powerplant. [Ed: NATO never distinguished it from the earlier class.] The submarine suffered a reactor accident (nine killed) in the Northern Fleet on 24 May '68 and was stricken that year. After fifteen years in reserve she flooded at Novaya Zemlya.

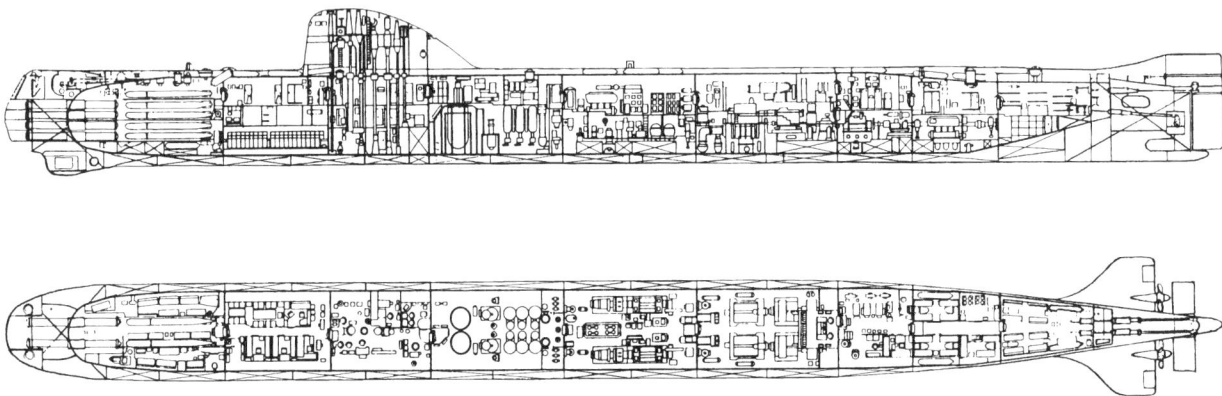

Project: 671RTM and 671RTMK*(SHCHUKA)

NATO Class Name: VICTOR-3

Names:

	completed
K-138*	
K-218	
K-242	named *50 Let Komsomolsk-na-Amur* May '82
K-244*	
K-247	
K-251	
K-254*	
K-255	
K-264	
K-292*	
K-298	
K-299	
K-305	
K-324	
K-355	
K-358	named *Murmanskiy Komsomolets* 1990–91
K-360	
K-388	
K-412	
K-414*	Jan. '91
K-448	
K-492	
K-502*	
K-507	
K-524*	named *60 Let Shefstva Vlksm* 1982–91
K-527*	

Twenty-six total. Built at Komsomolsk (prototype completed 1978) and at Admiralty Yard, Leningrad (lead unit K-524).

Displacement: 4950/6990

Dimensions: $107.2 \times 10.8 \times 7.4$

Diving Depth: 400/350

Armament: 4 533 mm TT, 2 650 mm TT (24 torpedoes and missile-torpedoes or 46 mines; Granat [SSN-21] in starred units)

Machinery: 2 reactors, 1 steam turbine, 2 screws on a single shaft (plus 2 auxiliary screws for creep motors), 31,000 HP = 18/30 kts. Endurance 80 days.

Complement: 100

Electronics: Sonar: Skat-KS; Sonar for Ice Observation: MT-70; Radar: MRK-50; ESM: Bulava; Periscope: PZKG-10; Communications system: Molniya-L (antennas: Kiparis, Anis, Sintez, plus Paravan towed antenna); Satellite communication system: Tsunami-B; Navigation system: Medvyed-itsa-671RTM

Project approved 1975, built through 1987. Chief designer was G. N. Tchyernyshov. The conning tower fairing and part of the superstructure are made of aluminum alloys. From K-292 on (Project 6717), these submarines have new equipment and new types of missile-torpedo armament. On 29 Aug. '91 these submarines were reclassified as Large Nuclear Powered Submarines of 1st Rank. K-242, K-247, K-251, K-264, K-305, K-355, K-360, K-412, K-492, K-507 are in the Pacific; the others are in the Northern Fleet.

[Ed.: According to an account of Russian nuclear submarine construction in *Military Parade*, this version of the Project 671 design was quieter than the preceding 671RT, had more powerful weapons, and had a better electronic warfare package. In the 1980s, unlike the earlier version, it was equipped with subsonic strategic cruise missiles (the TT-launched SS-N-21). Presumably the article refers in part to the new sonar, which included the first operational Soviet towed array.]

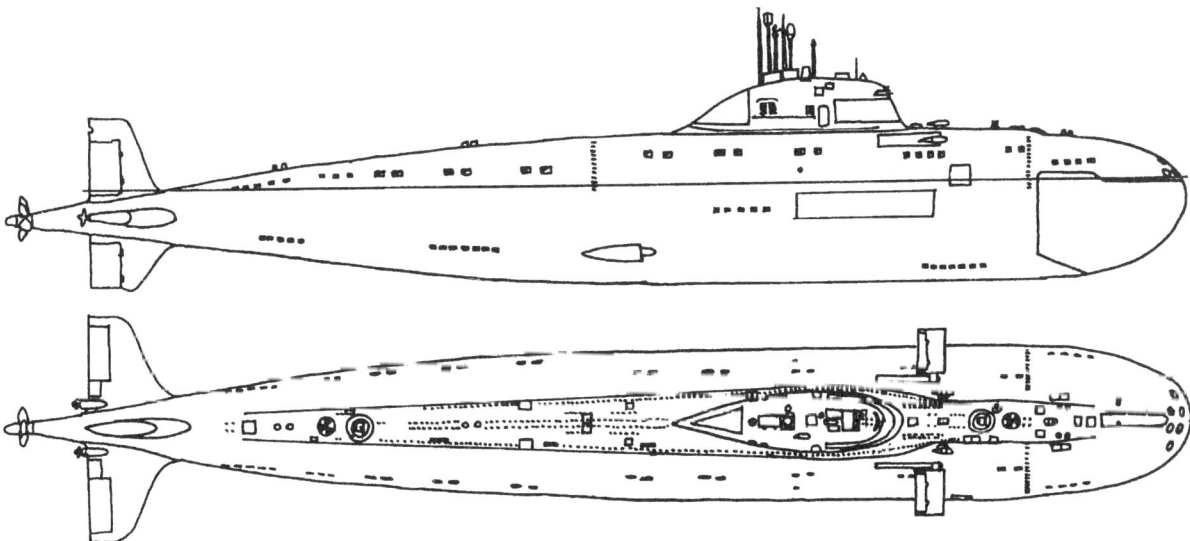

Project: 671RT (SEGMA)

NATO Class Name: VICTOR-2

Names:

	laid down	launched	completed
K-387	2 Apr. '71	2 Sept. '72	delivered 30 Dec. '72
K-371			1974
K-467			1975
K-488			1976
K-495			1976
K-513			1977
K-517			28 Oct. '78

Total seven units. Built in Leningrad (Admiralty) and Gorkiy (K-387, K-371, K-467, K-488).

Displacement: 4675/7190

Dimensions: 101.8 × 10.78 × 7.3

Diving Depth: 400/320

Armament: 4 533 mm TT, (18 53-65K or SET-65 torpedoes, Shkval, or MG-74 Korund decoys; or 32 Golyetz mines), 2 650 mm TT (6 65-76 torpedoes)

Machinery: 2 reactors, 1 turbine, 1 shaft (plus 2 auxiliary), 31,000 HP = 12/31.7 kts. Endurance 60 days.

Complement: 96 (27 officers)

Electronics: Sonar: Skat, MT-70; Radar: Tobol; Communications system: Molniya; Satellite communications system: Tsunami; Communications antennas: Kiparis, Anis, Sintez, Kora, and Paravan towed antenna; Navigation system: Medvyeditsa

Project approved 15 June '67. Chief designer: G. N. Tchyernyshov (TsKB-18). Hull has eight compartments: (i) torpedo room, battery; (ii) quarters, sick bay, galley, officers' mess; (iii) command center, navigation, and sonar rooms; (iv) reactors; (v) turbines; (vi) turbogenerators, auxiliary equipment, refrigerators; (vii) quarters, diesel generators; (viii) steering gear, creep motors. All in Northern Fleet. B-387 was stricken in 1995. B-467 is in refit.

K-387 (U. A. Pakhomov)

Project: 671, 671V*, 671K (ERSH)

NATO Class Name: VICTOR-1

Names:

completed

K-38 (l.d. Jan. '65, lch Oct. '65, delivered 5 Nov. '67; in service Aug. '67)

K-69	renamed B-369
K-147	
K-53	
K-306	
K-323	renamed *50 Let SSSR* in 1970
K-370	
K-138	
K-367	
K-314	
K-398	
K-454*	30 Oct. '73
K-462	
K-469	
K-481	

Project 671V:

K-314

K-454

K-469

All built at Leningrad (Admiralty); completed 1967–74.

Displacement: 4108/6085

Dimensions: 92.5 × 10.6 (16.5) × 7.3

Diving Depth: 400/320

Armament: 6 533 mm (18 rocket-torpedoes and torpedoes or 36 mines). Maximum launch depth 250 m.

Machinery: 2 reactors (VM-4T, 72 MW each), 1 steam turbine (OK-300), 31,000 HP = 12/32 kts; 2 electronic motors (PG-137) of 375 HP; 2 separate turbogenerators (2000 kW OK-2s), 1 DG-200 diesel generator; 2 storage batteries, each 112 cells (2×8000 amp-hr). Endurance 50 days, 38,880 nm/32 kts.

Electronics: Sonar: MGK-300 Rubin; Navigational system: Sigma-671

Complement: 76 (including 22 officers)

The TTZ was approved 3 Nov. '59. Building began in 1965. Chief designer G. N. Tchyernyshov (TsKB Malakhit). This was a second-generation submarine with a teardrop-shaped hull, a new powerplant, and anti-sonar hull covering. There are seven compartments: (i) torpedo room, quarters, battery; (ii) command center; (iii) reactors; (iv) turbines; (v) quarters and diesel generators; (vi) auxiliary equipment; (vii) electric motors. K-314 collided with USS *Kitty Hawk* 21 Mar. '89. In 1990 these submarines were reclassified as B (large) rather than K (cruisers). B-454 (Pacific Fleet) went into reserve 21 Mar. '89.

[Ed.: According to a recently published design history of Project 671 (in *Morskoi Sbornik*), this design was part of a larger series of follow-ons to the Project 627 *(November)* class first-generation nuclear attack submarine. SKB-143 (Malakhit), which had designed *November*, developed a number of sketch designs for successors in 1956–59; in May '58 it offered one of them to the State Committee on Shipbuilding. This was a U.S.-style design (with a cylindri-

K-292 (M. V. Yurtchyenko)

cal hull, a single reactor, and a single screw, with ballast tanks at the ends; unlike U.S. submarines, it did carry some ballast internally, between hull bulkheads). Unlike earlier Soviet submarines, this design could not satisfy the usual three-compartment standard for surface survivability; the bureau argued that surface considerations were now irrelevant. The State Committee showed no interest in the proposal, but did announce a competition for the next four submarine designs: Project 667 (SSBN), 669 (a large torpedo submarine, to succeed 627), 670 (a small torpedo submarine for mass production), and 671 (an ASW submarine). SKB-143, TsKB-18 (Rubin), and TsKB-112 (Lazurit, at Gorkiy) competed. Rubin got Project 667, Lazurit got 670, and 669 was amalgamated with 671. The OTZ for the latter seems to have been inspired by contemporary U.S. *Permit* class submarines: it called for a powerful new sonar, four torpedo tubes (eight torpedoes), a speed of about 30 kts, and a test depth of 300 m, on a displacement of about 2000 t, i.e., a bit more speed bought by drastically cutting the number of torpedoes and the test depth, on a smaller displacement. Similar optimism on displacement may have inspired the OTZ for Project 705 *(Alfa)*. SKB-143 proposed to return to its 1958 design study. It managed to beat back

proposed naval staff requirements that all nuclear submarines have two reactors and two shafts, for reliability. SKB-143 argued that the number of reactors (which happened, in this case, to be two) ought to be determined solely by the required speed. The single shaft was justified because it offered maximum speed and minimum noise; Admiral Gorshkov approved it on what he imagined would be a one-time exception to the proposed standards (though in fact Project 670 also had a single shaft). When Project 669 was folded into 671, the TTZ was revised to add more weapons. Maximum displacement was now set by the limitations of the White Sea Canal. The designers opted for a body-of-revolution hull, as in contemporary Western submarines, with their preferred cylindrical pressure hull inside a double hull with just enough volume to provide the preferred external hull form. Although the designers considered that a single reactor would give sufficient speed, they opted for two to provide growth margin. To minimize length, the reactors were arranged side by side, a new departure for Soviet practice. To provide bow space for a big sonar, the usual vertical arrangement of torpedo tubes was, in effect, turned on its side.]

Project: 627* and 627A (KIT)

NATO Class Name: NOVEMBER

Names:

	laid down	launched	completed
K-3*	24 Sept. '55	9 Aug. '57	
delivered 12 Mar. '59			
named *Leninskiy Komsomol* 9 Oct. '62			
K-14			31 Dec. '59
K-5			17 Aug. '60
prototype of 627A production series			
K-8			31 Aug. '60
K-52			23 Dec. '61
K-21			23 Dec. '61
K-11			23 Dec. '61
K-133			16 Oct. '62
K-181			16 Oct. '63
K-115			20 Dec. '62
K-159			4 Nov. '63
K-27	15 June '58	1 Aug. '62	30 Oct. '63
liquid metal version, Project 645			
K-42			4 Nov. '63
named *Rostovskiy Komsomolets* 8 May '81			
K-50			20 Dec. '63
renamed K-60 in 1970			
Built in Severodvinsk.			

Displacement: 3101/4069* (3087/3986)

Dimensions: 107.4 × 7.96 × 6.42

Diving Depth: 300/240

Armament: 8 533 mm TT (bow) (12 reloads: 53-65K or SET-65 torpedoes)

Machinery: 2 reactors (VM-A, 70 MW each), 2 geared turbines (60-D), 2 controllable-pitch screws (VRSh), 35,000 HP = 15.5/28 kts; 2 creep motors (PG-116, 450 HP each); 2 direct-current DG 400 diesel generators (M-820); 166,000 nm at 5.5/5.7 kts, 106,000 nm at 13.6/17.4 kts. Uninterrupted submerged time 1200 hr (1600 hr*). Battery: 224 cells in 2 groups (28-SM1). Endurance 50 days.

Complement: 110 (24 officers, 33 petty officers, 10 rated men)

Electronics: Sonar: MG-200 Arktika, passive sonar MG-10, sonar intercept receiver MG-13M, mine detection sonar Luch; Radar: RLK-101 Prizma; ESM: Nakat-M; IFF: Khrom-KM; Navigation system: Pluton-627 (Mayak gyrocompass, Tyeryek DRT, LG-8 log, EL-1 echo-icemeter)

Ordered built 25 Nov. '52. Chief designer: V. N. Peregudov, followed by R. A. Shmakov (SKB-143 Volna, which merged into TsKB-18 Malakhit). The preliminary outline design was developed in Mar.–Oct. '53, the technical project (design) from Nov. '53–June '54. Built of AK-25 steel with nine compartments: (i) torpedo room and quarters; (ii) officers' quarters and mess, sonar room, batteries; (iii) command center; (iv) diesel generators, refrigerators, compressors, evaporators; (v) reactors; (vi) turbines; (vii) electrical motors and quarters; (viii) quarters, galley, sick bay, air conditioner; (ix) quarters, steering gear, provisions, showers. A planned version (Project P-627A) to carry the big P-20 missile was canceled early in 1960.

K-3 was the first Soviet nuclear submarine. Her reactor was loaded with fuel in Sept. '57, and tests began in July '58. She was stricken in 1991, and is to become a museum. K-8 was lost off the coast of Spain on 8 Apr. '70 during Exercise Okean, and fifty-two were killed. K-115 was transferred to the Pacific via the North Pole. Also in the Pacific are K-14, K-42, and K-133. In 1968 K-181 was awarded the Order of the Red Banner. All units were stricken 1989–92.

[Ed.: Details of P627A and its successor, Project 653, were given in *Morskoi Sbornik*. P-627A was an attempt to place the 13 t Ilyushin P-20 long-range cruise missile on a modified Project 627 hull. Design work began at the end of 1957, and Malakhit began drawings early in 1958. The Project 627 hull could not be used unmodified due to submerged stability problems; the beam of the outer hull had to be increased from 7.9 to 9.2 m to increase reserve buoyancy to 40 percent. An extra group of batteries was added, and the torpedo armament was changed to a more defensive suit:

4 vice 8 533 mm, no reloads, plus 2 400 mm with decoys. Displacement rose over 400 t, to total 3950 t. The submarine was to have been built at Severodvinsk, for delivery in the third quarter of 1960. However, in 1960 P-20 was canceled in favor of ballistic missiles, and work stopped even though the submarine was already fitting out.

Project 653 was the production version, with a pair of P-20s side by side, on the inner hull, enclosed by the fairing containing the sail. The hull had to be widened further, to 12.2 m. Inner hull diameter was increased, and length was reduced to get a better length:beam ratio and thus to maintain the speed of the smaller Project 627 attack submarine. Project 627 components were used where possible, but Project 653 did adopt the improved VM-1M light-water reactor, autonomous turbogenerators (as in Project 645), and a new AK-29 high-strength steel. Design work began in 1958, and the technical design was complete by the end of 1959. Plans initially called for 4 ships; that was then increased to 18. The lead ship was scheduled for delivery in 1962 (the project was killed in 1960, however). Characteristics: 97.5×12.2×7.8 m = 5250 t normal; diving depth 300 m, 22–24 kts (2×16,500 HP); 4×53 cm, 4×40 cm TT.]

November class (U.S. Naval Institute Photographic Collection)

K-42 (V. V. Kostrichenko)

Project: 705 and 705K* (LIRA)

NATO Class Name: ALFA

Names:

	completed
K-377	
K-316	
K-373	
K-123*	26 Dec. '77
K-432*	
K-463	
K-493*	

Built at Leningrad (Admiralty) and Severodvinsk*, 1977–83.

Displacement: 2310/4320

Dimensions: 79.5 × 9.5 (13.5) × 6.9

Diving Depth: 350/420

Armament: 6 533 mm (bow)(18 torpedoes or mines)

Machinery: 1 liquid-metal (lead-bismuth) reactor (BM-40A* or OK-550; 155 MW), 2 steam turbogenerators (1500 kW, 400 Hz, 380 V), 1 geared turbine (OK-7), 1 shaft (plus 2 auxiliary 136 HP, with creep motors), 38,000 HP = 14/43 kts; 1 auxiliary diesel. Endurance 50 days.

Complement: 30 (all officers)

Electronics: Sonar system (complex): Okean (passive sonar: Yenisei; sonars Zhgut, Lutch, Rosa, Vint, Tissa); ESM: Bukhta; Combat data system: Accord; Communications system: Molniya; Navigation system: Sozh (including radar Chibis)

Project approved 27 May '61; technical project approved by Ministry of Defense 11 Dec. '61. Chief engineer: M. G. Rusanov (beginning in 1977, V. A. Romin of SKB-143 Volna, Leningrad). This design featured a titanium-alloy pressure hull and a high level of automation. All hatches in the compartments could be closed automatically and locked from the command center. K-377 (Yard 900) was laid down at Admiralty Works and dismantled after tests. K-123* (builder's number 105) was the first unit built at Severodvinsk. All units were stricken from the Northern Fleet and placed in reserve 1990–93. B-123 became a floating pier and was stricken in 1995.

[Ed.: According to Burov, the OTZ called for a 1500 t submarine capable of about 40 kts; the design then grew inexorably to 2300 t. According to a recent design history, Project 705/705K was conceived in 1958 by A. B. Petrov, an

Alfa class (U.S. Naval Institute Photographic Collection)

engineer in the Malakhit design bureau. In the interest of improving speed and maneuverability, he proposed halving the displacement of a second-generation nuclear submarine. He would cut tonnage to 1500 by adopting a single hull (which would also cut wetted area, hence resistance, as well as flow noise), by adopting titanium construction (for light weight), automation (to cut crew size to 15–17), and a single lightweight reactor (gas- or liquid-metal cooled). Among proposed innovations was the use of soft inflatable tanks to keep the submarine afloat on the surface in an emergency. V. N. Peregodov, the bureau chief, encouraged Petrov to form a special group within Malakhit to pursue the project. Against this, the fleet disliked both the single hull and the single reactor. Petrov first briefed his design concept within Malakhit in June '59. It was supported by both Admiral Gorshkov, chief of the Soviet fleet, and by B. Ye. Butoma, chairman of the state committee for the shipbuilding industry. The design study was completed in June '60.

Butoma pressed for completion of the project, but he also removed Petrov from it, replacing him in May '60 with chief designer M. G. Rusanov (who was completing work on the abortive Project 653 missile submarine). The project was formally authorized on 23 June '60; the concept design was completed on 31 Dec. '60. Petrov's radical concepts were diluted to some extent: the design that emerged had a double hull, six (rather than three) compartments, twice the crew, and 50 percent greater displacement. However, the emphasis on automation survived in the submarine's Akkord combat information system, which brought all control into a single console. For the first time in Soviet practice this one console controlled all of the ship's electronic equipment, including her navigation system, navigation radar, search radar, sonar system, and fire control system. It is not clear to what extent navigation included ship control. For the first time in Soviet practice, torpedoes were ejected hydraulically, so that they could be launched at any operational depth.

Another innovation was the escape capsule integrated into the submarine's sail. Very careful blending of a body-of-revolution hull, the sail (with covers for all retractable masts), and a slotted rudder preserved Petrov's goal of very high speed, comparable to that of torpedoes, and very high maneuverability.

Two liquid-metal power plants were already being developed in parallel: VM-40/A (modular two-section with two steam lines and circulating pumps) and OK-550 (modular, with branched first-loop lines and three steam lines and circulating pumps). They equipped, respectively, Project 705 and 705K submarines. To save weight, Project 705/705K adopted 400 Hz power in place of the 500 Hz systems of earlier Soviet submarines.

Apparently the project had lost much of its popularity by 1973. Visiting the laid-up prototype, D. F. Ustinov (then the central committee secretary for defense sectors) denounced the cramped design and the impossibility of repair (the prototype had suffered a reactor casualty and had to be withdrawn from service). Butoma (now minister of the shipbuilding industry), who had supported the project earlier, called for cancellation. Rusanov was relieved. The six surviving units were, however, modernized by 1982. It turned out that basing was difficult because the primary reactor loop (liquid-metal portion) had to be kept hot (to keep the alloy liquid) when the reactor was turned off; it was also necessary to keep the alloy from oxidizing (periodically regenerating it) and to monitor its state constantly. After the loss of the experimental *Komsomolets,* the main naval staff decided to withdraw these submarines by mid-1990 as potentially unsafe, despite the fact that their reactors and machinery had seen little use.

Projects 705 and 705K differ in using two different reactor plants, developed in parallel. Project 705 has three steam lines (three primary loops, each leading to its own steam generator); Project 705K has two.]

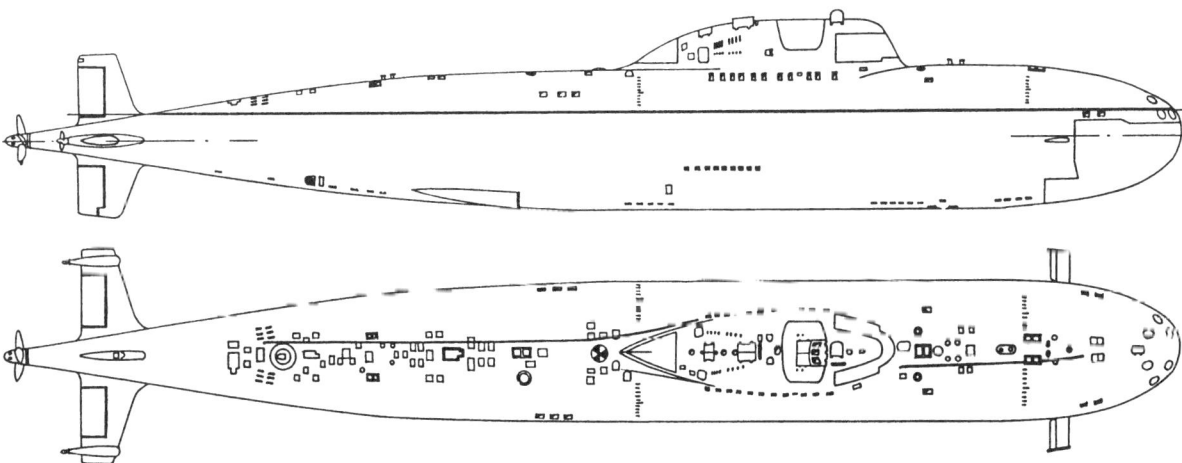

Project: 10831

NATO Class Name: None

Names:

AS-12

Displacement: 1600/2100

Dimensions: $60 \times 7 \times 5.1$

Diving Depth: 1000

Armament: None

Machinery: 1 reactor, 1 shaft, 15,000 HP = 30 kts

Complement: 25 (all officers)

Rated a Nuclear Deepwater Station 1st Rank; built at Severodvinsk.

Project: 1851

NATO Class Name: X-RAY

Names:

AS-11

Displacement: 550/1000

Dimensions: $40 \times 5.3 \times 5$

Diving Depth: – – –

Armament: None

Machinery: 1 reactor, 10 MW

This special submarine was built in Leningrad (Sudomekh) in 1982. She has a pressure chamber for deepwater divers.

Project: 1910 (KASHALOT)

NATO Class Name: UNIFORM

Names:

AS-15   built Nov. '82–July '83

AS-16   built Apr. '88–Nov. '89

Both built at Leningrad (Sudomekh). A third unit, which may be AS-19, was completed Dec. '93.

Displacement: 1390/2000

Dimensions: $69 \times 7 \times 5.2$

Diving Depth: – – –

Armament: None

Machinery: 1 reactor, 10,000 HP = 10/30 kts

Complement: 36

Special submarines for studies and tests of new types of reactors. Rated as Deepwater Stations of 1st Rank.

Project: 651

NATO Class Name: JULIETT

Names:

	laid down	launched	completed
K-156	16 Nov. '60	31 July '62	10 Dec. '63
renamed B-156 in 1987			
K-85			30 Dec. '64
K-24			31 Oct. '65
renamed B-124			
K-68			28 Dec. '65
K-63			12 June '66
K-70			31 Dec. '64
renamed B-270			
K-77			31 Oct. '65
K-58			23 Sept. '66
K-81			14 Dec. '65
K-73			15 Dec. '66
K-67			30 Sept. '67

Juliett class (U.S. Navy)

B-81 (Pavlov collection)

B-73 (Pavlov collection)

Juliett class (U.S. Naval Institute Photographic Collection)

K-78	1 Nov. '67
renamed B-478	
K-203	2 Dec. '67
K-304	21 Aug. '68
K-318	29 Sept. '68
K-120	26 Dec. '68

Sixteen units. Built in Leningrad (Baltic yard).

Displacement: 3174/3750

Dimensions: 85.9 × 9.7 × 6.29

Diving Depth: 300/240

Armament: 4 missiles (P-6, later replaced by P-500 or P-750), 6 533 mm TT (bow, 6 torpedoes), 4 406 mm TT (stern, 12 torpedoes). Number of torpedoes could be increased by placing them in compartment (ii).

Machinery: 2 diesels (D-43), 8000 HP; 2 electric motors (PG-141, 6000 HP total), also 1 battery-charging diesel (2D-42, 1750 HP); 2 shrouded propellers; 16.8/18 kts; 2 creep motors (PG-140, 1000 HP); 18,000 nm/7 kts (snorkelling), 27.8 nm/18 kts submerged, 810 nm/2.74 kts submerged. Endurance 90 days.

Complement: 78

Electronics: Sonar: Tuloma, Arktika-M, passive sonar MG-10, sonar intercept receiver MG-13; Underwater communication system: Svyet-2; Radar: RLK-101; ESM: Nakat; IFF: Nikhrom-M; Torpedo FCS: Leningrad-651; Navigation system: Sila-N651 (including Mayak gyrocompass, Sila GA gyroazimuth, LR-2 hydraulic log, Lira-11 astronavigational system, ARP-53 radio direction-finder, NEL-6 echo-log, and EL-1 echo-icemeter)

The preliminary design of a submarine with silver-zinc batteries was developed in May '58, and the technical project approved in Jan. '59. Chief designer A. C. Kassatsiyer. K-156 and K-85 had hulls of low-magnetic steel. Beginning with the fifth hull, these submarines had anechoic coverings. Using all sources of regeneration, a submarine of this type could remain submerged for 800 hr.

The missile launch system was similar to that of Project 675M: missiles were fired from the surface, at speeds of up to 8 kts, in sea states of up to 4, at a launch angle of 15°. B-68 tested the Kasatka satellite targeting system.

Assignments: B-124, B-77, B-81 in Baltic, B-58, B-67, B-318 in Black Sea, B-63, B-73, B-120, B-270 in Pacific; rest in Northern Fleet. These submarines were placed in reserve from 1991 on. In 1994 B-124 and B-77 were sold for conversion into floating restaurants in the Netherlands. Ships of this class are now on display at Copenhagen and Helsinki.

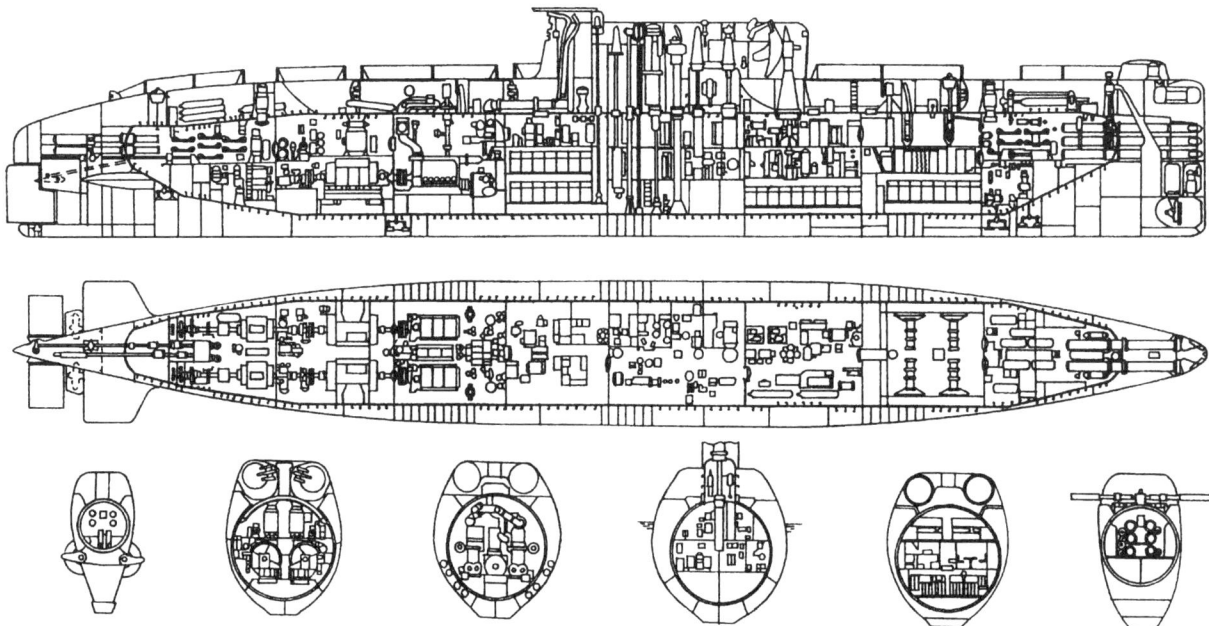

Project: 877, 877V, 877EKM (PALTUS)

NATO Class Name: KILO (VARSHAVYANKA)

Names:

completed

B-177

B-187

B-190

B-219

B-224

B-227

B-229

B-248   12 Sept. '80
 lead unit, built at Komsomolsk

B-260

B-345

B-354

B-394
 named *Komsomolets Tadjikistana* 26 Aug. '80–1991

B-401

B-402

B-404
 named *Tyumenskiy Komsomolets* until 1991

B-405

B-425

B-437
 named *Magnitogorskiy Komsolmolets* 9 June '80–1991

B-439

B-445

B-459

B-464

B-468

B-470

B-471

B-494

B-800

B-871

Total twenty-eight units, plus exports. Built in Komsomolsk (last of fifteen units completed 12 Mar. '94), Leningrad (Admiralty: export units), and Nizhni Novgorod (Gorkiy).

Displacement: 2325/3076

Dimensions: 72.6 × 9.9 (12.8) × 6.6

Diving Depth: 300/240

Armament: 6 533 mm TT (12 reloads: 53-65KE, 53-56V, 53VA, SET-53M, wire-guided TEST-71M; or 24 DM-1 mines); 8×1 launchers for 9M313 missile (Igla-1 system)

Machinery: 2 1500 kW diesel generators (type 4DL-42M); 1 PG-141 electric motor, 1 shaft, 5500 HP = 12/18 kts, also

B-425 (Pavlov collection)

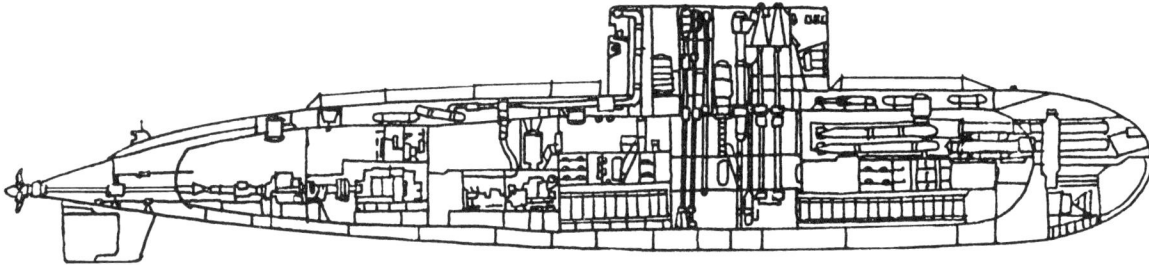

1500 HP low speed motor; 2 auxiliary screws (102 HP PG-140 motors), 6000 nm/7 kts (snorkeling), 400 nm/10 kts submerged. Endurance 45 days.

Complement: 53 (14 officers, 12 petty officers, 12 rated men, 15 seamen)

Electronics: Sonar: MGK-400 Rubikon system (MG-512, MT-533), MG-519 Arfa, passive sonar MG-53 (latest units have Ayaks sonar system); Radar: MRK-50 Tobol system; IFF: Khrom; Radio transmitters: P-654MR, P-680, P-625 (KV) (short waves); Navigation system: Andoga.

Technical assignment (staff requirement) approved by CinC 1974; technical project approved 20 Dec. '76. Chief designer Yu. N. Kormilitsyn (TsKB-18). There are six compartments: (i) living quarters, torpedo room, battery; (ii) command center; (iii) batteries; (iv) diesel generators; (v) main electric motor, switchboard; (vi) auxiliary electric motors, steering gear. This is the quietest Russian submarine. There are plans to install a small nuclear reactor (AEU, auxiliary atomic plant) in a submarine of this type. B-177,

the lead submarine built at Nizhni Novgorod, has a pump-jet (Black Sea Fleet). One boat is in use for training. Project 636 is an improved version, currently under development.

The export version is Project 877EKM. Exports: Algeria (2, in 1987 and in Jan. '88), China, India (6 in 1986–89), Iran (3, including B-219 in Oct. '92), Libya (1 in 1992), Poland (1, 21 June '86), Rumania (1).

B-354 suffered a fire on 4 Apr. '89. In 1994 B-459 visited Britain.

[Ed.: Russian accounts of this design emphasize that it is conceived around a central computer, into which fire control information is automatically entered, and which transmits torpedo settings. The computer also controls diving and machinery; most functions are controlled from a single central panel. Torpedoes can be reloaded from this station, using a Murena panel. The central computer can also hold the submarine on an ordered course, and can solve navigational problems.]

Project: 641B (SOM)

NATO Class Name: TANGO

Names:

B-30

B-97

B-146

B-215

B-225

B-290

B-303

B-307

B-312

B-319

B-380 named *Gor'kovskiy Komsomolets* until 18 Mar. '92

B-386

B-443

B-474

B-498

B-504

B-515

B-519

B-546

Nineteen units. Built in Gorkiy.

Displacement: 2750/3546

Dimensions: 90.2 × 9.6 × 6.9

Diving Depth: 300/240

Armament: 6 533 mm TT (24 torpedoes)

Machinery: 3 diesels (2D-42, 5250 HP total), 3 electric motors (total 5400 HP: center shaft driven by PG-102 motor, 2700 HP), 1 creep motor (140 HP), 3 shafts, 13/16 kts; 4 groups of battery cells. Endurance 80 days.

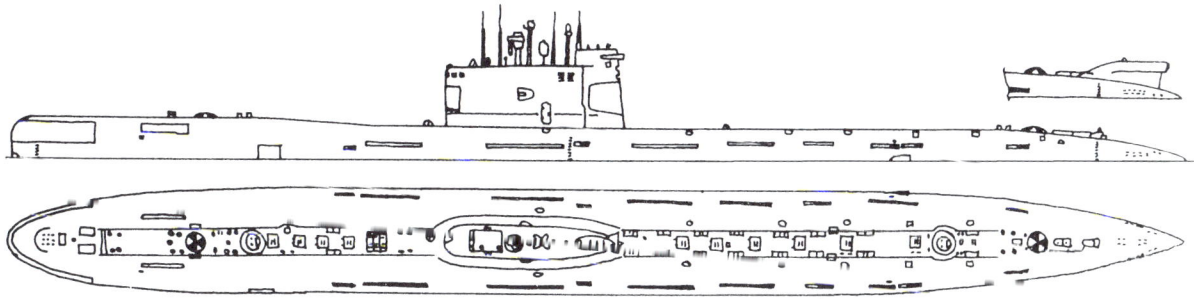

Complement: 78 (including 17 officers)

Electronics: Sonar: MGK-400 Rubikon; Torpedo FCS computer: Vol'fram; Autopilot computer: Pirit; Central computer complex: Uzel; Navigation system: Most-641B

The chief designer was Yu. N. Kormilitsyn. Two units have towed arrays. The lead unit, B-380, arrived in Sevastopol in July '73 and was repaired in 1992–94 (Black Sea Fleet).

[Ed: According to Burov, this class was conceived as a more automated version of the earlier Project 641 *Foxtrot*. For the first time in a Soviet diesel submarine, a sonar system ("complex") was installed, linked to a combat information control system. Data was automatically inserted into torpedoes before firing. The system automatically controlled ballasting, and there was an autopilot. The combat direction system may also have controlled combat maneuvering, e.g., the final stages of the pre-firing approach to a target. Torpedo load-out was increased by 20 percent. Ballast tank blow pressure was doubled and the batteries of earlier submarines superseded by modern ones. The machinery was specially silenced (some equipment was sound-isolated, and piping, foundations, and outer hull faced with sound-absorbing material); Burov claims that this class was recognized as the quietest of its time. For better habitability, officers had two-man staterooms and bunks were provided for all crewmen; half the chiefs and enlisted men were in cabins.]

B-146 (S. P. Bukan')

63

Project: 641, 641I, 641K

NATO Class Name: FOXTROT

Names:

	laid down	launched	completed
B-2			14 July '63
B-4			31 Aug. '61
named *Chelyabinskiy Komsomolets* 18 Jan. '63–Apr. '92			
B-6			30 July '64
B-7			15 Dec. '61
B-8			18 Dec. '62
B-9			30 Nov. '65
B-15			30 Sept. '64
B-21			31 Oct. '65
B-25			6 Sept. '65
B-26			24 Mar. '66
named *Yaroslavskiy Komsomolets* 15 Feb. '65			
B-28			18 June '66
B-29			28 Nov. '66
B-31			25 June '63
B-33			27 Nov. '61
B-34			31 Aug. '66
B-37			5 Nov. '59
B-38			30 Sept. '62
B-39			28 Dec. '67
B-40			6 Sept. '66
B-41			24 Dec. '66
B-46			30 June '67
B-49			30 June '67
named *Valdimirskiy Komsomolets* 23 Sept. '67			
B-50			8 Dec. '62
B-51			26 Oct. '67
B-53			5 Nov. '62
B-55			20 Sept. '63
renamed B-855 in 1970			
B-57			28 July '60
B-59			10 June '61
B-85			23 Dec. '60
B-94	3 Oct. '57	28 Dec. '57	25 Dec. '58
lead ship, built at Sudomekh			
B-95			30 Sept. '59
B-98			15 May '64
B-101			29 May '64
B-103			24 Dec. '64
B-105			15 June '62
B-107			28 Apr. '65
B-109			15 Apr. '65
B-112			5 Aug. '65
B-116			25 Aug. '60
B-130			22 Sept. '60
B-133			5 Nov. '59
renamed B-833 in 1970			
B-135			5 Nov. '59
B-139			15 Mar. '60
B-143			5 Nov. '60
B-153			30 Sept. '61
B-156			18 Apr. '61
B-164			16 Oct. '61
B-169			28 July '62
B-205			28 Dec. '69
B-213			11 Aug. '70
B-309			10 Dec. '78
B-311			11 Feb. '78
B-330			27 Oct. '77
B-397			31 Dec. '67
B-400			25 Sept. '68
B-401			19 Sept. '68
Yard 402			
B-402			5 Sept. '69
B-405			2 July '69
B-409			10 Sept. '71
B-413			25 Dec. '68
B-416			4 Dec. '69
B-427			4 Dec. '71
B-435			6 Nov. '70
B-440			25 Dec. '70
B-456			10 Oct. '72
B-464			16 Dec. '73
B-470			5 July '73
B-510			20 Oct. '83
B-522			20 Sept. '74
B-533			8 Oct. '76
B-586			30 Nov. '79
B-587			25 Oct. '81
B-588			28 Sept. '82
B-590			21 Nov. '80

B-94 was prototype: begun 3 Oct. '57, lch 28 Dec. '57.

Production for the Soviet Navy (sixty-two units) ended in 1971.

Export production: total twelve (included in the list above).

Transfers: Cuba (641K: B-309 on 7 Feb. '79, B-586 in Mar. '80, B-510 in Feb. '84), India (641I: B-51 in Apr. '68, B-401 in Mar. '69, B-405 in Nov. '69, B-402 in Feb. '70, B-456 in

B-51 (S. P. Bukan')

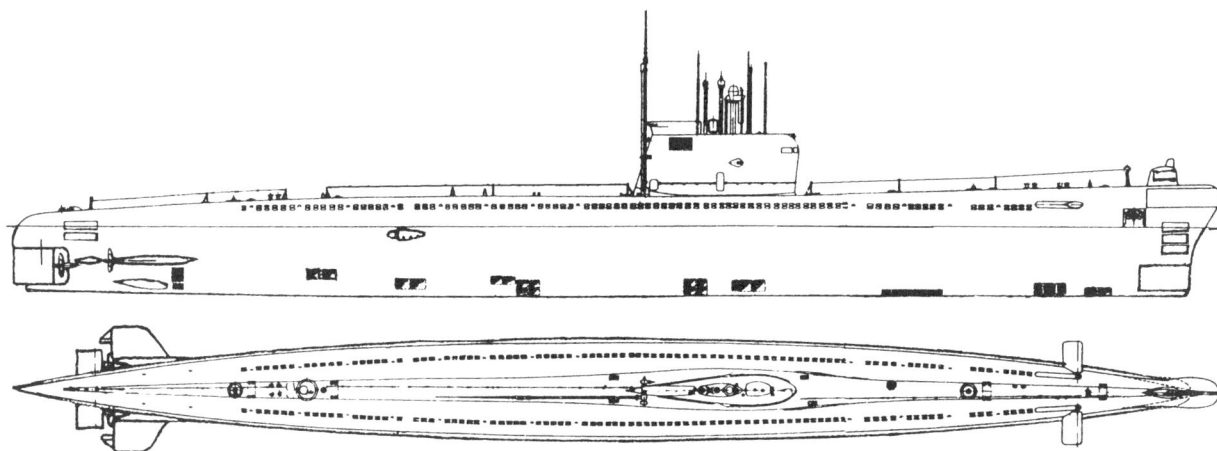

Design 641 (V. P. Tchyernyshov)

Nov. '73, B-470 in Dec. '73, B-464 in Oct. '74, B-522 in Feb. '75), Libya (641I: B-311 in Dec. '76, B-330 and B-533 in Feb. '78, B-587 in Feb. '81, B-588 in Jan. '82, B-590 in Feb. '83), Poland (ex-Soviet boats: 1987, 1988).

All were built in Leningrad (Admiralty and Sudomekh).

Displacement: 1950/2550

Dimensions: 91.3 × 7.5 × 5.1

Diving Depth: 280/250

Armament: 10 533 mm TT (6 bow, 4 stern)(22 torpedoes or 32 AMD-1000 mines). Torpedoes could be launched down to 80 m.

Machinery: 3 diesels (6000 HP 2D-42 in 45 units; from B-397 on had 40-D), 3 electric motors (5400 HP, with 2700 HP on the center shaft), 3 shafts, 16.4/16 kts, 30,000 nm/8.13 kts surfaced, 15.3 nm/16 kts submerged; 477 t oil fuel; 4 48-SM batteries (112 cells each). Endurance 90 days. Uninterrupted time submerged 575 hr.

Complement: 70 (12 officers)

Electronics: Sonar: Arktika, Tuloma (scanning); Sonar intercept receiver: Svyet-M (elsewhere listed as an underwater communications device); Radar: Burya; ESM: Nakat; IFF: Khrom-K; HF antenna (retractable): Iva; Gyrocompass: Kurs-5; Log: LR-2; Sounder: NEL-5; Echo-icemeter: EL-1

This project was approved in October 1954. Chief designer was S. A. Yegorov, succeeded by Z. A. Dyeribin. Double-hull boats with seven compartments. One unit (Project 641EEh) was a training boat.

B-37 blew up on 11 Jan. '62. B-33 sank in Vladivostok 26 Jan. '91. All are to be retired and scrapped. [Ed: Two are on view: one in London, at the Thames Barrier; and one in Sydney, Australia].

Foxtrot class (Friedman collection)

Project: 611, 611AV, 611-P, 611R

NATO Class Name: ZULU

Names:

	laid down	launched	completed
B-61	10 Jan. '51	26 July '51	31 Dec. '53
B-62			31 Dec. '53
B-63			30 June '54
renamed B-863 in 1970			
B-64			30 Dec. '54
B-65			6 Dec. '54
B-66			29 Dec. '54
renamed B-866 in 1970			
B-67			30 June '56
B-68			27 Nov. '55
B-69			31 Dec. '55
B-70			29 June '55
B-71			30 Sept. '56
B-72			30 June '56
B-73			30 Nov. '57
B-74			31 Oct. '56
B-75			6 Nov. '56
B-76			28 Nov. '56
B-77			30 Nov. '56
B-78			30 Nov. '57
named *Murmanskiy Komsomolets* 1978			
B-79			3 Dec. '57
B-80			13 July '57
B-81			13 July '57
B-82			17 Aug. '57
B-88			25 Sept. '57
B-89			13 Dec. '57
B-90			30 Oct. '57
B-91			15 July '58
renamed BS-891 in 1974			

Built in Leningrad (Sudomekh) and in Severodvinsk.

Displacement: 1831/2400

Dimensions: 90.5 × 7.5 × 5.1

Diving Depth: 200/170

Armament: 10 533 mm TT (6 bow, 4 stern)(22 torpedoes or 32 AMD-1000 mines plus 4 torpedoes), 1×2 57 mm (SM-24 ZiF, 250 rounds), 1×2 25 mm (2M-8, removed 1957)

Machinery: 3 diesels (37-D, 6000 HP), 3 electric motors (PG-102, 2700 HP, on center shaft, PG-101s, 1350 HP, on wing shafts, total 5400 HP), 3 shafts, 17/15 kts, surfaced 4230 nm/16.5 kts, 22,000 nm/9.2 kts, submerged 15 nm/15 kts or 443 nm/2.1 kts. 243 t fuel. Endurance 75 days. Uninterrupted time under water 200 hr.

Complement: 65

Zulu class (U.S. Navy)

Zulu class (U.S. Navy)

BS-68 (V. V. Zablotskiy)

Electronics: Sonar: Tamir-5LS and passive sonar Mars-24; Radar: Flag; ESM: Nakat; Periscopes: S-2 attack periscope with course angle indicator (DKU-5) and S-8 zenith periscope (DKU-7); Torpedo FCS: L-6/4; Radio transmitters: R-641, R-647, Rjejd-E; Radio receivers: R-670, R-673; Gyrocompass: Kurs-3; Log: GOM-III; Sounder: NEL-4

The technical assignment (staff requirement) for this first series of postwar large submarines was approved in Jan. '46. The design was completed at Sudomekh in Aug. '49. Chief designer was S. A. Yegorov. The double hulled submarines had seven compartments.

In 1956–57 B-64 was modified to a cruise missile submarine (Project 611P: one P-10 missile in a container); the missile was later removed. Under Project 611AV (chief designer N. N. Isanin; NATO Zulu V), B-62, B-67, B-73, B-78, B-79, and B-89 were converted into ballistic missile submarines, each carrying two surface-launched R 11FM in vertical tubes. Preparation to launch: 2 hrs underwater, then 5 min after surfacing (the second missile could be fired 5 min later). Missiles could be fired at speeds of up to 12 kts, in sea states up to 4. In 1958 B-67 was tested to her full rated diving depth and her missiles were tested against the shock effects of underwater explosions. B-78, the last of the missile submarine conversions, was stricken in 1990. Two units were used for ocean survey. BS-89 (Project 611R) was test ship for the Yenisei sonar system. From 1966 on, B-70, B-62, and B-68 were also used to test new sonars. B-863 became a test boat in June '78. BS-69 and BS-891 were modified as Northern Fleet frogman carriers. BS-82 was modified to search for underwater cables to cut in wartime.

One unit was sold to become a Dutch restaurant.

[Ed.: According to Shitikov et al., work on Project 611 began at TsKB-18 in 1943, and a TTZ was issued on 29 Jan. '44. It called for something slightly smaller than a K-class (1500 t) long range submarine (1100 t), armed with 6 bow (12 reloads) and 4 stern (2 reloads) TT, plus 1 100 mm and 4 25 mm guns, with a speed of 22/9–10 kts and an endurance of 15,000/200 nm. Diving depth would have been 150 m, and stores endurance forty-five days. With the end of the war it became obvious that this conventional submarine was obsolete, so a new TTZ was issued on 18 Jan. '46. Displacement increased to 1250–1300 t, gun armament would have been 2 100 mm (B-24-PS mounts) and 4 37 mm, and underwater endurance would have been 250 nm. The TTZ was recast again Jan. '47, this time calling for something closer to the wartime German Type XXI.]

Design 611 (Pavlov collection)

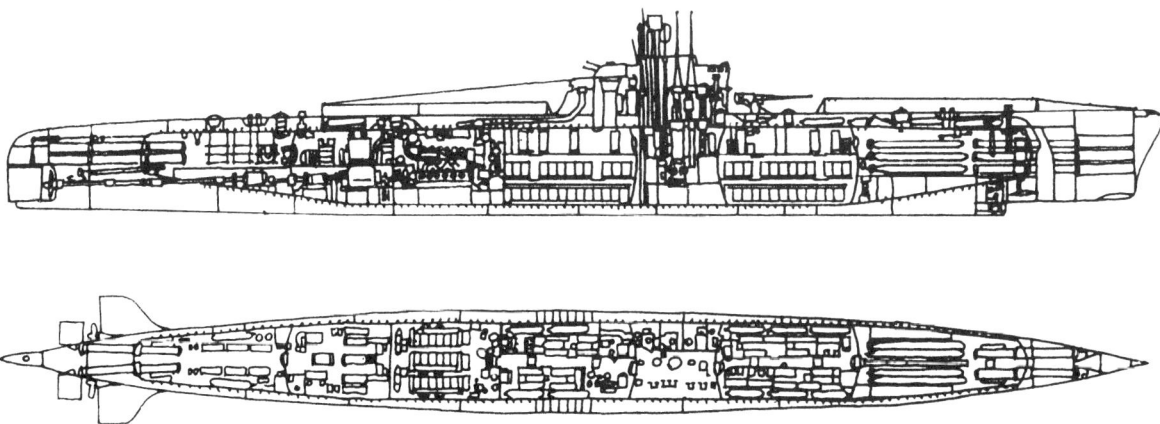

Project: 633 and 633RV

NATO Class Name: ROMEO

Names:

	laid down	launched	completed
S-4	22 Oct. '57	30 May '58	26 Dec. '59
S-6			
S-7			
S-11			
S-28			
S-34			
S-36			
S-37			
S-38			
S-41			
S-49			
S-53			
S-57			
S-101			
S-123			
S-212			
S-323			
S-350			
S-351			
S-352			
S-354			

22 units. All built at Gorkiy 1959–62.

Displacement: 1330/1730

Dimensions: 76.6 × 6.7 × 5.5

Diving Depth: 200/170

Armament: 8 533 mm (6 bow, 2 stern: 14 torpedoes or 28 AMD-1000 mines). Torpedoes can be launched at 40 m depth.

Machinery: 2 diesels (37-D, 4000 HP), 2 electric motors (PG-101, total 2700 HP), 2 shafts, 2 PG-103K 100 HP creep motors, 15/5/12.8 kts, 4500 nm/8 kts snorkelling, 13 nm/12.8 kts submerged; 7500 nm/8 kts snorkelling with extra fuel. Battery: 48-SM (2 groups, 112 cells each). Uninterrupted time under water, 300 hr. Endurance 60 days.

Complement: 54

Electronics: Sonars: Tamir-2, MG-15; Underwater communications: Svyet-M; Radar: Burya; ESM: Nakat; IFF: Khrom-K; Gyrocompass: Kurs-5; Log: LR-2; Sounder: NEL-5

Chief designer Z. A. Dyeribin, then A. K. Nazarov and E. V. Krylov. Double hull with 7 compartments. Plans originally called for 560 units of this class. S-37 was rebuilt in 1967 (Project 633L) with a new more streamlined outer hull, new torpedo FCS (Leningrad-633) and new sonars (Arktika, MG-15, and Svyet-M). SS-11 was modified to test new torpedoes (Project 06332). SS-128 (Project 06333) was modified with a massive bulged bow to test Granat missiles.

S-350 was sunk by explosion 11 Jan. '62. Remaining units were stricken in 1994.

Transfers: Algeria (S-7 and S-28, Jan. '82 and Feb. '83), Bulgaria (S-56 in May '72, S-212 in Nov. '72, S-38 in Jan. '83, S-36 in Dec. '85), Egypt (6 in 1966–68), Syria (S-4 in 1985, another in 1986). China and North Korea build this design from Soviet drawings. Four Chinese units were transferred to Egypt and Bangladesh.

S-49 (Pavlov collection)

S-38 (Pavlov collection)

Project: 613

NATO Class Name: WHISKEY

Names:

	laid down	launched	completed
S-43			29 Dec. '52
S-44			31 Dec. '52
S-45			31 Dec. '52
S-46			31 Dec. '52
S-61 KOMSOMOLETS lead unit	11 Apr. '50		24 May '52
S-62			18 Nov. '52
S-63			6 Nov. '52
S-64			4 Nov. '52
S-65			30 Dec. '52
S-66*			3 Jan. '53
S-67*			7 Feb. '53
S-68			20 Apr. '53
S-69			10 Apr. '53
S-70*			12 July '53
S-71*			6 Oct. '53
S-72			20 Sept. '53
S-73			5 Oct. '53
S-74			4 Nov. '53
S-75			14 Dec. '53
S-76*			31 Dec. '53
S-77			28 Feb. '54
renamed *Tyumenskiy Komsomolets* 23 Oct. '72			
S-78			29 May '54

	laid down	launched	completed
S-79			30 May '54
S-80 lead unit at Gorkiy	13 Mar. '50		2 Dec. '51
S-86			3 June '54
S-87			18 June '54
S-88*			30 Sept. '54
S-89			30 Aug. '54
S-98			31 Aug. '55
S-100			30 Dec. '54
S-140*			18 Mar. '54
S-141*			11 Apr. '53
S-142			19 May '53
S-143			8 Apr. '53
renamed *Ul'yanovskiy Komsomolets* 17 Sept. '76			
S-144			24 Apr. '53
S-145*			30 June '53
S-146			30 June '53
S-147			21 Dec. '53
S-148			30 Dec. '53
S-149			30 Sept. '53
S-150*			28 Sept. '53
S-153			31 Dec. '53
S-154*			31 Dec. '53
S-155			18 Dec. '53
S-156 *Komsomolets Kazakhstana*			31 Dec. '53
S-157			30 Nov. '53

S-98 (Pavlov collection)

	laid down	launched	completed		laid down	launched	completed
S-158			31 Dec. '53	S-187			20 Dec. '54
S-160			10 Mar. '54	S-188			8 Mar. '55
S-161			26 Mar. '54	S-189			9 Mar. '55
S-162			28 Apr. '54	S-190			29 Oct. '55
S-163			29 Mar. '54	S-191			4 Aug. '55
S-164			12 Apr. '54	renamed *Pskovskiy Komsomolets* 15 June '65			
S-165			10 May '54	S-192			31 Oct. '55
S-166			15 July '54	S-193			28 Apr. '55
S-167			30 July '54	S-194			17 Aug. '55
S-168*			23 July '54	S-195*			17 Aug. '55
S-169			29 July '54	S-196			25 May '55
S-170			26 July '54	S-197*			1 Apr. '54
S-171			10 Aug. '54	S-198			24 Mar. '55
S-172*			30 Aug. '54	S-199			28 Feb. '55
S-173			18 Sept. '54	S-200			23 Mar. '55
S-174			23 Sept. '54	S-217			31 Dec. '54
S-177			26 Sept. '54	S-218			17 Mar. '55
S-178*			20 Oct. '54	S-219			30 Apr. '55
S-179			5 Nov. '54	S-220			28 Apr. '55
S-180			9 Dec. '54	S-221*			31 May '55
S-181*			23 Nov. '54	*Komsomolets Tadjikistana*			
S-182			2 Dec. '54	S-222			31 May '55
S-183			14 Dec. '54	S-223			23 June '55
S-184			18 Dec. '54	S-224*			30 June '55
S-185*			20 Dec. '54	S-225			25 Sept. '55
S-186			10 July '55	S-226			30 July '55

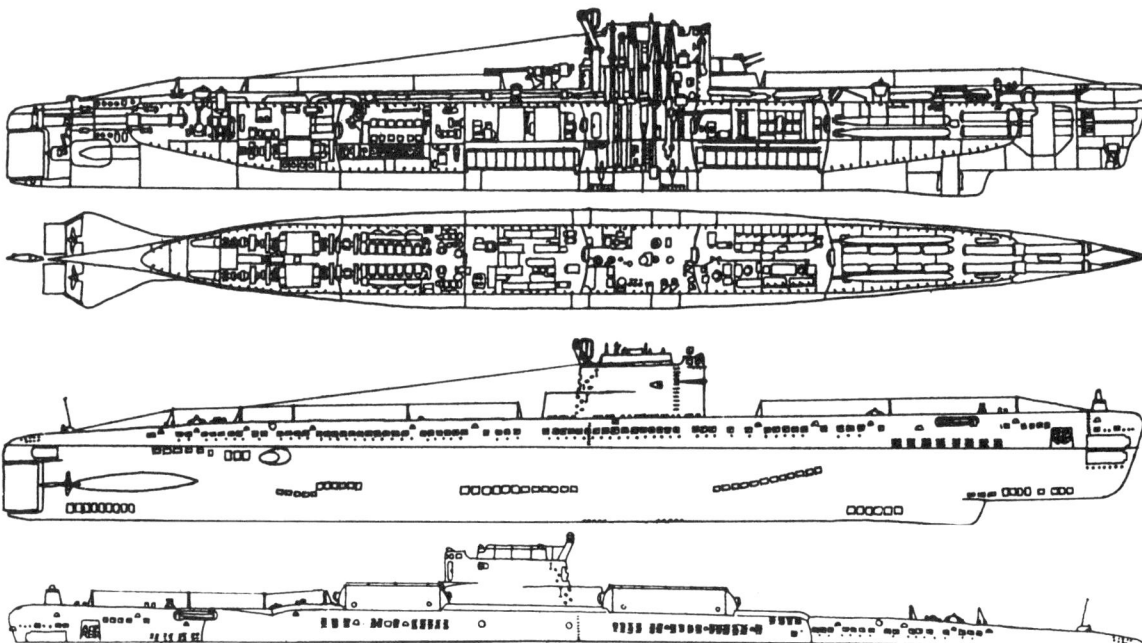

	laid down	launched	completed		laid down	launched	completed
S-227			31 Aug. '55	S-272			30 Sept. '55
S-228			16 Sept. '55	S-273			31 Aug. '55
S-229			25 Sept. '55	S-274			20 July '55
S-230			29 Sept. '55	S-275			25 Oct. '55
S-231			19 Oct. '55	S-276			21 Oct. '55
S-232			30 Nov. '55	S-277			30 Sept. '55
S-233			16 Dec. '55	S-278			12 Nov. '55
S-234			16 Dec. '55	S-279			20 Oct. '55
S-235			8 Feb. '56	S-280			2 Sept. '55
S-236			8 Feb. '56	S-281			7 Oct. '55
S-237			14 Feb. '56	S-282			25 Oct. '55
S-238			28 Apr. '56	S-283			31 Oct. '55
S-239			24 May '56	renamed *Vladimirskiy Komsomolets* 23 Sept. '67			
S-240			30 May '56	S-284			12 Nov. '55
S-241			29 May '56	S-285			31 Dec. '55
S-242			30 June '56	S-286			31 Dec. '55
S-243			25 Aug. '56	S-287			31 Dec. '55
S-244			14 Sept. '56	S-288			31 Dec. '55
S-245			14 Sept. '56	S-289			29 Dec. '55
S-246			30 Sept. '56	S-290			11 Apr. '56
S-250			24 July '56	S-291			2 Feb. '56
S-261			2 Apr. '55	S-292			31 Mar. '56
S-262			30 June '55	S-293			29 Feb. '56
S-263			30 June '55	S-294			11 Apr. '56
S-264			30 July '55	S-296			30 June '56
S-265			30 July '55	S-297			31 Aug. '56
S-266*			2 Aug. '55	S-300			8 Sept. '56
S-267			July '55	*Bryanskiy Komsomolets*			
S-268			31 July '55	S-325			17 Aug. '56
S-269			29 July '55	S-326			19 July '56
S-270			27 Aug. '55	S-327			17 July '56
S-271			31 Aug. '55	S-328*			24 Aug. '56

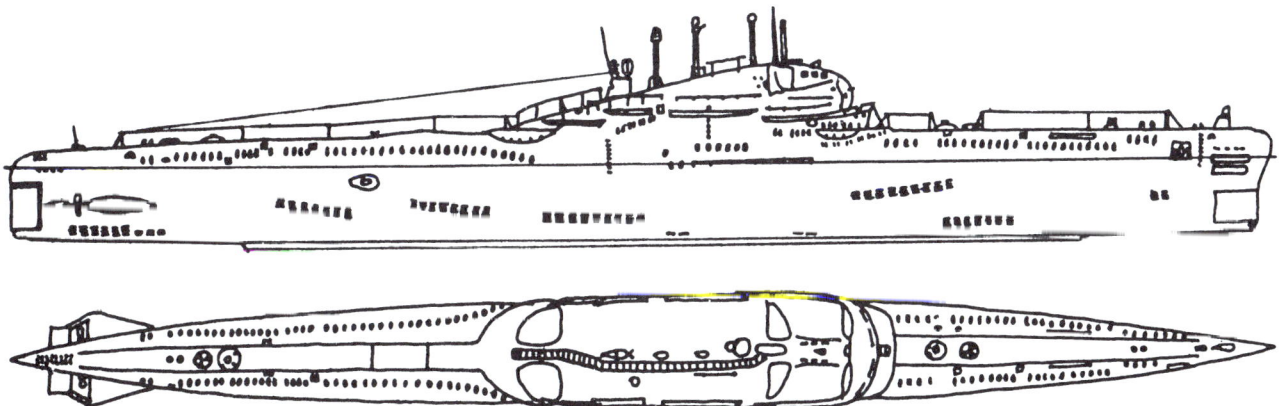

	laid down	launched	completed		laid down	launched	completed
S-329			28 July '56	S-364			31 Dec. '57
S-331*			31 Dec. '54	S-365			30 June '58
S-332			27 Nov. '55	S-374			31 Oct. '56
S-333			20 Nov. '55	S-375			23 June '57
S-334			9 Dec. '55	S-376			31 Dec. '56
S-335			28 Dec. '55	S-377			23 Feb. '57
S-336			3 Sept. '56	S-378			24 Mar. '57
S-337			31 Aug. '56	S-379			29 Apr. '57
S-338			24 Aug. '56	S-380			30 June '57
S-339			31 July '56	S-381			24 May '57
S-340			10 Aug. '56	S-382			29 June '57
S-341			8 Sept. '56	S-383			28 Aug. '57
S-342			18 Sept. '56	S-384	15 Apr. '57		not completed
S-343			25 Sept. '56	S-390			31 Oct. '56
S-344			24 Sept. '56	S-391			30 Nov. '56
S-345			11 Oct. '56	S-392			23 July '57
S-346			22 Oct. '56	S-393			24 July '57
S-347			26 Oct. '56				
S-348			30 Nov. '56				
S-349			31 Dec. '56				
S-355			12 Nov. '55				
S-356			28 Dec. '55				
S-357			26 Dec. '55				
S-358			24 May '56				
S-359			30 Sept. '56				
S-360			30 Sept. '56				
S-361			30 Nov. '56				
S-362			31 May '57				
S-363			17 Sept. '57				

Builders: See table below.

Total built for Soviet Navy, 215. Another twenty-one were assembled in China from Soviet-supplied components, 1956–64.

Displacement: 1080/1350

Dimensions: 76 × 6.3 × 4.6

Diving Depth: – – –

Armament: 6 533 mm TT (4 bow, 2 stern: 12 torpedoes or 24 AMD-1000 mines), 1×2 57 mm (SM-24 ZiF, 250 rounds), 1×2 25 mm (2M-8, 2000 rounds). Guns removed 1956–57.

Machinery: 2 diesels (37-D, total 4000 HP), 2 electric motors (PG-101, 1350 HP each), 2 shafts, 18.2/13 kts,

Builders: [Ed: following table taken from *Sudostroyeniye*.]

Yard:	Gorkiy	Nikolaev	Baltic	Komsomolsk
1951	1(S-80)	– – –	– – –	– – –
1952	4(S-43–46)	5(S-61–65)	– – –	– – –
1953	16(S-140–152, S-155, S-157, S-158)	11(S-66–76)	3(S-153, S-154, S-156)	– – –
1954	29(S-159–186, S-192)	14(S-77–79, 86–91, 95–97, 100, 217)	– – –	1(S-331)
1955	37(S-193–200, S-261–289)	18(S-98, S-218–234)	8(S-187–191, S-355–357)	4 (S-332–335)
1956	26(S-290–297, S-300, S-325–329, S-338–349)	15(S-235–246, S-250, S-374, 376)	4(S-358–361)	4 (S-336, S-337, S-390, S-391)
1957	– – –	9 (S-375, S-377–S-384)	3 (S-362–364)	2(S-392, 393)
1958	– – –	– – –	1 (S-365)	– – –
Totals	113	72	19	11

74

S-142 (G. G. Kisyelyov)

S-142 (G. G. Kisyelyov)

8580 nm/10 kts surfaced, 13.35 nm/13.1 kts submerged. Battery: 46-SU, 2 groups, 112 cells each. Endurance 30 days. Uninterrupted time underwater 200 hr.

Complement: 52

Electronics: Sonar: Tamir-5, passive sonar Feniks; Radar: Flag; ESM: Nakat; Torpedo FCS: L-4/2; IFF: Fakyel MO-1; Radio direction-finder: RPN-47-03; Gyrocompass: Kurs-3; Log: GOM III; Sounder: NEL-3

Technical project approved 15 Aug. '40. Chief designer was Ya. Ye. Yevgrafov, succeeded in 1950 by Z. A. Dyeribin. These double-hulled submarines had seven compartments.

[Ed.: According to a recent account of this design, Project 613 introduced torpedo-tube minelaying to Soviet practice, helping to cause the demise of alternative specialist minelaying submarines, the abortive Projects 632 and 648. The first Soviet tube-launched torpedo, PLT-3, had been adopted in 1944 but never became operational. It required a new type of torpedo tube (pneumatic but wakeless) which had been developed early in the 1940s for two abortive new classes, Projects 97 and 608. The follow-on AMD-1000 series included the first Soviet postwar ASW mines.

The Project 613 design evolved from a wartime project to replace the prewar S and Shch classes, as it was modified postwar in view of experience with captured German Type XXI submarines. The Soviets did criticize Type XXI on several grounds. They disliked its power plant, considered the drive-shaft arrangement too complex, rejected short-life engines and other machinery, and considered insulation grossly inadequate for high latitudes. They considered that

Type XXI lacked watertight integrity surfaced and submerged, that it was insufficiently seaworthy, and that it was difficult to handle on the surface. It was also criticized for inadequate surface reserve buoyancy.

Innovations in Project 613, compared with prewar Soviet types, included radar (Flag) and new active and passive sonars (Tamir-5L and Mars-24KIG, in a new bow configuration). Compared to Type XXI, Project 613 could dive deeper. Compared to prewar Soviet submarines, it enjoyed much longer underwater endurance, 200 versus 72 hours, using a new type of oxygen regenerator introduced in 1951. For the first time in Soviet practice, some machinery was sound-mounted. Also for the first time, each shaft had two electric motors, one for full power and one for quiet operation, driven via a belt.]

Some units (*) were modified (Project 613V) with new sonar and increased endurance. [Ed.: Other versions included 613-Ts, with increased diving depth; 613S, for the Navy Emergency Rescue Service; and 613RV, for tests of new types of torpedoes.]

In 1957 S-146 was modified at Gorkiy with one P-5 missile (Project P-613: NATO Whiskey Single Cylinder); in 1962 she was used to test the effects of underwater explosions. Under Project 644 (NATO Whiskey Twin Cylinder, designed by TsKB-18), boats were equipped with two cruise missile launchers from 1959 on: S-44, S-46, S-69, S-80, S-158, S-162; S-80 was flooded 27 Jan. '61, salvaged 27 July '69. S-162 (Project 644D) tested the P-5D missile. S-158 (Project 644-7, 1962–64) tested the P-7 missile. Project 665 (chief designer Leont'yev, TsKB-112: NATO Whiskey Long Bin) was a more elaborate 4-launcher conversion (1958–62): S-61, S-64, S-142, S-152, S-155, S-164: 1490 t, 85×6.7 m, 14.5/11 kts, 4 bow TT, with a new navigation system (Syevyer-N665). Project 613AD test-fired the Ametist missile submerged.

S-65 tested the R-21 (D-4 [SS-N-5]) ballistic missile (Project 613D-4). In 1957–58 S-229 (Project 613 RV) fired models of the R-11 missile submerged to test their motion, in preparation for submerged-launch operations by ballistic missile submarines. S-72 was converted to fire 2 Ametyst missiles (Project 513AD).

S-144 tested the T-5 nuclear-warhead torpedo off Novaya Zemlya.

Under Project 640 (chief designer Ya. Ye. Yevgrafov; NATO Whiskey Canvas Bag) boats were converted to radar pickets beginning in 1961: S-62, S-73, S-149, S-151: 1062 t, 76×6.3×5.1 m, 4 TT, Kasatka radar, stabilized against sea states up to 7.

S-384 tested an improved battery under Project 613TS.

S-296 (Project KATRAN) tested a new type of closed-cycle engine (using an electro-chemical generator, with fuel in extra tanks).

S-148 became the ocean survey ship (NES) Severyanka on 14 Dec. '58. S-63 became a frogman carrier (Project 666).

Transfers: Albania (S-241, S-358, S-360 left when the So-viets departed in 1960), Bulgaria (S-244, S-245), Egypt (10 units: S-175, S-180, S-182, S-184, S-193, S-226, S-227, S-228, S-280, S-380), Indonesia (12 units: S-79, S-91, S-218, S-219, S-223, S-225, S-235, S-236, S-239, S-290, S-292, S-391), Korea (S-75, S-90, S-325, S-326 transferred 1966; S-328 in 1988), Poland (4 units: S-265, S-278, S-279, S-355), Syria (3 units: S-167, S-171, S-183). Production documentation was given to China in 1954.

[Ed.: Western sources credit Albania with 4 units, China with 5 (transferred 1956–57), Cuba with 1 (for battery charging), Egypt with seven (6 in 1957–58, one in 1962), Indonesia with 14 (2 from Poland, and 2 used for spare parts), North Korea with 4, Poland with 5 (2 in 1962, 1 in 1964, and 2 in 1969), and Syria with 1 (1986, for battery-charging).]

SS-73 was stricken in 1978 (Pacific). S-45 was tested against underwater explosions in 1958–60. S-178 (Pacific) was sunk in a collision, 21 Oct. '81.

[Ed.: Wartime plans for postwar submarine construction called for Project 608, a conventional design. It was dropped in 1944, when the Soviets raised and examined a modern German submarine, U-250. Later some elements of the

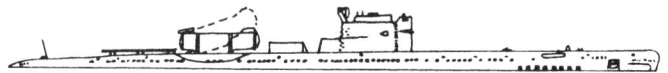

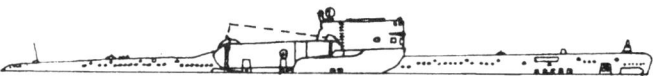

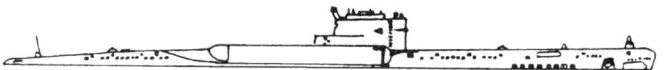

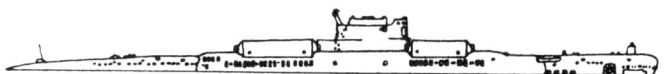

wartime German Type XXI were incorporated in the design. As of 1943, the TTZ for Project 608 called for a 640 t boat capable of 18/9.5–10 kts with a range (surfaced/submerged) of 6000/200 nm and a diving depth of 120/100 m, armed with 4 bow and 2 stern 533 mm TT (10 torpedoes in all), plus 1 76 mm and 1 25 mm gun, equipped with British-supplied Asdic and the passive Mars-16 sonar. In 1944 Project 608-1 met these requirements on a displacement of 687 t. As designed in 1948, Project 613 was considerably larger (1050 t), faster (18.25/13.1 kts), longer-ranged (8500/353 nm),

and deeper-diving (200/170 m), but retained the same number of TT (12 torpedoes) and substituted a 57 mm gun for the earlier 76 mm. Electronics were all modernized, with sonars and radars as shown above. Project 608 in turn could be traced back to a 1940 TTZ for a 500–600 t submarine, from which were developed Projects 98 and 106 in wartime. The TTZ called for a speed of 20/9–10 kts, endurance of 6000/120 nm, diving depth of 100/80 m, and armament (except for the 25 mm gun) as in Project 608.]

S-162 (Pavlov collection)

S-296 (N. U. Prokorov)

Project: 615 and A615

NATO Class Name: QUEBEC

Names:

Project 615:

	laid down	launched	completed
M-254 prototype	17 Mar. '50	31 Aug. '50	30 May '53

Project A615:

M-255–269

M-295–301

M-321

M-351–356

M-361   24 Aug. '62

delivered 1955:

M-255–259

delivered 1956:

M-260–268

M-351–354

delivered 1957:

M-269

M-295

M-297

M-298–300

M-355–356

delivered 1958:

M-301

M-321

M-354

Displacement: 392*, 405.8/503.9

Dimensions: 56.76 × 4.46 × 3.59 (2.78*)

Diving Depth: 120/100

Armament: 4 533 mm (bow: with 4 reload K-45 torpedoes), 1×2 25 mm (2M-8, removed 1956)

Machinery: Closed-cycle powerplant: 3 diesels (2 M-50, 1 32-D, each 900 HP), 3 shafts, 16.1/15 kts, 1 electric creep motor (PG-106, 78 HP). Battery: 23-MU (60 cells). Fuel: 19.54 t, 8.6 t of liquid oxygen, 14.4 t of chemical absorber. Endurance 10 days. Uninterrupted time underwater: 100 hr.

Complement: 29

Electronics: Sonar: Tamir-5L, passive sonar Mars-16KEG; Radar: Flag; Gyrocompass: Ghirya; Log: GOM-III; Sounder: NEL-4ug; Radio Direction Finder: RPN-47-03

Work began on this single powerplant (closed-cycle) submarine at TsKB-18 in Dec. '46. Chief engineer was A. S. Kassatsiyer. The conning tower fairwater was made of Duralumin. The submarine had a 1½- hull configuration with

seven compartments. In service these submarines were called "cigarette lighters."

M-361 was modified to Project 637 configuration [Ed.: to test a new solid oxidant, to replace liquid oxygen], then returned to her previous configuration; she became a memorial at Pushkin.

M-257 suffered a fire in 1956; that year M-259 suffered an explosion. M-258 was tested in 1958 to determine the effects of internal fires and explosions. M-296 was sunk in 1957. Salvaged, she became a memorial in Odessa (with hull number M-305) in Apr. '84. In 1959–71 all units were placed in reserve and stricken.

[Ed.: Early versions of the postwar building plan envisaged construction of Project 612, essentially an improved M-class submarine. Project 615 was an outgrowth of prewar work on closed-cycle diesel submarines (Projects 80 and 95). In effect this system of underwater propulsion (which the Russians called a single powerplant, to distinguish it from separate surface and submerged plants) competed postwar against the German-developed Walter system employed in Project 617.

An improved M-class submarine was developed as Project 96 in 1940, and a further improved design as Project 105 in 1942. A new small-submarine TTZ was issued in 1944: displacement was to be no more than 300 t, speed 16/8 kts, range 3000/140 nm, diving depth 100 m, stores endurance 15 days, armament 4 bow and 2 stern 533 mm TT (450 mm in Project 105, no stern TT in the M-class) plus 1 45 mm and 2 12.7 mm machine guns. Project 612 of 1946 called for a 400 t boat, 15.5/8.4 kts, 4000/170 nm, 2 900 HP diesels, 2 370 HP motors, diving depth 100/125 m, stores endurance 15 days, armament 4/2 533 mm TT, 2 25 mm machine guns. The data above suggest that Project 615 was in effect a closed-cycle diesel equivalent to Project 612, with an additional 900 HP diesel in place of the usual electric motors.

According to an account in *Sudostroyenie*, Projects 615/A615 were based on prewar work on closed-cycle submarine machinery, beginning with a proposal by S. A. Basilevskiy of TsKB-18 to store oxygen on board in liquid form. The powerplant was called REDO (Special Designation Single Regenerating Engine). Surplus carbon dioxide was collected with the aid of a compressor, to be dumped overboard. Oxygen was fed into the exhaust, which was fed back into the engine. In 1938 a Series XII submarine, M-92, was re-equipped with a REDO plant; she was renumbered S-92, but is often called R-1 in the records. Trials terminated with the outbreak of war. Postwar, M-92 was equipped with a YeD-VVD (single overboard exhaust engine, diesel), but "a positive evaluation of this installation was never obtained."

In 1938–39 the Special KB (OKB) of the NKVD, later incorporated into Plant 196, designed Project 95, a small fast closed-cycle submarine using a hard absorber to remove carbon dioxide from the exhaust. The diesel of this YeD-KhPI (single engine with lime water chemical absorber) operated on a mixture of inert nitrogen and added oxygen. M-401 was launched on 1 July '41 and ran trials in the

Caspian Sea during the war, reaching 12.5 kts submerged. The chief builder of the power plant, V. S. Dmitriyevskiy, died during a fire on the submarine on 23 Nov. '42.

After the war, the NKVD released the designers and builders from prison, and they moved the project to TsKB-18. M-401 was accepted into the fleet in 1946, and the group received a Stalin Prize (Second Degree) in 1948 for their work. A new YeD-KhPI submarine, Project 615, was begun under a July '46 decree. M-254, the prototype, as completed in May '53. As in the prewar M class, a major design requirement was that the submarine be transportable by rail in sections. In most features the new submarine followed the Project 613 ("Whiskey") design.

The powerplant consisted of three closed-cycle diesels: a 32D on the centerline and two M50 (torpedo boat diesels originally designed for aircraft) driving wing shafts from a separate compartment. The 32D diesel was used for cruising (up to 10 kts submerged) and for battery-charging using a snorkel; the two M50s were boost engines with a short operating life (300 hr). All diesels were shock-mounted, with special attention paid to silencing while running submerged. The submarine also had a PG-106 (68 HP) electric

motor and a 60-element battery (23-MU type).

Trials showed that liquid oxygen evaporated, so that full submerged cruising range could be achieved only for the first five days submerged. Compartments were criticized as too cramped, and the M50 engines had insufficient lifetime. A modified TTZ for the production version of the design, Project A615, was approved on 31 July '53.

To reduce evaporation, the two oxygen tanks of Project 615 were consolidated into one (which had less surface area and was better insulated). The M50 diesels were derated to 700 HP (as M50-Ps), which doubled their service life to 600 hr. New wing shaft reduction gears could be declutched when the submarine ran only on her center shaft. More chemical absorber and more fuel were provided. The resulting submarine could cruise underwater for 100 hours. Too, the electric motor/generator was uprated from 68 to 100 HP, so that it could charge batteries more quickly.

The system did suffer from frequent fires and small explosions ("knocks"). In 1956, M-259 suffered an explosion in her 32D diesel, which killed 4 crew members and injured 6. In 1957 M-256 was lost near Tallinn with almost her whole crew due to a fire in the 32D diesel space. M-257 was

M-296 (A. N. Sokolov)

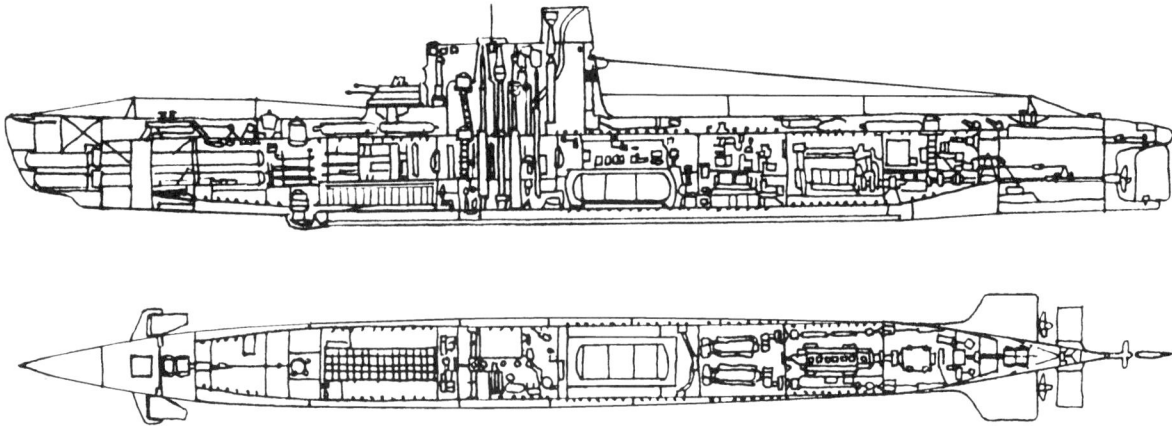

therefore reequipped for machinery tests. It turned out that an atmosphere in which the concentration of oxygen was either too low (below 18 percent) or too high (above 26 percent) could be explosive. Submarines were modernized to solve this problem, and by July '59 they were considered safe enough for unrestricted use. Thus in 1961 M-321 completed a fully submerged trip through the Baltic. M-356 made a similar voyage in 1962. It turned out that such a submarine could cruise for 100 hours at 3.5 kts on her 32D diesel, far beyond the submerged endurance of a conventional unit of similar size.

However, the fleet had already come to distrust these submarines as "cigarette lighters," and they were still susceptible to fire. Planned preventive repairs at shipyards were terminated in 1968, and in the first half of the 1970s practically all of these submarines were laid up.

Project 637 was an attempt to solve the liquid oxygen problem by using a hard granular substance, hyperoxide of sodium, which would absorb carbon dioxide while emitting oxygen. M-361, under construction, was re-equipped with this hard system, but just as trials were to begin (in 1960), they were canceled. Attention shifted to nuclear submarines.

Meanwhile other YeD-KhPI designs had been developed during 1954–58: Project 630 (a small torpedo submarine), Project 660 (an ocean-going ballistic missile submarine with Project 637 power plant), and Project 618 (a small submarine with a YeD-VVD power plant). These projects died when all work on closed-cycle submarines was stopped in 1960.]

Project: 617

NATO Class Name: WHALE (UNOFFICIAL)

Names:

	laid down	launched	completed
S-99	5 Feb. '51	5 Feb. '52	Dec. '55

Built at Sudomekh.

Displacement: 950/1500

Dimensions: 62.2 × 6.08 × 5.08

Diving Depth: 200/170

Armament: 6 533 mm (bow) (total 12 torpedoes or 20 AMD-1000 mines)

Machinery: Hydrogen peroxide (steam-gas turbine) powerplant: 1 turbine (7250 HP, for surface and submerged running), 1 diesel (8Ch-23/30, 600 HP), 1 main electric motor (PG-100, 540 HP), 1 creep motor (PG-105, 140 HP), 1 battery (type 26-SU, 112 cells); 1 diesel generator (DG-17). Range/speeds: 120 nm/20 kts or 198 nm/14.2 kts (steam-gas turbine), 8500 nm/8.5 kts (diesel), 8000 nm/5.8 kts (diesel, snorkelling), 13.4 nm/9.3 kts (electric motor, submerged). 88.5 t diesel fuel, 103.4 t hydrogen peroxide, 13.9 t kerosene (for the gas turbine). Uninterrupted time submerged 200 hr. Endurance 45 days.

Complement: 51

Electronics: Sonar: Tamir-5LS and passive sonar Mars-24-KEG; Radar: Flag; IFF: Fakyel-MO-1; Periscopes: attack periscope PANO and zenith periscope PZM-8.5; Radio transmitters (short wave): R-641, R-647; Radio receiver: R-670; Radio direction-finder: RPN-47-03; Gyrocompass: Kurs-3; Log: GOM-III; Sounder: NEL-4ug

Chief designer was A. A. Antipin (TsKB-18). This was the first Soviet combatant submarine with a speed of 20 kts. The powerplant was assembled from captured German parts [Ed: this was a single turbine of the type developed for the abortive Type XXVI U-boat]. At full speed the boat was quite noisy. The hull, with a rubber covering (captured from the Germans), was divided into six compartments: (i) torpedo room; (ii) quarters and batteries; (iii) control room; (iv) diesel; (v) turbine; (vi) electric motor and steering gear.

S-99 served in the Baltic Fleet. On 17 May '56 she suffered an explosion at 80 m depth. Although she returned to base under her own power, she could not be restored to service because it was impossible to duplicate her captured powerplant.

[Ed.: Project 616 was an earlier abortive effort simply to reproduce the German Type XXVI submarine. A new SKB-143, which later designed the first Soviet nuclear submarine, was hived off from TsKB-18 specifically to develop Project 617. When the nuclear project began, the Walter submarine was returned to TsKB-18. Sudomekh built a land-based Walter prototype, tests on which were completed in 1951. A follow-on Project 643 was canceled when all closed-cycle projects were closed down in 1960, to free personnel to work on the successful nuclear submarines.]

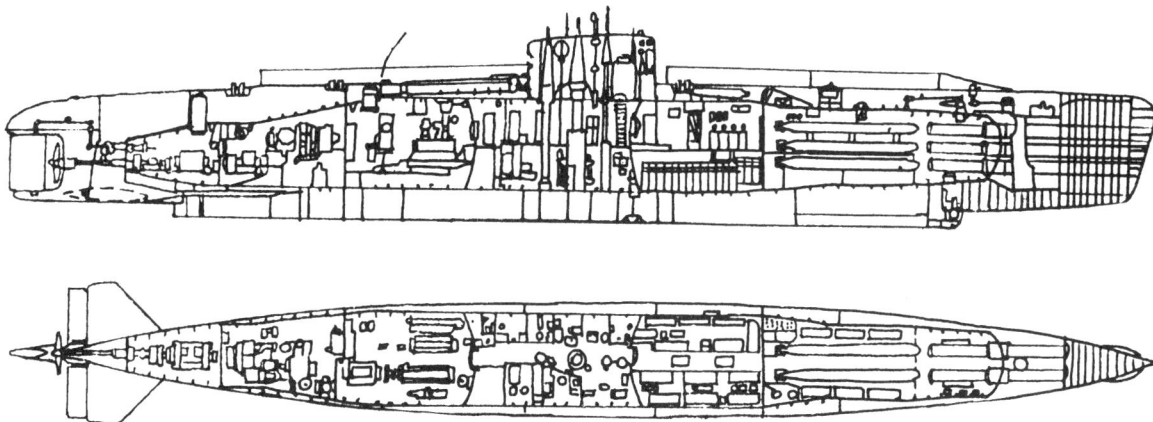

Project: 1840

NATO Class Name: LIMA

Names:

BS-555

Displacement: 1873/2300

Dimensions: 79 × 7.8 × 6.81

Diving Depth: 350

Armament: None

Machinery: 2 diesels (37-D, 4000 HP), 1 electric motor (PG-102, 2700 HP), 1 shaft, 11/17 kts; 400 t fuel, 25,000 nm/8 kts surfaced, 15 nm/14 kts submerged. Battery: 48-SM (2 groups, 112 cells each).

Complement: 41 (6 officers)

Built in Leningrad (Sudomekh) in 1979 for hydro-acoustic experiments. Six compartments. Pressure chamber for deep water work. No armament.

BS-555 (Pavlov collection)

Project: 940 (LENOK)

NATO Class Name: INDIA

Names:

	laid down	launched	completed
BS-257			
BS-486	22 Feb. '75	7 Sept. '75	21 Jan. '76

named *Komosomolets Uzbekistana* until 22 Apr. '92
Both built in Komsomolsk.

Displacement: 3950/4800

Dimensions: 106 × 9.8 × 7

Armament: None

Machinery: 2 diesels (D-42, 4000 HP), 2 electric motors (2700 HP total), 2 shrouded propellers, 15/10 kts; have taxi-up device

For salvage work and surveying. They carry deep-water salvage vehicles, similar to the U.S. DSRV, and are equipped for deep-water anchoring. BS-203 is in the Northern Fleet, and BS-486 in the Pacific Fleet; the latter participated in the rescue of the crew of S-178 in 1981. Both went into reserve in 1990. BS-486 stricken Nov. '94.

Project: 690 (KEFAL')

NATO Class Name: BRAVO

Names:

	completed
SS-368	
SS-256	
SS-310	31 Oct. '70
SS-356	

Built in Komsomolsk 1967–70.

Displacement: 2750/3300

Dimensions: 73 × 9.8 × 7.3

Armament: 1 533 mm TT, 1 406 mm TT, both in bow

Machinery: 1 diesel (3500 HP), 1 electric motor (2700 HP), 1 creep motor, 15 kts

Complement: 60

Electronics: Sonar: Arktika

Hull structure is designed to absorb the impact of training torpedoes. SS-310 is in the Black Sea.

SS-226 (Pavlov collection)

Bravo class (U.S. Naval
Institute Photographic
Collection)

Project: 1710 (MAKREL')

NATO Class Name: BELUGA

Names:

	completed
SS-533	Feb. '87

Built in Leningrad (Sudomekh).

Displacement: 1407/2480

Dimensions: 65.5 × 6.3 (11.3) × 5.6

Diving Depth: 240/300

Armament: None

Machinery: 1 diesel generator (2000 HP); 1 electric motor (2700 HP), 1 shaft, 10/24.5 kts, 185 nm/4 kts. Endurance 45 hr.

Complement: 30

Electronics: Radar MRK-50; Sonar: Rubikon

For hull tests of high-speed submarines, including work on laminar flow. [Ed.: Presumably using polymers.] Transferred to the Black Sea.

SS-533 (V. V. Kostrichenko)

Project: 865 (PIRAN'YA)

NATO Class Name: LOSOS

Names:

MS-520

MS-521

Built 1988–90 in Leningrad (Baltic Yard).

Displacement: 100/218

Dimensions: 28.3 × 3.7 × 2.5

Diving Depth: 200/180

Armament: 2 533 mm TT (2 torpedoes or Sirena-U devices)

Machinery: 1 diesel, 1 electric motor, 600 HP = 6.5/10 kts, range 1000 nm. Endurance 10 days.

Complement: 3 plus sabotage group

Chief designer Yu. K. Mineev (TsKB-16 Malakhit). Rated as Small Submarines of Third Rank. Hull is of low-magnetic steel. Expected to be built for export (one for Sweden in 1995).

MS-520 (V. V. Kostrichenko)

Project: 907 (TRITON-1) and 908 (TRITON-2)

NATO Class Name: None

Names:

V-483–490

V-520–543

30 units, built 1974–80 in Leningrad (LAO) and Nizhni Novgorod (Gorkiy)

Displacement: 1.6* (5.7)

Dimensions: 5 × 1.2* (9.5 × 1.9)

Diving Depth: 40

Machinery: Range 30*(60) nm

Complement: 2*(6)

Chief designer Yu. K. Mineev (TsKB-16 Malakhit). Serving in all fleets.

Project: 1855 (MIR)

NATO Class Name: None

Names:

MIR-1–5

Displacement: 18.7

Dimensions: 7.8 × 2.9 × 3.2

Diving Depth: 6100

Built in Finland (Rauma-Repola) to be used aboard salvage ships (including Alagyez class, *Akademik M. Keldysh*). MIR-1 participated in the search for the sunken submarine *Komsomolets*.

Project: 1832 (SEVER)

NATO Class Name: None

Names:

LS-17

LS-8

LS-28

LS-34

    Built at Leningrad (LAO).

Displacement: 28/40

Dimensions: 12.5 × 2.7 × 3.8

Diving Depth: 2000

Machinery: 4 kts

Complement: Up to 5

LS-28 (V. V. Kostrichenko)

Project: 1837 and 1837K

NATO Class Name: None

Names:

APS-2

APS-3

APS-5

APS-11

APS-18–27

Displacement: 35

Dimensions: 12.1 long

Diving Depth: 2000

    Submerged working time 11 hr. On board salvage ships Kommuna and El'brus class, OS-3, and Project 940 submarines (India class). APS-2 stricken 1989, APS-5 in 1992.

ARS-32 (V. V. Kostrichenko)

Project: 1839, 1839.2

NATO Class Name: EL'BRUS

Names:

ARS-1–4

ARS-7

ARS-9

ARS-10

ARS-12–16

ARS-29–33

ARS-35

ARS-36

Displacement: 45

Dimensions: 13.7 long

Diving Depth: 2200

    ARS-14 on salvage ship *G. Koz'min* and one on *El'brus* type salvage ship.

ARS (V. V. Kostrichenko)

Project: 1806 (POISK)

NATO Class Name: None

Names:

AGS-6

AGS-17

AGS-37

AGS-38

Diving Depth: 4000

Bathyscapes of different types. On board salvage ships Kommuna, El'brus, Alagyez class.

Project: 82

Class Name: STALINGRAD

Names:

	laid down	*launched*
STALINGRAD	25 Nov. '49	16 Mar. '54

Built in Leningrad (Baltic Yard).

Displacement: 36,500/42,300

Dimensions: 273.6 × 32.1 × 9.2

Armament: 3×3 305 mm (gun B-50, turret SM-31, 720 rounds), 6×2 130 mm (BL-109A, 2400 rounds), 6×4 45 mm (SM-20 ZiF, 19,200 rounds), 10×4 25 mm (BL-120, 48,000 rounds), 12×1 37 mm (70-K, 14,400 rounds)

Armor: Main belt 180 mm (at 15° angle) with 150 mm ends, bulkheads 140 mm forward and 125 mm aft; upper deck 50 mm, middle deck 70 mm (combined thickness of 3 decks, 135 mm); 50 mm longitudinal bulkhead behind main belt through citadel. Main caliber turrets 225(240) mm, barbettes 260 mm. Anti-torpedo protection 4 m deep including 100 mm bulkheads. Total weight of armor, 10,400 t (29 percent of displacement).

Machinery: 12 boilers (KV-68), 4 main geared turbines, 4 shafts, 280,000 HP = 35.5 kts, 5000 nm/18 kts; 4 DG-1000 generators; 5000 t of fuel. Endurance 20 days.

Complement: 1712

Electronics: Radars: Kliver, Don; Sonar: Tamir-2

Technical assignment approved on 31 Aug. '51 [Ed.: but note the laying-down date above]. Chief engineer was L. V. Dikovich (TsKB-16, then TsKB-17). The other two units, also laid down, were *Moskva* and *Arkhangelsk* (at Molotovsk [Severodvinsk]). Work stopped 23 Apr. '53. *Stalingrad* was used as a target and the other two were broken up on the slip. The main-caliber gun barrels were used to rearm the ex-Italian battleship *Novorossiysk*.

Stalingrad (A. N. Sokolov)

Project: 1143.5 and 1143.6 *(OREL)

Class Name: KUZNETZOV

Names:

	laid down	launched	completed
ADMIRAL FLOTA SOVYETSKOGO SOYUZA			
KUZNETZOV	1 Sept. '82	5 Dec. '85	25 Dec. '90
VARYAG	6 Dec. '85	25 Nov. '88	– – –

Kuznetzov was laid down as *Riga,* renamed *Leonid Brezhnev* 26 Nov. '82, then renamed *Tblisi* 11 Aug. '87, and then *Kuznetzov* 1 Jan. '91. *Varyag* was laid down as *Riga,* renamed Aug. '90. Both built at Nikolaev (Black Sea Shipbuilding Works). *Kuznetzov* was officially laid down 22 Feb. '83, after construction was already under way.

Displacement: 55,000/67,500

Dimensions: 304.5 × 38 (72 with angled deck) × 10.5

Armament: Typical air group: 52 aircraft: 18 Su-27K, 18 MiG-29K, 16 Ka-27 helicopters (including 3 for AEW and 2 SAR). 12 4K-80 Granit (SS-N-19) missile launchers, 4×6 Kinzhal AA missile launchers (total 192 missiles), 8 Kortik gun/missile AA weapons (including 2 30 mm guns, laser FCS), 6×6 30 mm guns (AK-630); 2 RBU-12000.

Machinery: 8 boilers, 4 steam turbines, 4 shafts, 200,000 SHP = 32 kts; 12,000 nm/10 kts

Complement: 2100

Electronics: Radar: Mars-Passat early warning, Fregat-MR auxiliary air search; Sonar: Orion long-range sonar, Platina towed body

Have 183×29×7.5 m hangar. Aircraft take off with the aid of a 15° ski-jump; there are no catapults. Types tested on board: Su-27K (fighter-interceptor), Su-25K (ground attack), MiG-29K (fighter); the ship can also operate Yak-41M vertical take-off aircraft. *Kuznetzov* received her air group in 1994.

Varyag has a modified superstructure, and is to carry Yozh AA missiles. Work on her has been suspended.

The nuclear carrier *Ul'yanovsk* (Project 1143.7) was laid down in 1988 but broken up 20% complete in 1992.

[Ed.: According to recent Russian accounts, the decision to build a full carrier was debated through the early 1970s. A TTZ was issued, and a Leningrad PKB (presumably TsKB-17) was assigned to develop a 75,000 to 80,000 t nuclear carrier to accomodate 60–88 conventional take-off aircraft under the code-name Orel (Project 1160 Eagle). She would have had 4 steam catapults. Admiral Gorshkov apparently personally decided that the ship would be armed with anti-ship cruise missiles in addition to her aircraft, at a slight cost in aircraft numbers. The preliminary design was approved in 1973. Minister of Defense D. F. Ustinov then objected to the cost of the ship, and asked whether instead the third KIEV could be modified with a waist catapult for

Varyag (B. E. Katayev)

Adm Kuznetzov (U.S. Navy)

Adm Kuznetzov (V. V. Kostrichenko)

Adm Kuznetzov (U.S. Navy)

В.И. КАТАЕВ

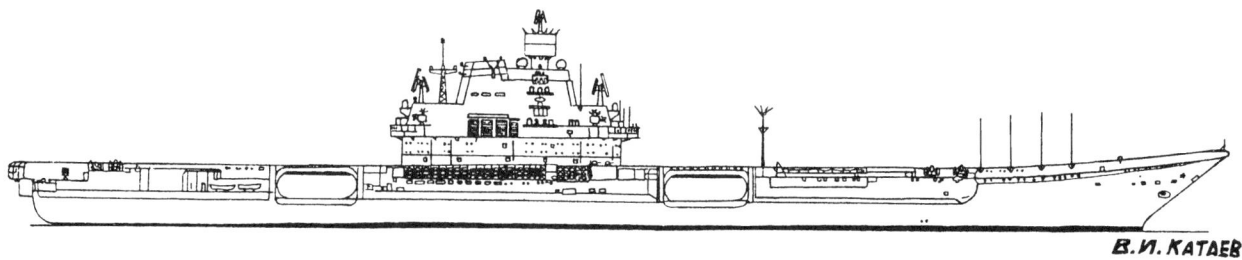

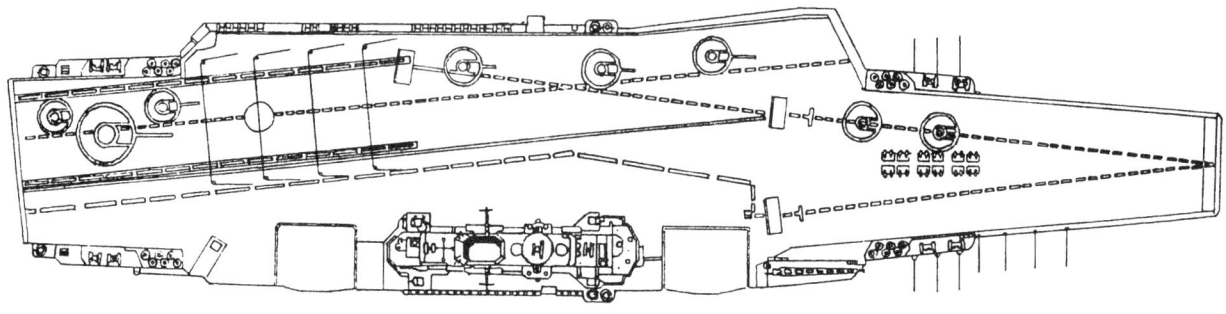

36 MiG-23A fighters. That proved unsuccessful, as did an attempt to fit 36 such aircraft into a ship of *Kiev* class dimensions. A revised TTZ for a smaller ship (still nuclear powered) was issued in June '74. A new TTZ for this Project 1153 (68,000 t, 2 catapults, 3 shafts, 29–30 kts, 50 aircraft, mainly fighters) was issued in Oct. '76, after an Apr. '76 Council of Ministers resolution approved two such ships (described as aircraft-carrying cruisers) for construction during the 1978–85 plan period (i.e., for the first half of the 1981–90 Ten-Year Plan). However, work on the program was stopped in 1976 after the concept design was approved.

In Jan. '79 a new TTZ was approved. The design was again revised downward to accomodate 42 aircraft plus cruise missiles. At this time the nuclear powerplant was dropped. Then work was again stopped, and a new TTZ approved in Apr. '80. This time it incorporated ski-jumps. Displacement was limited to 45,000 t. After visiting the carrier *Kiev* during a 1981 exercise, Minister of Defense Ustinov approved increasing displacement by 10,000 t. The abortive *Ul'yanovsk* presumably represented a return to the earlier concepts.]

Project: 1143.4

Class Name: ADMIRAL GORSHKOV

Names:

	laid down	launched	completed
ADMIRAL FLOTO SOVYETSKOGO GORSHKOVO
ex *Baku* — 26 Dec. '78 — 31 Mar. '82 — 11 Dec. '87
Renamed Aug. '90. Built at Nikolaev.

Displacement: 40,000/44,570

Dimensions: 273 × 32.7 × 10.2

Armament: Air group: 16 Yak-38, 1 Yak-38 trainer, 19 Ka-27 or Ka-29 helicopters, 3 Ka-25 helicopters; 6×2 Bazalt missile launchers (no reloads), 4 blocks of 6×8 vertical launchers for Kinzhal AA missiles (192 missiles); 2×1 100 mm (AK-100, 500 rounds), 8×6 30 mm (AK-630, 16,000 rounds), 2×10 RBU Udav (anti-torpedo)

Machinery: 8 boilers, 4 steam turbines, 4 shafts, 180,000 HP = 30.7 kts; 13,500 nm/10 kts, 8000 nm/16.3 kts; 2 rudders

Complement: 1200 plus air wing

Electronics: Radars: Mars/Passat air/surface search, Podkat vs. low fliers, Fregat-MA secondary air search; Sonar: Orion plus Platina towed sonar

Chief designer A. V. Marinichyev (Nevskiy PKB). Begun as a unit of the Kiev class, but completed to a new design, midway between Kiev and Kuznetsov. Flight deck: 195×20.7 m. In Northern Fleet.

Helicopters:

	Take-off Wt	Speed	Range	Ceiling
Ka-25	9.83 t	220 km/hr	650 km	
Ka-27	11.3 t	250 km/hr	6 km	
Ka-29	11 t	280 km/hr	600 km	4.3 km
	(2 engines, 4400 HP)			

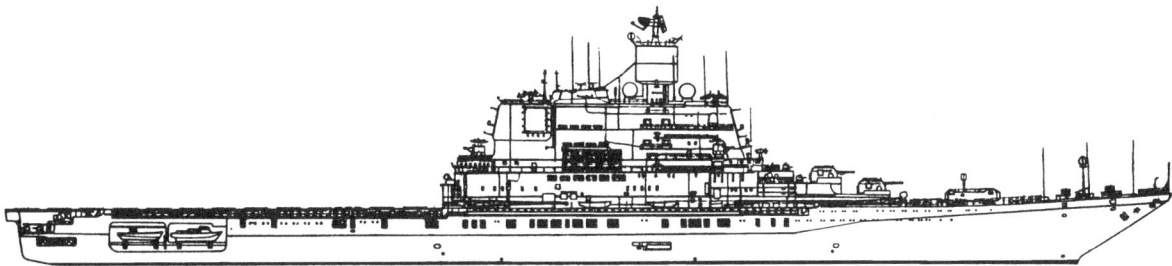

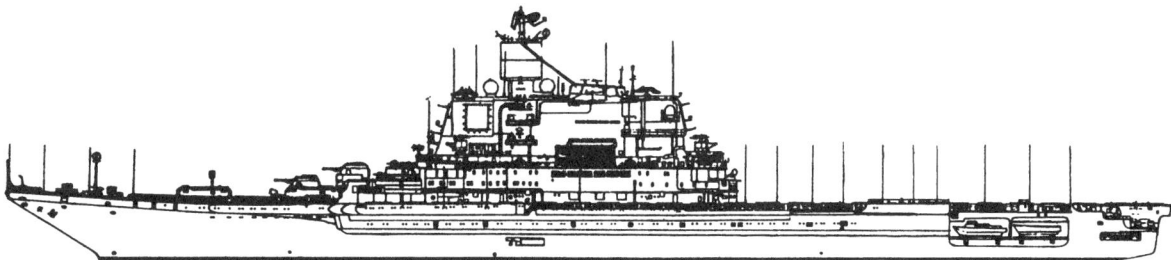

Baku (V. V. Kostrichenko)

Project: 1143, 1143.2 (KRECHET)

Class Name: KIEV

Names:

All built at Nikolaev.

	laid down	launched	completed	str
KIEV	21 July '70	26 Dec. '72	28 Dec. '75	30 June '93
MINSK	28 Dec. '72	30 Sept. '75	27 Sept. '78	30 June '93
NOVOROSSIYSK	30 Sept. '75	26 Dec. '78	14 Aug. '82	30 June '93

was named *Kharkov* until 1978

Displacement: 36,300/41,370

Dimensions: 273.1 × 32.7 wl (49.2 m with angled deck) × 10

Armament: Air group (designed): 24 Yak-38, 2 Ka-25 helicopters; actual air group: 12 Yak-38, 1 Yak-38 trainer, 19 Ka-27 helicopters, 3 Ka-25; 4×2 SM-241 launchers for Bazalt missile system (1 reload each, total 16 missiles system in Uragan-1143), 2×2 launchers for Shtorm AA missile system (72 missiles), 2×2 launchers for Osa-M missiles (40 missiles), 2×2 76 mm (AK-726), 8×6 30 mm (AK-630), 1×2 launcher for Vikhr' ASW missile-torpedo system, (48 82-R missiles) 2×12 RBU-6000, 2×5 533 mm TT (none on *Novorossiysk*)

Machinery: 8 boilers, 4 steam turbines, 4 shafts, 180,000 HP = 30.7 kts (maximum 32.5 kts); 6 turbo-generators (1500 kW each), 4 diesel generators (DG-1500); 7000 t fuel, 1200 t aviation fuel; 8000 nm/14.2 kts, 4000 nm/31 kts; 2 rudders.

Complement: 1433 (including 300 officers)

Electronics: Radar: Fregat, Voshkod, Volga; Landing system: Privod-SV; Sonar: MG-342 Orion plus MG-335 Platina towed body; Communications system: Tsunami; Navigation system: Salgir

TTZ approved 16 Oct. '68. Designed by TsKB-17 (Nevskiy PKB). Flight deck: 189×20.7 m. Rated as Heavy Aircraft-Carrying Cruisers (1st Rank) until 1991, then as Heavy Helicopter Carriers. *Kiev* was awarded the Order of the Red Banner in Jan. '85. *Minsk* and *Novorossisk* (Pacific) were placed in reserve in 1991 and will be scrapped. [Ed: They were towed to South Korea.] *Kiev* was stricken after her 1993 fire.

[Ed.: Despite the enormous difference in size, these ships are direct descendants of the much smaller *Moskva* class, via an intermediate design, Project 1133, for the third ship, *Kiev*. According to a recent account written by Arkadi Morin, the

Novorossiysk (U. A. Pakhomov)

Novorossiysk (U. A. Pakhomov)

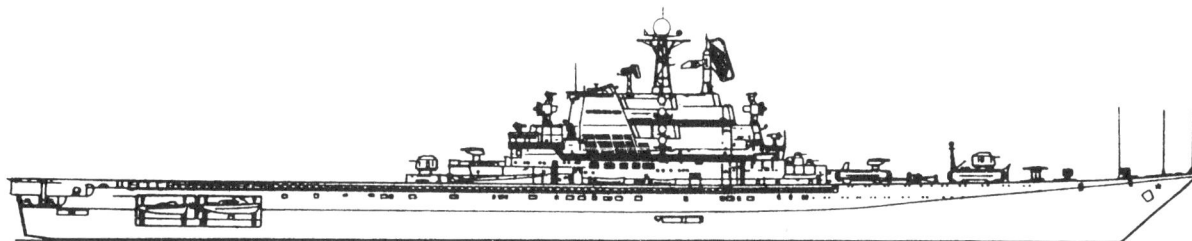

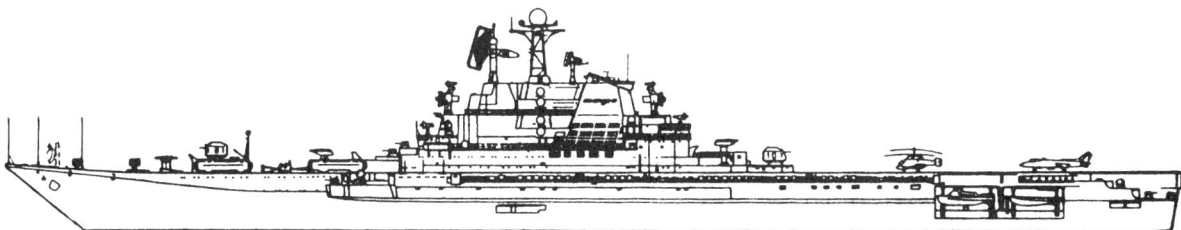

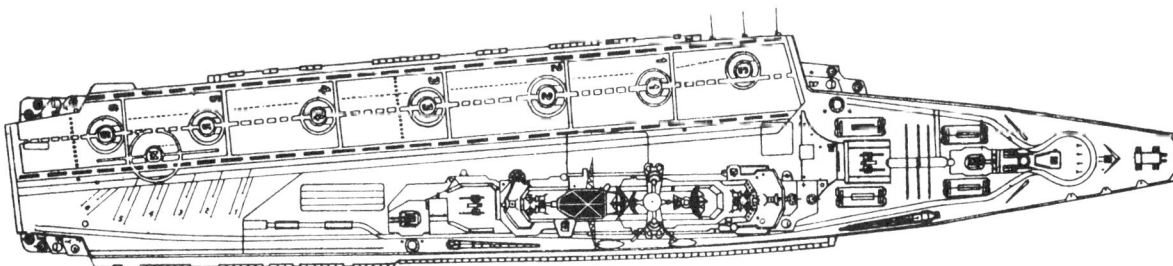

Kiev (A. B. Zagvozdkin)

ship's preliminary designer, work on this design began in July '67; it was intended to have a stronger anti-aircraft battery, better sea-keeping, and greater autonomy. The *Moskva* hull was to have been lengthened by 10 m and broadened by 1 m. Displacement would have increased to 19,500 t. This ship was to have been laid down on 20 Feb. '68, the 60th birthday of the First Secretary of the Ukrainian Communist Party. However, the project was suspended because Alexander Yakovlev, designer of the Yak-36 VTOL prototype (which was demonstrated in the summer 1967 Domedovo air show), proposed that this aircraft be developed into a naval attack bomber. By this time, with Khrushchev gone, such concepts could once more be entertained.

Initially, Admiral Gorshkov limited standard tonnage to 15,000. The addition of fixed-wing aircraft would make it possible for the ship to engage surface ships and shore targets and to support amphibious operations. The initial study called for a total of 20–22 aircraft, an anti-ship missile system, an "Osa" (SA-N-4) defensive missile system, and 76 mm and 30 mm (8–10) guns. Compared to *Moskva*, the new design would need twice the endurance, and it would also need spaces for troops which might be landed by heli-

copter. It soon became obvious that the ship would need six rather than the original four take-off spots plus a spot for a plane guard helicopter. The hull began to grow. Versions of a possible design were developed as a basis for a TTZ. Some had catapults and arresting gear for MiG-23 fighter-bombers. Some could accomodate as many as fifty aircraft, and displacement reached 45,000 tons.

As of Sept. '68 plans developed by the Northern PKB called for a total of 20–22 aircraft (Yak-36M and Ka-25 helicopters), a Vikhr ASW system (NATO SUW-N-1), two RBU-6000, eight P-15M anti-ship missiles (SS-N-2), 2 Shtorm (SA-N-3) and 2 Osa-M (SA-N-4) anti-aircraft missile systems, 2 AK-176, and 8–10 AK-630 AA cannon. The ship would attain 27 kts, and she would displace 20,000 to 25,000 t. Construction would begin in 1973.

Review of the design led to a decision (in 1970) to substitute the new "Bazalt" anti-ship missile (SS-N-12) for P-15M, tonnage increasing to 28,000. In this form the design was designated Project 1143. Design work was completed on 30 Apr. '70. Note that the ship gained considerable tonnage (to 31,700) during detail design and construction.]

Project: 1144 and 1144.2 (ORLAN)

NATO Class Name: BALCOM-1

Names:

	laid down	launched	completed

All built at Baltic Yard, Leningrad.

KIROV

        26 Mar. '74   27 Dec. '77   30 Dec. '80

now *Adm Ushakov*

FRUNZE

        26 July '78   26 May '81   31 Oct. '84

now *Adm Lazarev*

KALININ

        May '83   26 Apr. '86   30 Dec. '88

now *Adm Nakhimov*

YURI ANDROPOV

        24 Apr. '86   29 Apr. '89   1996

now *Petr Velikiy Admiral Flota Sovetskogo Soyuza Kuznet-zov.* Ordered 31 Dec. '88, canceled 4 Oct. '90. The name *Dzerzhinskiy* has also been given for this unit.

    Ships were renamed 22 Apr. '92.

Displacement: 24,300/28,000

Dimensions: 251.2 × 28.5 × 9.1

Armament:

Adm Ushakov:

20 SM 233 launchers for Granit system, 12×8 B-203A launchers for Fort AA missile system (96 rockets), 2×2 launchers for Osa M AA system (40 9M33 missiles), 1×2 launchers for Metel' (85R, 10 missiles) ASW rocket-torpedo system, 2×1 100 mm (AK-100), 8×6 30 mm (AK-630), 2×5 533 mm TT (10 torpedoes), 1×12 RBU-6000 (96 RGB rounds), 2×6 RBU-1000

Adm Lazarev*:

20 launchers for Granit system, 12 launchers for Fort AA missile system, 8×8 launchers for Kinzhal AA system

Kirov (U.S. Naval Institute Photographic Collection)

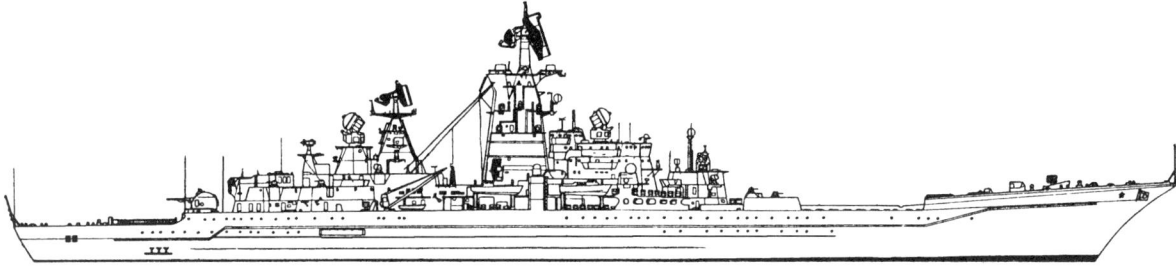

(3595), 2×2 launchers for Osa-M AA system (40 9M33 missiles), 1×2 130 mm (AK-130), 8×6 30 mm (AK-630), 2×5 ASW missile launchers (for Vodopod missiles, instead of TT), 1×6 RBU-6000, 2×6 RBU-1000

Adm Nakhimov*:

20 launchers for Granit system, 12×8 B-203A launchers for Fort AA missile system, 16×8 2S-95 Kinzhal launchers (8 forward, 8 aft), 2×2 launchers for Osa-M AA system (40 9M33 missiles), 6 Kortik mountings, 1×2 130 mm (AK-130), 2×5 Vodopod launchers, 1×10 RBU-12000, 2×6 RBU-1000

P. Velikiy*:

20 launchers for Granit system, 12 launchers for Fort AA missile system, 16×8 Kinzhal launchers, 6 Kortik mountings, 1×2 130 mm (AK-130), 2×5 Vodopod launchers, 1×10 RBU-12000, 2×6 Udav anti-torpedo weapons

Armor: Side over the reactor section, 100 mm (35 mm at ends); steering gear 70 mm sides and 50 mm deck, conning tower 80 mm

Machinery: 2 reactors (KN-3, 300 MW each), 2 auxiliary oil-burning boilers, 2 shafts, 140,000 HP = 32 kts, 14,000 nm/30 kts, or 1000 nm/17 kts on oil-burning boilers alone; 8 turbogenerators (4×3000 kW, 4×1500 kW). Endurance 60 days.

Complement: 610 (including 82 officers); *Lazarev, Nakhimov:* 655 (105 officers, 130 petty officers)

Electronics: Radar: Flag, Voshkod, Fregat (Fregat-M in *Lazarev, Ushakov*), Vaigach; Sonar: Polinom; Communications system: Faifun; Space communications system: Kristall (Tsunami in *Nakhimov, Ushakov*)

Tactical-technical requirement approved by Minister of Defense 25 May '71. Chief designer B. I. Kupyenskiy (after 1981, V. A. Perevalov)(Northern PKB). All but the first unit, *Ushakov* (ex-Kirov) are Project 114.2.

[Ed.: According to a Russian account, design work actually began in 1968, on the basis of a contemporary design for a multi-purpose ("all-singing") surface combatant armed with 6–8 long-range (150 km) anti-ship missiles, possibly a pre-design for what became the *Sovremennyy*. Admiral Gorshkov personally rejected it as too weak, as in effect it would be a nuclear powered *Kynda*. The design team thought that the ship should not displace more than 8000 t, and attempts to remain within that limit cost considerable time. They soon realized that the weapon systems they wanted (for AAW and effective ASW, as well as good ASUW) would demand a displacement of at least 20,000 t. That would have required four to six of the existing submarine reactors, a plant rejected as cumbersome and dangerous. Fortunately a nuclear power design bureau came up with the elegant solution (nuclear base plant plus steam boost) which they adopted.]

Project: 1123 (KONDOR)

Class Name: MOSKVA

Names:

Built in Nikolaev (Nosenko Yard).

	laid down	launched	completed
MOSKVA	15 Dec. '62	14 Jan. '65	25 Dec. '67
LENINGRAD	15 Jan. '65	31 July '68	2 June '69
str 24. June '91			
KIEV	1 Aug. '66	– – –	canceled, BU 1969

Displacement: 13,110/14,655

Dimensions: 189.1 × 21.5 (wl)/34 (extreme) × 7.17 m (13.6 with sonar lowered)

Armament: 14 Ka-25PL helicopters, 2×2 B-187 launchers for the Volna-M (Shtorm) AA system (96 V-611 missiles), 2×2 57 mm (AK-725), 1×2 launcher for Vikhr ASW system (48 82-R rocket-torpedoes), 2×5 533 mm TT (SET-65, 53-65K torpedoes, removed 1970), 2×12 RBU-6000 Smerch-2 ASW rocket launchers (120 RGB-60 bombs)

Machinery: 4 boilers, 2 steam turbines, 2 shafts, 91,000 HP = 28.8 kts (search speed 19.5 kts); 2600 t fuel; 9000 nm/15 kts, 6000 nm/18 kts, 4000 nm/28.5 kts. Endurance 15 days.

Complement: 541

Electronics: Radars: MR-600 Voskhod, MR-310 Angara; Sonars: Orion (retractable) under keel plus towed MG-325 Vyega

Built under resolution of 3 Dec. '58; TTZ approved by CinC 25 Jan. '60 and technical project (design) approved 25 Jan. '62. Chief designer A. S. Savichev, followed (from 1967

Moskva (V. V. Kostrichenko)

on) by A. V. Marinichyev (TsKB-17). Flight deck: 81×34 m; hangar: 67×25 m; main deck hangar: 41×12 m. Two 10-ton elevators.

Both ships operated in the Black Sea Fleet.

Moscow was modified in 1972 to operate Yak-38 aircraft. She suffered a fire on 2 Feb. '75. *Leningrad* was stricken in 1991.

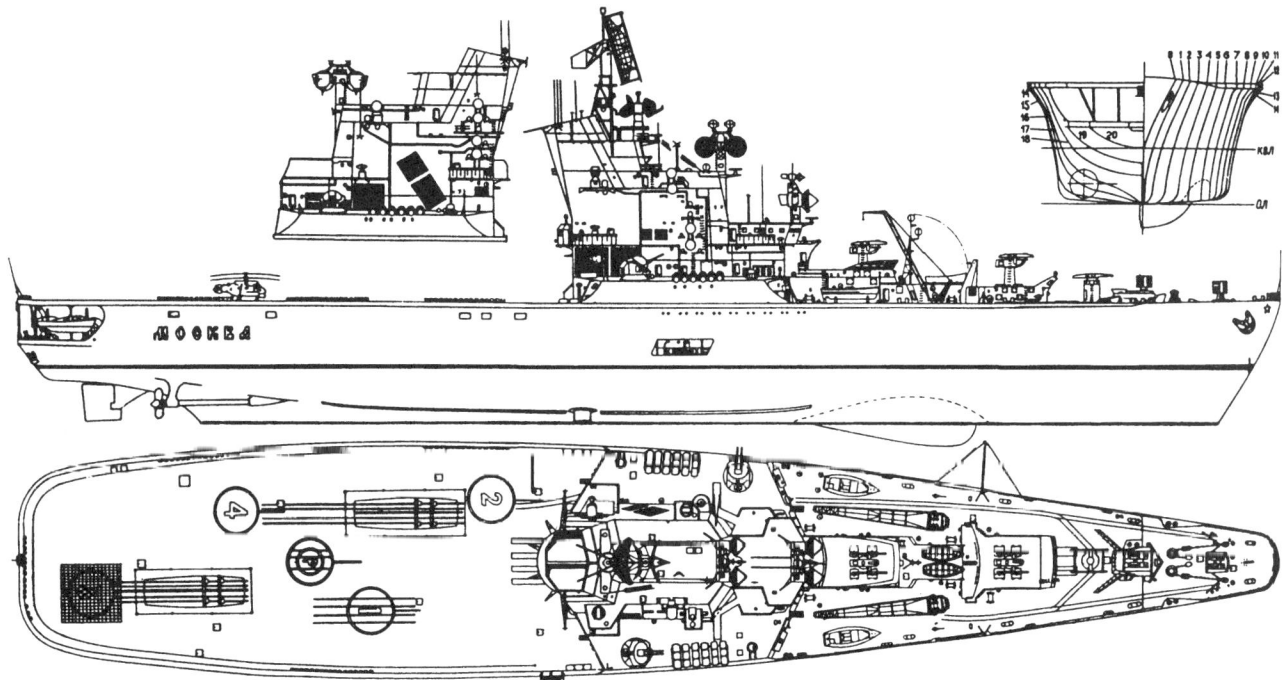

Moskva class (Siegfried Breyer)

Moskva (V. V. Kostrichenko)

[Ed.: According to a 1994 *Morskoy Sbornik* article, the advent of the Polaris missile led the Soviet Navy to reexamine an ASW program begun in the late 1950s which had included conversion of some first-generation missile ships (presumably Project 57bis *Krupnys*) into ASW ships. Suddenly it became necessary to develop long-range ASW ships with greater endurance. A navy NII (currently NII-1) conducted research into this problem jointly with TsKB-17, as well as with other navy and air force agencies. The conclusion was that ship-based aircraft would be essential; the search for an SSBN would take several days and would require integration with other ships and aircraft (i.e., would require command functions in the new unit). Based on this work, in 1958 TsKB-17 submitted two sketch designs, one based on a Project 68bis (*Sverdlov*) hull, the other on a specially designed hull.

The OTZ approved 31 Jan. '59 was for a ship to attack enemy SSBNs and attack submarines as part of a surface search strike force and to cooperate with land-based naval aircraft. The main requirement was to maintain two helicopters continuously airborne throughout a mission (i.e., a total of 8). TsKB-17 proposed adding a long-range sonar, an ASW missile system, torpedoes, rocket bombs (presumably RBUs), and air defense weapons. Both the TsKB and the co-operating naval research institute (TsNII-45) wanted more helicopters, and the total was increased to 10–14. The TTZ included a design displacement of 7000–8000 t, which the navy's main shipbuilding directorate wanted reduced. To this end, TsKB-17 (which had developed the sketch design) was ordered to compete with TsKB-53 (in effect, a destroyer bureau) for the detailed design. To limit displacement, TsKB-17 tried an aluminum-magnesium hull (which was rejected); it also pointed out that a steel hull with the required performance would have to use a gas turbine powerplant. This, too, was rejected, as was the alternative TsKB-53 design. Finally a pressure-fired steam plant like that on the new Project 58 (*Kynda*) missile cruiser was adopted. Basic specifications were approved on 29 Sept. '60 and a preliminary design was approved on 1 Dec. '60. However, more questions were raised (e.g., adoption of larger helicopters and a drastic reduction in crew size through automation), and a 9300 t design was approved only in Mar. '61 as the basis for a contract design. It in turn was substantially modified (not least because of difficulties in deciding exactly which aircraft facilities should be provided) and was approved (at 10,600 t standard displacement) on 25 Jan. '62.

For a short time about 1961 there was also interest in a companion AAW escort, Project 1126, armed with M11 (SA-N-3) missiles.]

Project: 1164 (ATLANT)

Class Name: SLAVA

Names:

	laid down	launched	completed

All built at Nikolaev.

SLAVA

| | 5 Nov. '76 | 27 July '79 | 30 Dec. '82 |

Was at Nikolaev for refit when USSR broke up, begun Dec. '90 but stopped and in Ukrainian hands as of 1995.

ADMIRAL LOBOV

| | 5 Oct. '78 | 25 Feb. '82 | 15 Sept. '86 |

Renamed *Marshal Ustinov* 6 May '85

CHERVONAYA UKRAINA

| | 31 July '79 | 28 Aug. '83 | 25 Dec. '89 |

KOMSOMOLETS

| | 29 Aug. '84 | 11 Aug. '90 | – – – |

Renamed *Admiral Flota Lobov* 23 Mar. '85, taken over by Ukraine for completion Mar. '93; was renamed *Poltava*, then *Bohdan Khmenytsky,* then *Vilna Ukraina*

ROSSIYA — – – – — – – – — – – –

Renamed *Oktyabrskaya Revolutsiya* 30 Dec. '87, stopped 4 Oct. '90

ADMIRAL FLOTA SOVETSKOGO SOYUZA GORSHKOV
— – – – — – – – — – – –

Stopped 4 Oct. '90

Displacement: 9800/11,300

Dimensions: $186 \times 20.8 \times 7.6$

Armament: 1 helicopter in hangar; 16×1 launchers for Bazal't missile system (1 salvo), 8×8 vertical launchers for Fort AA missile system (64 S-300F missiles), 2×2 ZiF-122 launchers for Osa AA missiles (40 9M33M5 missiles), 1×2 130 mm (AK-130, 350 rounds), 6×6 30 mm (AK-630, 1200 rounds), 2×12 RBU-6000, 2×5 533 mm TT. *Adm Flota Lobov* is to have Vulkan anti-ship missiles instead of Bazal't.

Machinery: 2 power trains (each comprising 2 22,500 HP and 1 10,000 HP M-9 gas turbines), 2 shafts, total 110,000 HP = 32 kts, 2500 nm/30 kts, 6800 nm/18 kts; 2 GTG-1500, 1 GTG-1250, 3 DG generators. Endurance 30 days.

Complement: 416 (38 officers)

Electronics: Radars: Voskhod, Fregat (Fregat-M on all but Slava), RLK MR-800 Flag, Sonar: Platina; Space communications system: Tsunami

Tactical-technical requirement (TTZ) approved in 1972, technical project (design) approved Aug. '74. Chief designer

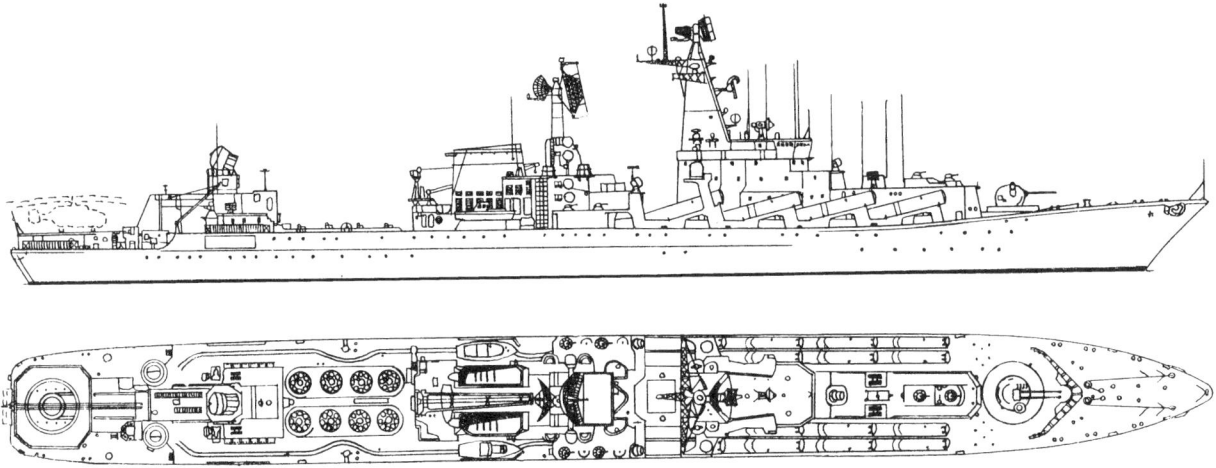

A. K. Per'kov (beginning in 1979, V. M. Muhtikhin. The Fort system is intended for area defense; using a phased-array fire control radar, it can engage six targets with twelve missiles, simultaneously launching missiles at different targets. Reaction time (under watch conditions) is 16–19 sec. The missile magazine is 5.2 × 5.2 × 7.42 m. Assignments: *Slava* in Black Sea, *Ustinov* in Northern Fleet, *Chervonaya Ukraina* in Pacific Fleet. [Ed.: *Ustinov* visited the United States several times.]

Slava (Pavlov collection)

Project: 68 bis

Class Name: SVERDLOV

Names:

	laid down	launched	completed	str

Baltic Yard:

SVERDLOV
| 15 Oct. '49 | 5 July '50 | 15 May '52 | '91 |

ZHDANOV
| 11 Feb. '50 | 27 Dec. '50 | 31 Dec. '51 | Mar. '89 |

ADM USHAKOV
| 31 Aug. '50 | 29 Sept. '51 | 8 Sept. '53 | '88 |

ALEKSANDR SUVOROV
| 26 Feb. '51 | 15 May '52 | 31 Dec. '53 | BU Mar. '92 |

ADM SENYAVIN
| 31 Oct. '51 | 22 Dec. '52 | 30 Nov. '54 | '89 |

DMITRI POZHARSKI
| 31 Mar. '52 | 24 June '53 | 31 Dec. '54 | 5 Mar. '87 |
to Indian breakers Jan. '90

KRONSTADT
| Oct. '53 | 11 Sept. '54 | – – – | BU '61 |

TALLIN
| 1953 | 28 May '55 | – – – | BU '61 |

VARYAG
| Dec. '52 | 5 June '56 | – – – | BU '61 |

Admiralty Yard:

ORDZHONIKIDZE
| 19 Oct. '49 | 17 Sept. '50 | 30 June '52 | |
Indonesia 1962 *(Irian)*, BU '72

ALEKSANDR NEVSKI
| 30 May '50 | 7 June '51 | 31 Dec. '52 | '91 |

ADM LAZAREV
| 6 Feb. '51 | 29 June '52 | 30 Dec. '52 | 12 Oct. '86 |

SCHERBAKOV
| June '51 | 17 Mar. '54 | – – – | BU '61 |
Nikolaev (Marti)

DZERZHINSKIY
| 31 Dec. '48 | 31 Aug. '50 | 18 Aug. '52 | '87 |

ADM NAKHIMOV
| 27 June '50 | 29 June '51 | 27 Mar. '53 | str 29 Aug. '60 |
dismantled Feb. '62

MIKHAIL KUTUZOV
| 23 Feb. '51 | 29 Nov. '52 | 30 Dec. '54 | |
From 1994 in preservation in Black Sea

ADM KORNILOV
| 6 Nov. '51 | 17 Mar. '54 | – – – | Jan. '57 |
BU 12 Sept. '57   Hulk PKZ 13

Severodvinsk:

MOLOTOVSK
| 15 July '52 | 25 May '54 | 30 Nov. '54 | 16 Sept. '87 |
renamed *Oktyabrskskaya Revolutsiya* 3 Aug. '57   BU '90

MURMANSK
| 28 Jan. '53 | 24 Apr. '55 | 22 Sept. '55 | '91 |

ARKHANGELSK
| 1954 | – – – | – – – | BU '61 |

VLADIVOSTOK
| 1955 | – – – | – – – | BU '61 |

Displacement: 14,290/17,970

Dimensions: 210.1 × 22.1 × 7.8

Armament: 4×3 152 mm (MK-5 bis, 1980 rnds), 6×2 100 mm (SM-5-1, 3600 rounds plus 30 ready-use), 16×2 37 mm (V-11M, 44,250 rounds), 2×5 533 mm TT (PTA-53-68 bis, removed 1956–58), 68 KB mines, 48 UDM mines, 63 VKSM mines. *Scherbakov* and later units (Project 68-ZiF) were to have had quadruple 45 mm mounts (ZiF-68) in place of the V-11s (13,720 t).

Adm Senyavin (G. G. Kiselev)

Zhdanov (G. G. Kiselev)

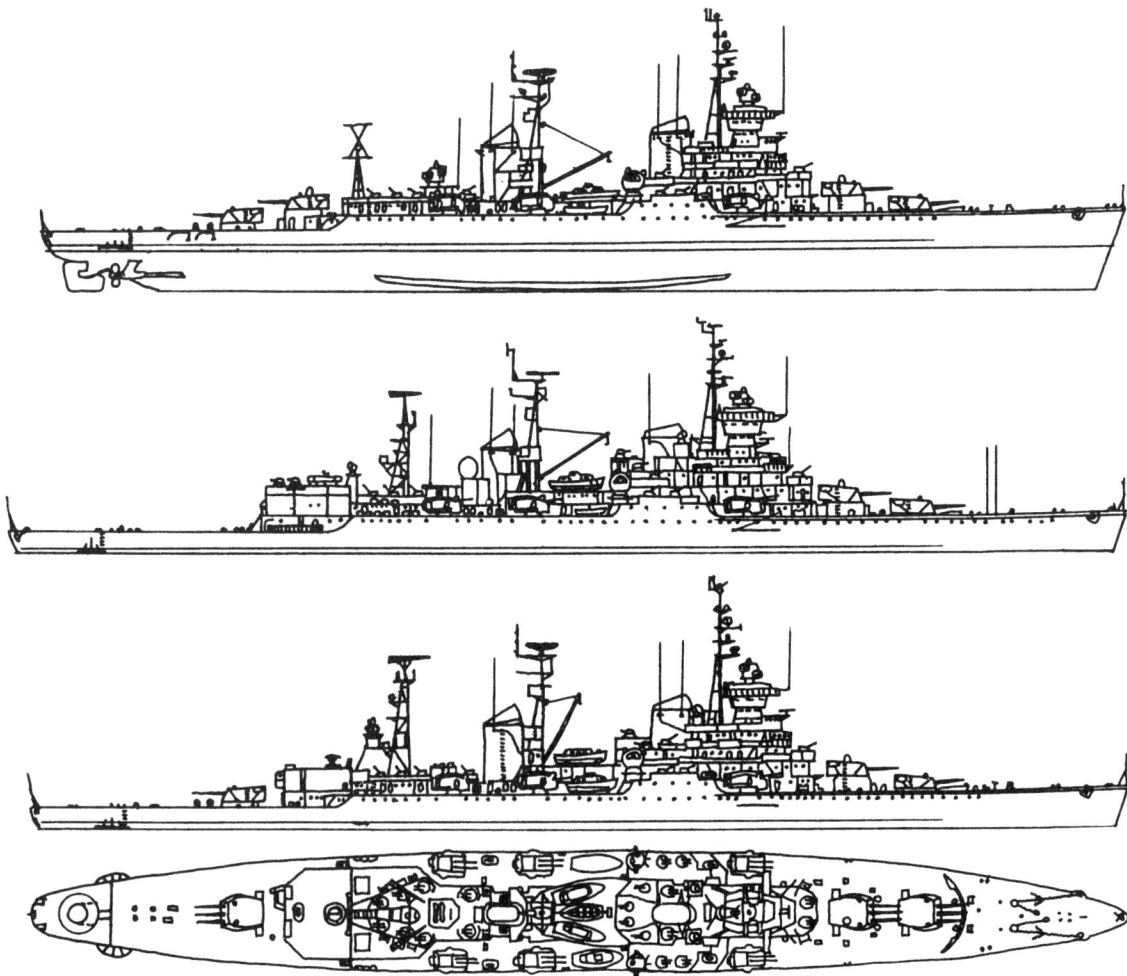

Sverdlov (U.S. Naval Institute Photographic Collection)

Dzerzhinskiy (G. G. Kiselev)

Armor: Sides 100 mm at waterline, 32 mm at ends; armored bulkheads 120 mm (forward), 100 mm (aft); lower (armor) deck, 50 mm; conning tower 130 mm sides, 30 mm deck, 100 mm roof; steering gear 100 mm sides, 50 mm deck; main turrets 175 mm face, 50 mm sides, 75 mm roof; 130 mm barbettes (main armament); secondary armament barbettes 20 mm; stabilized directors 10 mm

Machinery: 6 boilers (KV-68), 2 steam turbines (TB-72), 2 shafts, 110,000 HP = 33.7 kts; 3900 t fuel, 62.5 t oil, 417 t boiler water, 150 t fresh water; 5220 nm/18.2 kts, 4100 nm/23.2 kts, 2080 nm/32 kts, 1975 nm/33.5 kts; Generators: 5 TG-300 (turbo-generators), 4 DG-250. Endurance 30 days.

Complement: 1270 (50 officers, 75 petty officers, 154 rated men)

Electronics: Radars: Gyus-2 air warning, Ryf surface search, Neptun navigational; ECM: Machta; Sonar: Tamir-5N

Thirty units were planned. Chief designer was A. S. Savichev. These ships had welded hulls with twenty-four bulkheads; armor joints were welded. They had degaussing coils.

Modifications:

Zhdanov (Project 68-U1, No.3 turret replaced by 2×2 Osa [SA-N-4] missile launchers

Adm Ushakov (Project 68-A), 8×2 30 mm (AK-230)

Adm Senyavin (Project 68-U2, 1972), Nos. 3 and 4 turrets removed, Osa missiles, 4×2 30 mm (AK-230), and helicopter added. Suffered an explosion in No. 1 turret 13 June '78.

Adm Lazarev had a P-20 radar in place of her V-11 AA mounts.

Adm Nakhimov was modified under Project 67-EP

Dzerzhinskiy (Project 70E, under chief designer K. K. Troshkov of TsKB-16, 1962): No. 4 turret and after director and 8 V-11 removed, replaced by M-2 Volkhov SAM system (10 V-750 missiles, APG-1 radar with Kaktus antenna): 12,970/16,070 t.

Project: 58

NATO Class Name: KYNDA

Names:

	laid down	launched	completed	str
GROZNY	23 Feb. '60	26 Mar. '61	30 Dec. '62	24 June '91
ADMIRAL FOKIN	5 Oct. '60	19 Nov. '61	28 Dec. '64	30 Dec. '93

l.d. as *Steregushchiy*, renamed *Vladivostok* 31 Oct. '62, then renamed again 11 May '64

ADMIRAL GOLOVKO	20 Apr. '61	18 July '62	30 Dec. '64	'91

ex-*Doblestnyi*, renamed 18 Dec. '62

VARYAG	13 Oct. '61	7 Apr. '63	20 Aug. '65	

Decomm 14 Oct. '90 (ex-*Soobrazitelnyy*, renamed 31 Oct. '62)

Guards missile cruiser, laid up at Dal'zavod Mar. '89, stricken 1991

Displacement: 4300/5550

Dimensions: 142 × 15.8 × 5.3

Armament: 2×4 missile launchers (SM-70) firing P-35 missiles (Progress-M, with 1 reload each), 1×2 missile launcher for Volna SAM (16 missiles), 2×2 76 mm (AK-726, 1250 rounds), 4×6 30 mm (AK-630, 3000 rounds, installed after modernization), 2×1 45 mm (21-KM saluting guns), 2×12 RBU-6000, 2×3 533 mm TT (TTA-53-57 bis)

Machinery: 4 high-pressure boilers, 2 steam turbines (TV-12), 2 shafts, 91,000 HP = 34 kts, 6000 nm/14.5 kts, 1500 nm/34 kts

Complement: 304 (including 25 officers)

Electronics: Radars: MR-500 Kliver, MR-302 Rubka, Don, Uspekh-U (radar down-link for Tu-95Ts and Ka-25Ts); ECM: Zaliv (ESM), Krab (ECM), Konuhs; R/st: Tyul'pan, Yasyen', Vishnyn, Orekh; Radio direction finder: Vizir-1; Sonar: GAS-372 Gerkules-2M

TTZ approved 6 Dec. '56; chief designer was V. A. Nikitin (for modernization, Zhukov). Ten units were planned. These ships were built with nuclear/chemical protection. They had a landing pad for a Ka-25 helicopter aft. They also had an active anti-roll device. *Grozny* was modernized 1976–84 (chief engineer Zhukov); she was broken up in Liepaya in 1993). *Admiral Golovko* served in the Black Sea.

[Ed.: According to Burov, the TTZ for the missile system was issued in Oct. '56. (The short-range AA missile on 16 October, the strike missile, which became P-35, on 24 October.) Another article dates the decree authorizing the ship design to 25 Aug. '56. The sketch design was developed between Dec. '56 and June '57, and approved in Oct. '57; the technical design, completed Mar. '58, was approved 15 Aug. '58. Basic characteristics were officially approved on 18 Sept. '58. The ships were initially intended to destroy enemy surface combatants; only later was the anti-carrier mission added. Hull lines were based on those of the Project 56 (Kotlin) destroyers, with fuller bow lines to reduce wetting and spray. The first two ships had two added control spaces, one (GKP, main command post) to coordinate missile strikes and air defense, the other (FKP, flagman's command post) for an admiral commanding a group of ships. They and the CIC (BIP, battle information post) were located in the hull, a departure from previous practice. *Varyag* and *Admiral Golovko* also had special missile control coordination systems using helicopters, for which they had pads. Up to four missiles could be fired in a single salvo.

Because more power was needed to reach the 34 kt design speed, this class introduced pressure-fired boilers, as well as lighter-weight turbines and gearing. On trials, the lead ship

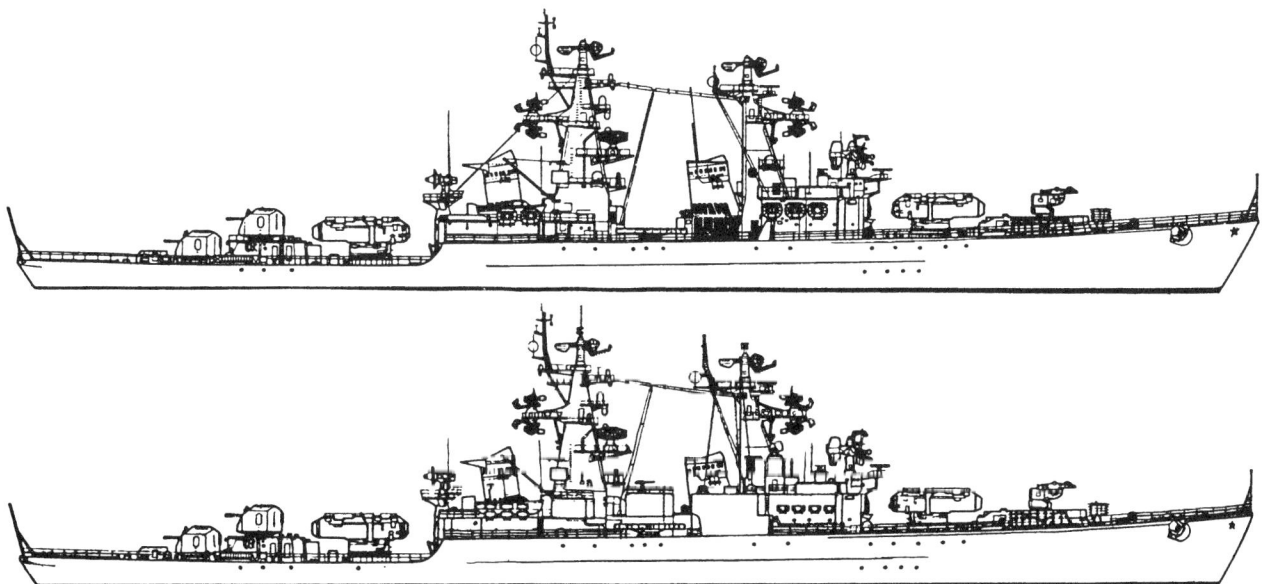

Varyag (G. G. Kiselev)

made 34.5 kts at 95,000 SHP, and cruising range at 18 kts was 3650 rather than the required 3500 nm.

The new P-35 missile system employed a supersonic version (4K44) of the submarine-launched P-6 (SS-N-3A) missile. It enjoyed much greater range than the earlier version. The ship could guide 4 such missiles simultaneously, the Binom radar on each mast directing two. At sea, all the launch tubes were kept loaded with fueled missiles; missiles in magazines were kept unfuelled. Missiles were fired at a 25° launch angle.

Proposed shipbuilding programs included as many as sixteen ships of this class. The direct successor to this class was the Kresta-1 (Project 1134) class cruiser, which was described as a multi-purpose ship (AAW/ASW) rather than as a strike cruiser.]

Project: 1134 (BERKUT)

NATO Class Name: KRESTA-1

Names:

laid down	launched	completed	str

All built at Zhdanov, Leningrad.

ADMIRAL ZOZULYA

26 July '64	17 Oct. '65	8 Oct. '67	Sept. '94

Baltic   BU '95

VITSE-ADMIRAL DROZHD

26 Oct. '65	18 Nov. '66	27 Dec. '68	1 Oct. '90

Sank under tow for BU, Mar. '92

VLADIVOSTOK

24 Dec. '64	1 Aug. '67	11 Sept. '69	1 Jan. '91

Sold to Australian breakers

SEVASTOPOL

8 June '66	28 Apr. '67	25 Sept. '69	28 May '90

BU '91

Had transferred from Northern to Pacific Fleet 19 Oct. '80.

Displacement: 6140/7600

Dimensions: 155.6 × 16.8 × 6.8

Armament: 1 helicopter, 2×2 missile launchers firing P-35 (Progress-M) missiles, 2×2 launchers for Volna SAM (32 V-601 missiles), 2×2 57 mm (AK-725, 4200 rounds), 4×6 30 mm (AK-630, on *Drozd* and *Zozulya* as modernized), 2×12 RBU 6000 (192 RGB-60), 2×6 RBU-1000, 2×5 533 mm TT

Machinery: 4 boilers, 2 steam turbines (TV-12), 2 shafts, 91,000 HP = 32 kts, 5000 nm/18 kts, 2400 nm/32 kts; 2065 t fuel; generators: 2 TG-750, 4 DG-500. Endurance 30 days.

Complement: 360 (39 officers, 50 petty officers, 271 sailors)

Electronics: Radars: MR-310 Angara, MR-500 Kliver, MR-302 Rubka-M, Don navigational radar; IFF: Khrom-2M (Parol as modernized); Sonars: MG-312 Titan, MG-26.

These ships are an intermediate type between cruisers and large ASW ships (BPK). *Sevastopol* was transferred from the Northern to the Pacific Fleet on 19 Oct. '80.

[Ed.: According to Burov, the TTZ for this design was approved in Dec. '61.

According to a 1996 Russian account, this design was produced on virtually a crash basis to help counter enemy strategic submarines. Apparently it was hoped that the new class could be developed directly from the Kynda hull (in fact the hull had to be lengthened considerably). Thus the preliminary design phase was skipped. The ship was described as an anti-aircraft/anti-submarine combatant, to support submarines in combat (by destroying enemy ASW forces), to support ASW ships (e.g., to escort the *Moskva* class), and also to prosecute AAW and ASW in the protection of Soviet sea routes. The problem was that weapon design and development was not at all coordinated with ship development. This class did not show much improvement in ASW weaponry simply because organizations developing those weapons were concentrating on those launched by submarines. As for AAW, the desired weapon, Shtorm (SA-N-3), only began development in 1961 (the preceding weapon, Volna [SA-N-1], was not yet ready). It was to have been ready in 1964–65. In fact, by the time the ships were being built, it was clearly running so late that the Volna system of the earlier "Kynda" had to be adopted. Thus this class was subjected to major redesign during construction. The hull grew (to the largest which could be built under cover at the Zhdanov yard in Leningrad) because required cruising range increased from 3500 to 5000 nm, specifically for the *Moskva* escort mission.

Plans apparently originally called for twin Shtorm launchers (18 missiles each); the missiles were to have been stowed horizontally below SM-136 box launchers. When plans switched to the earlier Volna, there was some interest in supplementing the usual sixteen missiles (in twin revolving drums) with upper-deck boxes loading their weapons horizontally; ultimately the drums were replaced by vertical containers, holding a total of thirty-two missiles per launcher. The shift back to the earlier missile did somewhat simplify radar design. The ship was originally to have had a 2-D radar, Kliver (MR-500 [NATO Big Net]) for long-range search and a 3-D radar (Angara-A, later renamed MR-600

V.Adm Drozd (U. A. Pakhomov)

Adm Zozulya (V. E. Katayev)

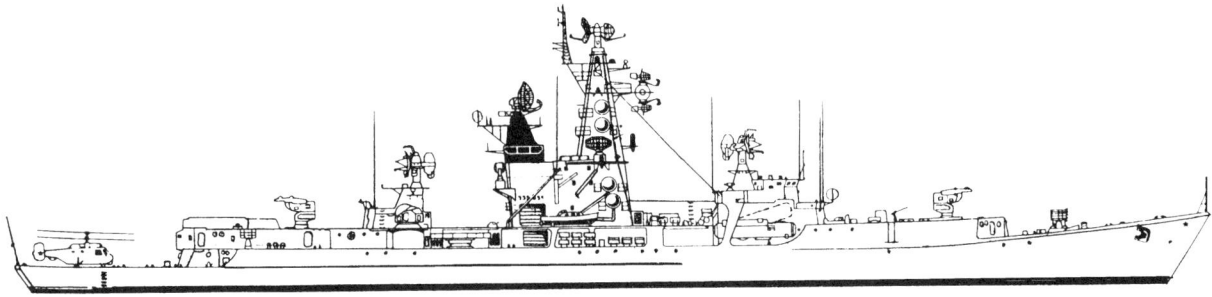

Voshkod [NATO Top Sail]) to direct the Shtorm system. Voshkod development was slow, and as a stop-gap a 3-D version of Angara (NATO Head Net), MR-310 (NATO Head Net C) was developed. It was unsuitable for Shtorm because it did not give good high altitude data and its altitude data was difficult to obtain. However, it was good enough for Volna. This radar was therefore used on board Project 1134 as well as on other Volna ships. Angara-A grew to become a primary long-range air search set in ships armed with Shtorm, such as the *Moskva* class, with MR-310 as backup. The history of this class, however, explains why it was soon combined with a 2-D antenna, to provide long-range air search.

Similarly, plans initially called for reloads, in upper-deck boxes, for the four P-35 (SS-N-3) launchers. However, reloading took several hours, and the reloads were dropped from the design.

Because there were no new surface ASW weapons under design, Project 1134 initially was to have carried the same armament as Project 58, albeit with better sonars. With the deletion of the reload P-35s, the earlier triple torpedo tubes were replaced by quintuple tubes firing ASW torpedoes, and RBU-1000 replaced the earlier RBU-6000: despite its reduced range, it offered four times the explosive weight of the earlier weapon. Far more importantly, Project 1134 was the first Soviet ship with a helicopter hangar (apparently fitted because it could be accomodated in the lengthened hull). There was stowage for five ASW torpedoes (PLAT-1) and 54 sonobuoys.

The silhouette was reduced by leading all uptakes into a single stack. The machinery plant was that of Project 58, but length was reduced by placing the turbochargers directly above the boilers. Generating capacity had to be increased.

Plans initially called for building at least ten ships, but as the project was delayed for 2–3 years it became clear that it was only transitional.]

Project: 1155 (FREGAT)

Class Name: UDALOY

Names:

	laid down	launched	completed
Kaliningrad:			
UDALOY	23 July '77	5 Feb. '80	31 Dec. '80
ADMIRAL SPIRIDONOV	1981	1983	30 Dec. '84
MARSHAL SHAPOSHNIKOV	1983	Jan. '85	30 Dec. '85
SIMFEROPOL*	12 June '84	24 Dec. '85	30 Dec. '87
ADMIRAL VINOGRADOV*	5 Feb. '86	4 June '87	30 Dec. '88
ADMIRAL KHARLAMOV	7 Aug. '86	29 June '88	30 Dec. '89
ADMIRAL PANTALEYEV	1987	1988	19 Dec. '91
ADMIRAL CHABANENKO**	1988	1992	– – –

originally to have been named *Admiral Basistiy*. Note that she was christened 16 June '94, several years after launch.

ADMIRAL BASISTIY	– – –	– – –	1990

originally to have been named *Admiral Kucharov*

	laid down	launched	completed
Zhdanov:			
VITSE-ADMIRAL KULAKOV	4 Nov. '77	16 May '80	29 Dec. '81
MARSHAL VASILYEVSKIY	22 Apr. '79	29 Dec. '81	8 Dec. '83
ADMIRAL ZAKHAROV	16 Oct. '81	4 Nov. '82	30 Dec. '83

In reserve 1992 after a fire.

ADMIRAL TRIBUTS	19 Apr. '80	26 Mar. '83	30 Dec. '85
ADMIRAL LEVCHENKO	27 Jan. '82	21 Feb. '85	30 Sept. '88

was to have been named *Khabarovsk,* renamed 24 May '82

Starred ships are Project 1155 bis. Double stars indicate Project 1155.1.

Udaloy (U. A. Pakhomov)

Adm Chabanenko (G. P. Savochkin)

Adm Vinogradov (G. G. Kiselev)

Vitse Admiral Kulakov (U.S. Navy)

Displacement: 6945/7570

Dimensions: 162.8 × 19 × 7.5

Armament: 2 helicopters in 2 hangars (Ka-27PL and Ka-27RTs), 2×4 missile launchers (KT-R-1134A) for rocket-torpedo system 85-RU Metel', 8×8 vertical launchers (3S95) for Kinshal (64 missiles), 2×1 100mm (AK-100), 4×6 30mm (AK-630), 2 saluting guns (21-KM), 2×12 RBU-6000, 2×4 533mm TT (ChTA-53-1155), 26 mines

Project 1155.1: 1×2 130mm (AK-130), Moskit missiles, 2 Kortik AA systems (7700/8900 t)

Machinery: 4 gas turbines (2×9000 HP cruise and 2×22,000 HP boost), 2 shafts, 62,000 HP = 30 kts; 2000 t fuel; 3000 nm/14 kts (5700 nm with overload fuel). Endurance 30 days.

Complement: 220 (29 officers)

Electronics: Radars: MR-760 Fregat-MA, MR-350, Volga (later Vaygatch), MR-212, Topaz; Sonar: Polinom; Communications systems: Taifun, Kristall

TTZ approved 17 Oct. '72; chief designer was V. P. Mishin. Aluminum superstructure, air-conditioned. Rated as Large ASW Ships of 1st Rank (BPK). *Adm. Zakharov* (laid up 1992) stricken 5 June '94.

Project: 1134B, 1134.2, 1134.7, 1134.8 (BERKUT-B)

NATO Class Name: KARA

Names:

	laid down	launched	completed
All built at Nikolaev.			
NIKOLAEV	25 June '68	19 Dec. '69	31 Dec. '71
str 29 Oct. '92 l.d. as *Novorossisk*			
OCHAKOV	19 Dec. '69	30 Apr. '71	4 Nov. '73
KERCH	30 Apr. '71	21 July '72	26 Dec. '74
AZOV	21 July '72	14 Sept. '73	25 Dec. '75
PETROPAVLOVSK*			
	9 Sept. '73	22 Nov. '74	29 Dec. '76
TASHKENT	22 Nov. '74	5 Nov. '75	21 Dec. '77
str 3 July '92			
TALLIN	5 Nov. '75	5 Nov. '76	31 Dec. '79
Renamed *Vladivostok* 2 Aug. '90			

Displacement: 6700/8565

Dimensions: 173.4 × 18.5 × 5.74

Armament: 1 helicopter in hangar (Ka-25 or Ka-27*), 2×4 missile launchers (KT-100M-1134) for rocket-torpedo 85-R Metel' (rocket-torpedo Rastrub*), 2×2 missile launchers (B-92) for Shtorm V-611 SAM (72 missiles); 1 twin launcher on *Azov* (36 missiles); *Azov:* 6×4 launchers for Fort system (24 missiles); 2×2 launchers for Osa 9M33 system (40 missiles), 2×2 76mm (AK-726, 4800 rounds), 4×6 30mm (AK-630, 8000 rounds), 2×12 RBU-6000 (144 RGB-60), 2×6 RBU 1000 (60 RGB-10), 2×5 533mm TT (2×2 on AZOV) for 53-65K and SET-65 torpedoes

Machinery: 6 gas turbines (4x GTU-12A, 20,000 HP each, and 2 M-5, 8000 HP each), 2 shafts, 96,000 HP = 32 kts; 1830 t fuel, 14 t boiler water, 19 t oil, 16.8 t kerosene for helicopter, 50 t water; 6500 nm/18 kts (cruise turbines only), 3000 nm/32 kts. Endurance 30 days.

Complement: 380 (47 officers, 47 petty officers, 286 sailors)

Petropavlovsk (G. G. Kiselev)

Kerch (Friedman collection)

Kerch (Pavlov collection)

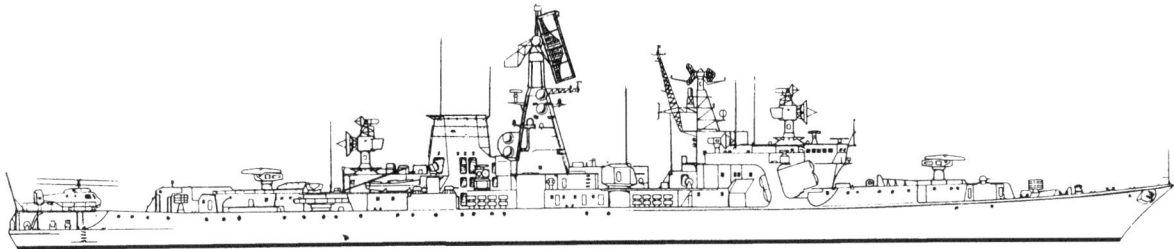

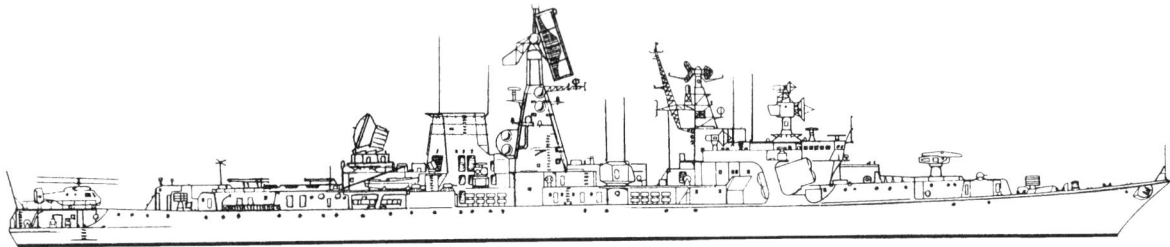

Azov (Pavlov collection)

Electronics: Radars: MR-600 Voskhod, MR-310A Angara, MR-700 on *Kerch*; navigational radars: Volga (2) and Don; Sonars: MG-332 Titan, MG-325 Vega VDS, MG-26 for communication/IFF; Non-acoustic sensor: MI-110K to detect a submarine wake; Radio direction finder: ARP-50P; Gyrocompass: Kurs-5; Log: MGL-50M; Sounder: NEL-5.

Rated as Large ASW ships (BPK); chief designer was A. K. Per'kov. *Azov* was modernized June '86 (Project 1134.7). Transfers to Pacific: 1979, *Petropavlovsk* and *Tashkent;* 1981, *Talinn;* 1983, *Nikolaev. Tashkent* and *Nikolaev* began repairs at Nikolaev 1987 after a July '86 collision with BPK *Stroigy* during fleet exercises. They were included in the Ukrainian Fleet and stricken in 1992, then broken up in India 1994, to pay debts. *Ochakov* was repaired in Sevastopol 1980–84. *Azov* and *Kerch* are in the Black Sea Fleet.

Project: 1134A (BERKUT-A)

NATO Class Name: KRESTA-2

Names:

	laid down	launched	completed
All built at Zhdanov Yard, Leningrad.			
KRONSTADT	12 Dec. '66	10 Feb. '68	29 Dec. '69
str 24 June '91			
ADMIRAL ISAKOV	15 Jan. '68	22 Nov. '68	28 Dec. '70
str 30 June '93			
ADMIRAL NAKHIMOV			
	15 Jan. '68	15 Apr. '69	29 Nov. '71
str 31 Jan. '91			
ADMIRAL MAKAROV			
	23 Feb. '69	22 Jan. '70	25 Oct. '72
str 3 July '92 BU in India			
MARSHAL VOROSHILOV			
	20 Mar. '70	8 Oct. '70	15 Sept. '73
Renamed *Khabarovsk* 24 Jan. '91 str 3 July '92			
ADMIRAL OKTYABRSKIY			
	2 June '70	21 May '71	28 Dec. '73
str 30 June '93			
ADMIRAL ISACHENKOV			
	30 Oct. '70	28 Mar. '72	5 Nov. '74
str 3 July '92 BU in India			
MARSHAL TIMOSHENKO			
	2 Nov. '72	21 Oct. '73	25 Nov. '75
str 3 July '92			
VASILIY CHAPAEV			
	22 Dec. '73	28 Nov. '74	30 Nov. '76
str 30 June '93			

Marshal Voroshilov (G. G. Kiselev)

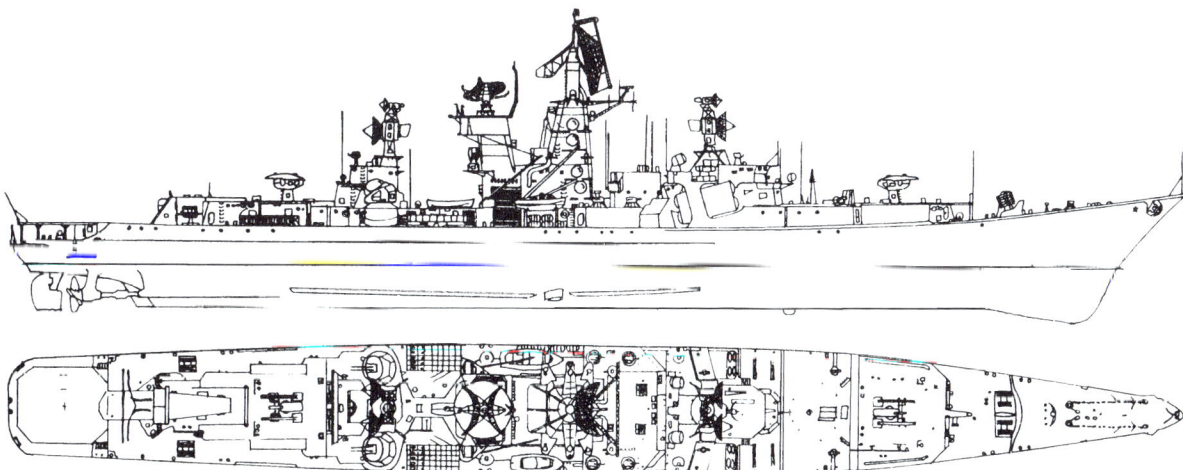

ADMIRAL YUMASHEV

                    17 Apr. '75   30 Sept. '76   30 Dec. '77
str 23 Feb. '93

Displacement: 5600/7535

Dimensions: 158.9 × 16.8 × 7.8

Armament: 2×4 launchers (KT-100) for Metel' 85-R, 2×2
launchers (B-187A) for Shtorm SAM (96 missiles),
2×2 57 mm (AK-725, 2200 rounds; with another 2200 in
overload condition), 4×6 30 mm (AK-630, 8000 rounds),
1 45 mm (21-KM) saluting gun, 2×12 RBU 6000 (144
RGB-60), 2×6 RBU 1000 (60 RGB 10), 2×5 533 mm
(PTA-53-1134, firing SET-53 and SET-65 torpedoes)

Machinery: 4 boilers, 2 steam turbines (TV-12), 2 shafts,
91,000 HP = 32 kts; 1830 t fuel, 13 t oil, 6 t kerosene;
5200 nm/18 kts, 2400 nm/32 kts; Generators: 2 TG-1000
(400 V, 50 Hz), 4 DG-500, 1 TG-750 (for sonar).

Complement: 343 (33 officers, 29 petty officers, 281 sailors)

Electronics: Radars: MR-600, MR-310A, navigational
radars: Volga and Don; Sonars: MG-322 Titan-2, MG-35
Shtil', MG-26 for communications
    Rated large ASW ships (BPK); chief designer V. F. Anikiyev.
There were sixteen compartments. These ships were air-
conditioned and had water desalinization plants.

Project: 956 (SARICH) and 956A*

Class Name: SOVREMMENNY

Names:

	laid down	launched	completed
All built at Zhdanov.			
SOVREMENNYY			
	3 Mar. '76	18 Nov. '78	25 Dec. '80
OTCHAYANNYY			
	4 Mar. '77	29 Mar. '80	30 Sept. '82
OTLICHNYY			
	22 Apr. '78	21 Mar. '81	30 Sept. '83
OSMOTRITELNYY			
	27 Oct. '78	24 Apr. '82	30 Sept. '84
BEZUPRECHNYY			
	1980	Aug. '83	6 Nov. '85
BOYEVOY			
	26 Mar. '82	4 Aug. '84	28 Sept. '86
STOYKIY			
	28 Sept. '82	27 July '85	31 Dec. '86
OKRYLENNYY			
	16 Apr. '83	31 May '86	30 Dec. '87
BURNYY			
	1984	Feb. '87	30 Sept. '88
GREMYASHCHIY			
	23 Nov. '84	30 May '87	30 Dec. '88

originally named *Vedushchiy,* renamed 18 Aug. '88

BYSTRYY			
	29 Oct. '84	28 Nov. '87	30 Sept. '89
RASTOROPNYY			
	15 Aug. '86	4 June '88	30 Dec. '89
BEZBOYAZNENNYY			
	1987	Mar. '89	28 Nov. '90

BEZUDERZHNIY			
	1987	June '90	25 June '91
BESPOKOYNYY			
	1988	1990	28 Dec. '91
NASTOYCHIVYY			
	1989	1991	30 Dec. '92

renamed *Moskovskiy Komsomolets* 30 Dec. '87, name later
restored

BESSTRASHNIY*			
	1992	30 Dec. '93	
VAZHNYY*			
	1989	– – –	1996
VDUMCHIVYY*			
	1989	– – –	1997
BULINIY*			
	1991	1994	– – –

VNUSHITELNIY

l.d. at Nikolaev 30 Aug. '83, was launched 17 Oct. '87 but
never completed; she was hulked as a floating warehouse. A
second unit was dismantled on the slip.

Displacement: 6500/7940

Dimensions: 156.5 × 17.2 × 5.96

Armament: 2×4 launchers (KT-190) for Moskit missiles,
2×1 launchers (3S90) for Uragan/Shtil' SAM missiles (44
missiles), 2×2 130 mm (AK-130, 500 rounds), 4×6 30 mm
(AK-630, 8000 rounds), 2×1 45 mm saluting cannon (21-
KM, 100 rounds), 2×2 533 mm TT, 2×6 RBU 1000 (120
rounds), 40 mines

Machinery: 4 boilers, 2 steam turbines, 2 shafts, 110,000 HP
= 32 kts; 1740 t fuel; 4500 nm/18 kts (maximum fuel load;
3920 nm with normal fuel load), 10,000 nm/14 kts.
Endurance 30 days.

Complement: 296 (including 25 officers)

Electronics: Radar: MR-750 Fregat (first 3, Fregat-M in units 4 and 5, MR-760 in others), Volga or Vaiygach; Sonar: Platina; Communications system: Taifun (in 956A), Burau; Space communication system: Pritsep

Chief designer: I. I. Rubis. A planned modernized version, Project 956U *(Vechniy)* will have Kinzhal AA missiles.

[Ed.: According to an article in *Military Parade* describing this class, this design evolved from a 1970–71 TTZ for a 5000 t ship armed with three single guns, an air defense missile (presumably SA-N-4), and rocket launchers, intended mainly to support amphibious assaults. Subsequent cost-benefit analysis led to drastic revision of the TTZ, and the ship became a multi-purpose destroyer. In this form the design was completed in 1974 and shipyard work began in 1975. According to a recent Polish account of the class, difficulties with the AK-130 gun led to a project to mount a single 180 mm gun instead.

Burnyy (G. G. Kiselev)

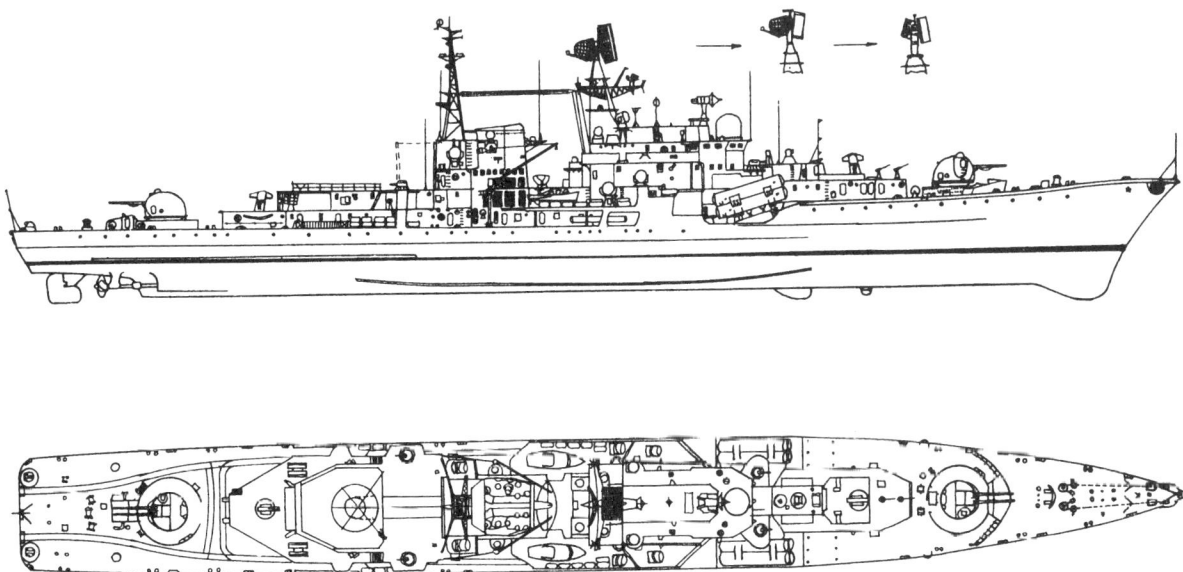

Project: 61, 61E, and 61M*

NATO Class Name: KASHIN

Names:

	laid down	launched	completed	original name
Zhdanov, Leningrad:				
OGNEVOIY*	9 May '62	31 May '63	31 Dec. '64	SKR-31
conversion completed Feb. '73; str 24 May '89, BU Turkey Oct. '90				
OBRAZTSOVYY*	29 July '63	23 Feb. '64	29 Sept. '65	SKR-2
str 30 June '93				
ODARENNYY*	22 Jan. '63	11 Sept. '64	30 Dec. '65	
str 19 Apr. '90; had become SM-449 30 May '78				
SLAVNYY*	9 July '64	24 Apr. '65	30 Sept. '66	
conversion completed Sept. '75, str 24 June '91				
STEREGUSHCHIY*	9 July '64	20 Feb. '66	21 Dec. '66	
str 30 June '93				
Nikolaev:				
KOMSOMOLETS UKRAINY	15 Sept. '59	31 Dec. '60	31 Dec. '62	SKR-25
str 24 June '91				
SOOBRAZITELNYY	20 July '60	25 Sept. '61	26 Dec. '63	SKR-44
str 3 July '92				
PROVORNYY	10 Feb. '61	23 Mar. '62	25 Dec. '64	SKR-37
str 21 Aug. '90				
OTVAZHNYY	10 Aug. '63	17 Oct. '64	31 Dec. '65	*Orel*
lost 30 Aug. '74 by fire				
STROYNYY	20 Mar. '64	28 July '65	15 Dec. '66	
conversion completed '80; str 12 Apr. '90; BU Turkey Jan. '91				
KRASNYY KAVKAZ	25 Nov. '64	9 Feb. '66	25 Sept. '67	
RESHITELNYY	25 June '65	30 June '66	30 Dec. '67	
SMYSHLENYY	15 Aug. '65	22 Oct. '66	27 Sept. '68	
conversion completed '74; str 22 Feb. '93				
STROIGY	22 Feb. '66	29 Apr. '67	24 Dec. '68	
str 30 June '93				
SMETLIVYY	15 July '66	26 Aug. '67	25 Sept. '69	
SMELYY	15 Nov. '66	6 Feb. '68	27 Dec. '69	
conversion completed '74; to Poland Dec. '87 as *Warszawa*				
KRASNYY KRIM	23 Feb. '68	28 Feb. '69	15 Oct. '70	
str 10 Apr. '94				
SPOSOBNYY	10 Mar. '69	11 Apr. '70	25 Sept. '71	
str 3 July '92				
SKORYY	20 Apr. '70	26 Feb. '71	23 Sept. '72	
SDERZHANNYY*	20 Oct. '70	29 Feb. '72	30 Dec. '73	

Stars indicate modernization to Project 61M. Note that apart from *Sderzhannyy*, which was completed to this design, *only* Leningrad-built units were modernized. *Komsomolets Ukrainy* was lead ship: began trials 15 Oct. '62.

Displacement: 3440/4290

Dimensions: 144 × 15.8 × 4.46

Obrastzovyy (U.S. Naval Institute Photographic Collection)

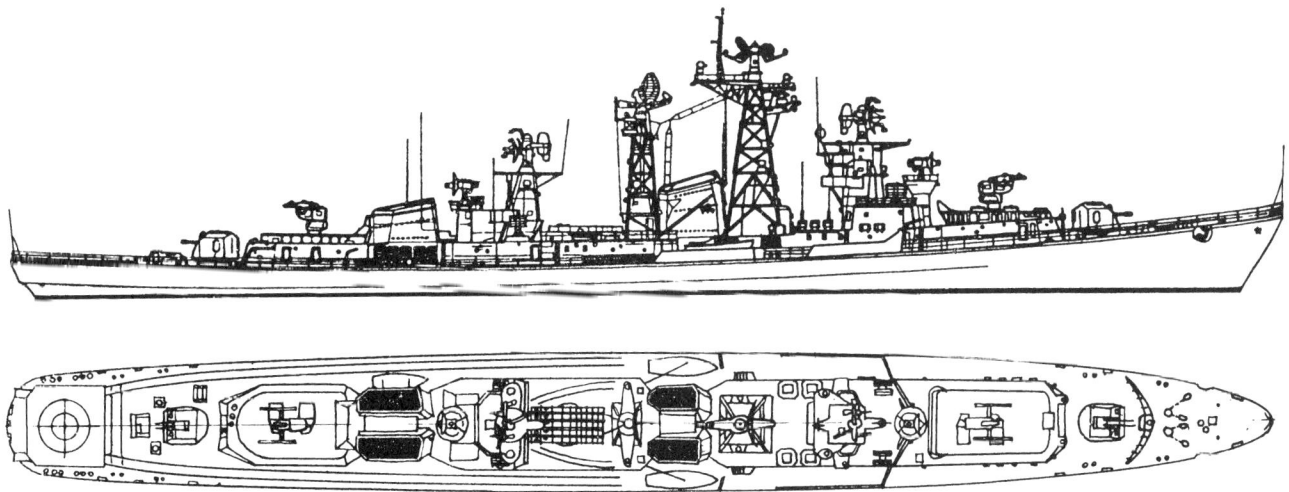

Odarennyy (Pavlov collection)

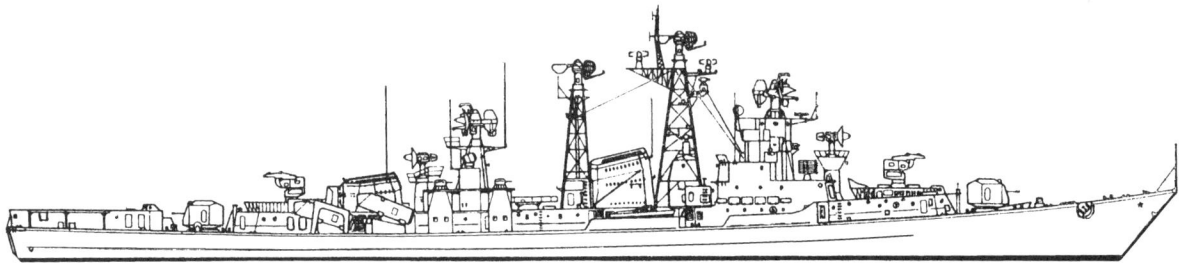

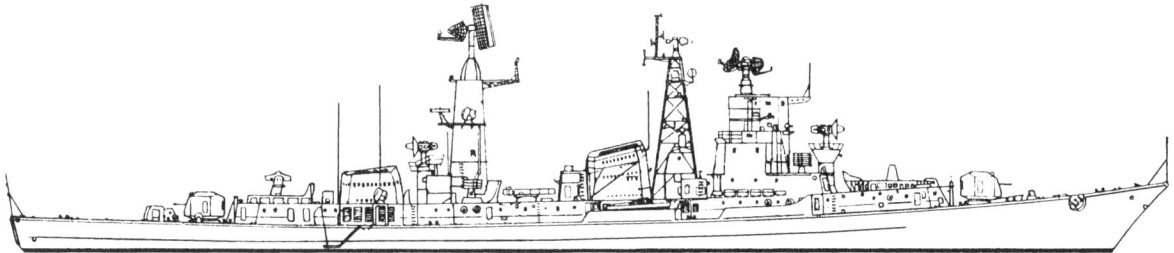

Smelyy (Pavlov collection)

Armament: 2×2 launchers (ZiF-101) for Volna M-1 missiles (32 missiles, type 4K90), 2×2 76 mm (AK-726, 1200 rounds), 2×12 RBU-6000 (196 RGB-60), 2×6 RBU 1000 (48 RGB-10*), 1×5 533 mm TT (PTA 53-61, for SET-53 or 53-57 torpedoes)

Machinery: 2×2 M-3 gas turbines, 2 shafts, 72,000 HP = 34 kts (up to 35.3 kts in service), 3500 nm/18 kts, 2000 nm/30 kts, 2500 nm/25 kts, 1500 nm/35 kts; 840 t fuel, 38 t water, 10 t lubricating oil, 5 t kerosene for helicopter. Endurance 10 days.

Complement: 266 (22 officers, 18 petty officers, 226 sailors)

Electronics: Radars: Angara (2), MR-300, Don (navigational), later replaced by Volga; Sonars: MG-312 Titan, MG-311 Vychegda; Underwater communications: MG-26 Khost; IFF: Nikel-Khrom; Sounder: NEL-5; Gyrocompass: Kurs-3

Chief designer: B. I. Kupyenskiy (TsKB-53). Built under Council of Ministers Resolution of 18 Sept. '57. Technical project (design) approved 22 Apr. '58. First large combat-ants in the world powered entirely by gas turbines. Initially classified as SKR (guardships), reclassified as BPK (large ASW ships) 19 May '66. They have aluminum superstructure and masts, active anti-roll devices, and water desalination equipment.

Sderzhanniy was completed under Project 61M and modernized under Project 61MP. Project 61M: 4010/4974 t, 146.2 × 15.8 × 4.84 m, 32 kts, 4000 nm/18 kts, 320 men (29 officers). 4 launchers for P-15M cruise missiles, 4×6 30 mm (AK-630, 3000 rounds) were added. New radars: Kliver and Volga instead of Don navigational set. New towed sonar: Platina. In 1975 *Provornyy* was fitted with a launcher for Shtil AA missiles. In 1991 *Smetliviy* had her after AK-726 replaced by a new sonar and her 533 mm TT replaced by 1×7 406 mm TT. *Sposobnyy* was modernized in 1990.

Black Sea units: *Reshitelnyy, Sderzhanniy, Krasniy Krim, Krasniy Kavkaz, Smetliviy, Komsomolets Ukrainy, Provornyy.*

Five ships were built for India (in 1980, 1982, 1983, and 1986: *Tverdiy, Gubitelniy, Lobkiy, Nadezhniy, Tolkoviy*).

Project: 57 bis and 57A*

NATO Class Name: KRUPNY and KANIN*

Names:

	laid down	launched	completed

Zhdanov, Leningrad:

GREMYASHCHIY
25 Feb. '58 · 30 Apr. '59 · 30 June '60
str 2 Oct. '91; became OS-315 in Northern Fleet 1989

ZHGUCHIY · 23 June '58 · 14 Oct. '59 · 23 Dec. '60
str 30 July '87; BU Spain 1988

ZORKIY · 17 Apr. '59 · 30 Apr. '60 · 30 Sept. '61
str 30 June '93

DERZKIY · 10 Oct. '59 · 4 Feb. '60 · 30 Dec. '61
str 19 Apr. '90; sunk as target (Northern Fleet)

Nikolaev:

GNEVNYY · 17 Dec. '57 · 30 Nov. '58 · 10 Jan. '60
str 8 Apr. '88; target ship 1987, Project 57A.

UPORNYY · 9 Apr. '58 · 14 Oct. '59 · 3 Dec. '60
str 29 June '93; became PZK-12 1991 (Pacific)

BOYKIY · 2 Apr. '59 · 15 Dec. '60 · 26 June '61
str 17 July '88; grounded en route to BU 14 Nov. '88 in Norwegian Sea

Komsomolsk:

GORDYY · May '59 · 24 May '60 · 6 Feb. '61
str 30 July '87; completed reconstruction 23 Mar. '74; target ship 1987

KHRABRYY · 1959 · 1961 · Canceled 1963

Gremyashchiy (A. N. Sokolov)

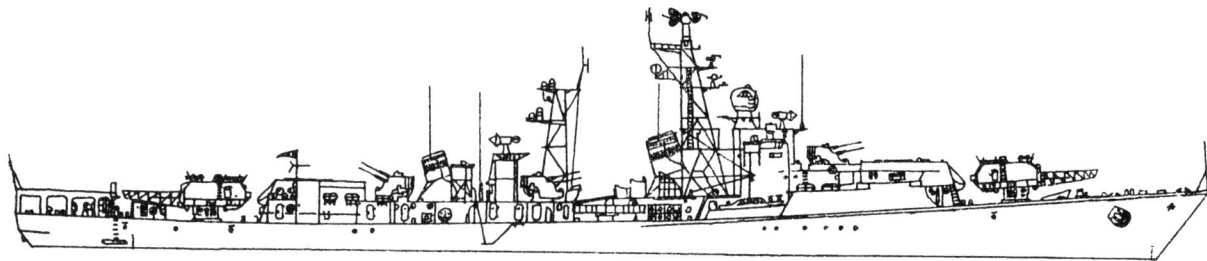

Gremyashchiy (G. G. Kisyelov)

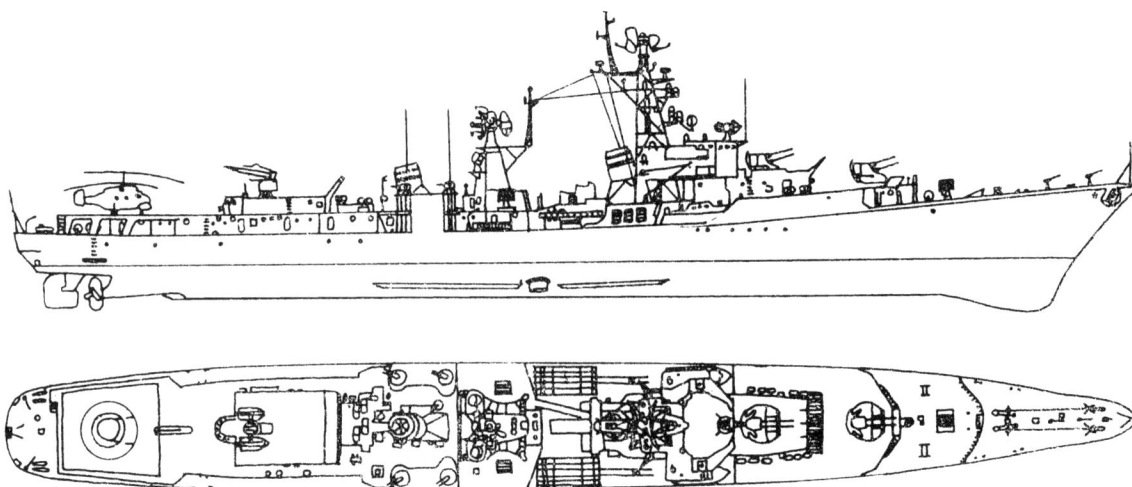

Displacement: 3500/4192

Dimensions: 138.9 × 14.85 × 4.2

Armament: 2×6 missile launchers (SM-59-1a) for KSSh missile (4 extra missiles as overload), 4×4 57 mm (ZiF-75, 9500 rounds), 2×3 533 mm TT (TTA-53-57bis), 2×16 RBU-2500 (128 RGB-25), helicopter pad (originally for Ka-15, then for Ka-25*)

Machinery: 4 boilers (64 kg/sq cm), 2 steam turbines (TV-8), 2 variable-pitch propellers, 72,000 HP = 32 kts, 2800 nm/14 kts, 700 nm/32 kts; 690 t fuel, 30 t oil, 110 t water; 2 DG-300 generators. Endurance 10 days.

Complement: 302 (28 officers, 24 petty officers, 250 sailors)

Electronics: Radars: Angara, Zalp-Shch, Fut-B, Neptun (navigational); ESM: Bizan'-4a; Sonar: Gerkules-2M

Chief designer: O. F. Yakob (TsKB-53). TTZ approved by Navy staff 25 July '55; project approved by CinC 26 Feb. '57. A total of twelve were planned. The canceled *Khrabryy* be-

came a self-propelled generating plant docked at the Komsomolsk yard. These ships were originally rated as destroyers; in 1966 they were re-rated as Large Missile Ships (BRK).

Ships were rebuilt 1967–77 as Large ASW Ships (BPK)*: 3760/4550 t, 140.6 × 14.85 × 4.8 m, 1×2 M-1 Volna AA launchers (16 missiles), 4×2 30 mm (AK-230, 4000 rounds) with Rys radar, 2×2 57 mm (ZiF-75 with 6400 rounds), 3×12 RBU-6000 (216 RGB) and new radars: MR-300 air search, Volga navigational, and Nikel-KM IFF; MG-332T Titan-2 bow sonar; and underwater detectors MI-110K (wake detector) and MGS-47. The DG-300 generator was replaced by a DG-500, and another DG-500 was installed to power the Titan-2 sonar; a DG-200 was added for harbor use. The chief designer of the modified version was V. G. Korolyevich (Northern PKB, ex-TsKB-53). At the end of their careers these ships were designated SKR of 2nd Rank.

Project: 41

NATO Class Name: TALLIN

Names:

	laid down	launched	completed
NEUSTRASHIMYY	5 July '59	29 Jan. '52	31 Jan. '55

Built at Zhdanov Yard (Leningrad).

Displacement: 3010/3830

Dimensions: 133.83 × 13.57 × 4.42

Armament: 2×2 130 mm (SM-2, 1700 rounds), 4×2 45 mm (SM-16, 2000 rounds/bbl), 2×4 25 mm (4M-120, 20,000 rounds, later removed), 2×5 533 mm TT (PTA-53-41),

mines (48 KB-3 or 48 GMZ), 105 depth charges (BB-1), 6 depth charge throwers (BMB-1, with 48 BGB charges); in 1959, 2×16 RBU-2500 (128 RGB-25 bombs) were installed.

Armor: On deckhouse and bridge: 8–20 mm on main command post, 68 mm on main gunhouses

Machinery: 4 boilers (KV-41), 2 steam turbines (TV-8), 66,000 HP (actually 64,200 HP) = 33.55 kts, 5280 nm/14 kts, 1010 nm/33.5 kts. Endurance 20 days.

Complement: 328 (23 officers)

Electronics: Radars: Fut-N air search, Ryf surface search, Zarya FCS; Sonar: Pegas

Chief designer V. A. Nikitin (TsKB-53). TTZ approved 14 June '47. Technical project (design) approved 28 Sept. '49. A

Neustrashimyy (G. G. Kiselev)

total of 110 units were planned. The hull had thirteen bulkheads, and the ship was fitted with fin stabilizers. The ship failed to reach her design speed (36 kts) on trials due to propeller-rudder interaction. The series was not built. The ship was modernized in 1959 with 4×4 45 mm SM-20 ZiF in place of SM-16s, new radars and communications antennas, and new propellers. She was used as Baltic Fleet staff ship and as training ship for new construction crews, and went to the breaker in 1975.

[Ed.: According to several published Russian accounts, the decision not to series-produce this design was made in 1951, before the first unit was completed, on the ground that it was too large and too expensive. The ship actually placed in production, Project 56 (Kotlin), was essentially a smaller hull into which much the same weapons, sensors, and machinery had been packaged.]

Neustrashimyy (G. G. Kiselev)

Project: 56, 56E*, 56M*, 56K, 56A, 56U

NATO Class Name: KOTLIN and KILDIN*

Names:

	laid down	launched	completed

Project 56:

Zhdanov:

SPOKOYNYY 4 Mar. '53 28 Nov. '53 27 June '56
  str 19 Apr. '90

SVETLYY 4 Mar. '53 27 Oct. '53 17 Sept. '55
  decomm 25 Apr. '89

SPESHNYY 30 May '53 7 Aug. '54 30 Sept. '55
  str 25 Apr. '89

SKROMNYY** 27 July '53 26 Oct. '54 30 Dec. '55
  str 25 Apr. '89

SVEDUSHCHIY**
  7 Dec. '53 17 Feb. '55 31 Jan. '56
  str 8 Apr. '92

SMYSHLENYY*
  23 Feb. '54 2 May '55 28 June '56
  str 22 July '86 (29 Oct. '58 *Moskovskiy Komsomolets*)

SKRYTNYY 25 July '54 27 Sept. '55 30 Sept. '56
  str 25 Apr. '89

SOZNATELNYY**
  25 Sept. '54 15 Jan. '56 31 Oct. '56
  str 1 Mar. '88

SPRAVEDLIVYY**
  25 Dec. '54 12 Apr. '56 20 Dec. '56
  25 June '70 to Poland as *Warsawa*

NESOKRUSHIMYY**
  15 June '55 20 July '56 30 June '57
  str 30 Dec. '87

NAKHODCHIVYY**
  19 Oct. '55 30 Oct. '56 18 Sept. '57
  str 25 Apr. '89

NASTOYCHIVYY**
  3 Mar. '56 23 Apr. '57 30 Nov. '57
  str 25 Apr. '89

Nikolaev:

BLESTYASHIY*
  20 Feb. '53 27 Nov. '53 30 Sept. '55
  str 30 July '87

Spokoynyy (A. B. Zagvozdkin)

Blagorodnyy (Pavlov collection)

Prozorlivyy (B. P. Tiurin)

Kotlin class (U.S. Navy)

BYVALVYY*   6 May '53   31 Mar. '54   21 Dec. '55
   str 17 July '88

BRAVYY   25 July '53   28 Feb. '55   9 Jan. '56
   str 30 July '87 (SAM Kotlin prototype)

BESSLEDNYY* 1 Apr. '54   5 Nov. '55   31 Oct. '56
   str 8 Apr. '88; sank while in tow to Philippine breakers.

BURLIVYY*   5 May '54   28 Jan. '56   28 Dec. '56
   str 25 May '89

BLAGORODNYY*
              5 Mar. '55   30 Aug. '56   18 July '56
   str 25 Apr. '89

PLAMENNYY*
              3 Sept. '55   26 Oct. '56   31 Aug. '57
   str 24 June '91

NAPORISTYY*
              17 Aug. '55   30 Dec. '56   31 Oct. '57
   str 30 July '87

Komsomolsk-on-Amur:

VYZYVAYUSHCHIY*
              25 July '53   20 May '55   31 Mar. '56
   str 25 Apr. '89

VESKIY
              30 Jan. '54   31 July '55   30 Mar. '56
   str 30 July '87

VDOKHNOVENNYY*
              31 Aug. '54   7 May '56   31 Oct. '56
   str 5 Mar. '87

VOZMUSHCHENNYY*
              30 Dec. '54   8 July '56   31 Dec. '56
   str 5 Mar. '87

VOZBUZHDENNYY**
              29 July '55   10 May '57   31 Oct. '57
   str 25 Apr. '89; sunk as target 1990–91

VLIYATELNYY
              29 Oct. '55   10 May '57   6 Nov. '57
   str 17 July '88; sunk as target 1990–91

VYDERZHANNYY
              30 June '56   24 June '57   10 Dec. '57
   str 25 Apr. '92 (20 Feb. '67 renamed *Dalnevostochnyy
Komsomolets;* became PKZ-7 1992)

Single asterisks in the list of names indicate the 56PLO ASW
modernization. Double asterisks indicate 56A AAW missile
conversions.

Project 56M (NATO KILDIN)

Zhdanov:

BEDOVYY   1 Dec. '53   31 July '55   30 June '58
   str 25 Apr. '89 fitted out to Project 56EM configuration;
she was never in service as a Project 56 destroyer.

NEULOVIMYY
              23 Feb. '57   27 Feb. '58   30 Dec. '58
   str 19 Apr. '90

NEUTOMIMIY   ordered but not built

Nikolaev:

PROZORLIVYY
              1 Sept. '56   30 July '57   30 Dec. '58
   str 24 June '91 built to 56M design

Komsomolsk:

NEUDERZHIMYY
              23 Feb. '57   24 May '58   30 Dec. '58
   str 8 Dec. '85

SPOKOYNYY   began builder's trials 27 Aug. '54

NEUKROTIMYY   ordered 1955 but not built

Displacement: 2667/3249

Dimensions: 126.1 × 12.7 × 4.26

Armament: 2×2 130mm (SM-2-1, 850 rounds plus 200 in
overload condition), 4×4 45mm (SM-20 ZiF, 13,200
rounds), 2×5 533mm PTA-53-56, 50 mines (KB-3, AMD-
500, AGSB, GMZ) or 36 mines (AMD-1000) or 48 depth
charges (6 BMB-2 throwers)

Armor: Superstructure sides 10mm, deck 6mm, gunhouses
40mm

Machinery: 4 boilers (KV-76), 2 steam turbines (TV-8),
2 shafts, 72,000 HP = 39 kts; 584 t fuel, 3880 nm/14.3 kts,
3090 nm/17.3 kts, 642 nm/38 kts; generators: 2 TG-400, 2
DG-200. First of class had 2 rudders, others 1. Endurance 10
days.

Complement: 284 (22 officers, 19 petty officers, 243 sailors)

Electronics: Radars: Fut-N (air search), Neptun (navigational); Sonar: Pegas-2

   Chief designer O. L. Fisher (TsKB-53). A total of 100
units was planned. These destroyers had aluminum superstructures, 15 bulkheads, and anti-roll devices.

   Project 56PLO ships (1961–62) had their after TT and
depth charge throwers removed, an ASW control station
added, and 2 RBU-2500 or RBU-6000 plus 2×2 25mm
(2M-3, later removed).

   Bravyy (Project 56K, 1960) was the prototype AA missile
conversion, with 1 launcher replacing her after gun mount
(16 missiles in 2 drums). She displaced 2890/3480t as converted. The production version, Project 56A (1969–71), also
had the after 130mm mount replaced by an M1 Volna AA
missile launcher. Of this group, *Nesokrushmyy, Skrytnyy,*
and *Soznatelniy* had 2 SM-20 ZiF replaced by 4 AK-630. All
56A units had new Angara radars, 2 RBU-6000 (96 RGB-
60), and Gerkules-2 sonars. Displacement changed to
3060/3625t.

   Bedovyy (Project 56E, chief designer O. T. Yakob) was
completed as a missile ship, an SM-59-1 launcher for
KSShch missiles replacing her after 130mm mount, and
an additional quadruple 45mm SM-20ZiF replacing her
forward mount; her 1×5 533mm TT was replaced by
2×2 533mm TT; displacement was 2850/3390t. Project
56M ships were similar but had all 45mm guns replaced by

4×4 57 mm ZiF-75 (9600 rounds) and Pegas-2M sonars instead of the earlier Gerkules-2M. Machta replaced the earlier Bizan-4A ESM.

Bedovyy, Neulovimyy, and *Prozorlivyy* (all Black Sea) were modified 1972–74 (Project 56U, chief designer V. G. Ko-rolyevich) with 4 P-15M missiles, 2×2 76 mm (AK-726, 2000 rounds), 2 2 533 mm TT (SET-53 torpedoes), 2×16 RBU-2500 (128 RGB-25), new radars and sonars: 2940/3447 t. They were stricken 1989–91.

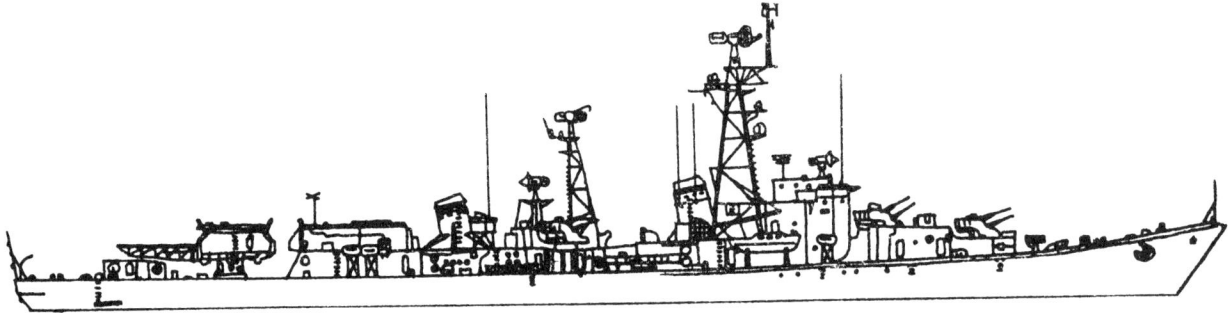

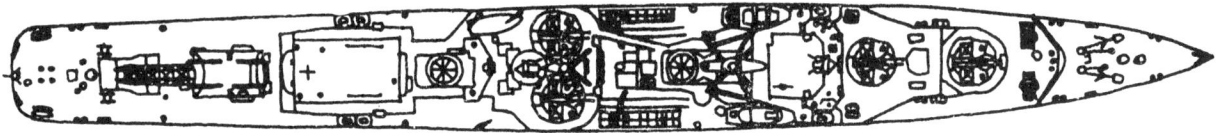

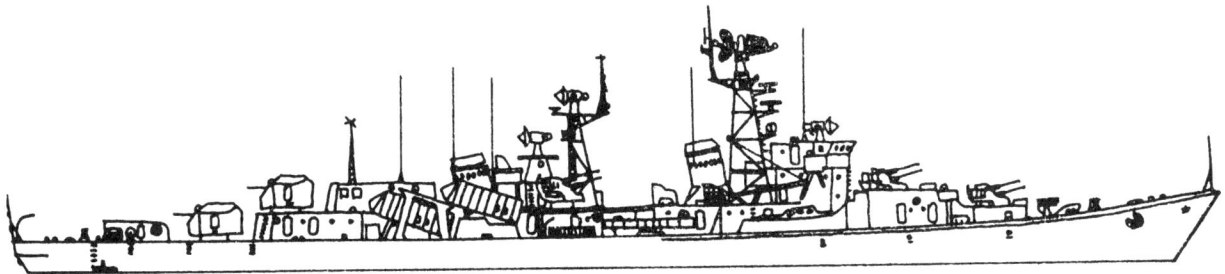

Project: 30 bis and 31

Class Name: SKORY

Names:

	laid down	launched	completed	stricken
Leningrad Yard 190 (Zhdanov)(16 units):				
SMELYY	16 May '48	29 Sept. '48	21 Dec. '49	10 Feb. '65
accomodation ship Murmansk, flooded at Novaya Zemlya				
STOYKIY	16 Nov. '48	1 Feb. '49	18 Apr. '50	22 Feb. '80
SKORYY	30 Mar. '49	14 Aug. '49	26 Sept. '50	to Poland '58 (Wicher)
SUROVYI	17 Aug. '49	1 Oct. '49	31 Oct. '50	11 Feb. '88
SERDITYI	22 Dec. '49	15 Apr. '50	20 Dec. '50	14 Mar. '75
SPOSOBNYY	1 Mar. '50	30 Apr. '50	20 Dec. '50	to Poland 26 Dec. '57 (Grom)
STREMITEL'NYI*	15 May '50	15 Apr. '51	4 July '51	decomm 25 June '84
SOKRUSHITELNYI	15 Sept. '50	30 June '51	28 Nov. '51	18 July '77
SVOBODNYI	27 Nov. '50	20 Aug. '51	23 June '52	19 Jan. '83; to SM-132 1988(?)
STATNYI	1 Mar. '51	23 Oct. '51	4 Aug. '52	8 July '82
SMETLIVYI	24 May '51	17 Nov. '51	5 Aug. '52	to Egypt '56 (Al Zaffer)
SMOTRYASHCHCHII	21 June '51	19 Feb. '52	4 Nov. '52	14 Feb. '78
SOVERSHCHENNYY	16 July '51	24 Apr. '52	20 Dec. '52	5 Mar. '87
SER'EZHNIY	25 Oct. '51	13 July '52	18 Dec. '52	5 Mar. '87
SOLIDNIY	4 Jan. '52	17 Aug. '52	31 Dec. '52	to Egypt '56 (Al Nasser), returned '68, str 15 Apr. '87
STEPENNIY	11 Feb. '52	22 Sept. '52	11 Feb. '53	14 Mar. '86
Nikolaev Yard 200 (61 Kommunar)(18 units):				
BDITELNYY	10 June '48	30 Dec. '48	25 Oct. '49	planned for India; became TsL-83 1960; str 12 Oct. '68
BEZUDERZHNIY	20 July '48	31 Mar. '49	30 Dec. '49	decomm 2 June '76; became PKZ-127 1966
BUIYNIY	15 Apr. '49	23 Sept. '49	29 Aug. '50	hulk at Sevastopol '82 –'83, str 7 Mar. '86
BEZUPRECHNIY	15 July '49	31 Dec. '49	9 Sept. '50	14 Mar. '75
BESSTRASHNIY	19 Sept. '49	31 Mar. '50	2 Nov. '50	decomm 2 June '76
BOEVOIY	21 Dec. '49	29 Apr. '50	19 Dec. '50	to Indonesia '62 (Darmuda)
BYSTRYY	20 Feb. '50	28 June '50	19 Dec. '50	31 July '79
BURNYY	18 May '50	29 Aug. '50	4 June '51	to Egypt '62 (Suez)
BESPOSHCHADNIY	28 May '50	30 Sept. '50	27 June '51	to Egypt '62 (Damietta), returned 1968, str 9 Feb. '88
BEZZHALOSTNIY	12 July '50	30 Dec. '50	6 July '51	to Indonesia '64 (Brawidjaja)
BEZZAVETNYY	28 Sept. '50	30 Mar. '51	11 Nov. '51	to Indonesia '59 (Sultan Iskandar Muda)
BESSHCHUNMIY*	31 Oct. '50	31 May '51	30 Nov. '51	disarmed 15 June '79; to UTS-538 1 Oct. '85
BESPOKOYNYY	16 Jan. '51	30 June '51	21 Dec. '51	to Indonesia '59 (Sandjaja)
BEZBOYAZNENNYY*	28 Mar. '51	31 Aug. '51	11 Jan. '52	decomm 12 Aug. '77; became SM-274 29 July '76
BEZOTKAZNIY	22 June '51	31 Oct. '51	4 Oct. '52	25 Apr. '85
BEZUKORIZNENNYY	29 July '51	31 Jan. '52	10 Dec. '52	3 Jan. '67; became TsL-78 1961
BESSMENNYY	12 Sept. '51	31 Mar. '52	10 Dec. '52	to Egypt '68 (Damietta)
PYLKIY	29 Apr. '52	31 July '52	31 Dec. '52	to Indonesia '64 (Diponegoro)
Komsomolsk-on-Amur (18 units):				
VSTRECHNIY*	29 Apr. '48	20 May '49	7 Dec. '49	planned for India; to SM-302 17 Oct. '72
VEDUSHCHIY	31 July '48	21 Aug. '49	26 Dec. '49	14 Mar. '75
VAZHNYY	30 Oct. '48	4 Sept. '49	29 Dec. '49	14 Mar. '75

VSPYL'CHIVIY	15 Feb. '49	14 May '50	30 Sept. '50	12 Mar. '74; became TsL-77 1960
VELICHAVIY	4 Aug. '49	14 May '50	31 Oct. '50	decomm 12 Aug. '77, str 10 Feb. '78
VERTKIY	5 Nov. '49	22 July '50	14 Dec. '50	decomm 1 Sept. '78, to UTS-286 1975
VECHNIY	12 Jan. '50	30 Aug. '50	15 Dec. '50	to PTB-12 1960, to UTS-27 15 July '71, str 22 Aug. '89
VIKHREVOIY*	28 Feb. '50	15 Sept. '50	27 Dec. '50	7 June '83
VIDNIY	27 May '50	17 May '51	21 Dec. '51	to TsL-90 1961, to UTS-262 12 Feb. '71, decomm 30 May '83
VERNIY*	15 July '50	17 May '51	26 Dec. '51	21 Mar. '81
VNEZAPNIY	23 Sept. '50	14 June '51	28 Dec. '51	to Indonesia '59 (*Sawunggaling*)
VNIMATEL'NIY	31 Oct. '50	2 Aug. '51	26 Dec. '51	to UTS-538; decomm 21 May '81, str 27 July '86
VYRAZIMITEL'NIY	14 Dec. '50	26 Aug. '51	29 Dec. '51	to Indonesia '62 (*Singamangaradja*)
VOLEVOIY	1 Mar. '51	11 Sept. '51	29 Dec. '51	to Indonesia '59 (*Siliwangi*)
VOLNYIY	12 June '51	4 June '52	31 Dec. '52	15 Dec. '81
VKRADCHIVIY	14 July '51	4 June '52	31 Dec. '52	30 Jan. '79
VDUMCHIVYY	5 Nov. '51	31 July '52	31 Dec. '52	decomm 28 Apr. '77; became OT-1 29 July '76
VRAZUMITELNIY	15 Dec. '51	3 Sept. '52	31 Dec. '52	7 Feb. '77

Severodvinsk (18 units):

OGNENNIY*	14 Aug. '48	17 Aug. '49	28 Dec. '49	25 Dec. '79
OTCHETLIVNIY	29 Oct. '48	14 Sept. '49	28 Dec. '49	decomm 19 May '72, to PTB-7 1970
OSTRIY	21 Dec. '48	16 Apr. '50	25 Aug. '50	4 June '83
OTVETSTVENNIY	11 June '49	16 Apr. '50	31 Aug. '50	decomm 12 Apr. '63; to TsL-42 1961; to PKZ-48 1966
OTMENNIY	8 Oct. '49	18 June '50	6 Nov. '50	9 Feb. '78
OTRYVISTIY	3 Dec. '49	28 Aug. '50	10 Dec. '50	7 Feb. '77
OTRAZHAYUSHCHIY	3 Mar. '50	3 Oct. '50	17 Dec. '50	decomm 20 Apr. '67, to TsL-20 31 Aug. '61
OTRADNIY	10 May '50	4 Jan. '51	20 July '51	12 June '84
OZHARENNIY	6 July '50	10 Apr. '51	28 July '51	decomm 31 July '80
OBEREGAYUSHCHIY*	23 Sept. '50	14 May '51	28 Oct. '51	13 Mar. '75; renamed PKZ-12
OKHRANYAYUSHCHIY	25 Nov. '50	26 July '51	28 Nov. '51	27 Feb. '87
OSTOROZHNIY	25 Jan. '51	25 Sept. '51	20 Dec. '51	15 Dec. '81
OKRILENNYY	24 Mar. '51	17 Oct. '51	31 Dec. '51	25 Dec. '78
OTZHIVCHIVIY	30 May '51	29 Dec. '51	20 Dec. '52	18 July '77
OTCHAYANNYY	25 Aug. '51	29 Dec. '51	25 Nov. '52	to Egypt '68 (*Al Nasser*)
OPASNIY*	20 Oct. '51	1 June '52	9 Dec. '52	5 Mar. '87
OZHIVLENNIY	12 Jan. '52	4 Aug. '52	24 Jan. '53	2 June '76
OZHESTOCHENNIY	3 Apr. '52	26 Sept. '52	14 Mar. '53	12 Mar. '71; to TsL-22 1966; later OS-19

Starred units were modernized under Project 31.

Burnyy (Pavlov collection)

Bezboyaznennyy (N. N. Pobyeda)

Suroviy (V. P. Tchernyshov)

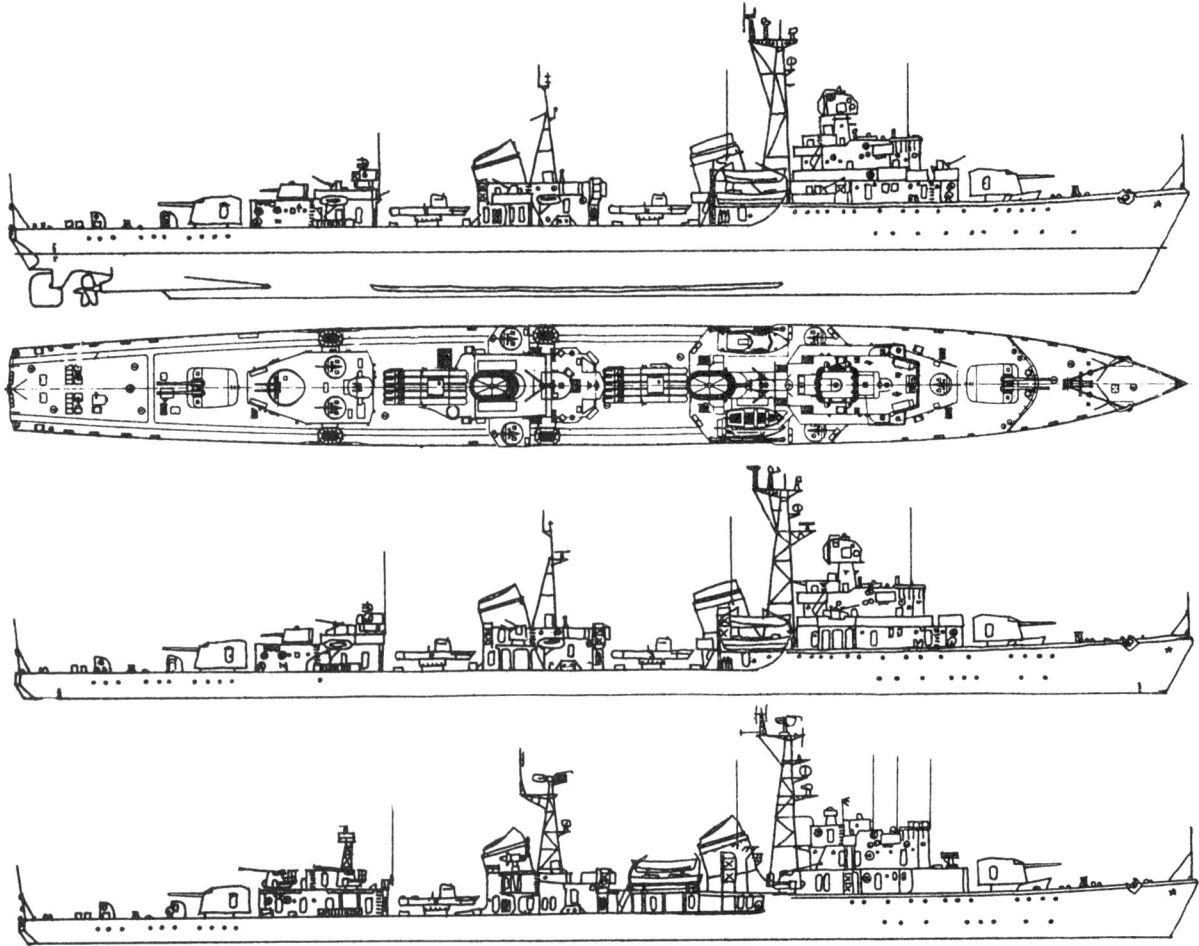

Displacement: 2316/3066 (2495/3273*)

Dimensions: 120.5 × 12 × 4.25 (4.49*)

Armament: 2×2 130 mm (B-2LM, 600 rounds), 1×2 85 mm (92-K, 600 rounds), 7×1 37 mm (70-K) or 4×2 37 mm (V-11, 8000 rounds), 3×2 25 mm (2M-3M, 6000 rounds), 2×5 533 mm TT (PTA-53-30bis, SET-53 and SET-65 torpedoes), 50 depth charges (BB-1) or 52 mines (KB-Krab) or 60 mines (M-26)

Machinery: 4 boilers, 2 steam turbines (TV-6), 2 shafts, 60,000 HP = 35.5 kts, 778 t fuel, 3660 nm/15.7 kts, 940 nm/30 kts

Complement: 280 (18 officers)

Electronics: Radars: Gyuis-1M4, Ryf; ECM: Korall-14*; IFF: Nikel-KM with Khrom-K transponder; Sonar: Tamir-5N (GS-572 Gerkules-2M*)

Chief designer O. L. Fisher (TsKB-53). Units modernized in 1956–61 (Project 31*) had 1×5 533 mm TT removed, 5×1 57 mm (ZiF-71, 3500 rounds) added, and Fut-B radar.

Project: 1135, 1135M (BUREVESTNIK)

NATO Class Name: KRIVAK

Names:

	laid down	launched	completed

KRIVAK I (Project 1135 Burevestnik):

Kaliningrad:

	laid down	launched	completed
BDITELNYY			31 Dec. '70
BODRYY		31 Dec. '71	
SVIREPYY		1971	
STOROZHEVOY			30 Dec. '73
SILNYY*		1972	
RAZYASHCHIY			30 Dec. '74
RASUMNYY		30 Dec. '74	
DRUZHNYY		30 Sept. '75	

Eight units

Kamysch-Burun:

	laid down	launched	completed
DOSTOYNYY	1971		
DOBLESTNYY		1973	
DEYATELNYY		1973	
BEZZAVETNYY			1978
BEZUKORIZNENNYY			Dec. '79
LADNYY		1980	
PORVISTIY		10 Jan. '82	

Seven units

Zhdanov:

	laid down	launched	completed
ZHARKIY*	26 June '76		
RETIVYY		28 Dec. '76	
LENINGRADSKIY KOMSOMOLETS			29 Sept. '77
renamed *Legkiy* Apr. '92			
LETUCHIY		10 Aug. '78	
PYLKIY*		28 Dec. '78	
ZADORNYY		5 Sept. '79	

Six units

KRIVAK II (Project 1135M Burevestnik-M, all built at Kaliningrad):

	laid down	launched	completed
BESSMENNYY		26 Dec. '78	
GORDELIVYY		28 Sept. '79	
GROMKIY		1979	
GROZYASHCHIY			30 Sept. '77
NEUKROTIMYY			Feb. '78
named *Komsomolets Litvy* 1979–91			
PITLIVYY		16 Jan. '82	
RAZITELNYY	11 Feb. '75	1 June '76	31 Dec. '76
REVNOSTNYY		27 Dec. '80	
RESKIY		30 Sept. '76	
REZVYY		1975	
RYANYY		22 Feb. '80	

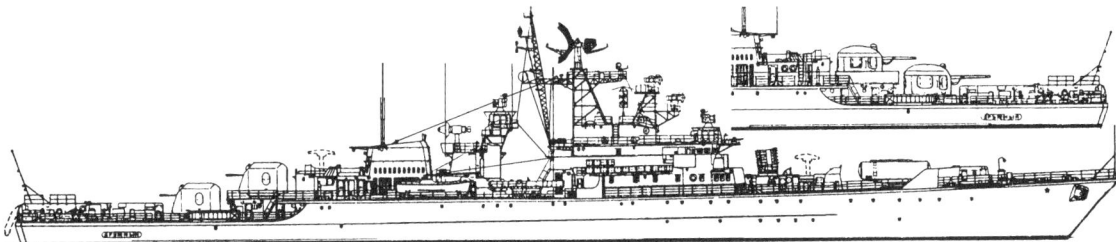

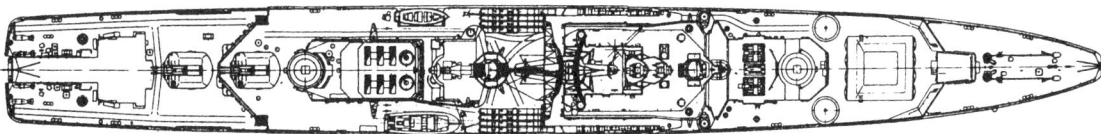

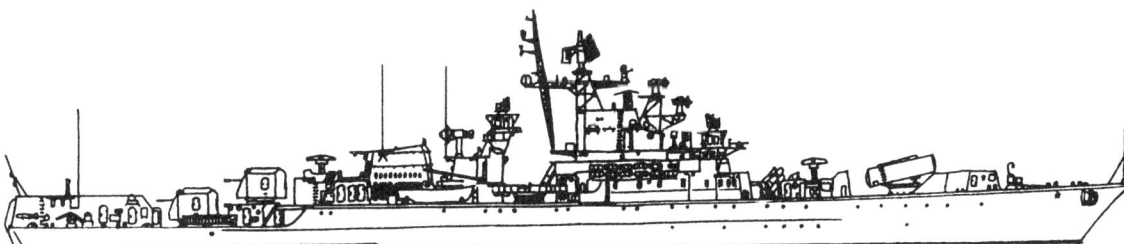

Eleven units

Displacement: 2735/3100

Dimensions: 123.1 × 14.2 × 7.2

Armament: 1×4 missile launcher (KTM-1135) firing rocket-torpedo 85-R Metel', 2×2 missile launchers (ZiF-122) of the Osa (4K-33) missile system (40 missiles: 9M-33), 2×2 76.2 mm (AK-726, 800) or (Project 1135M) 2×1 100 mm (AK-100, 600 rounds), 2×12 rocket launchers RBU 6000 (96 RGB-60), 2×4 533 mm ChTA-53-1135 (4 SET-65 and 4 53-65K torpedoes), plus mines (in overload condition: 16 IGDM-500 or 12 KSM or 14 KRAB

Machinery: 4 gas turbines (2×6000 HP RT-60 cruise, 2×20,000 HP M-3a for boost), 2 shafts, 52,000 HP = 32 kts, 4600 nm/20 kts, 1600 nm/30 kts; generators: 4 DG-600 plus 1 DG-600 for Vega sonar. Endurance 30 days.

Complement: 180 (22 officers, 28 petty officers, 130 sailors)

Electronics: Radar: MR-310U; Navigational radar: Don (later replaced by Volga); Sonar: high-speed search sonar MG-332 Titan-2, VDS Vega, MG-26, non-acoustic sensor MI-110KM; ECM: 4×16 chaff rocket launchers KL-101 (128 rockets); Radio system: Dolina; Gyrocompass: Kurs-5; Sounder: MEL-5; Radio direction-finder ARP-50R

Chief designer: N. P. Sobolev. Originally rated as BPK, then in 1978 redesignated SKR (guard ships). Assigned to Black Sea: *Bezukoriznennyy, Bezzavetnyy, Pitlivyy, Razitelnyy, Deyatelnyy*. Assigned to Pacific: *Grozyashchiy, Gordelivyy, Druzhnyy, Letuchiy, Porvistiy, Razyaschchiy, Reskiy, Ryanyy*. *Storozhevoy* transferred from Baltic to Pacific after 8 Nov. '75 mutiny. *Razyashchiy* was stricken Aug. '92. On 25 Nov. '94 *Porvistiy* was transferred to Vladivostok as a training base. *Grozyashchiy* was stricken in 1994. *Gordelivyy* and *Reskiy* were stricken in 1995 (Pacific).

Ships were modernized under Projects 1135.2, 1135.3, and 1135.6 (chief designer N. P. Sobolev; NATO Krivak IV): *Legkiy* (Feb. '87–Mar. '90), *Letuchiy* (Mar. '87–Apr. '90), *Pylkiy* (1990–92), *Zharkiy* (1991). The RBUs forward were replaced by 2×4 KT-184 launchers for Uran (Kh-35) missiles (3K24 system), and a new sonar was installed.

Bezukoriznennyy (Pavlov collection)

Porvistiy (V. V. Levchenko)

Project: 1135.1 (NEREIY)

NATO Class Name: KRIVAK-3

Names:

All built in Kerch (Zaliv Works).

	laid down	launched	completed	
MENZHINSKIY	1982	1983	Dec. '83	
DZERZHINSKIY	1983	1984	1985	
IMENI XXVII SYEZDA KPSS	– – –	– – –	1986	renamed *Orel* 1991
IMENI 70 LETTIYA VUK KGB	– – –	– – –	1988	*ex Andropov*
IMENI 70-LETTIYA PROGRANVOYSK	– – –	– – –	1988	
KEDROV	1987	1988	1989	
VOROVSKIY	– – –	– – –	Dec. '90	
HETMAN PETRO SAGAIDACHNYY	7 July '93	originally *Latsis*, then *Kirov*; renamed Mar. '92		
HETMAN BAYDA VYSHNEVETSKY	1995	originally *Berzin*, then *Krasny Vympel*; renamed 1992		

The last two units were taken over by Ukraine.

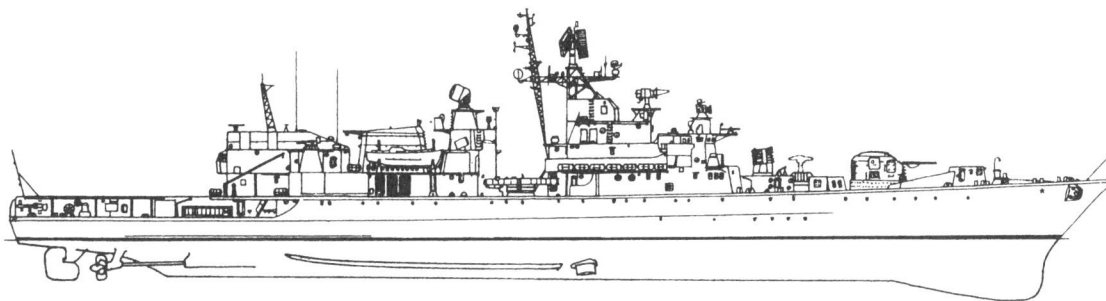

Krivak-3 class (U.S. Navy)

Krivak-3 class (Friedman collection)

Displacement: 2900/3500

Dimensions: 123.5 × 14.2 × 7.3

Armament: 1 helicopter in hangar, 1×2 missile launcher for Osa system (20 missiles), 1 100 mm (AK-100, 350 rounds), 2×6 30 mm (AK-630M, 4000 rounds), 2×12 RBU 6000, 2×4 533 mm TT (ChTA-53-1135)

Machinery: 4 gas turbines (2 RT-60 cruise turbines, 6000 HP each, 2 M-3A boost turbines, 20,000 HP each), 2 shafts, 52,000 HP = 32 kts, 4600 nm/20 kts, 1600 nm/30 kts

Complement: 190

Electronics: Radars: MR-310U Angara, navigational radar Volga; Sonars: MG-332 Titan-2, VDS MG-325 Vega; MI-110 KM non-acoustic detector; Radio system: Dolina; Underwater communications: MG-26, MGS-407, MG-35 Shtil

Border guards ships (PSKR) for the Sea Department of the Border Guard Forces. Chief designer A. K. Shnyrov. First of class arrived in the Pacific Sept. '84.

Project: 1154 (YASTREB)

Class Name: NEUSTRASHIMYY

Names:

	laid down	*launched*	*completed*
All built in Kaliningrad.			
NEUSTRASHIMYY	Apr. '86	May '88	24 Jan. '93
NEPRISTUPNIY	May '88	1990	1995?
TUMAN	1990	1995	1996?
NEUDERZHIMYY		1993	

Displacement: 3590/4200

Dimensions: 129.63 × 15.6 × 8.35

Armament: 1 helicopter in hangar, 4×8 missile launchers for Kinzhal system (32 missiles), 3×2 launchers for rocket-torpedo Vodopod, 4×8 launchers for Uran missile system (not installed), 2 Kortik combination missile-gun systems (32 Igla-M missiles, 3000 rounds), 1 100 mm (AK-100, 350 rounds), 2×6 30 mm (AK-630, 4000 rounds), 1×12 RBU 6000

Machinery: 4 gas turbines (2 M-70 cruise, 10,000 HP each, 2 M-90 boost, 18,500 HP each), 2 shafts, 57,000 HP = 30 kts; 580 t fuel; 3000 nm/18 kts; 2 DG-600 generators. Endurance 30 days.

Complement: 210 (35 officers, 34 petty officers, 141 rated men and seamen)

Electronics: Radar: MR-760 Fregat-MA, navigational radar Vaigach; Sonar system: M-1 Zvezda (with keel and towed arrays); Communications system: Buran; Navigation system: Beisur

Chief designer N. A. Yakovlevskiy (Zelenodolsk PKB). Rated as SKR 2nd Rank. Hull has twelve bulkheads.

[Ed.: According to a late 1996 Russian account, Project 1154 began as a replacement for the Project 1124 (NATO Grisha class) ASW ship. A TTZ released in 1972 called for a small ASW ship of about 800 tons, with a speed of 35 kts, with better armament and a more advanced weapon system (particularly an ASW helicopter, which was then in the final stage of development). By 1975, the approved concept design showed a displacement of 1500 tons, and the ship was reclassified as an ASW escort. In 1976 it was 1700 tons, and at the end of detailed design (1979) displacement was 2000 tons (2500 tons with a helicopter platform). Expected speed was only 27–28 kts. The new small escort was thus about the size of the Project 1135 (NATO Krivak class) SKR. In 1982 a joint resolution of the State Shipbuilding Committee called for parallel development of Project 1154 and of Project 1135.1 (NATO Krivak-3); it seems fairer to see Project 1135.1 as an interim attempt to put Project 1154 systems (such as the ASW helicopter) in the existing hull. Ultimately Project 1154 would use the Project 1135 powerplant. Both ships were described as convoy or task force escorts capable of anti-air, anti-submarine, and anti-ship warfare. In the event, Project 1135.1 was turned over to the Maritime Border Guards. However, her designed weapon system (except for the sonar, which would require a special hull form, and the AAW missiles and gun/missile system) probably matched that planned for Project 1154. The article credits Project 1154 with rocket-thrown torpedoes (RPK-7, NATO SS-N-15) as well as conventional ASW torpedoes. Note that the failure of the attempt to design a viable Grisha replacement may explain both the purchase of "Parchim" class corvettes from East Germany and the Grisha modernization program, the latter dating from about 1982.]

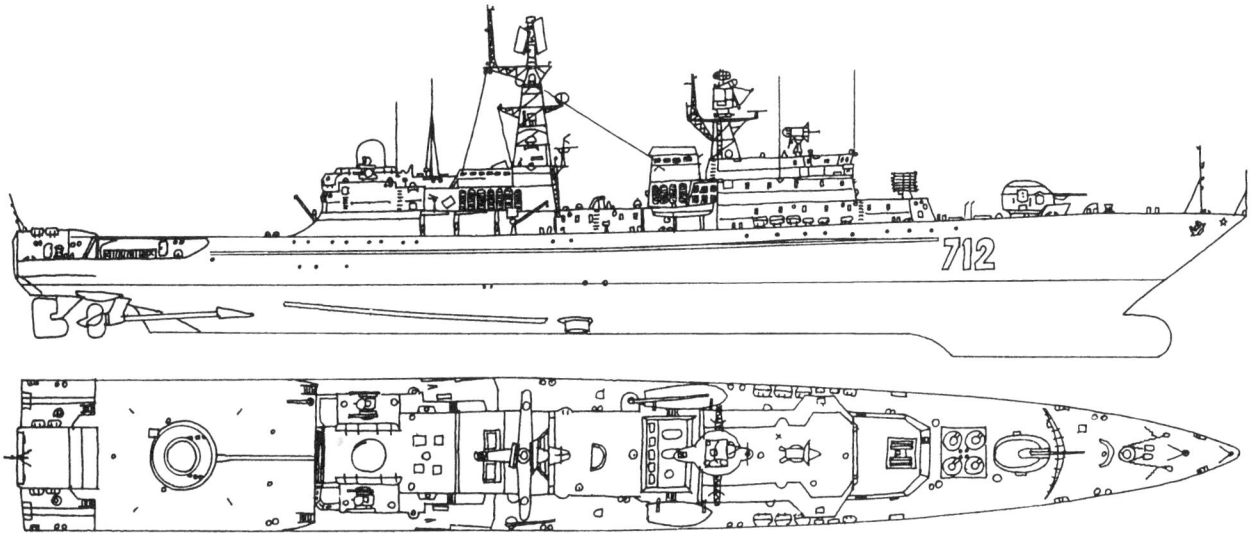

Nepristupniy (Pavlov collection)

Project: 42

NATO Class Name: KOLA

Names:

	laid down	launched	completed
SOKOL	17 Aug. '49	11 Sept. '50	delivered 30 Jan. '51

renamed *Komsomolets Azerbaidzhana* 1956

		launched	
BERKUT		10 May '52	
KONDOR		10 May '52	

renamed *Sovetskiy Azerbaidzhan* 1956

		launched	
GRIF		25 Oct. '52	
KRECHET		18 Dec. '52	

renamed *Sovietskiy Dagestan* 1956

		launched	
ORLAN		10 May '52	

renamed *Sovietskiy Turkmenistan* 1956

		launched	
LEV		17 Mar. '53	
TIGR		25 Apr. '53	

All were built at Kaliningrad.

Displacement: 1339/1679

Dimensions: 96.1 × 11 × 3.36

Armament: 4×1 100 mm (B-34 U-SM, 1080 rounds), 2×2 37 mm (V-11M, 5400 rounds), 1×3 533 mm TTA 53-42, 2×16 RBU-2500 (128 RGB-25), 4 BMB-1 depth charge throwers

Machinery: 2 KV-42 boilers, 2 TV-10 steam turbines, 2 shafts, 28,000 HP = 29.6 kts, 2265 nm/14 kts; 1 DG-100 generator. Endurance 10 days.

Complement: 211

Electronics: Radar: Ryf, navigational radar Visla; Sonar: Gerkules (originally Tamir-10); Radar: Ryf, Gius 1m-4, Visla; IFF: Nikel (interrogator)- Khrom-K (transponder); Radio transmitter: Tulpan; Gyro-compass: Kurs-3

Chief designer: D. D. Zhukovskiy (TsKB-32). Transferred from Baltic to Caspian Flotilla: *Sokol, Orlan, Krechet, Kondor* (stricken 1972–73). Pacific: *Grif, Berkut* (later UTS-7). Black Sea: *Lev, Tigr.*

[Ed.: According to Shitikov et al., this design was chosen instead of an improved Project 29, Project 29bis. As conceived in 1947, Project 29bis would have displaced 1300 t, would have had a speed of 27.5 kts and a range of about 2300 nm, and would have been armed with 3–100 mm, 6–37 mm, and 1 triple 533 mm TT. The OTZ for Project 42 called for 1900–2000 t, 27 kts, 5000 nm range, and an armament of 4–130 mm, 8–45 mm, 12–25 mm, and 1 triple 533 mm TT. TsKB-17 and TsKB-32 both submitted alternative steam and diesel designs; ironically, the one finally chosen was not too far from Project 29bis. Other alternatives were Projects 37 and 39. As in the case of the Project 41 destroyer, production of this design was ordered stopped in favor of a simpler and less expensive one, Project 50 *(Riga).*]

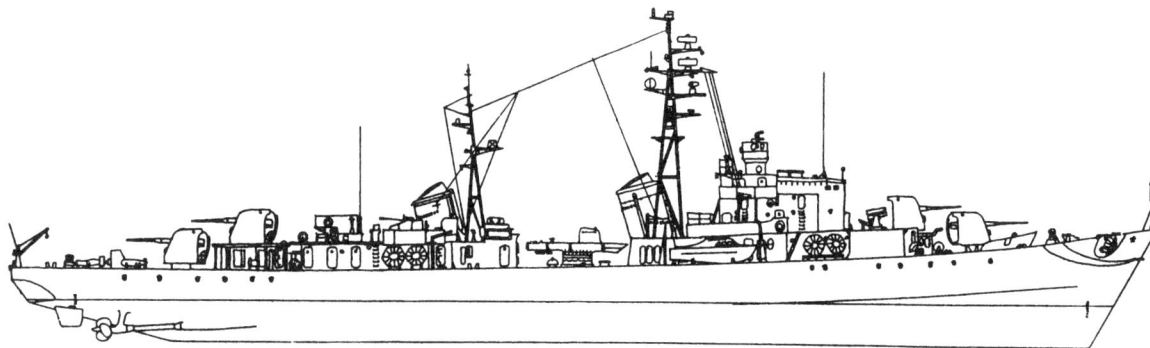

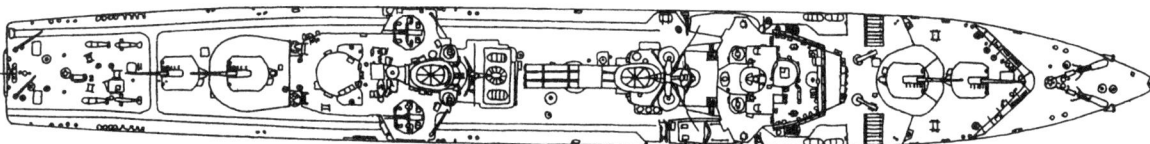

Kondor (A. N. Sokolov)

Project: 50
NATO Class Name: RIGA
Names:

completed

Nikolaev (20 units):

GORNOSTAY	
PANTERA	21 May '54
renamed *Komsomolets Gruzhiy* 28 Oct. '79	
RYS'	21 May '54
YAGUAR	24 Apr. '54
SARICH	31 Aug. '54
PUMA	31 Aug. '54
VOLK	31 Oct. '54
KUNITSA	23 Dec. '54
KORSAK	30 Dec. '54
NORKA	30 Apr. '55
GRIFON	30 June '55
SKR-51	28 Sept. '55
SKR-53	31 Dec. '55
SKR-57	28 Feb. '56
SKR-58	7 May '56
SKR-63	30 May '56
SKR-66	29 Sept. '56
SKR-67	22 Dec. '56
VORON	18 June '55
SKR-52	26 Nov. '55 renamed *Tuman* 10 Aug. '62

Komsomolsk (7 units):

ZUBR	31 May '54
BIZON	30 June '54

AIST	27 Aug. '54
LASKA	25 Oct. '54
PELIKAN	30 Nov. '54
PINGVIN	31 Dec. '54
GEPARD	31 Dec. '54

Kaliningrad (41 units):

LEOPARD	30 June '54
BARS	
l.d. 25 Apr. '52, lch 25 June '53, completed 30 June '54	
ROSOMAKHA	30 Apr. '54
SOBOL'	13 Oct. '54
BARSUK	15 Sept. '54
KUGUAR	31 Apr. '54
ENOT	30 Oct. '54
FILIN	9 Dec. '54
LUN'	27 Dec. '54
KOBCHIK	31 May '55
TUR	31 May '55
LOS'	31 June '55
OLEN'	27 Aug. '55
SKR-50	26 Oct. '55
SKR-54	1956
SKR-56	21 May '56
SKR-59	25 May '56
SKR-60	20 June '56
SKR-61	23 Aug. '56
SKR-62	25 Sept. '56
named *Irkutskii Komsomolets* 27 Oct. '69	
SKR-64	31 Oct. '56
named *Komsomolets Litvy* 12 Oct. '62	

SKR-65	27 Dec. '56
SKR-68	23 Mar. '57
SKR-69	30 May '57
SKR-70	20 June '57
SKR-71	13 July '57
SKR-72	13 July '57
SKR-73	30 Nov. '57
SKR-74	26 Nov. '57
SKR-55	1957
SKR-75	30 Dec. '57
SKR-76	15 June '58

named *Arkhangelskii Komsomolets* 25 Oct. '68

SKR-77	29 June '58
SKR-80	31 July '58
SKR-81	31 Aug. '58
SKR-10	21 Oct. '58
SKR-4	13 Dec. '58
SKR-5	31 Dec. '58
SKR-8	31 Dec. '58
SKR-14	
SKR-15	

The lead ship, *Gornostay,* was laid down on 20 Dec. '51, launched 30 July '52, and began builder's trials 13 Jan. '53.

Displacement: 1068/1200

Dimensions: 91 × 10.2 × 2.7

Armament: 3 100 mm (B-34 USM, 600 rounds), 2×2 37 mm (V-11M, 4500 rounds), 1×6 MBU-200, 4×1 BMB-2, 48 BGB, 26 mines, 1×3 533 mm TT (TTA-53-50) or 1×2 533 mm (DTA-53-50) with 3 or 2 SET-65, 53-51, or 53-39 (as modernized after 1960) U torpedoes

Machinery: 2 KBG-57/28 boilers (370°, 28 atm), 2 steam turbines (TV-10), 2 shafts, 20,000 HP = 29 kts, 2000 nm/14 kts, 320 nm/29 kts. Generators: 2 TG-150, 1 DG-100, 1 DG-25. Endurance 10 days.

Complement: 168

Electronics: Radar: Gius 1M-4 (later Ryf), Yakor´, Lin´ (later Neptune); Sonar: Pegas-2, MG-26; Gyro-compass: Kurs-3

Chief designer V. I. Neganov (TsKB-820). The TTZ was issued on 20 July '50, and the technical project (design) approved on 21 Aug '51. Note that these ships had 7–8 mm protection over their machinery, gunshields, and bridge. Surviving units were stricken 1986–92. Of these, SKR-50 was stricken in the Pacific in 1987. SKR-4, SKR-10, SKR-61, SKR-73, SKR-74, SKR-75 were stricken 1989. *Tuman*, SKR-57, SKR-70 were stricken in the Northern Fleet in 1988–90.

Transfers: Bulgaria (SKR-53 in 1957 [*Derzkiy*], SKR-66 on 15 Oct. '58 [*Smelyy*], *Kobchik* in 1986 [*Bodriy*]), East Germany (*Barsuk* [*Sassnitz*] 22 Nov. '56; *Enot, Tur, Olen'* in 1957), Finland (SKR-69, *Filin* in 1957), Indonesia (*Aist, Bizon, Grifon, Zubr, Korsak, Puma, Pelikan, Sarich* '64–'66).

Zubr (G. G. Kiselev)

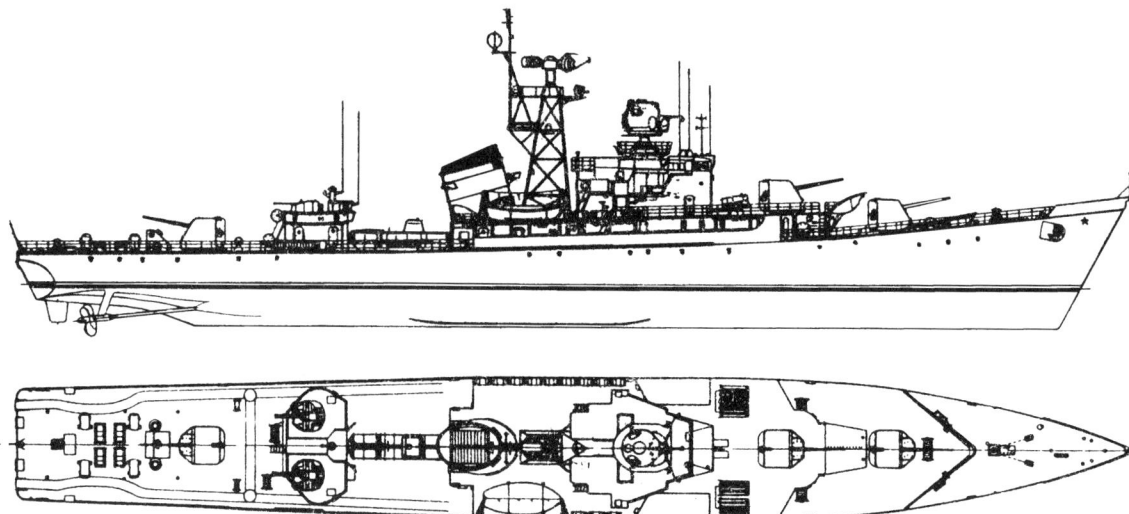

Project: 1159T

NATO Class Name: KONI

Names:

SKR-451

DEL'FIN

Displacement: 1515/1670

Dimensions: 95.51 × 12.55 × 4.12 (5.72 with sonar dome down)

Armament: 2×2 76.2 mm (AK-726, 1200 rounds), 2×2 30 mm (AK-230), 1×2 ZiF-122 missile launchers for 4K-33 system (20 missiles: 9M-33), 2×12 RBU 6000 (96 RGB-60 rockets), 2 depth bomb throwers, 20 mines

Machinery: 2 diesels (68-B, 6000 HP each, on wing shafts), 1 gas turbine (M-81E boost engine, 18,000 HP, on center shaft), 3 shafts, 27 kts (22 kts on diesels), 18,000 nm/14 kts

Complement: 130

Electronics: Radar: Fut-N; Sonar: Vychegda; ESM: Bizan-4B

Built in Zelenodolsk in 1976, on Black Sea to train foreign crews. To Bulgaria 1990 (*Smelyy*). Export units (including *Nerga*, SKR-29, SKR-125, SKR-195, SKR-471, SKR-481 temporarily in Soviet Navy):

Algeria: four: 20 Dec. '80, 24 Mar. '82, 2 in Oct. '84

Cuba: three: Sept. '81, Feb. '84, Apr. '88

East Germany: three: 25 July '78, 10 May '79, 23 Nov. '85

Libya: two: 30 June '87 and 28 June '88 (version with Termit missiles)

Yugoslavia: two: Apr. '80 and Dec. '82

[Ed.: Western sources list only three units to Algeria, and two to Cuba.]

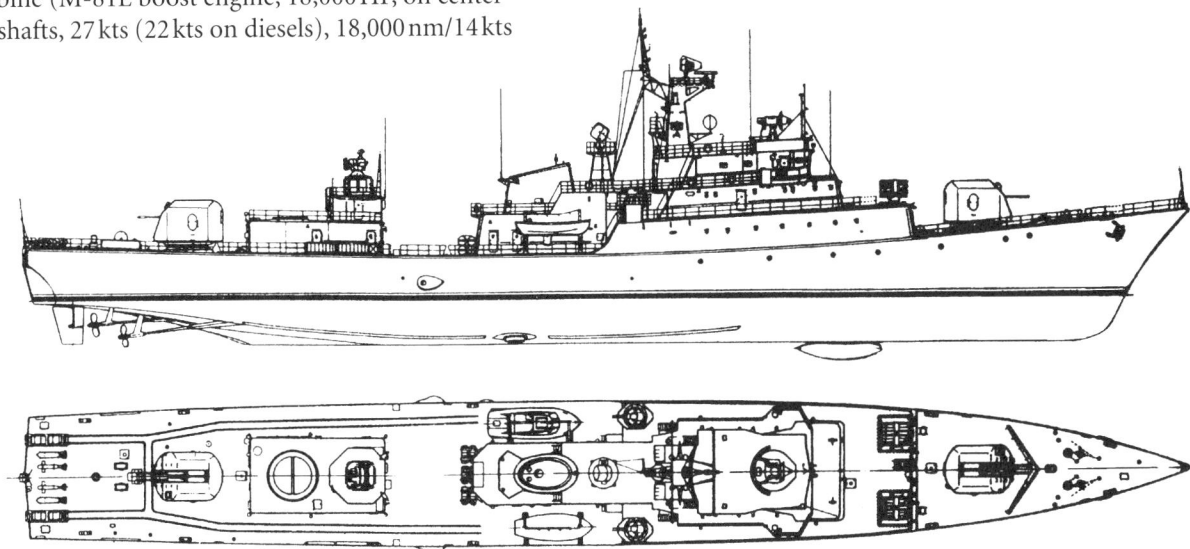

Delfin (V. V. Kostrichenko)

139

Project: 35 and 35-M*

NATO Class Name: MIRKA 1, 2*

Names:

GANGUTETS
   l.d. 26 Jan. '61, lch 23 Mar. '62, completed 25 Dec. '64

IVAN SLADKOV

SKR-6

SKR-7

SKR-9

SKR-12

SKR-13

SKR-19

SKR-20

SKR-22

SKR-26

SKR-32

SKR-48

SKR-83   named *60 Let Komsomola Belorussii* 9 June '80

SKR-84

SKR-86

SKR-87

SKR-117

Eighteen units. Built in Kaliningrad through 1967; nine units per year.

Displacement: 960/1140

Dimensions: 82.4 × 9.1 × 3 m (5.84 with sonar dome lowered)

Armament: 2×2 76 mm (AK-726), 4×12 RBU 6000, 1×5 406 mm TT, 2×12 RBU 6000, 2×5 406 mm TT*

Machinery: 2 gas turbines (D-3, 18,000 HP each) and 2 diesels (61-B, 6000 HP each), 2 shafts in tunnels for increased propulsive efficiency in rough seas; 48,000 HP = 32 kts (gas turbines; 20 kts on diesels); 2000 nm/14 kts, 1400 nm/18 kts, 500 nm/30 kts; generators: 1 DG-500, 1 DG-200, 1 DG-100. Endurance 10 days.

Complement: 96

Electronics: Radar: Rubka; ESM: Bizan'; Sonars: Titan and Vychegda

Modernized in 1974 with new radar (Palinas) and sonar (Rys'-K). Black Sea units: SKR-6, SKR-13, SKR-84, SKR-117. *Sladkov* was stricken in 1991.

[Ed.: Chief designer N. Kh. Zheliaskov. This design began as a modernized Project 159 (see below) using the two-shaft machinery of Project 204 *(Poti)*, which was expected to be quieter, to add about 3–4 kts on diesel power, and to offer better maneuverability since both shafts could reverse. The fixed sonar was replaced by a retractable type (which reduced draft by 3 m) and the RBU-2500s were replaced by RBU-6000s. On this basis an abridged technical design was conducted and approved in Dec. '57. This design included equipment to receive sonobuoy signals. Like the *Petyas* described below, these ships were modernized with improved sonars in the 1970s (mainly by installation of Vega towed sonars), increasing detection range at 18 kts by a factor of 3 to 3.5.]

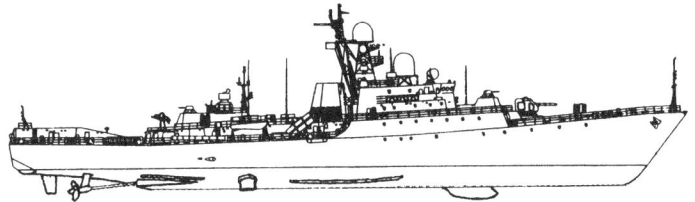

Design 35 (Pavlov collection)

Mirka-2 class (U.S. Navy)

Gangutets (G. G. Kiselev)

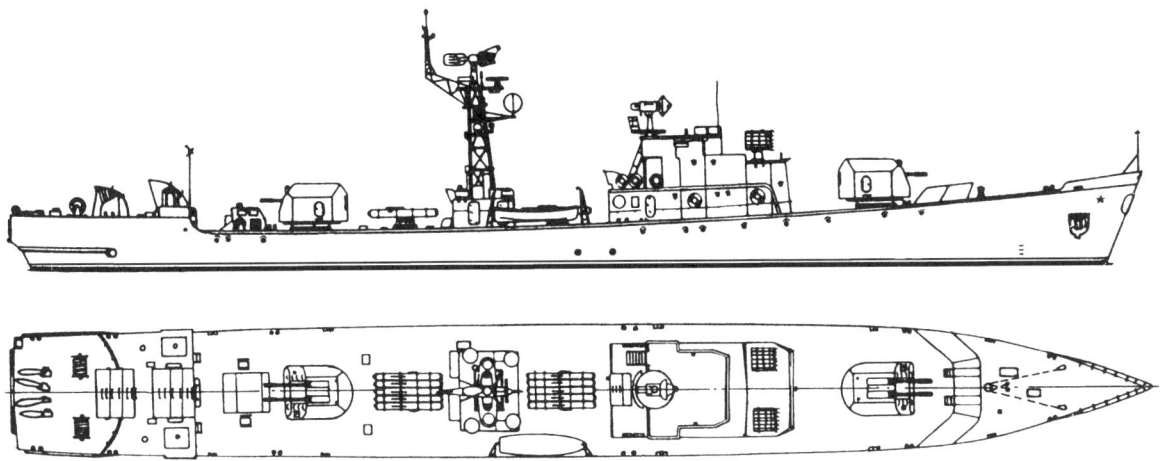

Mirka-1 class (U.S. Navy)

Project: 159, 159-A, 159 AE, and 159M

NATO Class Name: PETYA

Names:

	completed
SKR-2	
SKR-3	
SKR-11	
SKR-15	
SKR-16	
SKR-21	
named *Orlovskii Komsomolets* 12 Mar. '79–18 Mar. '92	
SKR-22 named *Timofey Ulyantsev*	
SKR-23	
SKR-27	
SKR-33–36	
SKR-38	
SKR-40	
SKR-41	
SKR-43	
SKR-46	
SKR-47	
SKR-78	
SKR-82	14 May '77
SKR-90	
SKR-92	
SKR-96	29 July '78
SKR-98	
SKR-103	
SKR-110	
SKR-112	
SKR-115	
SKR-120	
SKR-126	
SKR-128	30 Oct. '72
SKR-130	
SKR-133	31 Dec. '70
SKR-135	26 Dec. '72
SKR-138	30 Sept. '71
SKR-141	31 Dec. '71

Thirty-seven units. Built by Kaliningrad (twenty-two including exports) and Khabarovsk (thirty-two including exports): lead ship by Kaliningrad 1960–61. Khabarovsk production amounted to nine Project 159 Petya I completed 1961–66: SKR-3, SKR-11, SKR-15, SKR-21, SKR-23, SKR-41, SKR-43, SKR-46, SKR-47; eight Project 159A completed 1967–72; eleven Project 159AE completed 1968–77 for India; four Project 159M (completed 1973, 1974, 1976, 1982). Lead ship (159) l.d. 31 Aug. '57, lch 31 Aug. '59, completed 26 Dec. '61. Lead ship (159A) l.d. 10 Dec. '64, lch 27 Mar. '66, completed 30 Dec. '66.

Displacement: 900/1040

Dimensions: 81.8 × 9.2 × 2.72 (5.82 with sonar dome down)

Armament: 2×2 76 mm (AK-726), 4×16 RBU 2500 (Project 159) or 2×16 RBU 2500 (Project 159A) or 2×12 RBU 6000; 1×5 or 2×5 (Project 159A) 406 mm PTA-40-159 (5 SET-40 torpedoes), 22 mines [Ed.: As modernized beginning in '73: 2 after RBU 2500 and 1 depth charge track removed, Vega dipping sonar added.]

Armor: 15 mm on deckhouse

Machinery: 2 gas turbines (M-2, 15,000 HP each) and 1 diesel (61B, 6000 HP, on center shaft with controllable-pitch propeller), 3 shafts, 32 kts, 2000 nm/14 kts, 1500 nm/16.5 kts, 800 nm/18 kts; 130 t fuel. Endurance 10 days.

Complement: 96 (8 officers, 6 petty officers, 27 rated men, 55 sailors)

Electronics: Radar: Fut-N (Rubka in 159A); ESM: Bizan'-4b; Sonar: Titan (scanning search sonar), Vychegda [Ed: fire control sonar].

Chief designer A. V. Pkhov (TsKB-340), nine bulkheads. Compartments: (i) forepeak, chain locker, capstain; (ii) (Fr 20–22) crews' quarters, provisions; (iii) (Fr 22–36) magazines, refrigerators, quarters, power unit; (iv)(Fr 36–50) radio room, gyro, magazine; (v) (Fr 56–75) machinery control, DG-400, boiler, forward engine room with gas turbines; (vi) (Fr 75–81) machinery control room, magazines; (vii) (Fr 81–95) DG-100 and DG-200, after engine room; (viii) (Fr 95–115) storerooms; (ix) (Fr 121–130) sternpost

Rated as anti-submarine ships of 3rd Rank (PLK-3), then SKR. Rebuilt as test ships: OS-34, OS-332, OS-333. OS-332 was used to test the Vikhr' ASW system. Another was used to tow a sonar. All OS were armed with 1×2 76 mm.

Transfers: 3 for Ethiopia (1 July '83, 2 May '84; SKR-130, SKR-141, both 159A), 2 for Syria, 5 for Vietnam (2 in Dec. '78, 2 in Dec. '83, 1 in Jan. '84). Black Sea ships: SKR-27, SKR-110. Ukrainian Navy: SKR-112. Caspian Flotilla of Azerbaidzhan: SKR-116.

[Ed.: According to Burov, the first TTZ for this type, envisaged as a developed *Kronstadt* (Project 122bis), was drawn up in 1947 but abandoned because the required armament and machinery did not yet exist. It was revived in 1955; the sketch design was approved 30 Sept. '55 and the technical design on 7 Sept. '56. Initially only a single experimental ship was planned, but series construction was approved in 1957. Titan/Vychegda was the first Soviet second-generation sonar; Titan could detect submarines at 21 to 24 kts at 1.5 nm, providing data to the fire control system, whose Vychegda sonar could maintain contact at 24 to 32 kts. Their fixed dome used a titanium window, the first use of that metal in a surface combatant. All machinery was of a new type, specially designed for this class. Silencing measures included sound-mounted machinery and bubble screens for the propellers (initially using air bled from the leading edge, later air from holes in the blades). The main command post (GKP) was protected by 15 mm splinter armor. The improved Project 159A was designed in 1964 (after a Mar. '64 decision), and in 1968 the class was ordered modernized (the first unit was completed in 1973) with Vega dipping sonars. To maintain stability, 125 tons of solid ballast had to be carried, and overall displacement increased 70 tons.]

SKR-82 (V. V. Lyubimov)

SKR-112 (source unknown)

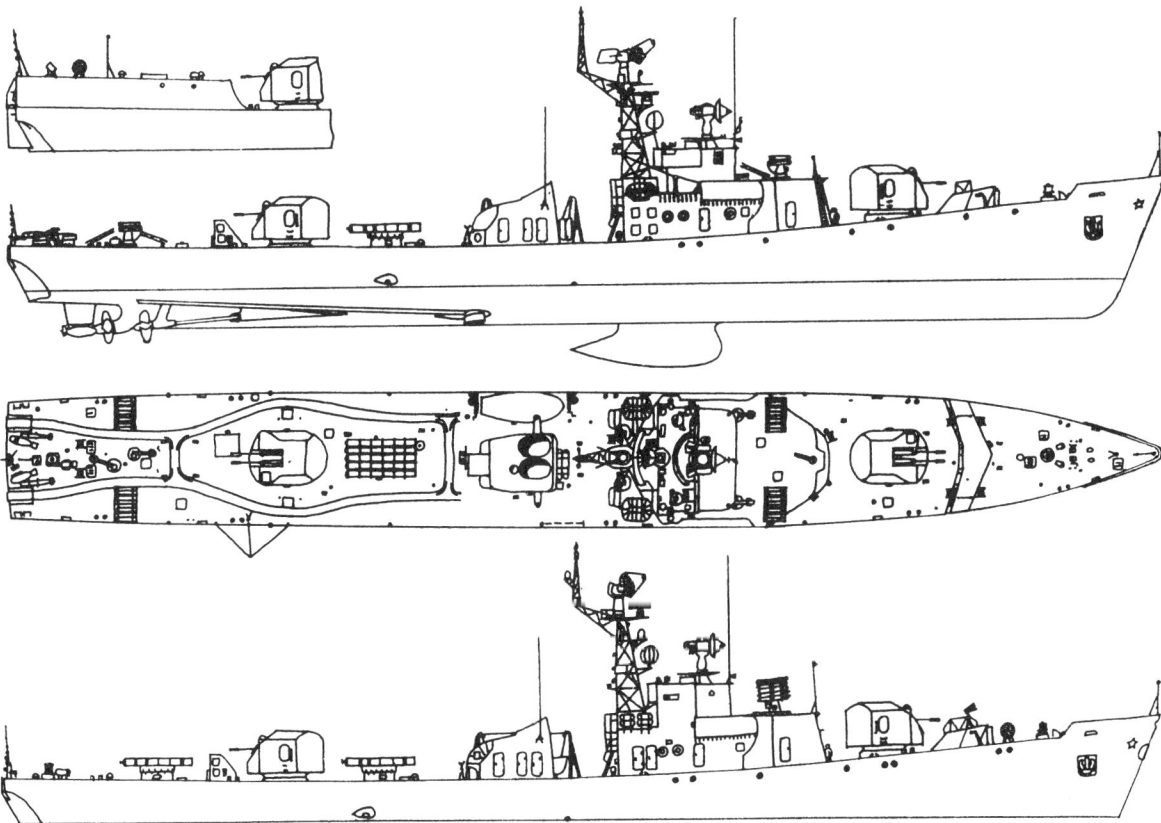

Project: 1239 (SIVUCH)

NATO Class Name: DERGACH

Names:

BORA   ex-MRK-27, renamed Mar. '92

SAMUM   1991   ex-MRK-17, renamed 1992
   Built in Zelenodolsk.

Displacement: 910/1260

Dimensions: 65.6 × 17.2 × 1.7

Armament: 2×4 launchers for Moskit missile, 1×2 launcher for Osa-M, 1 76 mm (AK-726), 2×6 30 mm (AK-630)

Machinery: 2 gas turbines (M-10-1, 20,000 HP each, with tandem propellers on retractable outboard legs), 2 diesels (M-504, 3300 HP each, for lift fans), 50 kts, 2500 nm/12 kts, 800 nm/45 kts

Complement: 35

Electronics: Radars: Ekran, navigational radar Don
   Technical assignment given 4 Jan. '74; project (design) approved 24 Dec. '80. A series of five units was planned. Models for Project 1239 *Ikar* and *Strelets* were tested. Chief designer L. V. Vel'skiy (TsKB Almaz). Twin-hulled surface-effect ship with skegs. Baltic and Black Sea Fleets.

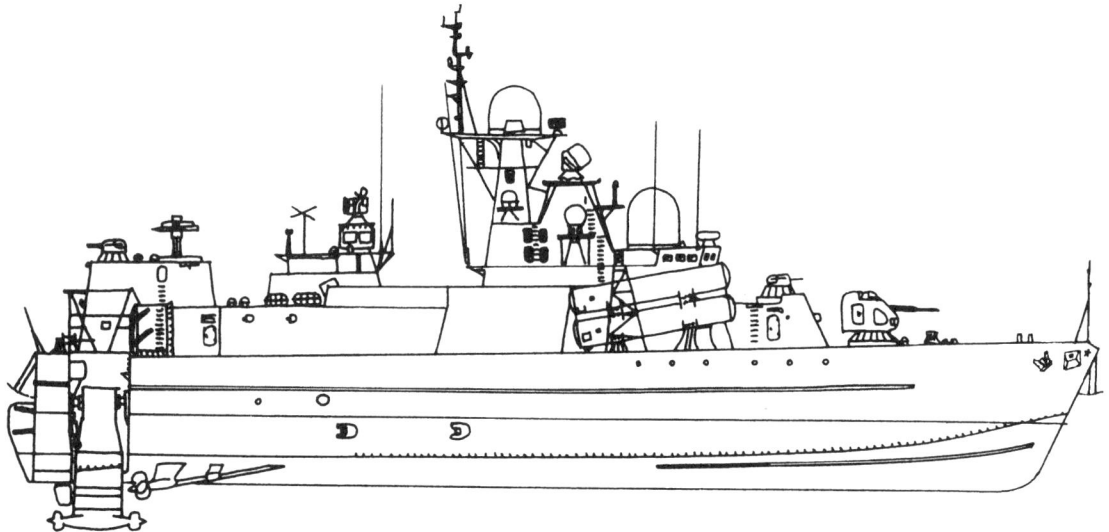

MRK-27 (V. V. Kostrichenko)

Project: 1240 (URAGAN)

NATO Class Name: SARANCHA

Names:

MRK-5

Displacement: 390/424

Dimensions: 44.4 × 14.2 × 2.8 (50.6 × 23.5 × 5.6)

Armament: 2×2 launchers for Malakhit P-120 missiles,
1×2 launchers for Osa-M missiles, 1×2 30 mm (AK-213)

MRK-5 (A. N. Sokolov)

MRK-5 (M. L. Makarov)

Machinery: 2 gas turbines (M-813, 18,000 HP each, driving tandem screws on retractable outboard legs folding aft), 2 diesels (M-401, 1200 HP each, driving pump jets), 55 kts foilborne (57 kts maximum); 8 kts hullborne. Generators: 3 TG- 100, 2 DG-100. 640 nm/45 kts.

Complement:—
   Chief designer: V. M. Burlakov (TsKB Almaz). Automatically stabilized for rough seas (kept roll to 2°). Due to high maintenance cost, was stricken after a pump jet broke down in 1991. Black Sea.

Project: 1234 (OVOD)
NATO Class Name: NANUCHKA 1
Names:

	completed	
BURYA ex-MRK-3	Sept. '70	renamed 25 Apr. '70
BRIZ ex-MRK-7, renamed 25 Apr. '70		
VIKHR'		
VOLNA		
GRAD		
GROZA		
GROM		
ZARNITSA		
ZARYA		
MOLNIYA		
METEL'		
RADUGA		
TAIFUN	30 Dec. '79	
TSIKLON		
SHTORM		
SHKVAL		
Sixteen units		

Displacement: 560/700

Dimensions: 59.3 × 12.2 × 2.6

Armament: 2×3 launchers for Malakhit missiles, 1×2 launcher for Osa-M system (20 missiles), 1×2 57 mm (AK-725)

Machinery: 3 diesels (M-507A, 10,000 HP each), 3 shafts, 35 kts, 4000 nm/12 kts, 1600 nm/18 kts, 900 nm/31 kts. Generators: 3 DG-300, 2 DG-75.

Complement: 60 (10 officers)

Electronics: Radar: Titanit

Chief designer I. P. Pyegov (TsKB Almaz). Built under a decree of 29 May '64. TTZ approved 17 Aug. '65. Built in Leningrad (Almaz Works, through 1976) and Vladivostok (1978–1981, lead ship *Taifun*). *Nanuchka II* (Termit missiles, Rangout radar) was built for export: three for Algeria (1981–83: *Zib', Leevyen, Burun)*, three for India *(Priliv, Priboiy, Uragan)*, four for Libya (1 in 1981, 1 in 1983, 1 in Feb. '84, and 1 in Sept. '85; 1 sunk 25 Mar. '86), four for Syria. *Grom, Groza, Zarnitsa, Burya* (lead ship) to breakers Sept. '91. *Briz* and *Vikhr'* to Pacific Sept. '91. *Briz* stricken 1992. *Tsiklon* and *Vikhr* stricken 1994. *Taifun* (Pacific) stricken 1995.

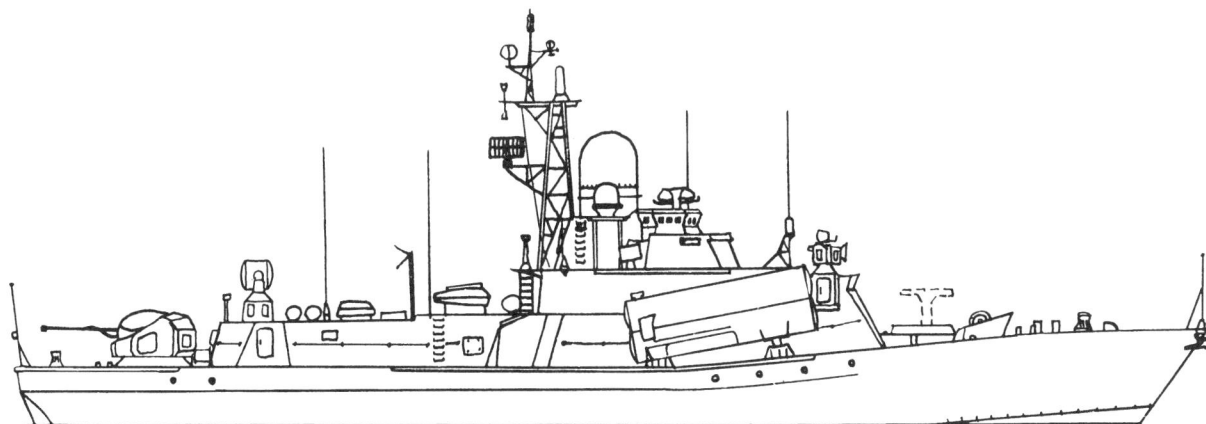

Burya (Pavlov collection)

147

Project: 1234.1 and 1234.7

NATO Class Name: NANUCHKA 3

Names:

	completed
	completed
BURUN	1977
VETER	1977
SHTIL'	1978 originally *Zib'*, renamed *Komsomolets Mordoviy* 28 Apr. '82, renamed 18 Mar. '92
AISBERG	1978
TUCHA	1978
URAGAN	1979
PRILIV	1980
NAKAT*	1980
MIRAZH	1981
MUSSON	30 Dec. '81
METEOR	1982
RASSVET	1982
GEIZER	1983
PASSAT	1983
PEREKAT	1983
PRIBOIY	1984
SMERCH	30 Dec. '84
MOROZ	1989
RAZLIV	1991
ENEIY	18 Feb. '88 originally *Leevyen*, renamed *XX S'yezd Vlksm* Apr. '87, renamed again 15 Feb. '92
ZIB'	1988
LEEVYEN'	1991

Total of 22 units, built in Leningrad (Almaz works; *Burun* was lead ship) 1979–91. Small missile ships of 3rd Rank.

Burun (U.S. Naval Institute Photographic Collection)

Nanuchka 3 class (U.S. Naval Institute Photographic Collection)

Displacement: 639/730

Dimensions: $59.3 \times 11.8 \times 2.9$

Armament: 2×3 launchers for Malakhit P-120 missiles, 2×6 launchers for Uran* missiles, 1×2 launcher (ZiF-122) for Osa missiles (20 missiles), 1 76 mm (AK-176), 1×6 30 mm (AK- 630)

Machinery: 3 diesels (M-507, 10,000 HP each), 3 shafts, 30,000 HP = 34 kts, 3500 nm/12 kts, 2100 nm/18 kts, 415 nm/34 kts

Complement: 60 (10 officers)

Electronics: Radars: Dubrava, Titanit

Garpun radar on *Nakat* (*) has outstanding ECCM. It can simultaneously track 15 targets and can obtain bearings on 6 under heavy jamming. Range: 120 km active, 500 km passive. Black Sea ships: *Mirazh, Shtil'*.

Musson sank in the Pacific after a direct hit by a missile on 16 Apr. '87; 39 men were lost.

Project: 1241RE, 1241.1, 1241.7, and 1241.9 (MOLNIYA)

NATO Class Name: TARANTUL 1, 2, 3, 4

Names:

R-5	named *Kalingradskiy Komsomolets* 9 June '80–Apr. '92
R-11	
R-14	
R-16	
R-18	
R-19	
R-20	
R-24	
R-26	
R-28	
R-33	
R-42	
R-45	
R-46	
R-47	
R-48	
R-52	
R-54	KRASNODARSKIY KOMSOMOLETS
R-66	
R-69	
R-71*	
R-74	
R-75	
R 76	
R 79	
R-83	
R-85	
R-86	
R-88	
R-98	

R-99	
R-100	
R-103	
R-104	
R-109	
R-113	
R-115	
R-141	KRONSTADSKIY KOMSOMOLETS
R-142	
R-143	
R-144	
R-145	
R-158	
R-160	POLTAVSKIY KOMSOMOLETS
R-162	
R-164	
R-176	
R-177	
R-179	
R-229	
R-230	
R-239	
R-240	
R-255	KIROVSKIY KOMSOMOLETS
R-261	
R-297	
R-298	
R-334	
R-442	

Displacement: 460/469

Dimensions: $56.1 \times 10.2 \times 2.65$

Armament: 2×2 launchers for Termit missiles or 2×2 launchers for Moskit missiles (Project 1241.9), 1×2 launcher for Strela-3 missiles, 1 76 mm (AK-176, 314

Molnija-II (Pavlov collection)

Design 1241.7 (Pavlov collection)

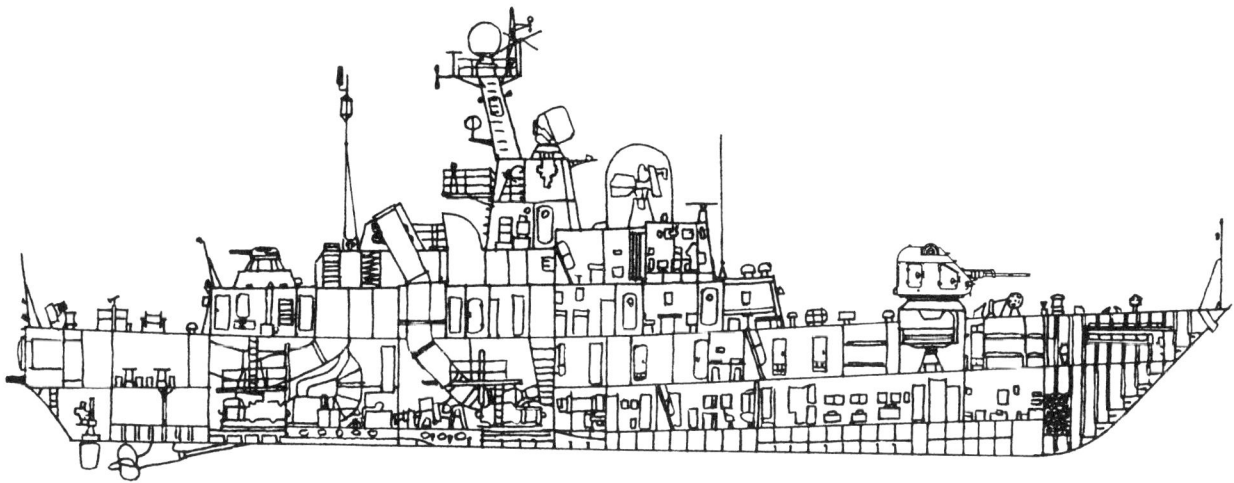

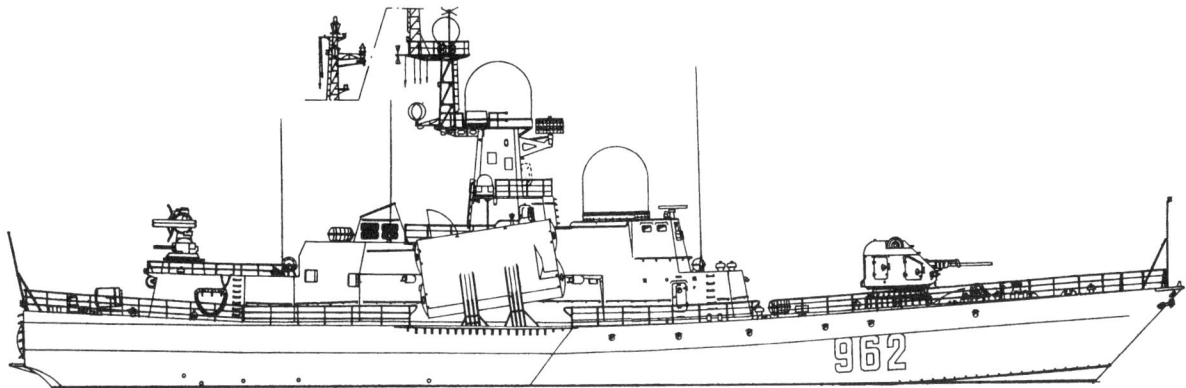

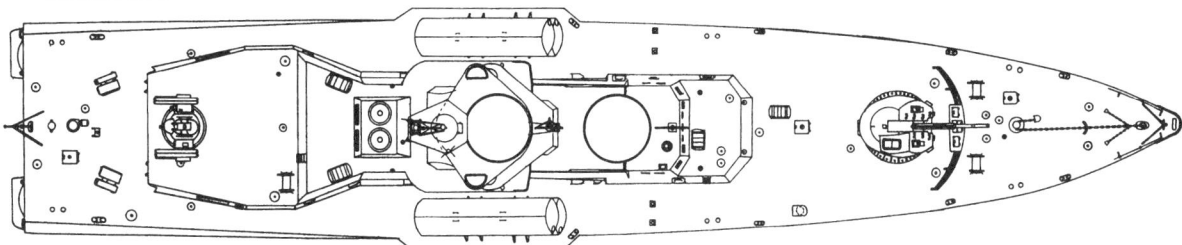

Molnija-III (V. V. Kostrichenko)

rounds), 2×6 30 mm (AK-630, 2000 rounds plus 1000 in overload)

Machinery: 4 gas turbines (2 M-70 cruise units, 6000 HP each, 2 M-75 boost turbines, 10,000 HP each), 2 shafts, 32,000 HP = 42 kts (on all 4 turbines), 2400 nm/13 kts, 400 nm/36 kts; generators: 3 DG-150 (380V, 50 Hz). Endurance 10 days.

Complement: 44 (5 officers)

Electronics: Radars: Positiv, Don

Chief designer Y. I. Yukhnin (TsKB Almaz). Aluminum superstructure, 9 compartments. Four Project 1241. One built in Leningrad beginning in 1970: first with Rangout radar, second with Monolit radar, third and fourth with Monolit and MR-105. Termit series (with improved radar system) built beginning in 1982 at Leningrad (Srednye-Neva Yard) and Khabarovsk (27 units: 2 in each of 1983 and 1984, 4 in 1985, 3 in 1986, 2 in each of 1987–93, 1 in each of 1994 and 1995). R-71 (Black Sea) has Kortik instead of 2×6 30 mm AK-630M (Project 1241.7). Some have Strela-3 or Igla anti-aircraft missiles. Project 1241.9 (Moskit missiles) built in Leningrad from 1981 on, 13 built so far and production is continuing. Boats of this type have M-510 diesels (4000 HP) in place of cruise gas turbines (CODAG system). Black Sea units: R-46, R-54, R-60, R-63, R-71, R-104, R-109, R-160, R-239, R-334. Pacific: 25 units. Caspian: 2 units.

Export version: Project 1241 RE were built in Rybinsk. Transfers: Bulgaria (2 in Mar. '90), East Germany (5: Sept.–Dec. '84, Sept. '85, Jan. and Nov. '86, now in Bundesmarine, one to U.S. Navy), India (5 in 1988–90; later built under license), Iraq (1990; 1 sunk by U.S. aircraft 1991), Poland (4: 28 Dec. '83, Apr. '84, Mar. '88), Romania (2 in Dec. '91: originally built for Iraq), Finland (1 in 1992), Yemen (2: Nov. '90 and Jan. '91).

[Ed.: Western sources list three to Romania and none to Iraq or Finland.]

Tarantul-II class (U.S. Naval Institute Photographic Collection)

Project: 206MR (VIKHR')

NATO Class Name: MATKA

Names:

R-15

R-25

R-27

R-30

R-44

R-50

R-85

R-161

R-166

R-172

R-174

R-180

R-185

R-221

R-240

R-251

R-254

R-260

R-262   TULA

R-265

　named *Komsomolets Tatariy* 1990–92

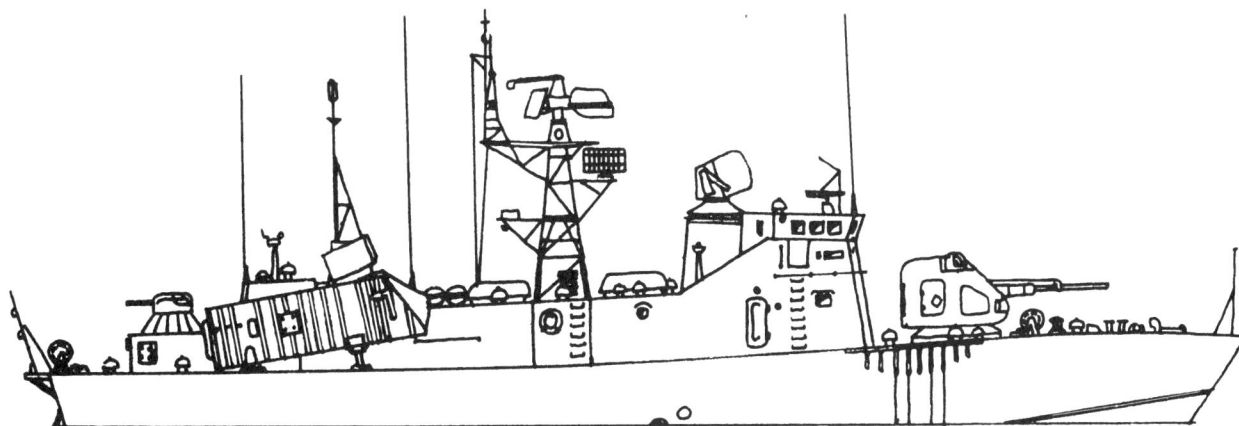

R-30 (Pavlov collection)

Displacement: 200/257

Dimensions: 38.6 × 7.6 (13.6) × 2.1 (3.2)

Armament: 2×1 launchers for Termit-Rubezh missiles, 1 76 mm (AK-176), 1×6 30 mm (AK-630)

Machinery: 3 diesels (M-520), 3 shafts, 15,000 HP = 42 kts, 1100 nm/35 kts (on hydrofoils), 700 nm/12 kts (hullborne), 38 t oil fuel

Complement: 25

Electronics: Radar: Rangout

Chief designer: A. P. Gorodyanko (TsKB Almaz). Built 1978–83 in Leningrad (Srednye-Neva Yard). R-44 has 2×4 Uran missiles and 2×6 30 mm experimental gun. Black Sea units: R-265, R-161, R-251, R-260, R-44, R-15.

Osa-2 (Pavlov collection)

Project: 205 (TSUNAMI)

NATO Class Name: OSA 1 and 2

Names:

R-1–5	
R-6	BRESTSKIY KOMSOMOLETS
R-10	
R-12–14	
R-17–23	
R-24	TAMBOVSKIY KOMSOMOLETS
R-25–32	
R-34–41	
R-43	
R-49–51	
R-53	
R-55	KOMSOMOLETS TATARIY
R-57	
R-59	
R-65	
R-67	
R-68	
R-70–73	
R-77	
R-78	
R-79	KIROVSKIY KOMSOMOLETS
R-80–84	
R-87	AMURSKIY KOMSOMOLETS
R-89	
R-91–93	
R-97	
R-104–114	
R-121–123	
R-141	KRONSHTADSKIY KOMSOMOLETS
R-146	
R-147	
R-161	
R-163	
R-166	
R-167	
R-169	
R-172	

R-173		
R-175		MICHURINSKIY KOMSOMOLETS
R-176		
R-178		
R-180		
R-183		
R-189		
R-193		
R-194		
R-196	24 Oct. '67	
R-199	26 Dec. '67	
R-201		
R-204		
R-206		
R-210	19 Nov. '68	
R-212		
R-218		
R-220–230		
R-288–333		
R-460–474		
R-494–537		
R-540–552		
239 units		

Displacement: 165/226 (200/245*)

Dimensions: 38.6 × 7.6 × 1.8

Armament: 4×1 launchers for Termit (P-15) missiles in hangars or (*) Rubezh (P-15U) missiles in containers, 2×2 30 mm (AK-230)

Machinery: 3 diesels (M-503A or M-504*), 12,000 HP (15,000 HP*) = 42 (47*) kts, 40 t fuel, 1800 nm/14 kts, 800 nm/30 kts, 500 nm/35 kts*

Complement: 26 (28*)

Electronics: Radar: Rangout; IFF: Nikel-Nikhrom-RM
   Chief designer: Y. I. Yukhnin. TTZ issued 24 May '56. Built from 1960 on in Vladivostok, Leningrad (Primorskiy and Almaz yards), and Rybinsk. Four boats had 1×8 Strela AA missiles. Rated as large torpedo boats before 1962, then as missile boats of 3rd rank. Seaworthiness: 5.
   Variants:
   Project 205 (Osa-1): 193 units
   Project 205U* (Osa-2) has P-15U missiles in containers; twenty-eight units built.
   Project 205E: P-25 missiles, bow hydrofoils (205ET, R-113): up to 50 kts. Eight units built.
   Project 205Ch: 400 Hz electrical system (R-105)
   Project 205M: to test P-15M missile and Graviy radar system.
   Exports:
   Osa-1: Algeria (3), Bulgaria (3), Cuba (5), Egypt (12), East Germany (15), India (8), Iraq(4), North Korea (8), Poland (14), Romania (6), Syria (6), Yugoslavia (10)

Osa-1 (G. I. Dianov)

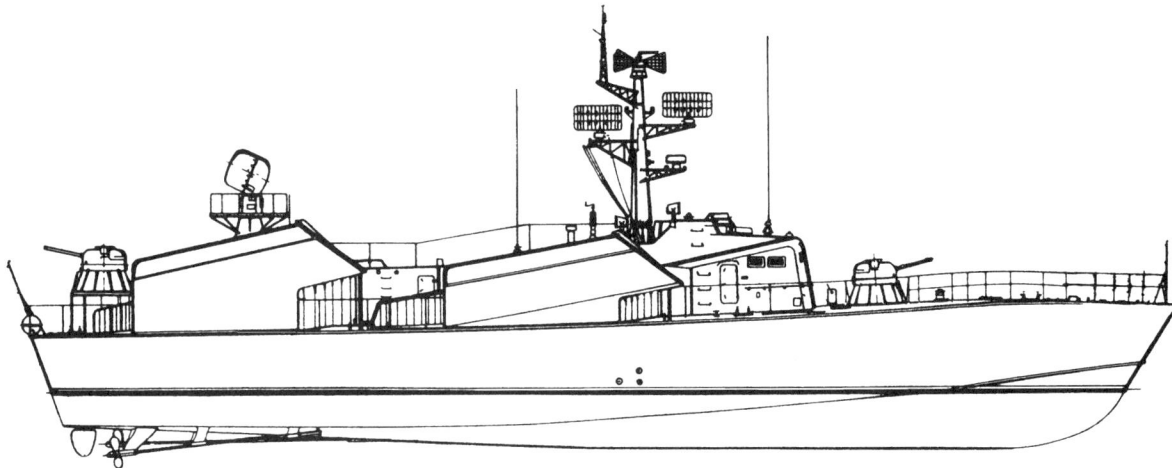

[Ed.: Western sources added Benin (2 in 1979) and China (4), omitted Cuba, and credited Egypt with 10 units, Iraq with 6, North Korea with 12, Poland with 13, and Syria with 8.]

Osa-2: Algeria (9), Angola (6), Bulgaria (4), Cuba (13), Iraq (8), Syria (10), Vietnam (8), North Yemen (2)

[Ed.: Western sources credited Bulgaria with 6, added India (8 in 1976), credited Iraq with 10, added Libya (12), Somalia (2), and credited Syria with 12.]

In 1982 R-2 burned in the Pacific. R-82 (Northern Fleet) burned out after a direct missile hit, 23 Mar. '83. R-39 was transferred to the *Vostok* club in 1989 in the Pacific. R-196 went to the *Meridian* club in Vladivostok, 1991. R-173 was handed to Azerbaidzhan.

Project: 183R

NATO Class Name: KOMAR

Names:

R-63

R-64

R-66

R-69

R-70

R-71

R-72

R-81

R-88

R-90

R-94–96

R-98

R-101–105

R-115–120

R-124–140

R-148–159

R-165–168

R-170

R-171

R-174

R-187–191

R-197

R-198

R-200

R-202

R-203

R-205

R-207–209

R-211

R-213–217

R-231–238

R-261–282

Built in Leningrad (58) and Vladivostok (52), Dec. '59–Dec. '65.

Displacement: 66.5/81

Dimensions: $25.5 \times 6.2 \times 1.5$

Armament: 2×1 launchers for P-15 missile, 1×2 25mm (2M-3M)

Machinery: 4 diesels (M-50F), 4800 HP = 39 kts, 1000 nm/12 kts, 500 nm/26 kts; 1 DG-100 generator. Endurance 5 days.

Complement: 27

Electronics: Radar: Rangout; FCS: Klon'

Project approved 6 Aug. '57. Chief designer: Y. I. Ykhnin (TsKB Almaz). Transfers: Algeria (6), China (20, then license-built), Cuba (18), Egypt (6), Indonesia (9), Korea (10), Syria (6 in 1966: R-81, R-90, R-95, R-96, R-117, R-118, R-140).

[Ed.: Western sources listed Algeria (6 in 1967), China (8 in 1960–61), Cuba (18 in 1962–66), Egypt (7 in 1962–67), Indonesia (12 in 1961–65), Iraq (3 in 1972), North Korea (10), Syria (9 in 1963–65), Vietnam (4 in 1972).]
Stricken 1968–72.

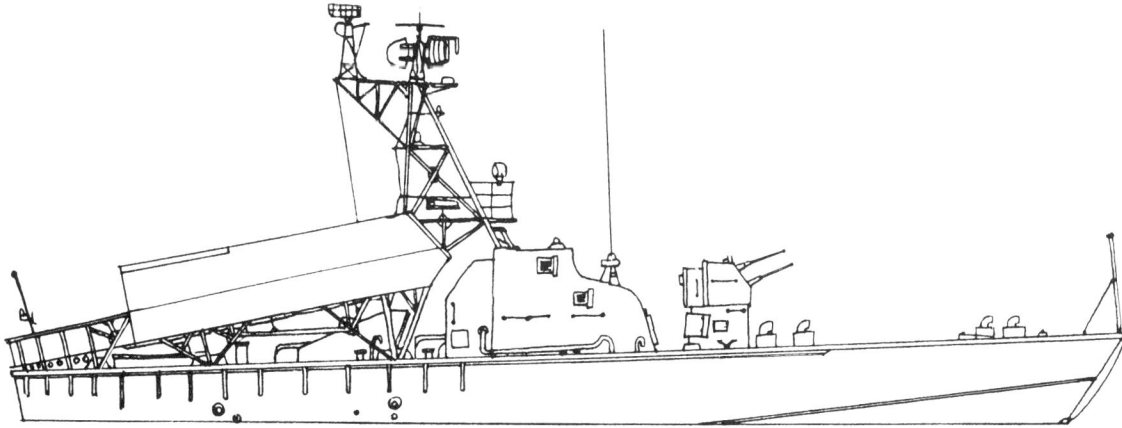

Design 183R (G. G. Kiselev)

Project: 1331M

NATO Class Name: PARCHIM 2

Names:

YUNGA

MPK-67

MPK-99

MPK-105

MPK-192

MPK-205

MPK-213

MPK-216

MPK-219

MPK-224

MPK-228

MPK-229

    Twelve units

Displacement: 960/1200

Dimensions: 72.5 × 9.4 × 3.5

Armament: 2×4 launchers for Strela missiles, 1 76 mm (AK-176), 1×6 30 mm (AK-630), 2×2 533 mm TT (ASW), 2×12 RBU 6000 (96 RGB-60 bombs), 2 depth charge throwers (10 depth charges), mines

Machinery: 3 diesels (M-504), 3 shafts, 15,000 HP = 25 kts; generators: 1 DG-500, 2 DG-200

    Built in East Germany (Peenewerft, Volgast) 1986, 1987 (three), 1988 (three), 1989 (three), 1990(one). Lead ships (Parchim-1) delivered to East German Navy Apr. '81.

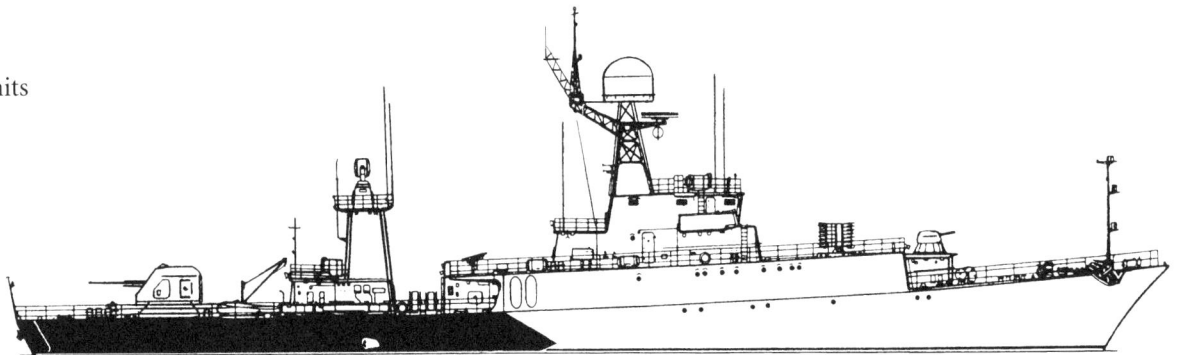

Parchim 2 class (M.O.D. Bonn)

Project: 1124A

NATO Class Name: GRISHA 2

Names:

AMETYST

BRILLIANT

BEZUPRECHNIY

BDITELNYY

DOZORNIY

ZORKIY

IZUMRUD

ZHEMCHUG

IZMAIL

DNEPR

RESHITELNYY

PROVORNYY

PREDANNIY

PRIMERNYY

RUBIN

SAPFIR

SMELYY

Seventeen units. Built in Zelenodolsk 1973–76.

Displacement: 880/960

Dimensions: 71.2 × 10.1 × 3.8

Armament: 2×2 57 mm (AK-725, 1000 rounds), 2×2 533 mm TT, 2×12 RBU 6000 (96 RGB-60 rockets), 20 depth charges

Machinery: 1 gas turbine (M-813, 18,000 HP), 2 diesels (M-507A, 10,000 HP each), 3 shafts, 38,000 HP = 35 kts, 2700 nm/14 kts, 950 nm/27 kts. Endurance 9 days.

Complement: 60

Electronics: Radars: Rubka, Don; Sonar: Shelon, Argun.

Border patrol ships (PSKR). *Sapfir* sank in a storm near Nevyel'sk in 1987. *Izmail* and *Dnepr* to Ukrainian Navy in 1994.

Grisha 2 class (French Navy)

Project: 1124, 1124M, 1124K, 1124MU (ALBATROS)

NATO Class Name: GRISHA 1, 3, 4, 5

Names:

BDITELNYY

BEZUPRESHCHNIY

DOZORNIY

ZORKIY

SMELYY

PROZORLIVYY

MPK-2–10

MPK-17

MPK-28

MPK-31

MPK-33

MPK-35

MPK-36	31 Dec. '71
MPK-37	19 Dec. '80
MPK-41	31 Dec. '72

MPK-43
  named *Odesskiy Komsomolets* until 18 Mar. '92

MPK-44
  named *Komsomolets Latvii* until Apr. '92

MPK-47

MPK-49

MPK-52

MPK-56

MPK-58

MPK-59

MPK-64

MPK-65

MPK-69

MPK-81	31 Dec. '74

MPK-82

MPK-85

MPK-89

MPK-101	23 Dec. '79

  named *Zaporozhskiy Komsomolets* until 1991

MPK-103

MPK-104*

MPK-107   IRKUTSKIY KOMSOMOLETS

MPK-108

MPK-113

MPK-114

MPK-117	31 Dec. '73

MPK-118   KOMSOMOLETS MOLDAVIY

MPK-122	31 Dec. '75

MPK-127
  named *Komsomolets Gruzhiy* 26 Aug. '80–18 Mar. '92

MPK-130

MPK-133

MPK-134   KIEVSKIY KOMSOMOLETS

MPK-136	11 Sept. '68

MPK-138

MPK-139

MPK-142

MPK-143	31 Dec. '76
MPK-145	30 Nov. '77

MPK-147
  lead ship: l.d. 1967, lch 13 Oct. '68, completed 10 Oct. '70

MPK-152

MPK-155	30 Sept. '80

MPK-161

MPK-170	14 Oct. '78
MPK-178	21 Dec. '84

MPK-190

MPK-191	21 Nov. '85

MPK-196

MPK-197

MPK-198

MPK-199
  named *Komsomolets Armeniy* until 18 Mar. '92

MPK-202

MPK-203

MPK-207

MPK-208

MPK-214
  named *Leninskaya Kuznitsa* 1990–1993

MPK-217

MPK-221

MPK-222

MPK-254
  named *Komsomolets Byelorussiy* until 1992

MPK-291

LUTSK

TERNOPOL

ZAPOROZHSKAYA SECH'

Eighty-six units. Built 1968–75 in Zelenodolsk: MPK-2–5, MPK-8, MPK-33, MPK-35, MPK-49, MPK-58, MPK-67, MPK-69, MPK-108, MPK-139, MPK-142, MPK-202. Project 1124MU were built in Kiev (Leninskaya Kuznitsa yard, lead ship MPK-139). Project 1124M boats were built in

Grisha 5 class (Allied Navy)

MPK-5 (V. V. Kostrichenko)

MPK-217 (V. V. Kostrichenko)

Grisha 1 class (M.O.D. U.K.)

Khabarovsk (three per year). *Bditelniy, Bezupreshchniy, Dozorniy, Zorkiy, Smeliy, Prozorliviy* are operated by Border Guards/Coast Guard.

Displacement: 954/1070

Dimensions: 71.2 × 10.15 × 3.72

Armament: 1×2 ZiF-122 launcher for Osa system (20 9M33 missiles), 1×2 57 mm (AK-725, 500 rounds) or (Projects 1124M and 1124MU) 1 76 mm (AK-176, 550 rounds) and 1×6 30 mm (AK-630M, 2000 rounds), 2×2 533 mm TT, 2×12 RBU 6000 (1124M: 1 RBU), 18 mines

Machinery: 1 gas turbine (M-813; M-83 in Project 1124M, 18,000 HP) and 2 diesels (M-507A, 10,000 HP each), 3 shafts, 38,000 HP = 32 kts (7 kts on one diesel, 16 kts on two diesels, 21 kts on gas turbine alone, 32 kts on all power-plants), 4000 nm/10 kts, 2750 nm/14 kts (diesels), 950 nm/27 kts; generators: 1 DG-500, 1 DG-300, 1 DG-200; 130 t fuel (143 t overload), 10.5 t oil, 27.2 t water. Endurance 9 days.

Complement: 70

Electronics: Radars: Rubka, Don; Sonars: Shelon', Argun, Khosta (Platina sonar and Topaz radar on Project 1124).

Chief designer V. I. Nesterenko. MPK-5 was completed as Project 1124.4 to test the Leevyen RBU (1×6). MPK-104 (Project 1124K) was equipped with 3×8 Kinzhal AA missile launchers forward and Podkat radar (Osa missiles and 57 mm gun were removed). Black Sea: twenty units. MPK-44 *(Zhemaiytis)* and MPK-108 *(Vietra)* were transferred to Latvia. U-200 *Lutsk* and *Ternopol* are in the Ukrainian Navy. Rest on completion.

Project: 1241.2 (MOLNIYA-2)

NATO Class Name: PAUK

Names:

G. GNATENKO

N. KARPLUNOV

G. KUROPATNIKOV

MPK-11

MPK-12

MPK-15

MPK-17

MPK-19

MPK-38

MPK-50

MPK-60   until 20 Apr. '92, *Komsomolets Bashkirii* MPK-61

MPK-62

MPK-68

MPK-72

MPK-75

MPK-76

MPK-88

MPK-90

MPK-93

MPK-95

MPK-100

MPK-106

MPK-116

MPK-124

MPK-144

MPK-146

MPK-157

MPK-159

MPK-222

MPK-291

MPK-345

PSKR-801–815

Forty-six units. Built in Yaroslavl 1979–92.

PSKR-806 (Pavlov collection)

Pauk class (U.S. Navy)

163

Displacement: 415/475

Dimensions: 57.5 × 10.2 × 3.59

Armament: 1×2 launcher for Strela 2M (8 missiles), 1 76 mm (AK-176), 1×6 30 mm (AK-630), 4×1 406 mm TT, 2×5 RBU 1200M, 1 MRG-1

Machinery: 2 diesels (M-507A, 10,000 HP each), 2 shafts, 20,000 HP = 33 kts, 2600 nm/14 kts (3000 nm with overload fuel). Endurance 10 days.

Complement: 38

Electronics: Radar: Positiv; Sonar: Bronza

Built under Council of Ministers decision 22 Aug. '73, on the hull of the Project 1241.1 missile boat. Transfers (all with Postiv-E radar and 2×2 533 mm TT): Bulgaria (2; MPK-146 in 1989 and MPK-124 in 1990, not export type), Cuba (1), India (4), Iraq (1), Libya (1). Eight units in Black Sea. *Kuropatnikov, Gatchenko,* and P-813 in Ukrainian Navy.

[Ed.: Western sources report no transfers to Iraq or to Libya; presumably plans for these transfers fell through.]

Project: 1145 (SOKOL)

NATO Class Name: BABOCHKA-2

Names:

MPK-215

MPK-220

Displacement: 415.1/468

Dimensions: 49.97 × 9.9 (21.2) × 4.5 (7.26)

Armament: 1 76 mm (AK-176), 1×6 30 mm (AK-630M), 1×8 launcher for Strela or Igla-M, 2×4 406 mm TT TR-224 (at stern)

Machinery: 2 gas turbines (NK-12, 18,000 HP each), 2 diesels (M-401, 1200 HP each), 40 kts (12 kts hullborne)

Complement: 50

Built in Feodosiya on the Black Sea, 1986–87.

MPK-215 (Pavlov collection)

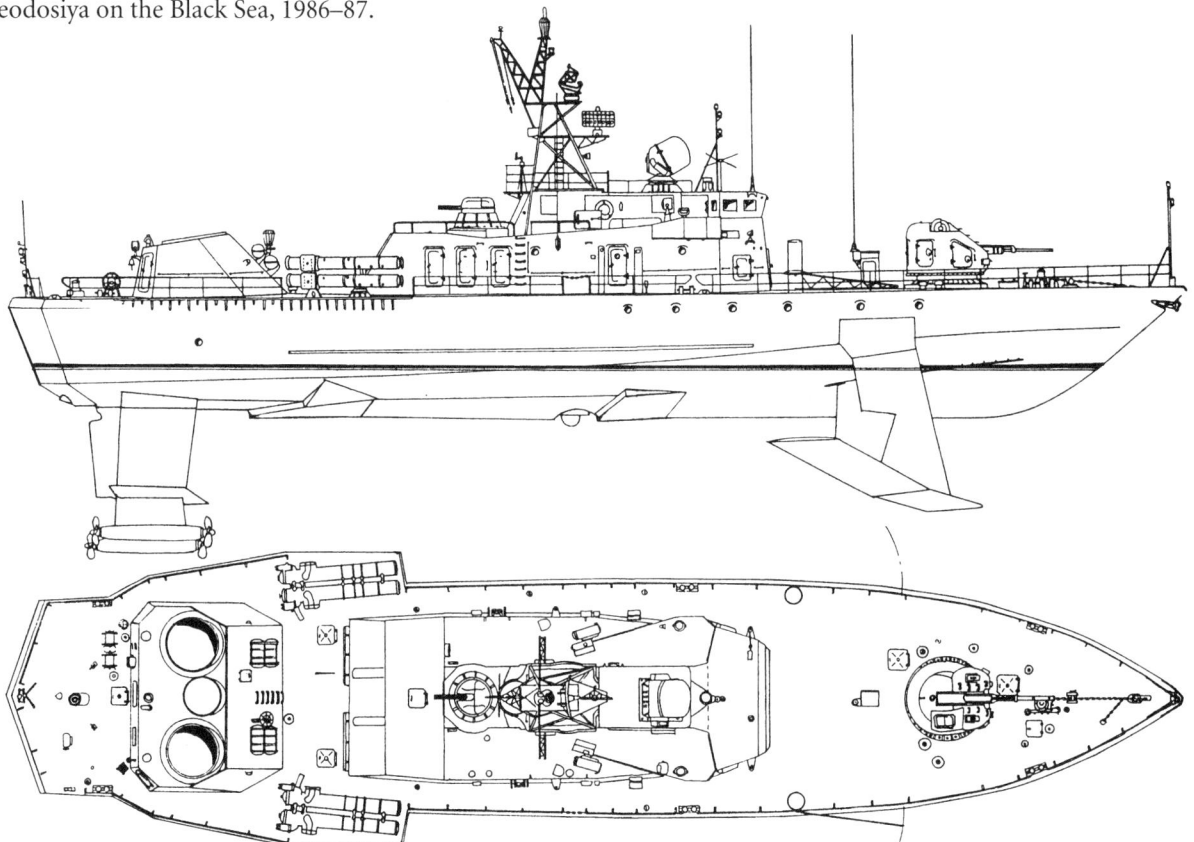

Project: 1141

NATO Class Name: BABOCHKA

Names:

	completed
ALEKSANDR KUNAKHOVICH	1977

Displacement: 320/465

Dimensions: 50 × 9.9 (21) × 4 (7.1)

Armament: 2×6 30 mm (AK-630), 2×4 406 mm TT (TR-224, for 8 SET-72)

Machinery: 3 gas turbines (NK-12, driving 3 tandem-type screws in fixed angled struts), 54,000 HP = 52 kts (60 kts maximum); 2 diesels for low-speed hullborne cruising, 1600 HP = 8 kts

Complement: 45

Electronics: Sonar: Sheksna

Chief designer: A. N. Kunakhovich, then Y. Ovsienko (Zelenodolsk PKB). TTZ approved 2 Feb. '67. Built in Feodosiya. Torpedo tubes were originally at the bow, but were moved to the stern in 1994. Turbine: 14 stages, with ringed combustion chamber. Black Sea.

Babochka class (B. P. Tiurin)

Babochka class (V. V. Kostrichenko)

Project: 204

NATO Class Name: POTI

Names:

MPK-1
MPK-10–12
MPK-14–20
MPK-38
MPK-44
MPK-50
MPK-58–62
MPK-68–77
MPK-85
MPK-88–100
MPK-103
MPK-106
MPK-107
MPK-109
MPK-111
MPK-112
MPK-114
MPK-124
MPK-125
MPK-128
MPK-134
MPK-136
MPK-148
MPK-156
MPK-157
MPK-158
MPK-159
MPK-160
MPK-215
MPK-375
MPK-431
MPK-435
MPK-440
MPK-446
MPK-449
MPK-481

Design 204 (Pavlov collection)

Poti class (U.S. Navy)

MPK-20 was later renamed SM-442, and MPK-107 became SM-450. Total of sixty-nine built 1961–68 at Kerch (24), Zelenodolsk (32), and Khabarovsk (8 in 1964–68).

Displacement: 439/555

Dimensions: 58.6 × 8.2 × 3.1

Armament: 1×2 57 mm (ZiF 31B or AK-725), 2×1 or 4×1 406 mm TT (OTA-40-204), 2×12 RBU 6000 (96 RGB-60 rockets)

Machinery: 2 gas turbines (D 2, 15,000 HP each), 2 diesels (M-250T, 4800 HP each), 2 screws in tunnels, 36 kts; 2500 nm/14.5 kts, 1500 nm/17.5 kts; generators: 2 DG-200; 107 t fuel, 6 t oil, 17 t water. Endurance 7 days.

Complement: 56 (4 officers, 6 petty officers, 46 sailors)

Electronics: Radar: Donets navigational; Sonar: Gerkules-2M; Gyrocompass: Kurs-4; Log: LG-4; Radio direction-finder: ARP-5; Sounder: NEL-5; DRT: AP-3; Autopilot: Albatros

Chief designer Byelodvorov, then A. N. Kunakhovich. Eight bulkheads. Transfers: Bulgaria (1973), Romania (1967). To breakers 1988–94.

[Ed.: According to Western sources, Bulgaria and Romania each received three units.]

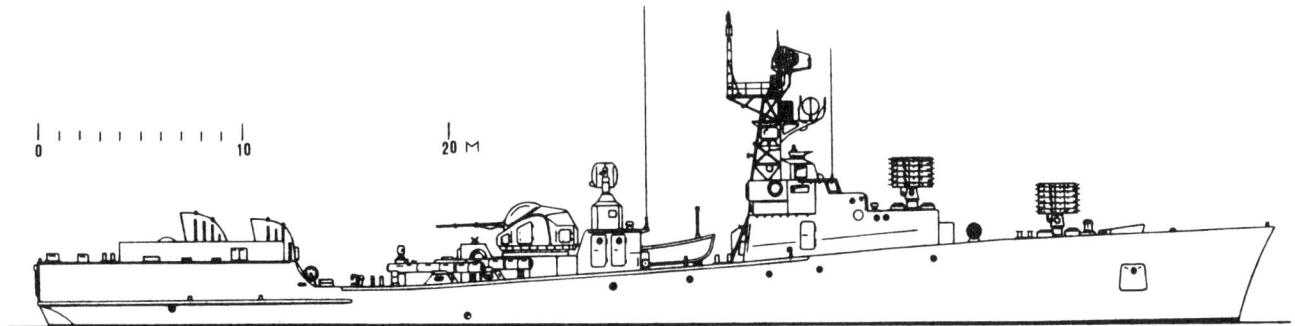

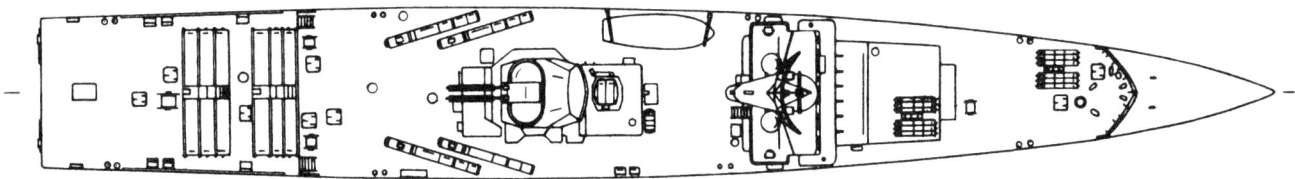

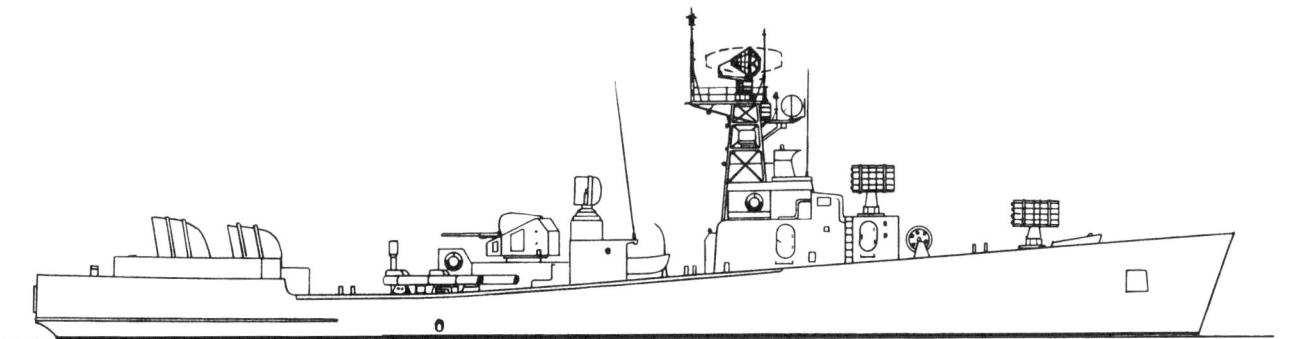

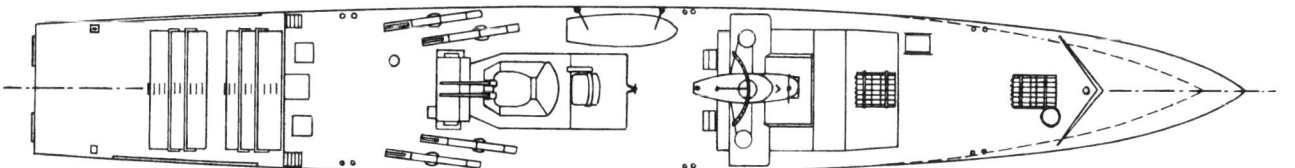

Project: 97-B* and 97-P

Class Name: IVAN SUSANIN

Names:

AISBERG

DUNAII

ANADYR
  named *Imenii 25 Svezda Kpss* until 11 Apr. '92, ex-*Dnepr*

IVAN SUSANIN

IRTYSH
  named *Imenii 26 Svezda Kpss* until 1992

NEVA

RUSLAN

VOLGA

SADKO

VLADIMIR KAVRAIYSKIIY*
  10 units, built in Leningrad, Admiralty Yard

Displacement: 3500

Dimensions: $70 \times 18.1 \times 6.4$

Armament: 1×2 76 mm (AK-726), 2×6 30 mm (AK-630) (not on *Ivan Susanin, Ruslan*)

Machinery: Diesel-electric (3 DG of type D-100), 3 shafts (1 bow, 2 stern), 5400 HP = 14.5 kts, 5500 nm/12.5 kts

Complement: 45

Ocean survey ships*, PSKR for Border Guards and naval icebreakers. Built in Leningrad (Admiralty Yard). Have a helicopter pad. *Imeni 26 Svezda Kpss* (ex-*Dnepr*) stricken 1991

Dunaii (Pavlov collection)

Project: 10410

NATO Class Name: SVETLYAK

Names:

AK-232

AK-233

AK-235

P-901–933

Thirty-six units. Built in Leningrad (Almaz) beginning 1988 and in Vladivostok (Uliss) beginning in 1990

Displacement: 328/382

Dimensions: 49.5 × 9.2 × 2.6

Armament: 1 76 mm (AK-176, 152 rounds), 1×6 30 mm (AK-630M, 2000 rnds plus 1000 overload), 2×1 406 mm TT, 2 grenade launchers (MPG-1), provision for 16 Igla-M missiles

Machinery: 3 diesels (M-520A), 3 shafts, 15,000 HP = 32 kts, 2200 nm/13 kts (with overload fuel); 1 DG-200, 2 DG-100 generators. Endurance 10 days.

Complement: 28 (4 officers, 4 petty officers)

Electronics: Radar: Mius, Khrom (IFF)

Replacement for Project 205P, built at the rate of three–four units per year. General designer K. Zh. Avenesov, later V. P. Lipiev and A. L. Ivchenko. Seaworthiness allowed use of weapons without speed restriction up to sea state 4, and up to 22 kts in sea state 5; can stay at sea up to sea state 7. Air conditioned, with aluminum superstructure. AK-232 on Caspian Sea.

Svetlyak class (Pavlov collection)

Project: 201, 201T, and 201M*

NATO Class Name: SO-1

Names:

P-175–190

P-255–259

P-260*

P-261–270

P-325–328

P-450–490

P-500–543

P-550–570

129 units. Built 1957–58 in Zelenodolsk and in Kerch.

Displacement: 170/215

Dimensions: 42.4 × 6 × 1.8

Armament: 2×2 25 mm (2M-3), 4×5 RBU 1200, 2×1 406 mm TT (Project 201T), 18 mines or 12 depth charges

Machinery: 3 diesels (30-D), 3 shafts, 7500 HP = 28 kts, 1100 nm/13 kts, 350 nm/28 kts

Complement: 31

Electronics: Sonar: Tamir-2 (Tamir-11 on export units)

[Ed.: According to Burov, this class was designed at Zelenodolsk; chief designer was A. N. Kunakhovich. The initial planned armament was a 45 mm gun, and planned displacement was 141/161 t. Alternative projected powerplants used 2000 HP 37-D and 1200 HP M-50F diesels. Project 201M grew to 213 t. Burov claims that a total of 160 units were built at Zelenodolsk, Kerch, and Khabarovsk. The difference between his figure and those above may be production at Khabarovsk, and may indicate Project 201P units built for the KGB.]

Armament varied: 57 mm instead of stern 25 mm mount and the two 406 mm TT. Yard 119 named *L'govskiy Pioner*. Transfers: Algeria (6), Bulgaria (6), Cuba (10), Egypt (12), East Germany (12 in 1959–60), Iraq (3), North Korea (15), Mozambique (2 in mid-1985), Vietnam (13), South Yemen (2).

[Ed.: According to Western sources, additional transfers amounted to Albania (4), China (2 in 1960), Cuba (18 total), East Germany (16 total), and North Korea (6 plus 12 built under license).]

Stricken 1977–91.

SO-1 class (U.S. Naval Institute Photographic Collection)

Design 201M (Pavlov collection)

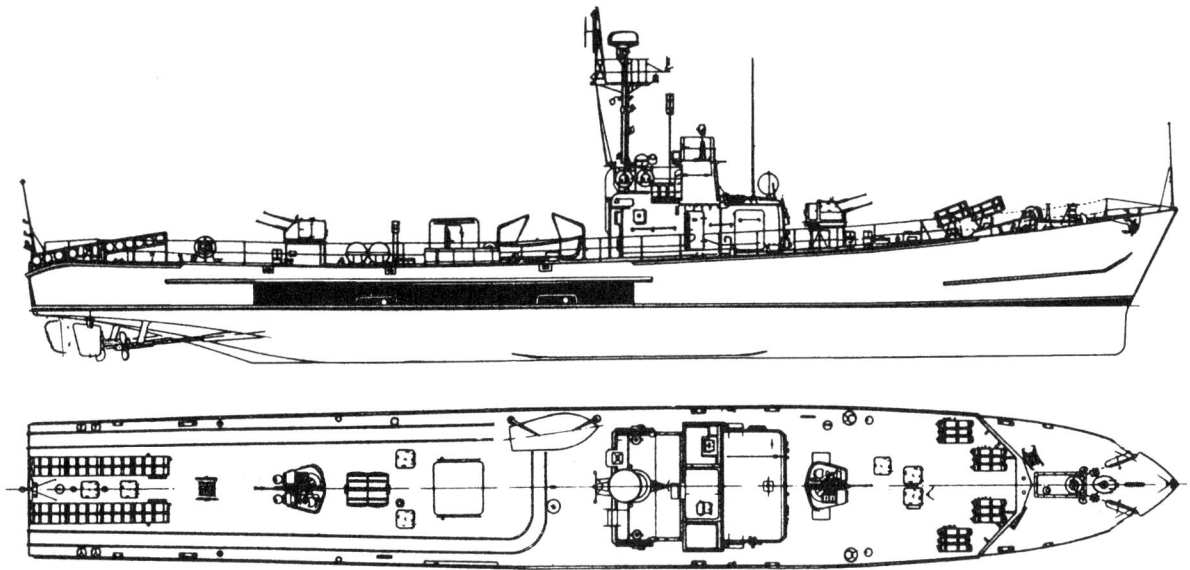

SO-1 class (Siegfried Breyer)

Project: 133 (ANTARES)

NATO Class Name: MURAVEY

Names:

P-101   DEL'FIN

P-102

P-103

P-105

P-107

P-108

P-109

P-110

P-115–121

16 units. Built at Feodosiya; lead ship laid down Aug. '76, completed 1979.

Displacement: 180/230

Dimensions: 40.3 × 8 (9 on hydrofoils) × 1.9 (4.7)

Armament: 1 76 mm (AK-176), 1×6 30 mm (AK-630), 2×1 406 mm TT

Machinery: 2 gas turbines, 2 shafts, 22,600 HP = 40 kts, 410 nm/40 kts

Complement: 34

Chief designer B. F. Orlov. For Border Guards. Have folding bow hydrofoils. Motion stabilizing system. Black Sea. Six units, including P-103, P-105, P-108 in Ukrainian Navy. P-102 stricken 1994.

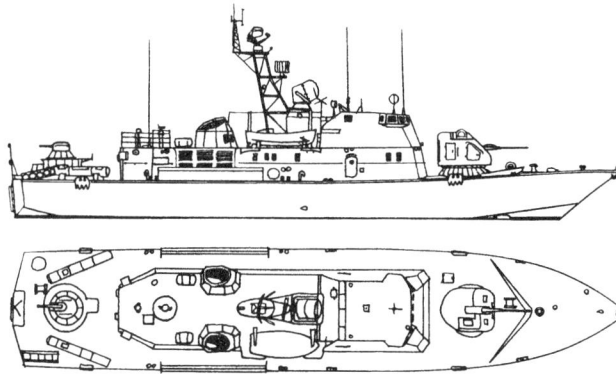

Muravey class (Pavlov collection)

Project: 205PE

NATO Class Name: SLEPEN

Names:

AK-225

Displacement: 175/210

Dimensions: 39 × 8.1 × 1.8

Armament: 1 57 mm (AK-157), 1×6 30 mm (AK-630)

Machinery: 3 diesels (M-504), 3 shafts, 15,000 HP = 36 kts

Complement: 30

Built in Leningrad (Primorskiy), 1970. Originally carried a twin 57 mm bow mount, replaced 1975 by a single experimental mount. Gunboat type AKA. On the Black Sea, to the breakers 1993.

AK-225 (Pavlov collection)

Project: 02065 (VIKHR' III)

NATO Class Name: ULISS or BOGOMOL

Names:

T-229   1988

Displacement: 207/251

Dimensions: $40.15 \times 7.6 \times 2.8$

Armament: 1 76 mm (AK-176M, 152 rounds), 1×6 30 mm (AK-630, 2000 rounds)

Machinery: 3 diesels (M-520TM-5), 3 shafts, 14,400 HP = 36 kts, 1700 nm/12 kts, 2500 nm/12 kts (with overload fuel); seaworthiness: 5; generators: 1 DG-100, 1 DG-200. Endurance 9 days.

Complement: 25

Electronics: Radars: Garpun, MR-102 navigational; ESM: Nakat; ECM: SPO-3; IFF: Nikrom-R; Communications system: R-784

Built in Vladivostok: export project. Aluminum superstructure, gyro-stabilizer (BAZA-02065), degausser, air conditioning. Provision for installation of 2 406 mm TT. Retained in Pacific for tests and to train foreign crews. From this prototype was developed a missile boat with 2×2 Uran missile launchers. Transfers: four to Guinea-Bissau 1988–90.

Uliss class (Y. V. Ivanov)

Project: 14310 (MIRAZH)

NATO Class Name: None

Names:

P-201

P-202

P-203

Displacement: 120

Dimensions: $34.2 \times 6.8 \times 2.1$

Armament: 1×6 30 mm (AK-630M, 2000 rounds)

Machinery: 2 diesels (M-504), 10,000 HP = 50 kts, 1500 nm/8 kts

Built from 1993 on for export and Border Guards in St. Petersburg (Almaz yard). General designer N. A. Serkov (TsKB Almaz). Hull of aluminum magnesium alloy.

Project: 205M and 205P (TARANTUL)

NATO Class Name: STENKA

Names:

AK-234

AK-301–350

AK-355–370

AK-374–376

AK-378

AK-379

AK-381

IVAN GOLUBETS

NIKOLAI KAPLUNOV

P-616

P-623

P-629

P-630

P-631

P-635–638

P-641–645

P-648–652

P-657

P-659

P-660

P-665

P-695

P-700

P-702

P-705

P-709

P-715

P-717

P-718

P-720

P-723

P-725

146 units. Built at Leningrad and Vladivostok.

Displacement: 170/210

Dimensions: 39 × 7.8 × 1.8

Armament: 2×2 30 mm (AK-230), 4×1 406 mm TT, 2 bomb throwers (12 depth charges)

Machinery: 3 diesels (M-503A, 4000 HP each, or M-504, 5000 HP each), 34/36 kts, 800 nm/20 kts, 500 nm/35 kts

Complement: 32 (5 officers)

Electronics: Radars: Baklan, Ksenon; Sonar: Gerkules-2 plus helicopter dipping sonar

Built from 1967 on (about five per year) in Leningrad (Primorskiy) and in Vladivostok on Project 205 hulls as gunboats and patrol boats for Border Guards (PSKR). Thirty units in the Black Sea.

AK-234 and AK-374 to Azerbaijan; P-623, P-629, P-630, P-635–637, P-642, P-722 to Ukraine after the breakup of the Soviet Union. *Karplunov* stricken 1992.

Transfers: Cuba (two in Feb. '85), Kampuchea (one in Oct. '85 without TT or dipping sonar)

Design 205P (Pavlov collection)

Project: 199

NATO Class Name: PO-8

[Ed: This is NATO MO-VI.]

Names:

P-301–351

P-402–406

P-417

P-723   ex-P-23

P-724   ex-P-24

  60 units

Displacement: 61.6/67

Dimensions: 25.4 × 6.24 × 1.26

Armament: 2×2 25mm (2M-3), 2 BMB-2, 36 depth charges

Machinery: 4 diesels (M-50F), 4 shafts, 4800 HP = 35 kts, 1000 nm/12 kts, 580 nm/33 kts; fuel 7 t; 1 DG-100 generator. Endurance 6 days.

Complement: 22

Electronics: ESM: Reya; IFF: Khrom; Sonar: Tamir-10

  Built at Leningrad on Project 183 hull up to Dec. '59. Genera; designer P. G. Goinkis. Seven units in the Caspian. P-326, P-329, P-330 stricken 1968 in Pacific; seven units in Caspian stricken 1972. One transferred to Metallurical Works in Shevchenko. Two to Indonesia 1965.

  [Ed.: Western sources listed as transfers: Bulgaria (10), Guinea (4 reported 1972–75), Nigeria (3 in 1967), North Korea (20 in 1957–60).]

Project: 1400 and 1400M* (GRIF)

NATO Class Name: ZHUK

Names:

AK-10–55

P-60–101

P-125

P-141

P-508

P-512

P-517

P-519

P-526–534

P-547

P-550

P-555

P-558

P-562

P-574

P-579

  Eighty-five units. Built 1971–1986.

Displacement: 50

Dimensions: 24 × 5.2 × 1.9

Armament: 2×1 14.5mm (2M-7) or 12.7mm (UTES-M)

Machinery: 2 diesels (M-508), 2 shafts, 2400 HP = 30 kts, 700 nm/28 kts, 1100 nm/15 kts

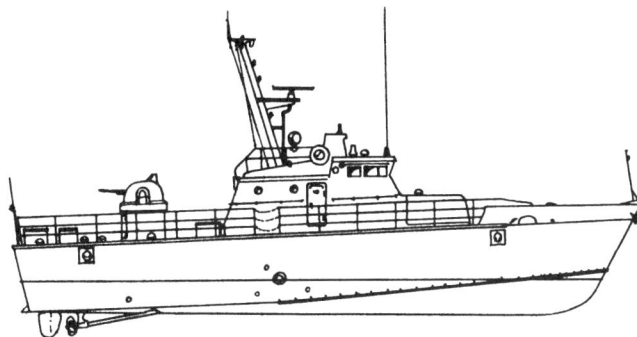

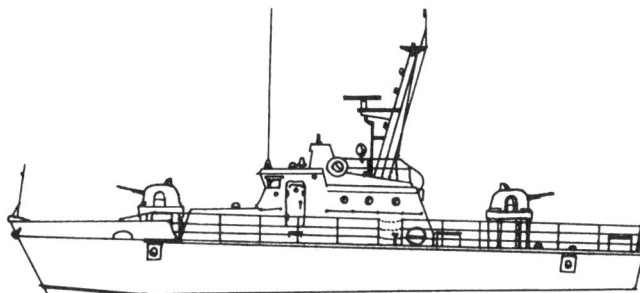

P-512 (Pavlov collection)

Complement: 17

Built for Border Guards 1971–86. On this hull ten units were completed as personnel launches: KSV-9, *Sokol,* KSV-12, KSV-485, *Tchaika,* KSV-1135, *Berkut,* KSV-1499, *Gurzuf,* KSV-1754. Thirty units on the Black Sea. AK-55* to Azerbaijan after the breakup of the Soviet Union.

Transfers: Angola (1 in 1977), Benin (4 in 1978–80), Bulgaria (6 in 1977–81), Cape Verde Islands (1 in 1980), Congo (6 in 1982–84), Cuba (35 in 1971–85), Equatorial Guinea (3 in 1974–75), Ethiopia (2 in Oct. '82), Iraq (5 in 1974–75), Kampuchea (1 in 1985), Mozambique (5 in 1978–80),

Nicaragua (3 from Cuba 1982, 1983, 1984, then 5 in 1986), Seychelles (2 in 1981 and 1982), Somalia (3 in 1976–79), Syria (6 in 1981–84), Vietnam (10 in 1978–86), North Yemen (6 in 1978–87), South Yemen (2 in Feb. '75).

[Ed.: Western sources also claim transfers to Algeria (1 in 1981), Bulgaria (5 rather than 6), Cuba (40 rather than 35), Ethiopia (they add 2 in June '90), Kampuchea (3 rather than 1), Mauritius (2 in Jan. '90), Somalia (1 rather than 3), Vietnam (14 rather than 10), North Yemen (5 rather than 6), and South Yemen (5 rather than 2).]

Project: 1208 (SLEPEN')

NATO Class Name: YAZ

Names:

	completed
MAK-1	1975
MAK-2	1975
MAK-3	1982
60 LET VchK	1978
MAK-5	1979
MAK-6	1976
MAK-7	1978
MAK-8	1984

Khabarovskiy Komsomolets
until Apr. '92

IMENII 60 - LETIYA POGRANIVOIYSK

| MAK-10 | 1981 |
| MAK-11 | 1983 |

Ten others (twenty-one units). Built 1978–90 in Khabarovsk (10 units) and Vladivostok.

Displacement: 390/440

Dimensions: 55.2 × 9.12 × 1.44

Armament: 2×1 100 mm (D-10-T2s, as in a T-55 tank), 2×6 30 mm (AK-630M), 2×2 12.7 mm (UTES-M), 2×1 30 mm grenade launchers (BP-30), 1×2 122 mm rocket launcher (ZiF-121, used for chaff rockets, Sneg system); 4 Strela AA missiles can be installed.

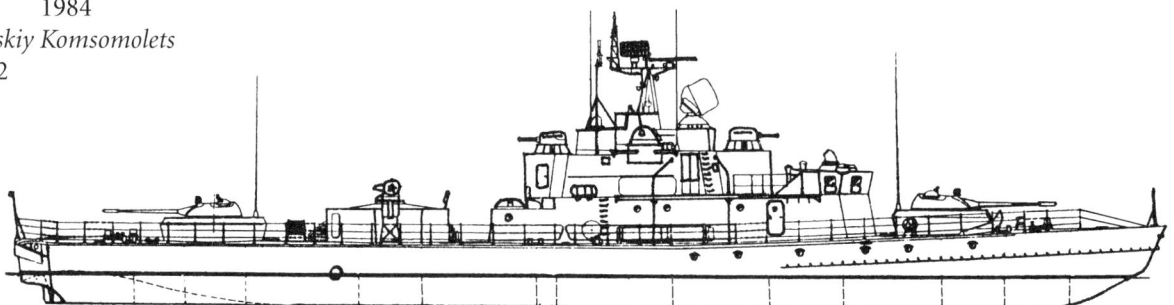

176

MAK-8 (Pavlov collection)

Armor: 8, 20, 35 mm on deckhouse, sides, turrets

Machinery: 3 diesels (M-512B), 3 shafts, 11,400 HP = 24.3 kts, 1000 nm/10 kts

Complement: 32 (4 officers)

Chief designer M. V. Koshkin. In divisional formations on Amur River. One placed in reserve 1992.

Project: 1248 (MOSKIT)

NATO Class Name: VOSH

Names:

BAK-313

BAK-320

BAK-440

BAK-459

BAK-467

BAK-469

One other (seven units)

Displacement: 150/230

Dimensions: 42 × 6.1 × 1.3

Armament: 1 100 mm (D10-T2s, as in a T-55 tank), 1×6 30 mm (AK-630M), 1×2 12.7 mm (UTES-M), 1 30 mm grenade launcher (BP-30), 1 bombardment rocket launcher ZiF-121

Machinery: 3 diesels, 3 shafts, 3300 HP = 17 kts

Complement: 34 (3 officers)

Built 1980–84 in Kokue (Sretenskiy yard). Assigned to the Amur River, in divisional formations of river boats.

BAK-320 (Pavlov collection)

Project: 1249

NATO Class Name: PIYAVKA

Names:

completed

Built at Vladivostok on *Vosh* hull.

PSKR-50	1979
PSKR-51	1980
PSKR-52	1981
PSKR-53	1982
PSKR-54	1982
PSKR-55	1983
PSKR-56	1983
PSKR-57	1984

Displacement: 150/210

Dimensions: 41.9 × 6.1 × 1.2

Armament: 1×6 30 mm A-219 (AK-630M), 1 grenade launcher (BP-30), 10 mines

Armor:—

Machinery: 3 diesels (M-401B), 3 shafts, 3300 HP = 17.5 kts, 500 nm/10 kts. Endurance 7 days.

Complement: 28 (2 officers) plus 12 staff

Built at Khabarovsk on Project 1248 hull: command/communications boats. Hull arrangement, fore to aft: forepeak, crew quarters with air conditioner unit, fuel tanks (12t), forward and aft engine rooms (latter with DG-75), stores, steering machinery. Main deck spaces: deckhouse, flag bridge, code room, cabin, wardroom, mess, sick bay.

For the Amur flotilla.

Project: 1204 (SHMEL')

NATO Class Name: None

Names:

119 built 1967–74 at Kerch (98) and Nikolaev (assembled at Khabarovsk):

AK-197–199

AK-201–203

AK-205–209

AK-211

AK-222–225

AK-234

AK-241–250

AK-255–273

AK-314

AK-316

AK-354

AK-374

AK-384

AK-385

AK-387

AK-397–399

AK-404–409

AK-483–485

AK-489

AK-500–509

AK-527

AK-563

AK-564

AK-581–585

AK-587–589

AK-599–602

PSKR-336–377

Displacement: 75/80

Dimensions: 27.7 × 4.3 × 0.8

Armament: 1 76.2 mm (D-56TM in tank turret, 150 rounds), 2×1 14.5 mm (2M-7); can install Malyutka (AT-3A) anti-tank missile (3M14), 2×1 14.5 mm guns (2M-7 or 2M-3M), 1 7.62 mm (PKT), 1×18 unguided rocket launcher (BM-14-17, 36 rounds); later had a 10 mm deckhouse for 4 AP-30 Plamya grenade launchers. Mines in overload condition: 4 UDM-500 or 2 UDM-1000 or 6 KPM or 8 YaM.

Armor: 8 mm sides, 5 mm deck

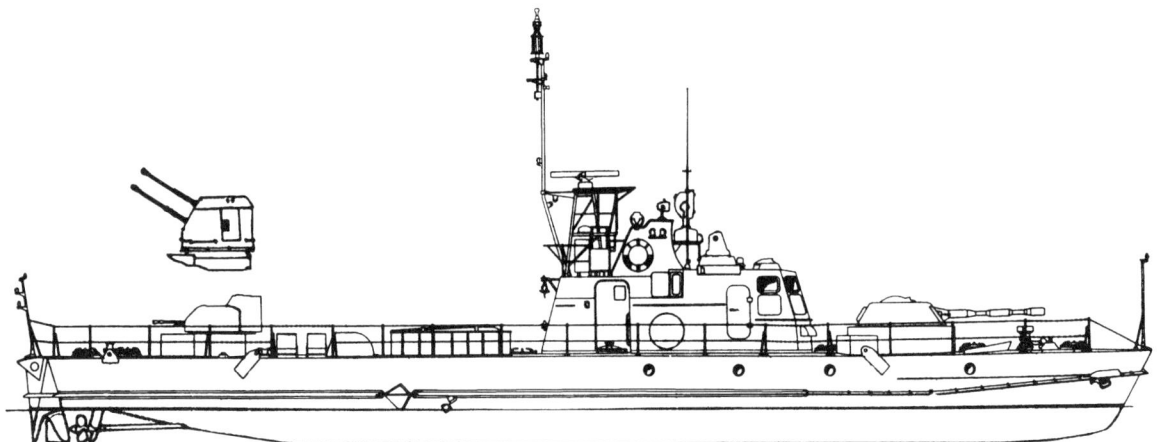

AK-397 (Pavlov collection)

Machinery: 2 diesels (M-50F), 2 shafts, 2400 HP = 23 kts, 240 nm/20 kts; 2 DG-25 generators; 4.75 t fuel, 0.3 t oil, 0.2 t water; seaworthiness: 3. Endurance 7 days.

Complement: 14 (1 officer, 2 petty officers, 3 rated men, 8 sailors)

Electronics: Radar: Donets-2; Night vision equipment; Short-wave radio: R-617; Ultra-shortwave radio: R-619; Gyrocompass: Gradus-2 (as modernized, Kurs); Sounder: NEL-7

Chief designer: L. V. Ozimov (TsKB-7). Ten bulkheads (11 compartments): forepeak; Fr 4–9 petty officers' living quarters; Fr 9–12 section under turret; Fr 12–17, living quarters; Fr 17–21.5, captain's cabin, radio room; Fr 21.5–25.5, living quarters; Fr 25.5–29, PVD, fuel; Fr 29–41, engine room; Fr 41–44, unknown; Fr 44–48, galley, refrigerator, provisions; Fr 48–52, after peak, steering gear. Fifty-nine units for the navy, PSKRs for Border Guards. PSKR-347 has an extra BM-14-17. Four to Kampuchea 1984–85. Twenty now in reserve.

AK-208, AK-245, AK-247–249, AK-407, AK-409, AK-489, AK-507–509 in Baltic; AK-209, AK-211, AK-223, AK-224, AK-246, AK-248, AK-335, AK-397, AK-506, AK-527, AK-563, AK-564, AK-582, AK-583, AK-599, AK-602 on Black Sea (Danube River flotilla). AK-234 and AK-374 on the Caspian Sea. Remainder on the Amur.

Project: 191 and 191M*

NATO Class Name: None

Names:

119 built at Perm' and Leningrad 1947–52:

BK-166–174

BK-275–300

BK-491–499

BK-544–549

BK-571–580

BK-590 598

BK-603–615

BK-617–628

BK-632

BK-633

BK-634

BK-925–960

BK-946 (V. V. Levchenko)

Displacement: 53.35/56.5

Dimensions: 25.9 × 4.3 × 0.7 (0.65*)

Armament: 1 85 mm (MK-85), 2×2 14.5 mm, 2×2 12.7 mm*

Armor: 10 mm deck, 14 mm sides

Machinery: 2 diesels (B-2*, 600 HP each, or M-50, 1000 HP each) = 16*/24 kts, 275 nm* or 175 nm/15; generators: 1 DG-6.5, 3 DG-1. Endurance 5 days.

Complement: 14

Chief designer Yu. Yu. Benua (TsKB-19). Lead ship(*) was built in Perm' Oct. '44, second in Nov. '47, then Project 191M in Perm and Leningrad. Forty units on Amur River (so-called *Gorbachiy*) from 1965. Gunboats (AK). One handed over to KYuM (junior sailors' club) of Odessa, named *Chernomorets*. Armament was changed periodically. Stricken 1970–73.

Project: 192

NATO Class Name: None

Names:

BK-922

BK-924

Displacement: 63/65

Dimensions: 30 × 5 × 0.95

Armament: 1 85 mm, 2×2 14.5 mm

Armor: deckhouse, sides, citadel 10 mm

Machinery: 3 diesels (M-50, 1000 HP each), 3 shafts, 23 kts, 200 nm/18 kts; 5 t fuel; 1 DG-6.5, 2 DG-4 generators. Endurance 5 days.

Complement: 16 (1 officer)

Chief designer Y. Y. Benua (TsKB-19). Built Dec. '91 at Kolpino (Izhora yard). Armored citadel is screened, with 15° sides, lower armored shelf, and vertical armor over hull sides.

Design 192 (A. N. Sokolov)

Project: 194

NATO Class Name: None

Names:

MO-105

MO-106

Displacement: 110/161

Dimensions: 27 × 6.2 × 1.7

Armament: 1 45 mm, 1 37 mm, 2×1 12.7 mm, 4 BMB-1 depth bomb throwers, 2 depth charge tracks (18 depth charges)

Machinery: 3 diesels (2 M-50F, 1200 HP each, 1 M-50E, 600 HP), 2 shafts, 24 kts, 1500 nm/10.5 kts; 2 DG-25 generators. Endurance 7 days.

Complement: 27

Electronics: Sonar: Tamir-5

Chief designer A. N. Kunakhovich. Built at Zelenodolsk 1955. Steel hull, based on MO-IV. Black Sea Fleet.

MO-114 (A. V. Bukhantsov)

Project: 14081 and 14081M (SAIGAK)

NATO Class Name: None

Names:
Twenty units

Displacement: 13

Dimensions: 14 × 3.5 × 0.55

Armament: None or 1 machine gun

Machinery: 1 M-401B diesel, 1000 HP = 35 kts, 200 nm/35 kts, 1.15 t fuel

Complement: 2

Built from 1986 on in Perm' (Kama works), 4–5 per year; seaworthiness: 3. Aluminum hull, can be moved by rail. One (Project 14082) is a target boat.

Saigak (M. L. Grif)

Project: 1398 (AIST)

NATO Class Name: None

Names:
Thirty units

Displacement: 3.55/5.8

Dimensions: 9.5 × 2.6 × 0.5

Armament: None or 1 machine gun

Machinery: 1 3D-20 diesel, waterjet, 235 HP = 20 kts, 0.37 t fuel

Built in Kokua (Sretenskiy yard) for Border Guards on Amur River.

Aist (A. Y. Zahikin)

Project: 206M (SHTORM)

NATO Class Name: TURYA

Names:

	completed
T-68	
T-70	
T-72	
T-73	
T-75	
T-88	1974
T-96	Dec. '72
T-100	1972
T-102	
T-116	
T-117	
T-119	

T-126	Aug. '71
T-140	1971
T-150	1973
T-163	
T-164	
T-166	
T-177	
T-178	
T-183	
T-201	
T-252	1975
T-253	1975
T-272	1976
T-273	1976

Three others (twenty-nine units)

T-119 (Pavlov collection)

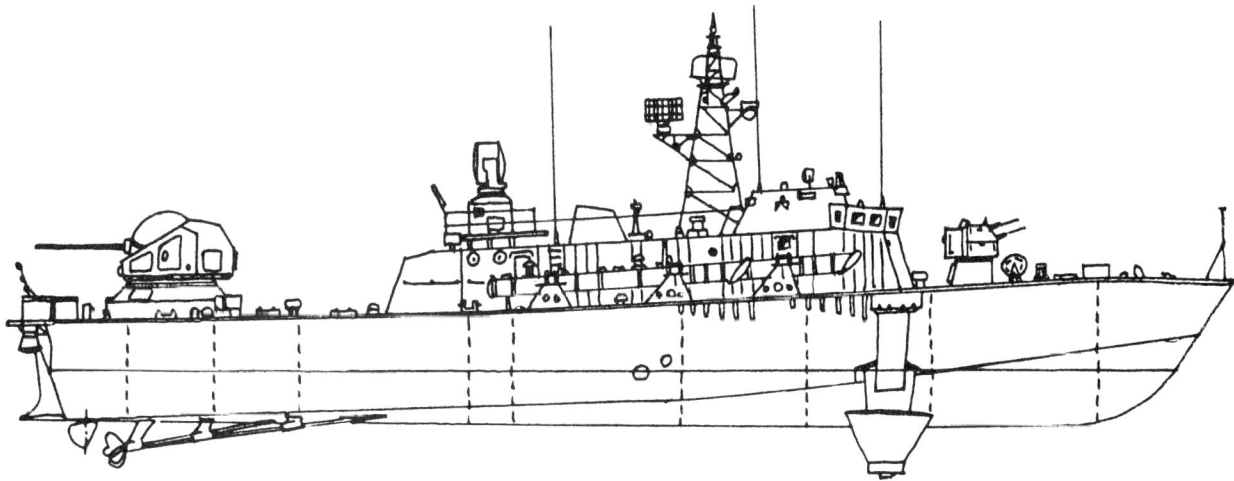

Displacement: 190/260

Dimensions: 38.6 × 7.6 (9.6 over foils) × 1.8 (3.3)

Armament: 1×2 57 mm (AK-725), 1×2 25 mm (2M-3M), 4×1 533 mm TT (OTA-206M), 2 torpedoes (53–56V or 53–56VA, 2 torpedoes 53-65K)

Machinery: 3 diesels (4000 HP M-503 or 5000 HP M-504), 3 screws, 48 kts (on foils), 600 nm/37 kts (foils), 1450 nm/14 kts (hullborne). Endurance 5 days.

Complement: 21

Electronics: Sonar: helicopter dipper (not on export units)

Built 1972–76 in Yaroslavl' and Vladivostok (ten units). Transfers: Cuba (2 each in Feb. '79, Feb. '80, Feb. '81, Jan. '83, 1 in Nov. '83), Ethiopia (1 each in 1985 and in Mar. '86), Kampuchea (1 each in 1984 and 1985), Seychelles (1 in Aug. '86; no TT), Vietnam (3 in 1984, 2 in 1986). T-72 and T-117 to Latvia 1993. T-75 on Caspian. T-116 sunk near Russkiy Island 1988. Remainder in Pacific stricken 1993–94.

Project: 184

NATO Class Name: None

Names:

	completed
TK-327	27 Aug. '56
TK-328	

Displacement: 31.5/34.1

Dimensions: 21.6 × 5 × 2.1

Armament: 2 533 mm TA, 1×2 14.7 mm (2M-1)

Machinery: 3 M-50F diesels, 3 screws, 3600 HP = 46 kts, 500 nm/33 kts, 300 nm/45 kts. Endurance 2 days.

Complement: 10 (1 officer)

Electronics: Radar: Zarnitsa; IFF: Nikel-Khrom

Chief designer V. M. Burlakov. Built in Feodosiya (Yard 831). Duralumin hull. Low seaworthiness (3–4). Black Sea. Stricken 1964.

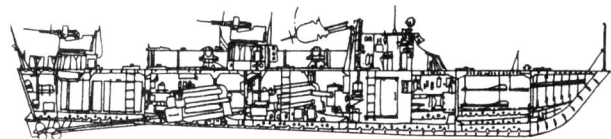

Project: 183 (BOL'SHEVIK)

NATO Class Name: P-6

Names:

T-61–67

T-69

T-72

T-112–114

T-151–161

T-172–175

T-192–199

T-221–254

T-266–271

T-701–749

T-851–889

T-901–939

T-962–981

T-1000–1316

T-1330–1450
  622 units

Displacement: 61.5/66.5

Dimensions: 25.4 × 6.24 × 1.24

Armament: 2×1 533 mm TT, 2×2 25 mm (2M-3, 4000 rounds), 8 depth charges (BB-1)

Machinery: 4 M-50F diesels, 4 shafts, 4800 HP = 43 kts; 1 DG-100 generator; 600 nm/33 kts, 1000 nm/14 kts; fuel 7.2 t. Endurance 5 days.

Complement: 20

Electronics: Radar: Zarnitsa (replaced by Reya); IFF: Fakel (later Nikel-K)-Khrom-K.

Chief designer: P. G. Goinkis (NKVD TsKB-5); lead unit built 1949, series production 1952–60 in Leningrad (Yard 5), Vladivostok (Uliss), and Sosnovskiy (TK-1244/1316). Wooden hull.

Project 183T: twenty-five units had boost gas turbines (4000 HP, 83 t, 52 kts, 5 screws); that included two with bow hydrofoils (Project 183-TK).

Project 183Ts: sixty converted to target boats (including KTs-4–9, KTs-23–25, KTs-29–31, KTs-37–39, KTs-44–48, KTs-50–52, KTs-54–61, KTs-74–103). Prototype KTs-23 was built in Leningrad in 1954.

Project 183A: one unit with Arktilita hull covering

Project 183U: one unit with 4×1 533 mm TT

Project 183E: two units for Black Sea tests with P-15 missiles (77.5 t, 38 kts), including T-69, stricken 1972

From 1964 forty-seat personnel launches were built on this hull: *Albatros, Burevestnik, Sokol, Taifun, Tsiklon, Chaika* (68 t, 39 kts).

Transfers: China (12, plus 80 built under license), Cuba (1962: TK-61, TK-1331, TK-1341, TK-1346, TK-1347, TK-1349, TK-1350, TK-1384, TK-1385, TK-1432, TK-1433), Egypt (24 in 1956 and 1960), Guinea (4), East Germany (13 on 5 Nov. '57, 18 in 1958–59), Indonesia (8 in 1961–62, including TK-1409, TK-1416, TK-1430, TK-1422, TK-1429, TK-1431), Iraq (2 in 1959, 4 in Nov. '60 and 6 in Jan. '61—all sunk), North Korea (10), Poland (20 in 1957–58), Somalia (4), South Yemen (2).

[Ed.: According to Western sources, transfers were Algeria (10 in 1963–68), China (few), Cuba (12 in 1962), East Germany (27 in 1957–60), Egypt (20 in 1956–58), Guinea (4 in 1965–67), Guinea-Bissau (4 in 1975–76), Indonesia (14 in 1961–62), Iraq (10 in 1960–62), North Korea (45 in the 1960s), Poland (20 in 1957–58), Somalia (4 in 1968), South Yemen (2 in 1973), Tanzania (3 from East Germany in 1974–75), and Vietnam (3 in 1967).]

Design 183T (Pavlov collection)

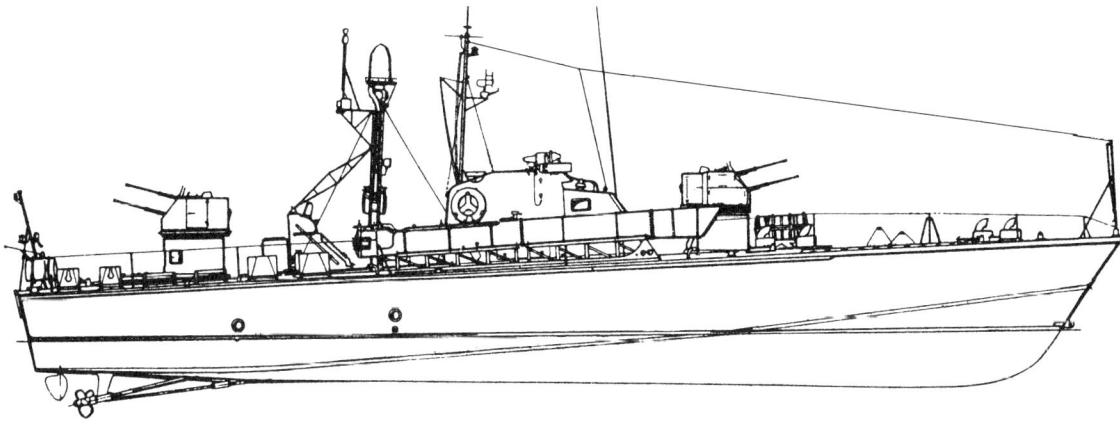

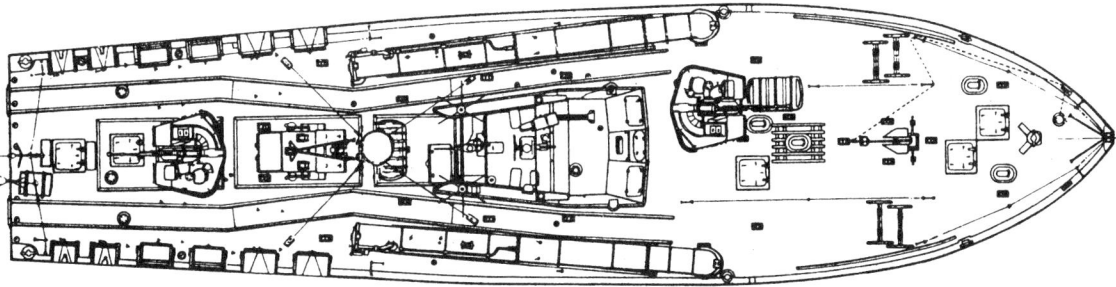

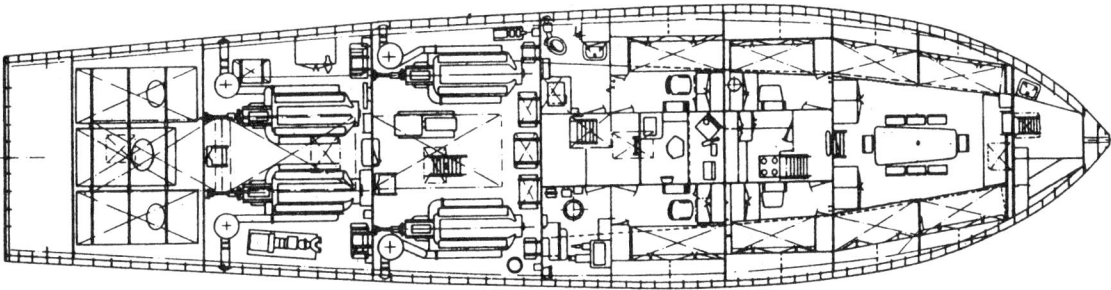

Design 183TK (Pavlov collection)

Project: 206

NATO Class Name: SHERSHEN

Names:

T-3
T-7
T-12–14
T-17–19
T-21
T-22
T-25–31
T-33
T-34
T-38
T-39
T-57
T-83–86
T-97–99
T-105
T-113–115
T-118
T-125
T-129
T-131
T-132
T-162
T-165
T-168
T-169
T-171
T-172
T-176

T-179
T-181
T-182
T-184
T-185
T-188–191
T-200
T-213
T-217
T-219
T-220
T-295
T-296
T-337
T-359
T-360
T-363
T-373
T-526–542

Eighty-seven units. Built at Zelenodolsk (1960–74) and Yaroslavl (fifteen units, 1960–70).

Displacement: 145/170

Dimensions: 34.6 × 6.75 × 3.75

Armament: 4×1 533 mm TT, 2×2 30 mm (AK-230, 2000 rounds), 12 depth charges or 3 mines

Machinery: 3 M-503A diesels, 3 shafts, 12,000 HP = 45 kts; 30 t fuel; 800 nm/30 kts, 600 nm/35 kts, 460 nm/42 kts; 3 DG-28 (220 V) generators.

Complement: 23

Electronics: Radar: Baklan
  Technical project developed 1955.
  Transfers: Angola (4), Bulgaria (6), Cape Verde Islands (2), Congo (3), Egypt (6), East Germany (18), Guinea (2), Guinea-Bissau (2), North Korea (3), Yugoslavia (2 plus 13 built under license). Three Northern Fleet units were destroyed 1972. Stricken 1984–94.
  [Ed.: Western sources added transfers to Vietnam (14).]

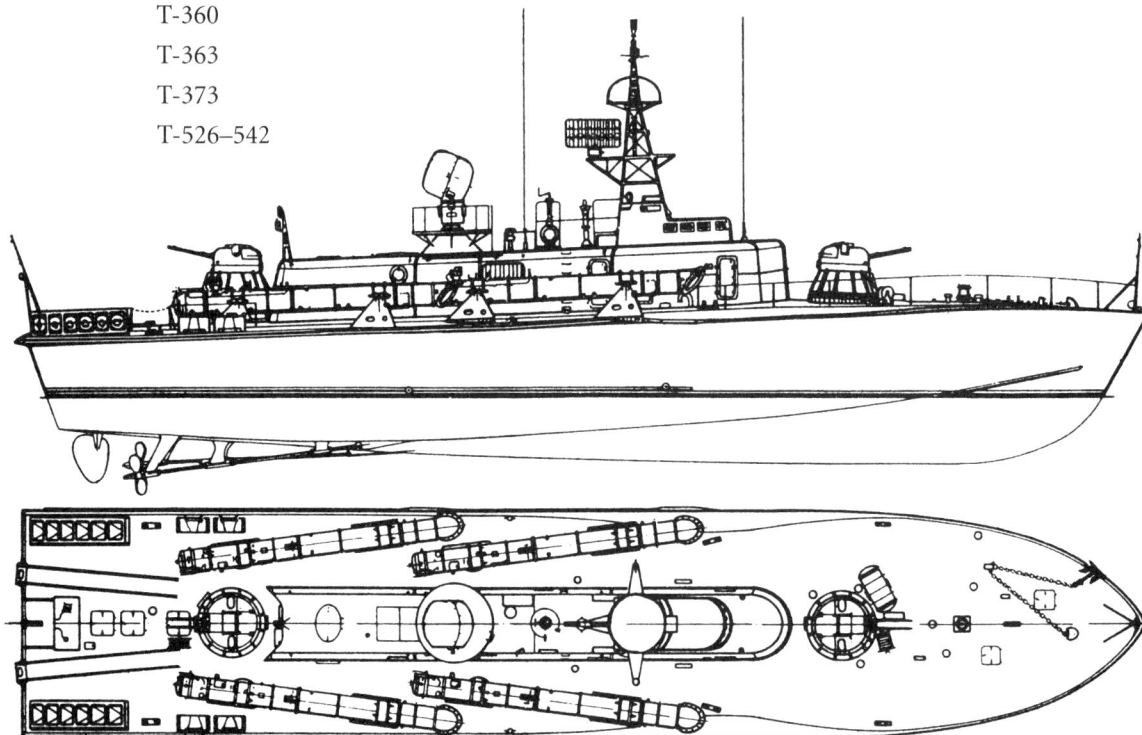

Shershen class (U.S. Navy)

Project: 206ER

NATO Class Name: MOL

Names:

TK-127

Displacement: 170/220

Dimensions: 38.5 × 7.7 × 1.8

Armament: 4×1 533 mm TT (OTA-53-206E), 2×2 30 mm (AK-230, 2000 rounds)

Machinery: 3 M-504 diesels, 3 shafts, 15,000 HP = 41 kts, 40 t fuel, 600 nm/35

Complement: 25

Electronics: Radar: Baklan

Built in Leningrad (Almaz yard) 1978. Escort-patrol boat on torpedo boat hull. Transfers: Ethiopia (2 in 1978), Somalia (4 in 1976–77), Sri Lanka (1 in 1975), South Yemen (1978). [Ed.: According to Western sources, boats listed as transfers to South Yemen were actually sent to Ethiopia.]

Design 206 (Pavlov collection)

TK-127 (Pavlov collection)

Project: 125 and 125A (KRY'LATIY)

NATO Class Name: PCHELA

Names:

T-330* and 1 other*

P-575–580

P-589–596 and 2 others
   Eighteen units

Displacement: 53.2/60.9

Dimensions: 25 × 4.9 × 2.6

Armament: 2×1 533 mm TA*, 2×2 25 mm*; other units: 2×2 14.5 mm (aircraft type)

Machinery: 2 M-503A diesels, 8000 HP, D-20P gas turbine, 20,000 HP = 73* kts or 68 kts (on foils), 2 DG-30 generators (400 Hz, 200 kW), 300 nm/45 kts

Complement: 12

Electronics: Radar: Ksenon-125

   Chief designer V. M. Burlakov (TsKB-19); in 1963–67 Feodosiya built two* torpedo boats for the navy and sixteen patrol boats/interceptors for the Border Patrol. Seaworthiness: 3. Twelve on the Baltic, remainder on the Black Sea; stricken 1988–91.

Pchela class (U.S. Naval Institute Photographic Collection

Pchela class (Pavlov collection)

Project: 317

NATO Class Name: ALESHA

Names:

completed

PRIPYAT

SUKHONA

VYCHEGDA   12 Jan.

Displacement: 2300/3860

Dimensions: 99 × 13.5 × 5.4

Armament: 1×4 45 mm (SM-20 ZiF), 4 mine tracks, 300 mines

Machinery: 4 diesels, 2 vertical-axis propellers, 8000 HP = 17 kts, 4000 nm/16 kts, 8500 nm/8 kts; have bow thrusters

Complement: 190

Electronics: Radar: Don-2

Chief designer: Ignatov. Built in Sevastopol 1967–76; fourth ship canceled and dismantled. Mine and net layers. *Pripyat* in Black Sea, *Vychegda* in Pacific, *Sukhona* in Northern Fleet. In reserve 1993.

Vychegda (Pavlov collection)

Project: 265*, 265K, 265A, I-265

NATO Class Name: SASHA

Names:

T-17

T-19

T-20

T-23

T-156–162

T-164–176

T-178

T-180–192

Thirty-seven units.

Displacement: 250/274* (265/289)

Dimensions: 42.5 × 6.4 × 1.77* (44 × 6.6 × 1.74)

Armament: 1 57 mm (ZiF-31B, or 1 45 mm SM-17), 2×2 25 mm (2M-3M; lead ship* had 2 14.5 mm 2M-7), 12 mines, 10 depth charges (BMB-1)

Machinery: 2 33-D diesels, 2 vertical-axis propellers (DKK 16/18), 1800 HP = 15.5 kts (with contact sweep, 8 kts), 1500 nm/10 kts, 2000 nm/8 kts; generators: 2 DG-25. Endurance 5 days.

Complement: 46

Electronics: Radar: Don; ESM: Bizan'-4; Sonar: Tamir-11

Chief designer: V. I. Blinov (TsKB-50, named Zapadnoye PKB after merger with TsKB-363). TTZ given 1946, lead boat built in Rybinsk 1953. Steel-hulled base sweepers. First combatants with vertical-axis propellers. Project 265A introduced new systems: new sweep AT-2, sonar MG-11, 57 mm gun, anti-nuclear protection (319 t). The three last units (Project E-265) were minehunters, with ET-3 television system. *Baltika* and *Saratovets* were handed over to civilian organizations.

Design 265A (A. N. Sokolov)

Project: 1256 (TOPAZ)

NATO Class Name: ANDRYUSHA

Names:

BT-10   named *Altaiskii Komsomolets* 13 Mar. '75–1992

BT-150 named *Komsomolets Estonii* 11 June '75–Apr. '91

Displacement: 373/400

Dimensions: 47.9 × 8.7 × 2.36

Armament: 1×6 30 mm (AK-630, 500 rounds; 500 in overload condition), 8 KSM mines or 6 KMD-1000 mines or 4 Kal'mar mines

Machinery: 2 diesels (M-504A-3, 4750 HP each) on wing shafts driving controllable-pitch propellers, 1 gas turbine (M-8NL, 20,000 HP) on center shaft, 29,500 HP = 38 kts, 500 nm/15 kts (normal fuel; 1000 nm with maximum fuel); fuel 26.5/50.5 t; seaworthiness: 6; 1 DG-200, 2 DG-100 generators. Endurance 3 days.

Complement: 16 (3 officers, 3 petty officers, 10 sailors)

Electronics: Radar: Don-D; IFF: Khrom-KMN; Ultra short-wave receiver/transmitter R-617, 619; Radio direction finder: ARP-58SB; gyrocompass (course indicator) GKU-2; Sounder: NEL-10

Chief designer Vilunas (KB P.O. Box A-1277); project approved 1970 and built 1975–76 at Srednye-Neva yard. Fiberglass hull. Used to create projected pressure waves to detonate pressure mines [Ed.: hence the unusually high power and speed]; also created powerful magnetic and acoustic fields. Sweep width 300–500 m. Can operate remote-control sweeps.

BT-150 (V. P. Chernyshov)

Project: 1252 (ALMAZ)

NATO Class Name: ZHENYA

Names:

	completed
KOMSOMOLETS TURKMENII	1966
BT-215	1968
Komsomolets Buryatii until 18 Mar. '92	
BT-177	1969

Displacement: 220/279

Dimensions: 38.9 × 7.8 × 4.7 m (with sonar dome down)

Armament: 1×2 30 mm (AK-230, 1000 rounds), 22 depth charges (in overload) or 4 KB mines; contact sweep MT-3U, acoustic sweep AT-3, looped magnetic sweep PEMT-4; or MT-2U, AT-3; or one solenoid magnetic sweep (ST-2) and acoustic sweep AT-3; surface net sweep MPST

Machinery: 2 diesels (M-870-FTK), 2 shafts, 2400 HP = 13.5 kts; generators: 2 DG-100, 1 DG-50; 1000 nm/10 kts; 14.4 t fuel, 1.5 t oil, 3.8 t water. Endurance 5 days.

Complement: 37 (4 officers, 2 petty officers, 31 sailors)

Electronics: Radar: Don; Sonar: Lan', MG-35, and Mezen'-2 bottom mine hunter (in system using a mine destroyer); Television to hunt bottom mines; IFF: Nikrhrom-M; Gyrocompass: Kurs-7; Sounder: NEL-M3b; Radio Direction Finder: ARP-50-06M

Chief designer: Vilunas (TsKB-363); project approved 1961. Experimental minehunters, built 1970, with fiberglass hulls. Stricken 1990.

BT-215 (V. V. Lubimov)

Project: 12660

NATO Class Name: GORYA (ex-BALCOM-7)

Names:

	completed
A. ZHELEZNYAKOV	30 Dec. '88
A. GUMANENKO	9 Jan. '94

Displacement: 780/950

Dimensions: 66 × 11 × 4.35

Armament: 2×4 launchers for Igla (9M39) AA missilc
system, 1 76 mm (AK-176), 1×6 30 mm (AK-630M),
2 406 mm TT (to launch minesweeping devices)

Machinery: 2 diesels, 2 shafts, 6000 HP = 15 kts

Complement: 65

Built 1988–91 at Srednye-Neva yard (T. Pontonniy) with
fiberglass hulls. Third ship dismantled incomplete. Systems
to hunt for and destroy mines of all types.

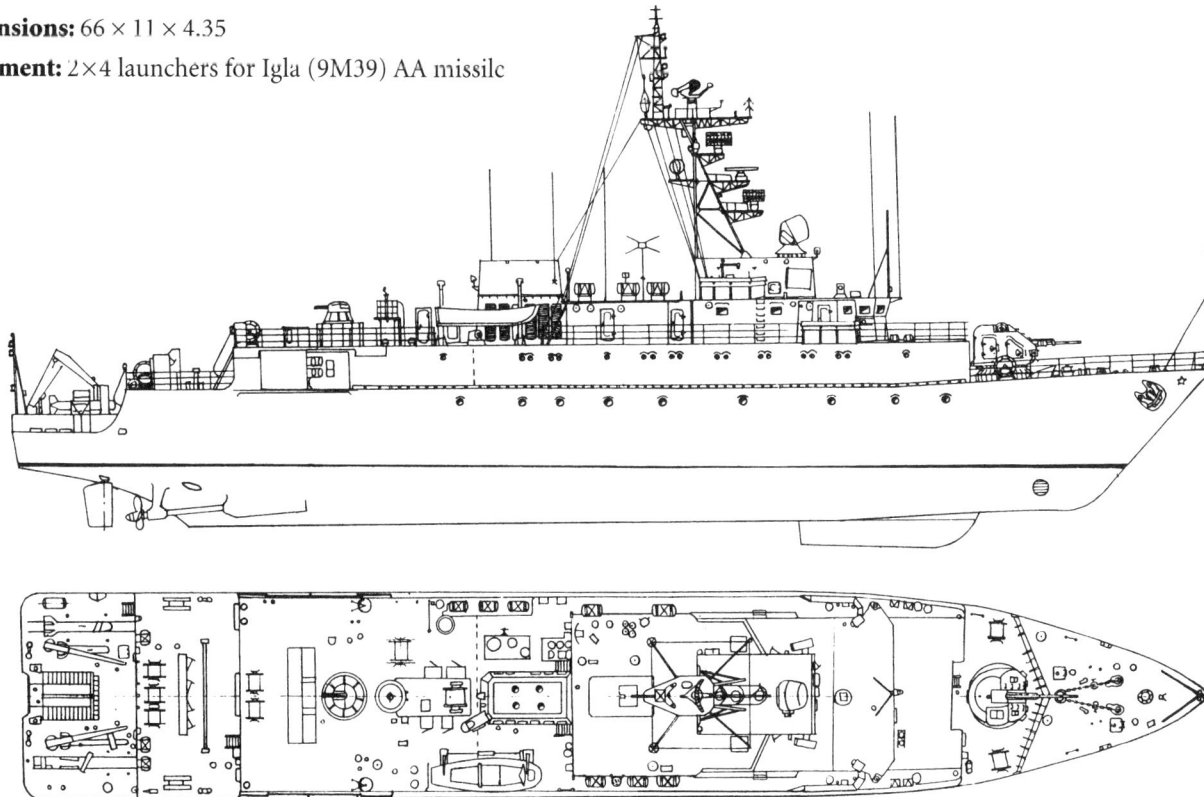

A. Zheleznyakov (V. V. Kostrichenko)

Project: 264 and 264A*

NATO Class Name: T-58

Names:

completed

T-1–T-12

T-14

T-15

T-22

T-50

T-71

T-108

T-110

T-112–130

PAVEL KHOKHRYAKOV

VASILII GROMOV

TIMOFEI UL'YANTSEV   16 Oct. '60

F. MITROFANOV

PAVLIN VINOGRADOV   16 Jan. '61

STARSHIY LEITENANT VLADIMIROV

STARSHIY LEITENANT LEKAREV

Forty-five units. T-6 (14 Apr. '60) was named *Vladimir Polukhin*. T-9 (l.d. 24 Sept. '57, lch 5 Sept. '58, completed 6 Aug. '60) was named *Primskii Komsomolets* in 1975.

Displacement: 773/842 (868*)

Dimensions: 70.2 × 9.61 × 3

Armament: 2×2 57 mm (ZiF-31B), 2×2 25 mm (2M-3, removed in *), 2×5 RBU 1200 (Uragan, with 120 RGB-12*), 12 large depth charges, MKT-1 sea contact sweep, TEM-2 magnetic sweep, BGAT high speed deep acoustic sweep

Machinery: 2 diesels (37-DR), 2 shafts, 4000 HP = 17.6 kts (11.4 kts streaming contact sweep), 2500 nm/12 kts; 2 DG-200, 1 DG-50 generators. Endurance 10 days.

Complement: 82

Electronics: Radars: Don, MR-103; ESM: Bizan'-4b; Sonar: MG-11

Chief designer: A. G. Sokolov (TsKB-263), built at Srednye-Neva yard. T-1 completed to Project 264A(*) in 1958. 2M-3 removed, new sonar installed, modified for anti-nuclear protection. Built through 1962. Originally rated Base Minesweepers, then Sea Minesweepers in 1966, then SKR in 1975. Re-equipped as radar pickets: T-50 (KVN-21), T-112 (KVN-23). T-4 became SKR-132; SKR-13 became UTS-399. *Vinogradov* and SKR-137 stricken in the Pacific in 1987. Last SKR and KVN stricken 1990. Transfers: Guinea (1), South Yemen (1).

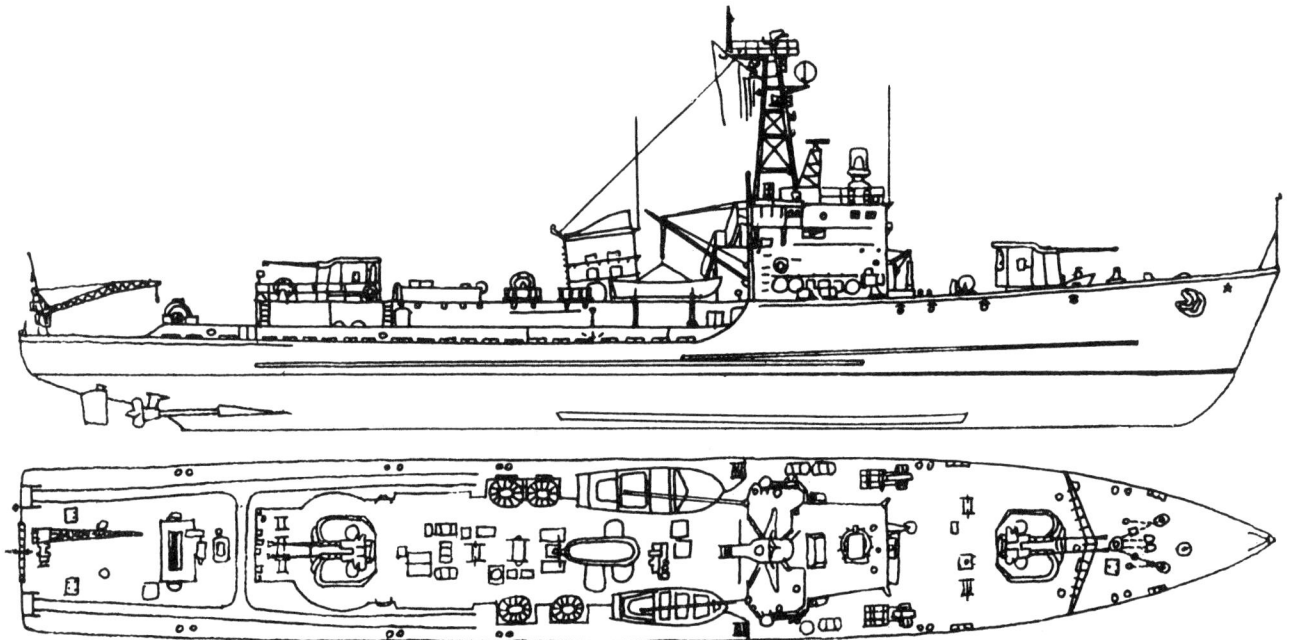

T-15 (A. N. Sokolov)

Project: 254, 254-K, 254-M*

NATO Class Name: T-43

Names:

MT-32

MT-43–49

MT-51

MT-52

MT-54–57

MT-59–69

MT-74–76

MT-78–86

MT-88

MT-89

MT-91–99

MT-102–107

MT-109

MT-131–141

MT-415–433

MT-480–500

MT-502

MT-503

MT-505–529

MT-750–752

MT-755

MT-801–837

VSEVELOD VISHNEVSKII

IVAN FIOLETOV

IVAN ROGOV

IVAN MASLOV

PROFESSOR PAPKOVICH

178 units. Names applied to numbered units after completion: *Dmitriy L'isov* (MT-46), *Komsomolets Kalmikii* (MT-69, renamed 14 Apr. '76), *Evgeniy Nikonov* (MT-94), *Kontr-Admiral Khoroshkhin* (MT-109), *Komsomolets Estonii* (MT-132), *Nikolai Markin* (MT-496), *Komsomolets Belorussii* (MT-502, renamed 12 Oct. '62), *Komsomolets Latvii* (MT-529), *Sakhalinskii Komsomolets* (MT-751), *Stepan Shaumyan* (MT-805), *Meshadi Azizbekov* (MT-818), *Kaliningradskiy Komsomolets* (MT-833), *Kontr-Admiral Yurkovskii* (MT-834), *A. Nikolaev* (MT-837). Built 1949–57 in Kerch (Zaliv yard: sixty-one units) and Izhora, Leningrad. In addition, twelve were built in Poland 1955–60.

Displacement: 535/569

Dimensions: 58 (59.1*) $\times$ 8.75 $\times$ 2.5*

Armament: 2$\times$2 37 mm (V-11M, 4000 rounds), 2$\times$2 25 mm (2M-3M, 4000 rounds*), 1$\times$2 12.7 mm (2M-1, 4000 rounds), 2 depth charge throwers (BMB-2, with 10 depth charges), 10 KB-3 mines. Sweeps: magnetic sweep TEM-52, sea contact sweep MT-1, acoustic sweep BGAT; or 2 BAT-2 acoustic sweeps.

Design 254 (V. P. Chernyshov)

T-43 class (U.S. Navy)

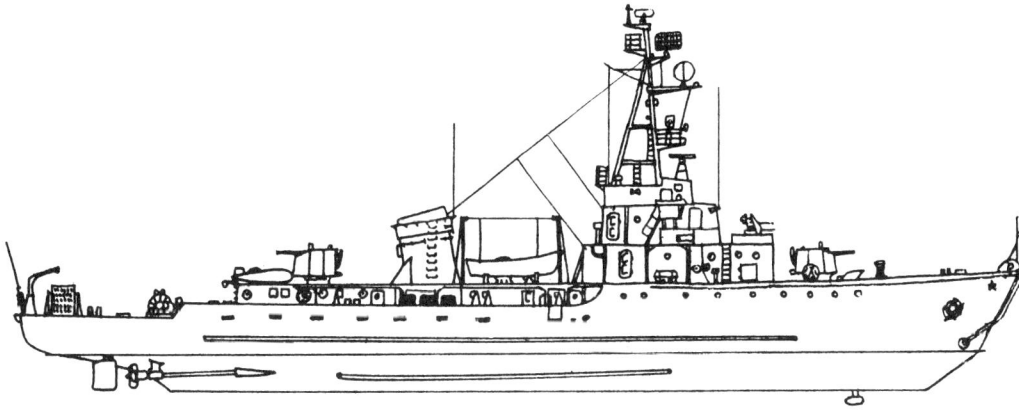

Armor: 8 mm deckhouse

Machinery: 2 diesels (9-D), 2 shafts (controllable pitch propellers on Project 254M), 2200 HP = 15 kts (10 kts with contact sweep, 12 kts with noncontact sweeps), 3500 nm/12 kts, 1900 nm/15 kts, 1500 nm*/14 kts, 4400 nm/8.3 kts; 68 t fuel; 2 DG-75, 1 DG-25 generators. Endurance 7 days.

Complement: 53 (5 officers, 7 petty officers, 11 rated men, 30 sailors)

Electronics: Radars: Lin', Fakel-MO, Ri'm; Sonar: Tamir-11
Chief designer G. M. Verasko (TsKB-50). Degaussing system. Ten bulkheads in hull.

Conversions to patrol ships 1963–72: MT-98, MT-419, MT-421, MT-751, MT-801, MT-802, MT-832 became P-499 *Kirov*, P-502 *Dzerzhinskiy, Brilliant, Korund, Sapfir, Izumrud, Rubin.*

Conversions to Project 258 radar pickets 1956–65: KVN-1 (MT-482), KVN-2 (MT-483), KVN-3 (MT-496), KVN-9 (MT-807), KVN-12 (MT-803), KVN-13 (MT-804), KVN-14 (MT-814), KVN-15 (MT-510), KVN-16 (MT-511), KVN-17 (MT-513), KVN-18 (MT-517), KVN-19 (MT-422), KVN-22 (MT-821), KVN-24 (MT-474), KVN-25 (MT-82), KVN-27 (MT-820), KVN-50.

Salvage ships (SS) based on this hull: SS-1, SS-2 (*Ivan Rogov*), SS-3 (MT-47), SS-13 (renamed *Chernomorets*).

Test ships based on this hull: *Som, Skat, Kasatka.*

On this hull were built or rebuilt 19 GKS (acoustic measurement ships, Project 513): GKS-11 (completed 20 June '56), GKS-12–26, GKS-45, GKS-48. In Nov. '90 GKS-23 burned in the Pacific.

Ivan Fioletov to Volgograd KUM 1990; *Moskva* and *Pogranichnik* to Moscow KUM. MT-31 became UTs-446, MT-102 became UTs-183 (1971), MT-56 became UTs-411, MT-60 became UTs-412. After ships were stricken, they were offered for use as boiler-cleaning ships, floating workships, etc.

Transfers: Algeria (2 in 1968), Albania (2 in 1960), Bulgaria (3 in 1953), China (4 in 1955, one returned 1960), Cuba (3: MT-416, 432, 433), Egypt (7 in 1962), Indonesia (6 in 1962), Iraq (2 in Mar. '69), Syria (2).

[Ed.: Shitikov et al. list two versions of a sketch design (300, 368 t) developed as early as 1944; the technical design was completed in 1947.]

Project: 266M, 266ME*, 266DM** (AKVAMARIN)

NATO Class Name: NATYA

Names:

	completed
MT-262	
MT-264	
MT-265	
MT-303*	
MT-417*	
MT-418*	
MT-461*	
MT-463* renamed MT-749 in 1990	
MT-712*	
ARTILLERIST	
VSEVELOD VISHNEVSKII	
VALENTIN PIKUL'	1990
VITSE-ADMIRAL ZHUKOV	
named *Elektrik* until 17 Mar. '85	
DISELIST	
DESANTNIK	
DAL'NOMERSHCHIK	
ZAPAL	30 Nov. '75
ZARYAD	30 Dec. '76
ZENITCHIK	
KOMENDOR	
KONTR-ADMIRAL VLASOV	
KONTR-ADMIRAL KHOROSHKHIN	1972
KONTR-ADMIRAL PERSHIN	1970
MASHINIST	
MINA	
MINER	
MARSOVIY*	
MOTORIST	
NAVODCHIK	
named *Kurskiy Komsomolets* June '82–18 Mar. '92	
PULEMETCHIK	
PARAVAN	31 Oct. '73
RAKETCHIK	
RULEVOIY	
RADIST	
named *Khar'kovskiy Komsomolets* until 18 Mar. '92	
RAZVEDCHIK	
SVYAZIST	
SEMEN ROSHAL'	17 Oct. '70
lead ship	
SIGNALCHIK	
SNAIYPER	
STRELOK**	
TRAL	30 Oct. '72
OS-99 named *Torpedist* until 1990	
TURBINIST until 1975 *Komsomolets Estonii*	
YAKOR'	30 Sept. '74

   Forty-six units.

Zenitchik (Pavlov collection)

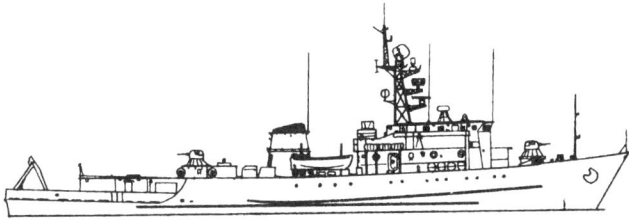

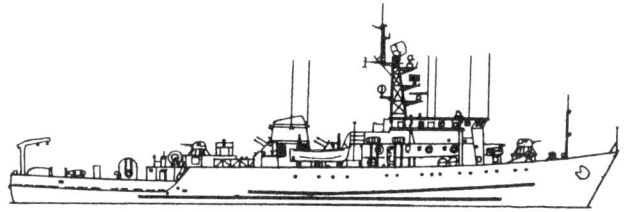

Displacement: 715/770 (745/800*)

Dimensions: 61 × 10.2 × 3.5

Armament: 2×8 launchers for Strela missiles (16 missiles), 2×2 30 mm (AK-230M, 2000 rounds), 2×2 25 mm (2M-3M, 2000 rounds), 2×5 RBU 1200M (30 RGB-12), 7 KMD-1000 mines or 32 BB-1 depth charges (overload). Submerged towed minehunter MKT-210. Sweeps: BKT, AT-3, TEM-4.

Machinery: 2 M-503 diesels, 2 screws, 5000 HP = 17 kts, 1500 nm/12 kts (with 48 t fuel; 2700 nm with 80 t fuel); seaworthiness: 9; 2 DG-200, 1 DG-100 (380 V, 50 Hz) generators. Endurance 10 days.

Complement: 68 (6 officers, 8 petty officers, 54 seamen)

Electronics: Sonars: MG-69 (to detect moored mines), MG-79 (to detect bottom mines), MG-26 (communications); Precision radio-navigation system: KPF-2 Shmel'.

Chief designer T. D. Pokhodun. Built in 1970–90 at Srednye-Neva and Khabarovsk (five units: one each 1972–76). Seagoing minesweepers (MTShch) with aluminum hulls. Three units had AK-630 gun mount. Twelve in Black Sea Fleet. *Rulevoiy* and *Signalchik* stricken 1994; *Tral* and *Paravan* stricken in Pacific 1993. *Khoroshkin* discarded 1994.

Transfers: India (two each 1978, 1979, 1980, 1986, 1987, 1988), Libya (two each 1981, Feb. '83; one each in Aug. '83, Jan. '84, '85, Oct. '86), Syria (one in 1985), Vietnam (*Mina* in May '80)

Natya class (U.S. Naval Institute Photographic Collection)

Project: 266, 266D (RUBIN)

NATO Class Name: YURKA

Names:

MT-6

MT-18

MT-27

MT-47

MT-58

MT-62

MT-63

MT-72

MT-73

MT-80

MT-82

MT-86

MT-94   named *Evgeniy Nikonov* 1965

MT-163

MT-179

MT-193

MT-200

MT-205

MT-208

MT-209

MT-214

MT-219

completed

MT-221   31 Aug. '70

MT-223   13 Apr. '68
   named *Grigorii Vakulenchik*

MT-226   named *Petr Mal'kov* 1968

MT-238   13 Oct. '67

MT-242   11 June '68

MT-253

MT-257   26 Dec. '69
   named *Vitse-Admiral Sabaneev* 1984

MT-262–264

MT-284   12 Sept. '68

ALEKSANDR KAZARSKII

ARSENII RASKIN

A. SOKOLOV

AFANASII MATIOSHENKO

BORIS SAFONOV

IVAN MASLOV 1966

IVAN SIVKO

MICHMAN PAVLOV   31 Dec. '70

   Twenty-five units. Built 1961–70 at Srednye-Neva (lead ship completed Dec. '63) and at Khabarovsk (four units, lead ship completed 30 June '64).

Displacement: 520/560

Dimensions: $52 \times 9.4 \times 2.6$

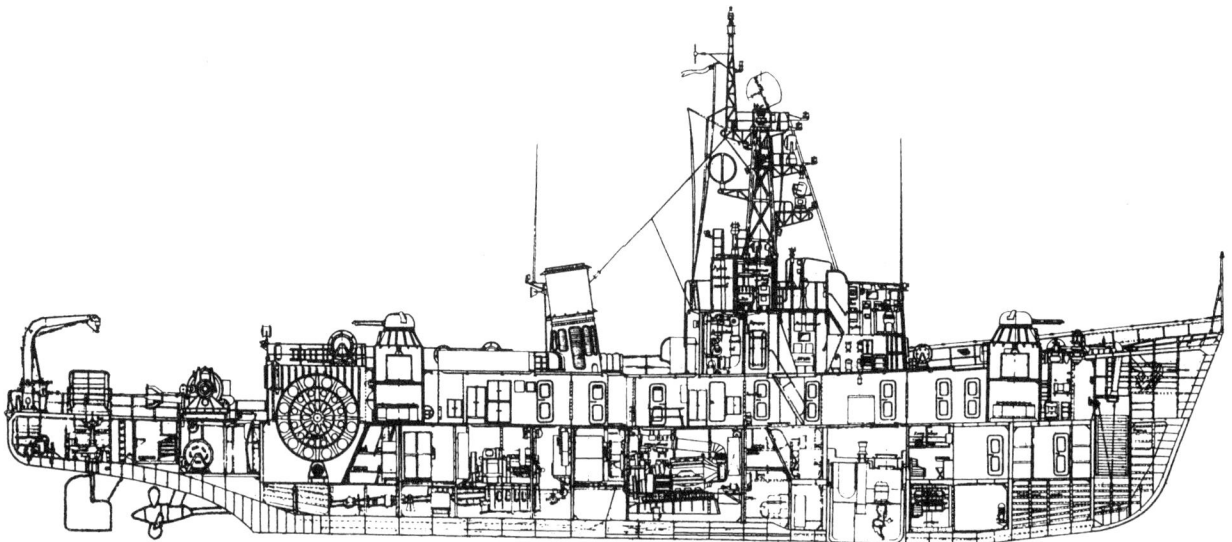

Design 266 (V. P. Chernyshov)

Armament: 2×8 launchers for Strela missiles (16 missiles), 2×2 30 mm (AK-230), 10 mines; sweeps: AT-5, TEM-3, PMR-2, PMT, GKT-2

Machinery: 2 M-503 diesels, 2 variable-pitch screws, 5000 HP = 16 kts (14 kts when towing contact sweep), 1500 nm/12 kts; 2 DG-200, 1 DG-100 generators. Endurance 7 days.

Complement: 60

Electronics: Radar: Don; IFF: Nikhrom; Sonar: Lan'
Chief designer Pegov (TsKB-363). Outline project (design) approved 1959. Aluminum-hulled ocean sweepers (MTShch).
Five units on the Black Sea. MT-80, MT-82, MT-200, MT-208, MT-242, MT-263, *Pavlov* (Pacific) were stricken 1991–93.
Transfers: Egypt (four in 1970–71), Vietnam (one in Dec. '79)

Project: 12650, 12655★ (YAKHONT)

NATO Class Name: SONYA

Names:

BT-15

BT-16   *Astrakhanskii Komsomolets* until Apr. '92

BT-21

BT-22

BT-31

BT-38   ex-*Sakhalinskii Komsomolets*

BT-48

BT-51

BT-56

BT-78

BT-96

BT-100

BT-103

BT-109

BT-114

BT-121

BT-123

BT-126   named *Orenburgskiy Komsomolets* 23 June '76–13 Mar. '92

BT-132

BT-152

BT-155

BT-202
named *Khersonskiy Komsomolets* 24 May '76–18 Mar. '92

BT-206

BT-212

BT-213

BT-215

BT-230

BT-232

BT-241★

BT-243–249

BT-251

BT-252

BT-255–261

BT-263

BT-266–270

199

Design 12650 (Pavlov collection)

BT-285	KOLOMENSKII KOMSOMOLETS
BT-79	

named *Sevastopolshiy Komsomolets* until 18 Mar. '92

BT-325   named *Komsomolets Buryatii* 30 Dec. '85

VLADIMIR POLUKHIN*

ALEKSEI LEBEDEV*

BT-294–296

BT-298–302

BT-315

BT-317–324

BT-327–330

BT-340–343

BT-347

BT-350

BT-438

BT-454

BT-470

BT-732   renamed *Komsomolets Kirgizii* 1987

BT-734

Seventy-four units. Built 1971–1991 at Vladivostok (Uliss: 22 units) and at Petrozavodsk (Avangard).

Displacement: 390/430

Dimensions: 49 × 10.2 × 2.75

Armament: 1×2 30 mm (AK-230), 1×2 25 mm (2M-3M), 5 mines; Project 12655 has 2×6 30 mm (AK-630M, 3500 rounds). Sweeps: BKT-2 contact, PEMT-4 looped magnetic, ST-2 solenoid magnetic, AT-5 acoustic, KIU-1 submerged towed television minehunting sensor (with mine-destruction explosives), surface net sweep TS-1.

Machinery: 2 diesels (9-D), 2 shafts, 2200 HP (2000 HP with DRA-210B installation) = 14 kts; 27.1 t fuel; 1700 nm/10 kts, 3 DG-100 generators; seaworthiness: 6. Endurance 15 days.

Complement: 45 (5 officers, 5 petty officers, 35 sailors)

Electronics: Radar: Mius; Sonars: MG-69 and MG-79; Underwater communications: MG-26

Chief designer V. Il Nemudrov. Wood- and fiberglass-hulled base minesweepers (BT) of 3rd Rank. Degausser has three coils. As modernized (*), sonars were replaced by MG-89 and underwater communications set was replaced by MG-35.

BT-325 suffered an engine room fire in 1984. BT-327 is a PKZ. BT-347 stricken 1995. BT-103 and 155 (Caspian Sea) were transferred to Azerbaidzhan.

Export units were Project 1265E (1500 nm range, endurance 10 days). Transfers: Bulgaria (four in 1983–86), Cuba (two in 1980, two in 1985), Syria (one in 1986), and Vietnam (one in Feb. '87, one in Feb. '88).

Project: 699, 257D, 257DM*

NATO Class Name: VANYA

Names:

completed	
BT-33–37	
BT-42	
BT-44	
BT-45	KOMSOMOLETS KIRGIZII
BT-70	
BT-77	
BT-85*	
BT-87	
BT-101	
BT-103*	
BT-111	
BT-116	
BT-142–149	
BT-168	
BT-194–199	
BT-203	

completed	
BT-206	
BT-216	
BT-218	
BT-220	
BT-222	
BT-224	
BT-227–231	
BT-235–237	
BT-239	
BT-240	
BT-277*	
BT-279*	
BT-283*	
BT-293	
BT-314*	20 June '70
BT-316*	30 Sept. '70
BT-338*	
BT-365	
BT-358*	

Vanya class (U.S. Naval Institute Photographic Collection)

Design 257D (Pavlov collection)

BT-415

BT-416

BT-442

BT-447

Sixty units. Built 1960–73 at Petrozavodsk and Vladivostok.

Displacement: 244/260 (254/270*)

Dimensions: 40 × 7.3 × 1.8

Armament: 1×2 30 mm (AK-230, low-magnetic version), 8–12 mines

Machinery: 2 M-870FTK diesels, 2 controllable-pitch screws, 2400 HP = 15 kts (10 kts with contact sweep), 1400 nm/12 kts, 2400 nm/9 kts; 2 DG-100, 1 DGR-50 (380V, 50 Hz) generators. Endurance 5 days.

Complement: 30

Originally minesweepers, then minehunters (TM-44 and others), then base sweepers (BT). Redesigned 1965 as Project 699 (six built in Petrozavodsk): 2500 HP. Seven units on the Black Sea, including one on the Danube River. BT-116 (Caspian) handed to Kiev DOSAAF 1981. *K. Kirgizii* stricken 1987.

Export construction: Bulgaria (seven in 1971–85), Syria (two in Dec. '72), Vietnam (one in 1986).

Project: 1258 (KORUND)

NATO Class Name: YEVGENYA

Names:

	completed
RT-29	
RT-32	
RT-41	1980
RT-52	1980
RT-136	
RT-155	
RT-172	
RT-297	
RT-349	
RT-361	
RT-402	1978
RT-403	1978
RT-420	
RT-433	
RT-444	
RT-471	1979
RT-435	
RT-473	
RT-583	
RT-585	
RT-587	
RT-588	
RT-602	
RT-823	

202

RT-1202–1210

RT-1215

RT-1244

RT-1256

RT-1258

Forty-five units. All built 1976–80 at Srednye-Neva.

Displacement: 88.5/91.5

Dimensions: 26.13 × 5.9 × 1.38

Armament: 1×2 25 mm (2M-3M) (or 14.5 mm 2M-7, 2000 rounds), 1×7 MRG-1 grenade launcher, twelve depth charges (including eight in overload condition); Neva-1 television minehunting system; sweeps: GKT-3 contact sweep, AT-2 acoustic sweep, SEMT-1 solenoid magnetic sweep

Machinery: 2 diesels (3D-12), 2 shrouded screws, 600 HP = 12 kts; also a low-speed propulsion unit with 1 diesel (6Ch-12/14); 300 nm/10 kts; 2.7 t fuel; 2 DG-50 generators. Endurance 3 days.

Complement: 10 (1 officer)

Electronics: Radar: Donets-2; Sonar: MG-7; Ultra-short wave transmitter and receiver: R-615, R-619-1; Gyrocompass: Gira-MA; Log: LR-2; Sounder: NEL-7; IFF: Khrom-KMN

Chief designer V. I. Blinov (KB P.O. Box A-1277); rated Roadstead Sweepers of 4th Rank. Three units were on the Black Sea. RT-136 and -473 were transferred to Azerbaidzhan. RT-52 and RT-403 were stricken 1994.

Transfers: Angola (2 in Sept. '87), Bulgaria (4 in 1977), Cuba (10 in 1977–84), India (6 in 1983–84), Iraq (3 in 1975), Mozambique (3 in Sept. '86), Nicaragua (2 ex-Cuban units, 1984), Syria (4 in 1978–86), Vietnam (2 in Nov. '89), North Yemen (3 in May '82).

RT-52 (B. P. Tiurin)

Project: 10750 (SAPFIR)

NATO Class Name: LIDA

Names:

RT-233

RT-234

RT-765–775

Twenty-two units. Built from 1989 on at Sredniye-Nevskiy, four per year.

Displacement: 85/135

Dimensions: 31.5 × 6.5 × 2.4

Armament: 1×6 30 mm (AK-630M, 2000 rounds); 1×8 launcher Igla-M missiles; submerged television minehunter, 1 contact sweep GKT-3MO, 1 non-contact sweep SEMT-1 (including acoustic sweep AT-6)

Machinery: 3 diesels (3D-12), 900 HP = 12 kts; 3 DG-50 generators; 650 nm/10 kts; seaworthiness: 5. Endurance 5 days.

Complement: 11

Electronics: Radar: Mius; Sonar: mine locator Kabarga-1

Fiberglass hull. Crane pull 5.3 t at 9 kts. Can carry spetsnaz divers and mine specialists.

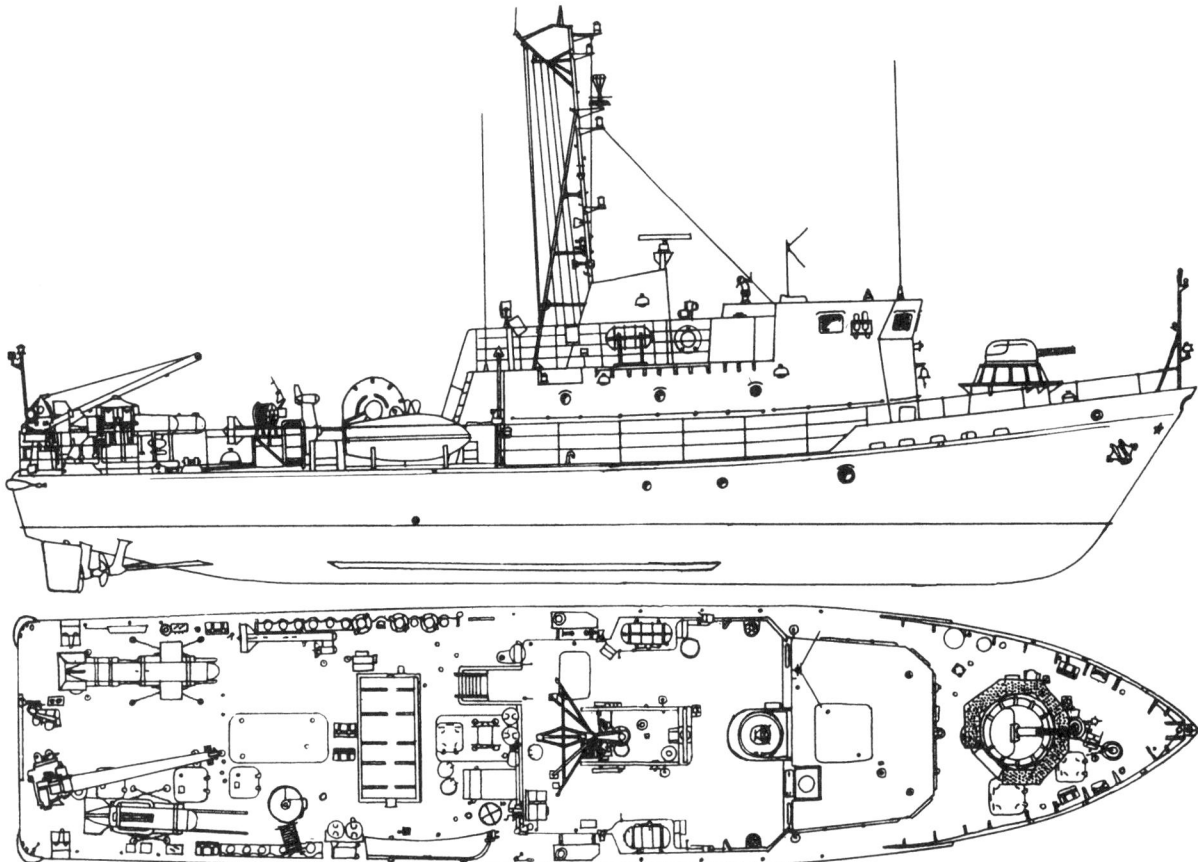

BT-757 (Pavlov collection)

Project: 1427

NATO Class Name: ILYUSHA

Names:

completed 1966–69

RT-168

RT-293

Eight others
Ten units

Displacement: 70/85

Dimensions: $26.4 \times 5.9 \times 1.4$

Armament: none

Machinery: 1 diesel, 500 HP = 12 kts

Complement: 10

Fiberglass hull. Can be used as radio-controlled sweepers.
Two on the Black Sea, one in Caspian.

Project: 1259 and 12592 (MALAKHIT)

NATO Class Name: OLYA

Names:

RT-450

RT-710

RT-722

Four others
Seven units. Lead ship built 1973 at
Srednye-Neva

Displacement: 62/64

Dimensions: $22.8 \times 4.5 \times 1.4$

Armament: 1×2 25 mm (2M-3M) or
1×2 12.7 mm (UTES-M)

Machinery: 2 diesels (3D-6N), 470 HP =
10 kts, 2 DG-50 generators, 400 nm/8 kts

Complement: 15

Electronics: Radar: Mius
Fiberglass-hulled Roadstead Sweepers
of 4th Rank.

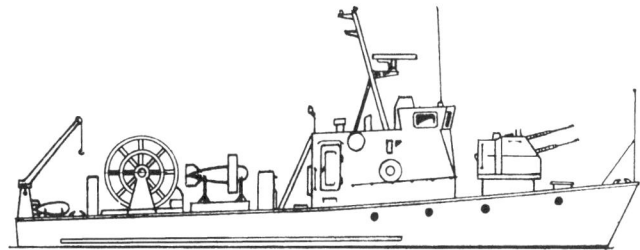

RT-172 (I. B. Neiy)

Project: 151

NATO Class Name: TR-40

Names:

RT-20–28

RT-33–35

RT-145–154

RT-157–170

RT-175–196

Displacement: 49.8/51

Dimensions: 27.7 × 4.1 × 0.72

RT-158 (Pavlov collection)

Armament: 1×2 25 mm (2M-3, 1000 rounds), 1×2 14.7 mm (2M-7, 1000 rounds), 24 depth charges or mines (YaM-25 or KPM-13 or AMD-1000); RKT-1 contact sweep; BAT-1 acoustic sweep, SAMT-1 magnetic sweep; explosive line charge (1000 m)

Armor: 7 mm deckhouse, 4 mm turret and barbette

Machinery: 2 diesels (3-D12), 600 HP = 16 kts, 400 nm/14.8 kts, 500 nm/10 kts; 2.75 t fuel; 2 DG-12.5 generators; seaworthiness: 2. Endurance 5 days.

Complement: 12 (2 petty officers, 3 rated men, 8 seamen)

Chief designer D. I. Rudakov (TsKB-19). Nine bulkheads. Built 1954–58 in Poland (Visla yard). Wooden hull with degaussing coils. [Ed.: Burov describes these units as river minesweepers.]

Project: 361T

NATO Class Name: K-8

Names:

KT-62–65

RT-1216

125 others

Displacement: 19/26

Dimensions: 16.9 × 3.2 × 1.2

Armament: 1×2 12.7 mm (2M-7)

Machinery: 2 diesels, 700 HP = 18 kts, 300 nm/10 kts

Complement: 6

Design 361T (Pavlov collection)

Built 1954–59 in Soviet Union and Poland (Visla yard, Gdansk). Launch minesweepers. Personnel and medical boats built on this hull: SN-33, SN-88, SN-126, SN-391, SN-397, SN-1306. Four boats on Danube. Transfers: Nicaragua (four in 1984), Vietnam (five in Oct. '80).

Project: 1253

NATO Class Name: None

Names:

SH-1–7

One other

    Built in Petrozavodsk 1966–70.

Displacement: 111.5/115.8

Dimensions: 25 × 5.4 × 1.63

Armament: None

Machinery: 1 diesel, 600 HP = 18 kts,
2 DG-50 generators

Complement: 6

Electronics: Radar: Donets-2; IFF: Khrom KMN.
    Chief designer V. V. Siderov. Remote-controlled
line charge layers with wooden hulls.

SH-3 (Pavlov collection)

Project: 696, 696DB

NATO Class Name: None

Names:

4 units built 1976 at Srednye-Neva

Displacement: 293/315

Dimensions: 43 × 7.2 × 1.5

Armament: 1×6 30 mm (AK-630), up to 20 mines

Machinery: 2 diesels, 2200 HP = 16.5 kts, 1000 nm/12 kts

Complement: 27

    Simplified hull construction with stabilizer. Roadstead
Sweepers 4th Rank.

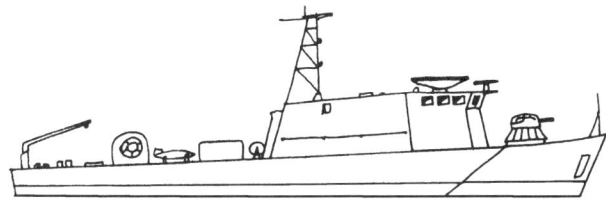

Project: 1250

NATO Class Name: None

Names:

RchT-46

RchT-139

RchT-141

RchT-187

RchT-189

RchT-190

RchT-214

RchT-220

RChT-249

Displacement: 120

    The Soviet Navy operated Roadstead Sweepers of Projects
1225.5, 13000, 697, 1330 (on a trawler hull), 911V, R-33,
1741, T-63, mainly using lake and river tugs with 150–600 HP
powerplants and other vessels, as well as unpowered line
charge layers, mine rafts (Project 355), etc.

Project: 572/34

NATO Class Name: None

Names:

RT-720

One other

Displacement: 90.4/119

Dimensions: 25.2 × 5.6 × 2.1

Machinery: 1 diesel (6 NVD-24), 150 HP = 9 kts; 1 DG-27
generator. Endurance 7 days.

Complement: 12

    Built on SChS-150 hull, in Caspian and in Pacific.

Project: 388/1

NATO Class Name: None

Names:

		completed
BT-459	ex-LENOK	7 Sept. '73

Displacement: 225/318

Dimensions: $34 \times 7.1 \times 2.9$

Armament: 1×2 25 mm (2M-3M)

Machinery: 1 diesel (8 NVD-36), 300 HP = 9.5 kts; 23.3 t fuel. Endurance 10 days.

Complement: 18

    Built in 1958 at Petropavlovsk, in 1967 at Nikolaevsk-on-Amur, type RS-300 (seiner). In Pacific Fleet. Stricken 31 May 1984.

Project: 1338P

NATO Class Name: None

Names:

RT-223

Displacement: 69.3/93

Dimensions: $21.8 \times 6 \times 1.8$

Armament: 1×2 12.7 mm (2M-7)

Machinery: 1 diesel (3D-6), 150 HP = 9 kts. Endurance 1 day.

Complement: 7

    Built at Vladivostok (Okyabrskoi Revolut-siya yard). Stricken July '92.

Project: 1328

NATO Class Name: BALTICA

Names:

BT-225

Displacement: 130.2/175

Dimensions: $25.5 \times 6.8 \times 2.4$

Armament: 1×2 12.7 mm (2M-7)

Machinery: 1 diesel (MBD-26), 1 shaft, 300 HP = 10 kts, 1350 nm/10 kts

Complement: 10

    Built in Kiev (Leninskaya Kuznitsa yard) 1983 on a trawler hull; this type was also built at the Sosnovskiy yard.

Project: 1174 (EDINOROG)

NATO Class Name: None

Names:

	completed
IVAN ROGOV	15 June '78
ALEKSANDR NIKOLAEV	30 Dec. '82
MITROFAN MOSKALENKO	1989

    Built in Kaliningrad.

Displacement: 8600/13,880

Dimensions: $158 \times 24.5 \times 4.2$ (5.5)

Armament: 4 helicopters, 2×1 launchers (ZiF-122) for Osa-M missiles (20 missiles); 2×8 launchers for Strela missiles; 1×2 76 mm (AK-726, 1200 rounds), 4×6 30 mm (AK-630), 2×30 122 mm rocket launchers (BM-21) (320 rockets)

Machinery: 2 gas turbines, 2 screws, 36,000 HP = 21 kts, 4000 nm/18 kts, 12,500 nm/14 kts. Endurance 30 days.

Complement: 400

Electronics: Radars: MR-310, Volga; Direction-finder: Rumb

    Chief designer V. V. Maksimov. Discharges through bow ramp and stern well dock. Load: 440 naval infantry men, 79 vehicles, or 46 medium tanks with crews. Tank space $54 \times 12 \times 3$ m. 34 t crane. Can deliver air cushion vehicles (KVP; 2 Lebed' type) or 1 small landing ship of Ondatra type, or Serna in well deck ($75 \times 12.6 \times 8.2$ m). *Mitrofan Moskalenko* in Northern Fleet, others in Pacific.

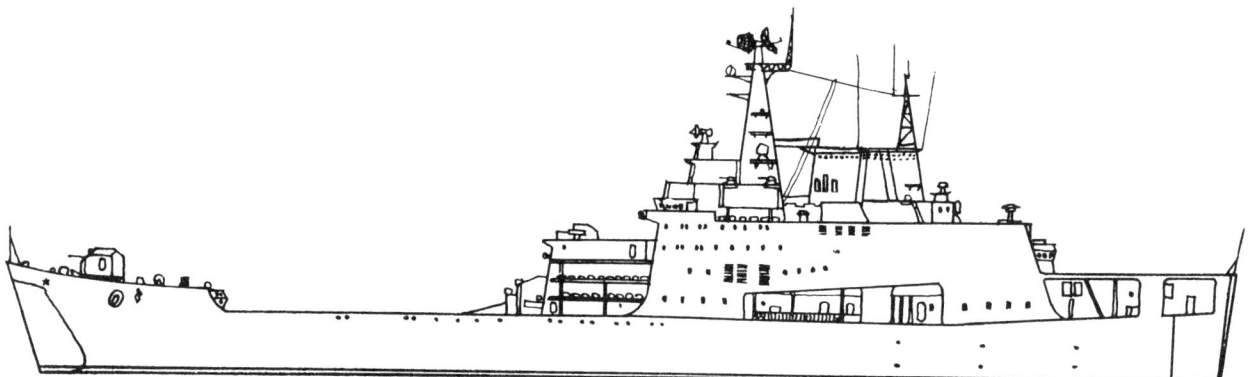

Ivan Rogov (U.S. Navy)

Project: 775-III*, 775-II, 775

NATO Class Name: ROPUCHA

Names:

	completed		
BDK-11*	Apr. '90		
BDK-14	31 Aug. '81		
BDK-32			
BDK-43			
BDK-45			
BDK-46			
BDK-57			
BDK-48	30 June '75		
BDK-54*			
BDK-55			
BDK-56	KONSTANTIN OL'SHANSKII		
BDK-58			
BDK-60			
BDK-63	30 July '75		
BDK-64	TSEZAR KUNIKOV		
BDK-67			
BDK-90	30 Nov. '75		
BDK-91			
BDK-99			
BDK-105			
BDK-119			
BDK-121			
BDK-122*			
BDK-181			
BDK-182			
BDK-197		17 Aug. '78	
BDK-200			

Twenty-eight units

Displacement: 3450/4080

Dimensions: 112.5 × 14.9 × 3.6

Armament: 4×8 launchers for Strela missiles (32 missiles), 2×2 57 mm (AK-726) or 1 76 mm (AK-176)*, 2×6 30 mm (AK-630)*, UMS-73 Grad*

Machinery: 2 diesels (16 ZVB 40/48), 2 screws, 19,200 HP = 18 kts, 3500 nm/16 kts, 6000 nm/12 kts; 3 DG-800 generators. Endurance 30 days.

Complement: 98 (17 officers), 225 Naval Infantry

Electronics: Radar: Positiv, Don

Built in Poland (Gdansk): first series 1974–78 (twelve units), second 1980–85, third (*) 1988–91. Load through bow. Large landing ships (BDK) of 2nd Rank. An improved landing ship (Project 778 ADM GREN) was dismantled on the slip. BDK-11, BDK-14, BDK-48, BDK-63, BDK-90, BDK-98, BDK-101, BDK-181, BDK-197 (of which BDK-48 stricken 1994) in the Pacific. BDK-46, BDK-54, BDK-56, BDK-64, BDK-67 in Black Sea. BDK-119 to South Yemen 1979.

Ropucha class (Pavlov collection)

Ropucha class (U.S. Naval Institute Photographic Collection)

Ropucha class (U.S. Navy)

Project: 1171 (TAPIR)

NATO Class Name: ALLIGATOR

Names:

completed

Type 1:

BDK-6   KRIMSKIY KOMSOMOLETS

BDK-25   named *Tomskiy Komsomolets* until Mar. '92
    ex-BDK-13   Sept. '67

BDK-65 named *Voronezhskiy Komsomolets* until 18 Mar. '92
    ex-BDK-10

BDK-62   *Komsomolets Karelii* until Apr. '92

Type 2:

BDK-66   1968
    named *Sergei Lazo* 13 Feb. '75

BDK-69

Type 3:

ALEKSANDR TORTSEV   Dec. '71

DONETSKIY SHAKHTER

KRASNAYA PRESNYA

PETR IL'ICHEV

BDK-80   named *50 Let Shefstva Vlksm* 23 Oct. '72–Mar. '92
    ex-BDK-77   1969

ILYA AZAROV

Type 4:

NIKOLAI FIL'CHENKOV

NIKOLAI VILKOV   30 May '74

Displacement: 3040/4650

Dimensions: 113.1 × 15.6 × 4.5

Armament: 3×8 launchers for Strela missiles (24 missiles) on BDK-62, *Lazo,* and *D Shakh;* 2×8 launchers for

Alligator class (U.S. Naval Institute Photographic Collection)

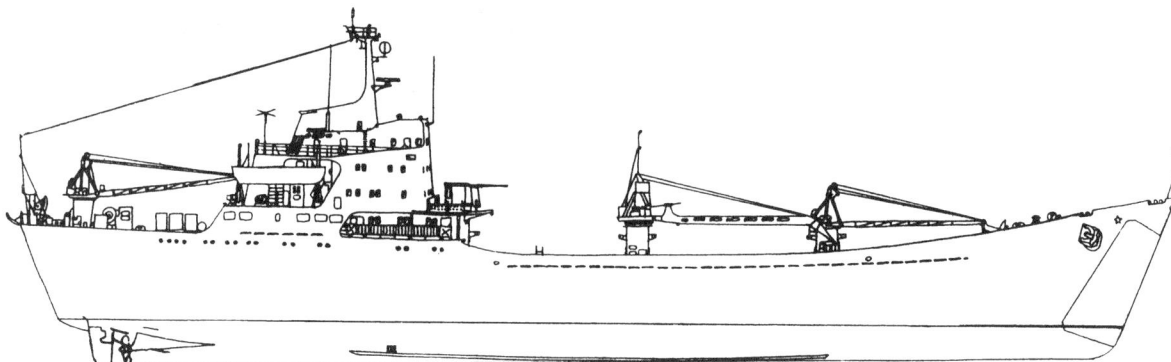

Strela missiles (16 missiles) on *Petr Il'ichev* only; 1×2 37 mm (V-11M), 2×22 rocket launchers, 2×2 25 mm (2M-3M on Type 4)

Machinery: 2 diesels, 2 screws, 9000 HP = 16.5 kts, 10,000 nm/15 kts

Complement: 100

Built 1966–76 in Kaliningrad (Yantar' yard). Ramps at bow and stern. Load: 1750 t. Tank deck: 90 m. Accomodates 20 MAZ-543 or 52 ZIL-131 or 85 GAZ-66. Time to unload on an unprepared shore: 1.5 hr. *Ilya Azarov* taken over by Ukraine. BDK-25, BDK-80, *Lazo*, and *Tortsev* stricken 1994. *Presnaya* sold to a private firm in 1994.

Project: 773

NATO Class Name: POLNOCNY-C

Names:

SDK-20

SDK-22

SDK-61

SDK-62

SDK-82

SDK-88

SDK-154

SDK-164

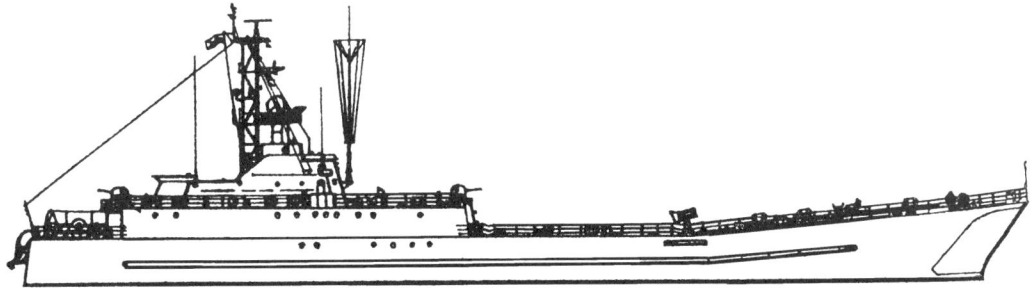

Polnocny-C class (U.S. Navy)

Displacement: 1120/1150

Dimensions: 82 × 10 × 2

Armament: 4 launchers for Strela missiles (32 missiles), 2×2 30 mm (AK-630), 2×18 rocket launchers (140 mm)

Machinery: 2 diesels, 2 screws, 5000 HP = 18 kts, 900 nm/17 kts, 2000 nm/12 kts

Complement: 42

Built in Poland 1970–76. Load: 350 t; six tanks, 180 Naval Infantry. Bow ramp. Landing deck: 53.3 × 6.7 m. Medium landing ships (SDK). Two ships have helicopter pads. SDK-82, SDK-88, SDK-154, SDK-164 on Black Sea. SDK-135 sold to a private firm in 1994.

SDK-82 (Pavlov collection)

Polnocny-C class (U.S. Naval Institute Photographic Collection)

Project: 770D, 770MD

NATO Class Name: POLNOCNY-A

Names:

MDK-36

MDK-37

MDK-68

MDK-78

MDK-79

MDK-81

MDK-85

MDK-86

MDK-87

MDK-88

MDK-92

MDK-93

MDK-94

MDK-107

Displacement: 740/794

Dimensions: 73 × 8.5 × 1.8

Armament: 2×8 launchers for Strela missiles (16 missiles), 2×2 30 mm (AK-230), 2×18 rocket launchers

Machinery: 2 Skoda diesels, 2 screws, 5000 HP = 18.5 kts, 1000 nm/18 kts, 1500 nm/14 kts

Complement: 38

Built in Poland 1963–68 by Northern Yard (Polnocny Yard in Polish). Load: 183 t; 9 ZIL-131 or 20 GAZ-66 trucks. Landing deck: 36.6 × 5.2 m. One equipped as a minelayer. Medium landing ships, redesignated small landing ships (MDK) 3rd Rank from 1990 on. MDK-107 to Azerbaidzhan. MDK-2, MDK-7, MDK-10, MDK-21, MDK-24 to breakers 1993–94.

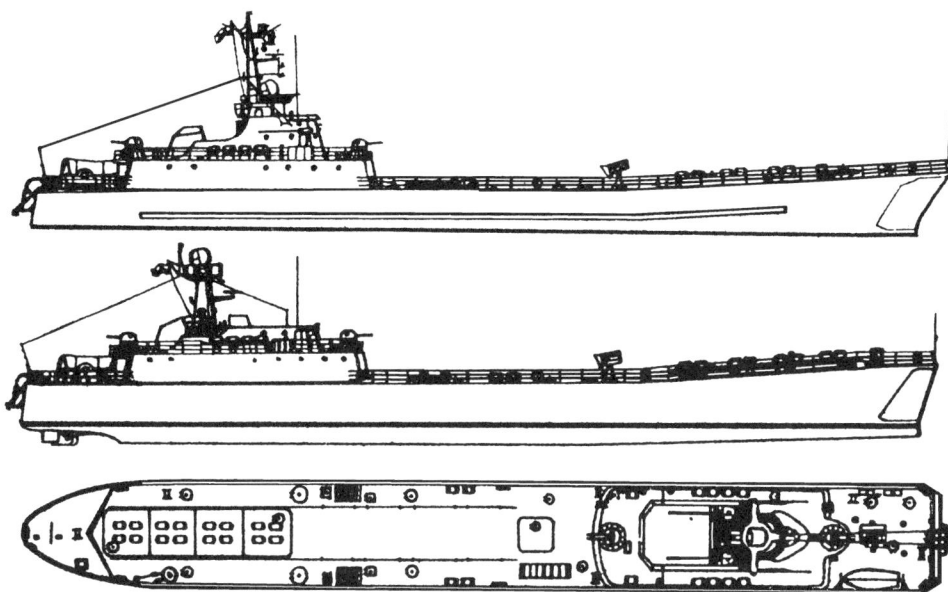

MDK-79 (V. P. Chernyshev)

Project: 771, 771A

NATO Class Name: POLNOCNY-B

Names:

	completed
SDK-19	
SDK-21	
SDK-39	
SDK-44	
SDK-45	
SDK-70–74	29 May '70
SDK-83	
SDK-84	
SDK-96	
SDK-99	
SDK-102	
SDK-111	
SDK-112	
SDK-119–121	
SDK-137	
SDK-171	30 June '68
SDK-172	

Displacement: 750/800

Dimensions: 74 × 8.5 × 1.8

Armament: 4 launchers for Strela missiles (32 missiles), 2×2 or 4×2 30 mm (AK-230), 2×18 140 mm rocket launchers (BM-18)

Machinery: 2 diesels, 2 screws, 5000 HP = 19 kts, 1000 nm/18 kts, 1500 nm/14 kts

Complement: 40

Built in Poland 1968–70. Load: 180 t, up to 100 Naval Infantry. Landing deck: 45.7 × 5.2 m. Three ships re-equipped as minelayers. Twenty-three built for Polish Navy. Transfers (of Polish-built ships): India (10), Indonesia (1), Iraq (4), Libya (4). Transfers from Soviet Union: Algeria (1), Angola (3), Cuba (2), Egypt (3), Ethiopia (2), Somalia (1), South Yemen (3, including SDK-44 and -45 in 1973), Syria (3), Vietnam (3, including SDK-74 in Apr. '80 and SDK-112 on 4 Jan. '80). [Ed.: Western sources list 4 for South Yemen and 3 for Libya.]

SDK-73, SDK-96, SDK-99, SDK-111, SDK-172 stricken 1992–94. SDK-84 stricken after accident in Pacific 1979. Black Sea units: SDK-83 (to breakers 1993), SDK-102, SDK-137, SDK-154, SDK-164.

Project: 188

NATO Class Name: MP-8

Names:

SDK-8
SDK-9
SDK-12
SDK-24
SDK-25–35
SDK-75
SDK-76
SDK-85

Displacement: 1020/1430

Dimensions: 74.7 × 11.3 × 2.43

Armament: 2×2 57 mm (ZiF-31B)

Machinery: 2 diesels (37-DR), 4000 HP = 14 kts, 2000 nm/10 kts

Complement: 35

TsKB-50 design, built in Vyborg. Lead ship completed 31 Dec. '58, series completed 1963. Load: five medium tanks, three heavy tanks, or 350 men with ammunition.

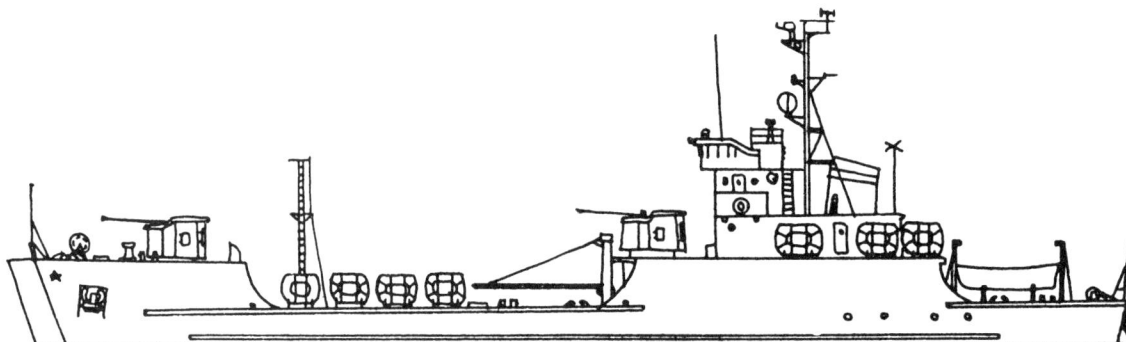

MP-8 class (U.S. Naval Institute Photographic Collection)

Project: 572

NATO Class Name: MP-6

Names:

SDK-2

SDK-4

BUREYA

KHOPER

BIRA

IRGIZH

VOLOGDA

SDK-38

Displacement: 1400/2030

Dimensions: 70.9 × 12.3 × 3.8

Armament: 1×2 57 mm (ZiF-31B), 2×2 25 mm (2M-3M)

Machinery: 2 diesels (8-DR), 1600 HP

Built in Oktyabrskiy 1956–59 on the basis of the Project 568 freighter. Load: 5 medium or 4 heavy tanks or 225 men. 1 10t crane, 2 t cranes. *Bureya* and *Khoper* re-equipped as missile transports (VTR-29, VTR-297), two more converted to military transports (VTR-298, VTR-299), stricken 1992. One to experimental ship (OS-15, in the Caspian). *Bira* on the Black Sea.

OS-15 (V. V. Muratov)

Project: 450, 450 bis*

NATO Class Name: MP-2, MP-4*

Names:

MPK-16

MPK-17

MPK-23

MPK-40

MPK-41

MPK-46

MPK-48

MPK-49

MPK-50

MPK-52

MPK-53

MPK-114

MPK-115

MPK-116

MPK-124

MPK-128*

MPK-130–136*

MPK-142

MPK-143*

MPK-144

MPK-145

MPK-146*

MPK-147

MPK-148

MPK-149

MPK-150

MPK-162

Thirty-three units

Displacement: 505/620

Dimensions: $56 \times 8 \times 2.7$

Armament: 2×2 25 mm (2M-3), 3×2 25 mm*

Machinery: 2 diesels, 1100 HP = 10 kts, 1500 nm/8 kts

Complement: 40

Built in Vyborg 1956–58. Originally designated MDK, redesignated SDK 1963. 4 3t cranes.* SDK-114, SDK-115, SDK-124 stricken 1970 (Pacific). MDK-50 to ocean survey ship 1972. MDK-162 became a test ship. MDK-52, MDK-53, MDK-144, MDK-145 became target ships. MDK-49 and MDK-146 became seagoing barges MBSS-252400 and MBSS-253400.

MP-4 class (Royal Danish Navy)

MP-2 class (A. N. Sokolov)

Project: 106K, 106KM*

NATO Class Name: VYDRA

Names:

MDK-4

MDK-27

MDK-155–166

MDK-168–170

MDK-176–175*

MDK-172–217

    Sixty-three units

Displacement: 308/442

Dimensions: 54.5 × 7.7 × 2.4

Armament: None

Machinery: 2 diesels, 2 shafts, 1000 HP = 10.5 kts, 2500 nm/10 kts, 1900 nm/11 kts

Complement: 5 (1 officer)

    Built in East Germany 1967–69. Load: 200 t, up to 100 Naval Infantry. 6 ZIL-131 or 10 GAZ-66. Unloading time on an unprepared shore, 1 hr. Transfers: Bulgaria (twenty-one), Egypt (ten). Two are base supply ships in Amur River flotilla.

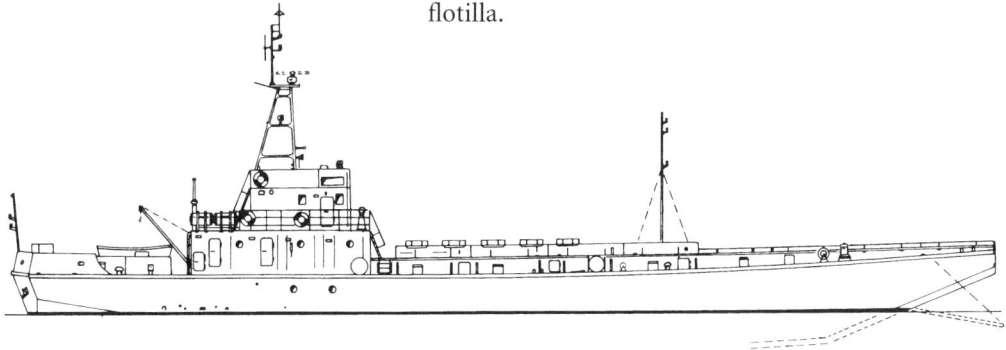

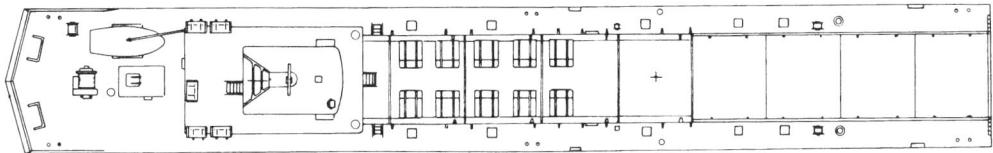

Vydra class (Royal Danish Navy)

Project: 106

NATO Class Name: SMB-1, MP-10

Names:

MDK-4

MDK-22

MDK-23

MDK-28

MDK-29

MDK-30

Nine others

    Fifteen units

Displacement: 280/300

Dimensions: 48.2 × 6.5 × 1.6

Armament: None

Machinery: 2 3D-12 diesels, 600 HP = 10 kts

Complement: 16

    Built 1958–68. Load 180 t. Five transferred to Egypt.

Project: 1176 (AKULA)

NATO Class Name: ONDATRA

Names:

Forty units

Displacement: 115

Dimensions: 24.5 × 5.2 × 1.55

Armament: None

Machinery: 2 3D-6 diesels, 2 shrouded screws, 300 HP = 10 kts, 500 nm/5 kts. Endurance 2 days.

Complement: 5

Production begun 1979. One tank. Cargo deck 13.7 × 3.9 m.

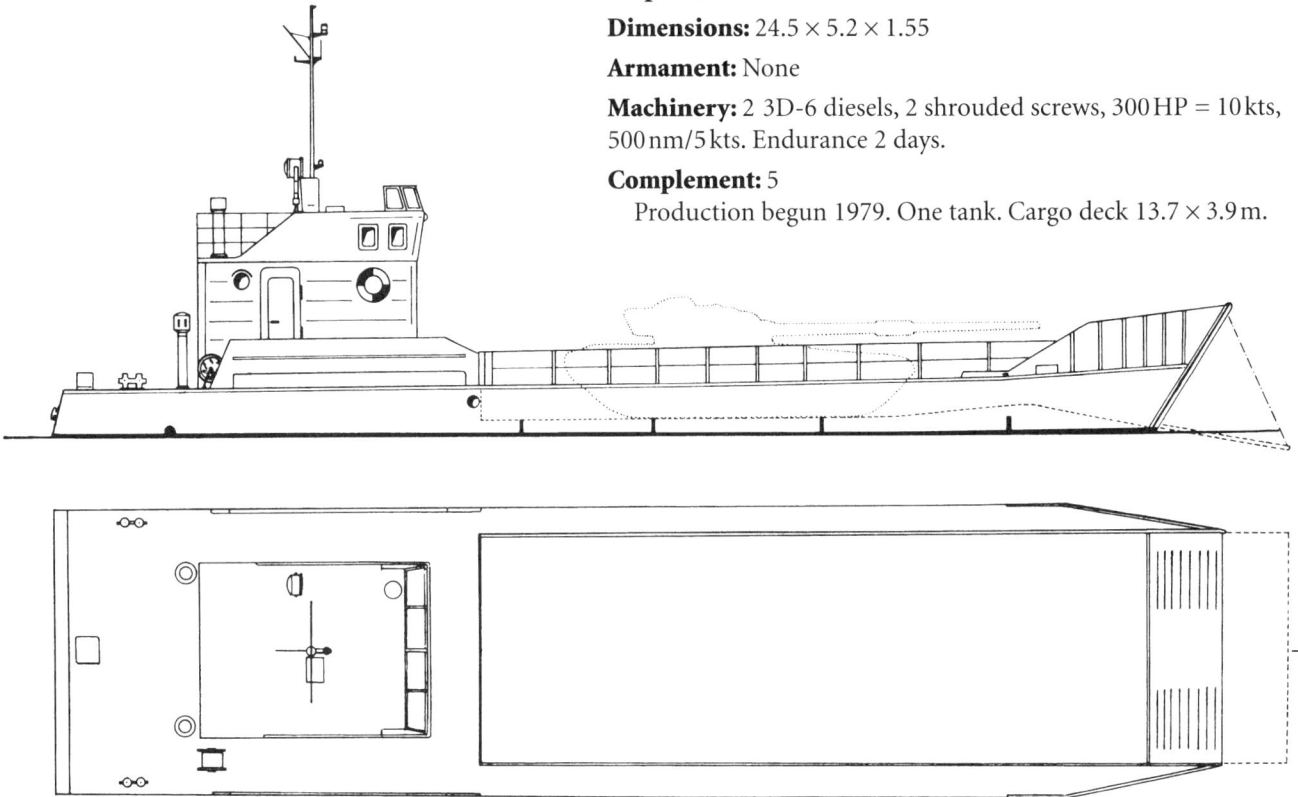

Project: 1733 (VOSTOK)

NATO Class Name: None

Names:

Forty-six units

Displacement: 18.56/38.9

Dimensions: 16.5 (with ramp) × 4.78 × 1

Armament: None

Machinery: 1 diesel (3D6-N), 1 shaft, 235 HP = 8.2 kts

Complement: 2

Production began 1969 at Vladivostok (Slavyanskom SRZ). Load: 19.2 t (cargo deck 9.5 × 3.9 m)

Project: 1785

NATO Class Name: T-4

Names:

D-342–345

D-501–515

D-519–581

D-601–608

Eighty-six units

Displacement: 40/80

Dimensions: 20.4 × 5.4 × 1.2

Armament: None

Machinery: 2 3D-6 diesels, 2 screws, 300 HP = 8 kts

Complement: 2

Built 1968–72. One T-72 tank. D-603 to Azerbaidzhan. Experimental prototype air-cushion landing craft (Serna type), designed and built in Nizhni Novgorod, were sold for export in 1994.

Project: 1232.2 (ZUBR)

NATO Class Name: POMORNIK

Names:

completed

MDK-95

MDK-97

MDK-103

MDK-104

MDK-106

MDK-108

MDK-109

MDK-116

MDK-117

MDK-118

MDK-123

DONETSK   26 June '93

IVAN BOGUN

Displacement: 415/550

Dimensions: 57.3 × 25.6 × 2

Armament: 4 launchers for Igla-M missiles (32 missiles), 2×2 30 mm (AK-630), 2×22 rocket launchers, up to 10 mines

Machinery: 3 gas turbines for propulsion (MT-70) driving 3 air propellers, 30,000 HP = 63 kts (maximum), 55 kts (cruise); 2 lift gas turbines (20,000 HP); 56 t fuel; 300 nm range. Endurance 5 days with landing party.

Complement: 31 (4 officers, 7 petty officers)

Electronics: Radar: Ekran

Built beginning 1985 in Leningrad (Almaz) and Feodosia; lead ship completed 1988. *Donetsk* and *Bogun* building for Ukrainian Navy. Carries eighty Naval Infantry, three tanks, and ten BTR; or 360 Naval Infantry and 25 t cargo. Three in the Black Sea.

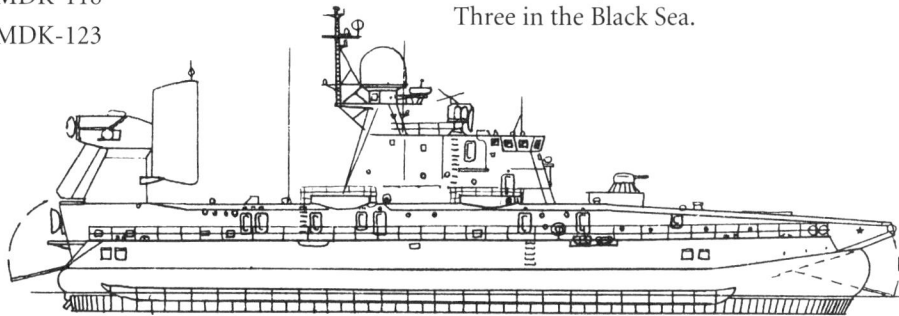

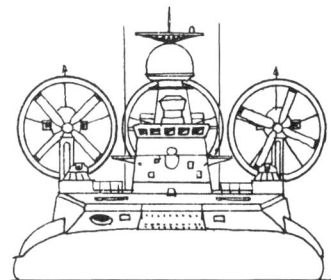

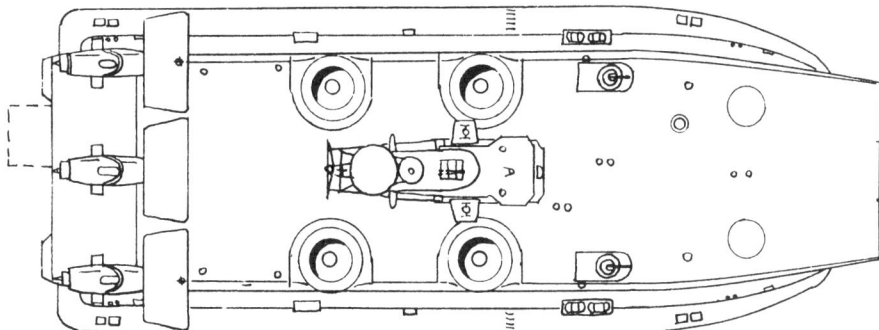

Pomornik class (Pavlov collection)

Project: 1232.1 (DZEIYRAN)

NATO Class Name: AIST

Names:

MDK-18

MDK-80

MDK-82

MDK-89

MDK-100

MDK-102

MDK-110

MDK-111

MDK-122

MDK-125

MDK-126

MDK-127

MDK-136

MDK-138

MDK-141

MDK-172

MDK-173

MDK-516

MDK-518

Displacement: 298/350

Dimensions: 47.8 × 17.5 × 1.6

Armament: 2×2 30 mm (AK-230)

Machinery: 2 DT-4 gas turbines, 4 air propellers, 32,000 HP = 70 kts (maximum)/50 kts (cruise); 300 nm/50 kts; 2 DG-30, 2 gas turbine generators (40 kW); 47 t fuel. Endurance 5 days.

Complement: 15 (3 officers)

Built in Leningrad (Almaz): lead ship completed 1970, series production begun 1974. Load: four PT-76 tanks and fifty Naval Infantry or two medium tanks and 200 infantry. Originally rated as Landing Assault Ships (DShK), then as Small Landing Ships (MDK). One burned 1981 at Baltisk (Baltic) and was repaired; one burned in Leningrad in 1991. Five on the Black Sea.

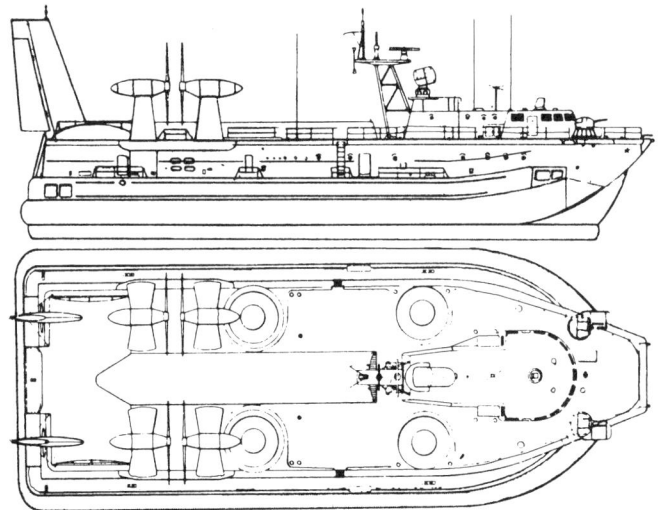

Aist class (U.S. Naval Institute Photographic Collection)

Project: 12061 and 12061E (MURENA)

NATO Class Name: TSAPLYA

Names:

	completed
D-453	1985
D-458	1986
D-259	1987
D-285	1988
D-447	1989
D-323	1990
D-142	1991
D-143	1992

Displacement: 110.5/140

Dimensions: 31.6 × 14.5 × 1.6

Armament: 2×6 30 mm (AK-306), 2 30 mm grenade launchers (BP-30)

Machinery: 2 gas turbines, 20,000 HP = 55 kts, 200 nm/50 kts (with 24 t load). Endurance 1 day.

Complement: 8–9

Built in Khabarovsk. Load: 24 t (one T-72 or two PT-76b tanks or three BRDM-2 or 130 Naval Infantry). Rated Landing Craft 4th Rank. D-142 crashed on the Amur River 4 Aug. '91 (three killed, repaired). Handed to Border Guards 1994.

Tsaplya class (U.S. Naval Institute Photographic Collection)

Tsaplya class (Siegfried Breyer)

D-142 (A. P. Kiselev)

Project: 1206T (KAL'MAR-T)

NATO Class Name: PELIKAN

Names:

Two units

Displacement: 131

Dimensions: 24.6 × 11.3 × 1.2

Armament: 1×6 30 mm (AK-630M)

Machinery: 2 gas turbines, 20,000 HP = 54 kts (with sweep, 30 kts), 100 nm/54 kts. Endurance 1 day.

Complement: 7

Electronics: Radar: Ekran

Built 1981–82 in Feodosiya. Load: 40 t (one tank in landing version). Used as air cushion roadstead sweepers (4th Rank). On the Black Sea.

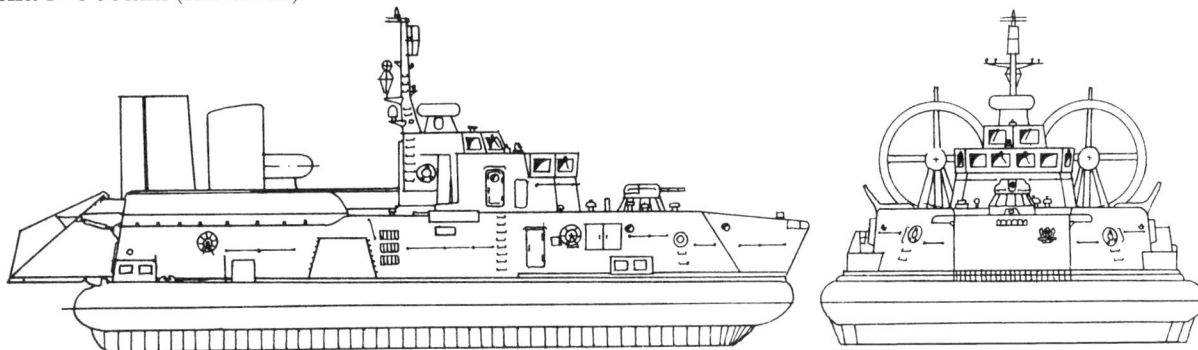

Project: 1209 (OMAR)

NATO Class Name: UTENOK

Names:

D-346

D-349

Displacement: 43/55

Dimensions: 26.3 × 11.7 × 1

Armament: 1×2 12.7 mm (UTES-M), 1 30 mm grenade launcher (BP-30)

Machinery: 1 M-35 gas turbine, 2 air propellers, 6000 HP = 65 kts, 11 t fuel

Complement: 7 (3 officers)

Built 1980–81 in Feodosiya, in reserve 1992 (Black Sea). Can carry sixty Naval Infantry.

D-346 (V. V. Kostrichenko)

Project: 1206 (KAL'MAR)

NATO Class Name: LEBED

Names:

D-52

D-277

D-347

D-348

D-379

D-435

D-633

D-703

Eleven others

Displacement: 87/117

Dimensions: 24.5 × 10.8 × 1.3

Armament: 1×2 12.7 mm (UTES-M)

Machinery: 2 MT-70 lift gas turbines, 20,000 HP = 55 kts, 100 nm/55 kts; fuel 12.7 t. Endurance 1 day.

Complement: 6 (2 officers)

Built in Feodosiya 1975–81 (14) and Leningrad (5). Load: 37 t; two light tanks or 120 Naval Infantry. Six units on Black Sea, of which three stricken after fire. D-379, D-633 stricken 1988, D-435 in 1992.

D-277 (U. A. Pakhomov)

Project: 1238 (KASATKA)

NATO Class Name: None

Names:

AK-16

Displacement: 90

Dimensions: 23 × 11 × 1.2

Armament: 1×6 30 mm (AK-630, 2000 rounds), 2 BP-30 grenade launchers, 2×22 Grad rocket launchers

Machinery: 2 MT-70 gas turbines, 24,000 HP = 56 kts, 120 nm/50 kts

Complement: 6

Built in Feodosiya 1990 as a landing and fire support ship; a planned sister (for salvo fire) was not built. On the Black Sea.

Project: 1205 (SKAT)

NATO Class Name: GUS

Names:

D-226–228

D-337

D-369

D-418–434

D-435–448

D-555

D-556

D-702

   Thirty-eight units

Displacement: 27

Dimensions: 20.4 × 8.4 × 0.5

Armament: None

Machinery: 2 gas turbines (TVD-10M, 1560 HP) for propulsion, 1 gas turbine (TVD-10, 780 HP) for lift, 40 kts, 200 nm/49 kts

Complement: 7

   Built in Zelenodolsk and Feodosiya 1969–74. Carry 25 naval infantry. One unit (Project 1205P) used for search and salvage of space objects on Caspian Sea. D-423, D-424, D-426 stricken 1994. MVD river formations also used Gepard and Bars type air-cushion vehicles (2 t, 100 HP, 60 km/hr).

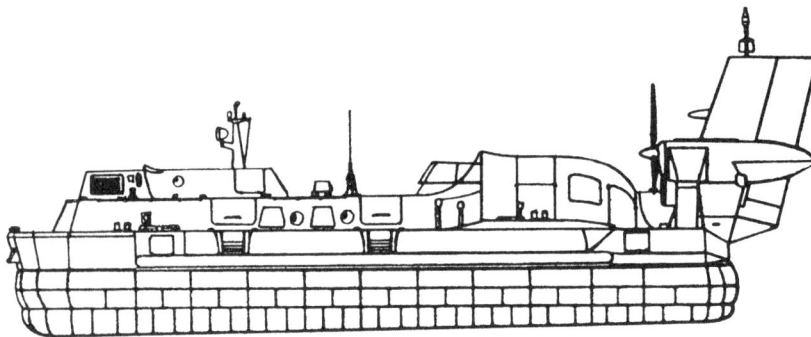

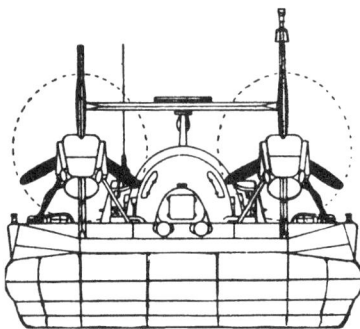

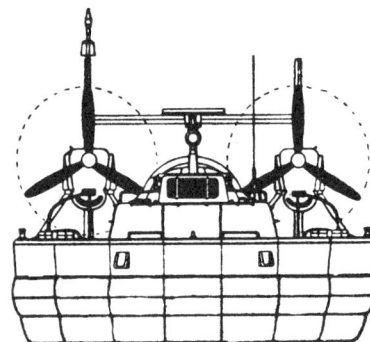

Gus class (U.S. Naval Institute Photographic Collection)

Project: Unnamed

NATO Class Name: None

Names:

MK-01

MS-01

Displacement: 27, 22

Dimensions: $21 \times 8 \times 0.5$, $21 \times 7.3 \times 0.5$

Armament: None

Machinery: 41, 40 kts

Built at Nevskiy Yard, Leningrad (1962) to test air-cushion chamber (MK-01) and nozzle (MS-01) configurations. Lift and propulsion plants are identical.

MS-01 (G. G. Kiselev)

Project: KM-1 Type

NATO Class Name: None

Names:

One unit

Displacement: 544

Dimensions: $92 \times 37 \times 2$

Armament: None

Machinery: 8 turboprops (NK-8, 60,000 HP), 2 NK-8 (15,400 HP), 400–450 km/hr

General designer R. E. Alekseeyev. Built 1963–65 at Gorkiy (Volga yard); test vehicle for Ekranoplan (WIG). Crashed and sank 1980 after a Caspian Sea test flight. Another eighteen test vehicles were built. During 1961–72, under the supervision of chief designer R. E. Alekseeyev, a series of test Ekranoplanes were built: SM-1 (1961) for tests and studies of aircraft configuration; SM-2 (1962) two vessels for studies of takeoff and landing on water; SM-4 (1963) for studies of motion at high speed; SM-5 (1964) for work on overall configurations; SM-6 (1965–66) was two mockups; 6M79 and 6M80 (prototype of *Orlonok*) for work on configuration of cruise engines; SM-8 (1968) for studies of hull construction. In addition a UT training Ekranoplane and a small patrol Ekranoplane (*Strizh*, chief designer V. V. Bulanov) were built. There was also a commercial SDVP.

KM-1 type (*Military Parade*)

Project: 902R*(LUN') and 902S

NATO Class Name: UTKA-2

Names:

	completed
S-31	1993
SPASATEL'	1995

Displacement: 242/400

Dimensions: 73.8 × 44 × 2.8*(2.5)

Armament: 3×2 Moskit launchers in S-31

Machinery: 8 turbojets (NK-87M) with 104t thrust (60,000 HP) = 300 kts, range 3000 km. Endurance 5 days.

Complement: 9

Built at Nizhni Novgorod (Volga yard). Missile version of Project 902 (but second unit, laid down as a missile shooter, will be completed as a salvage type). Chief designer V. Kirillovich. Cruises at altitude .25 m, maximum up to 100 m (*Spasatel'*). Seaworthiness on take-off/landing: 5.

Project: 902D

NATO Class Name: UTKA

Names:

MD-160

Displacement: 240/370

Dimensions: 73.5 × 44 × 2.5

Machinery: 4 turbojets (NK-87M), 30,000 HP = 280 kts, range 3200 km. Endurance 5 days.

Complement: 7

Built at Gorkiy (Volga yard), can carry 900 troops. Chief designer V. V. Sokolov. In the Caspian.

Utka class (*Military Parade*)

Utka class (*Military Parade*)

Project: 904 (DRAKON)

NATO Class Name: ORLAN

Names:

		completed
S-20	DUBL'	1972
S-23		1975
S-21		1978
S-25		1979
S-26		1980

Displacement: 140

Dimensions: 58.1 × 31.5 × 1.5

Armament: 1×2 14.5 mm (UTES-M)

Machinery: 2 take-off turbojets (NK-8-4K, 20 t thrust), 1 cruise turbofan (NK-12MK, 15,000 HP), auxiliary powerplant (TA-6A), 500 nm/180 kts

Electronics: Radar: Ekran; Collision-avoidance system: Ekran-4
  Chief designer V. V. Sokolov. Experimental ships built in Gorkiy (Volga yard). Carry up to 400 Naval Infantry or 20 t cargo. Landing time 1.5 min. Flight altitude 2.5 m. Turning radius 50 m. Has wheels for ground landing. Cargo is loaded and unloaded through bow ramp (bow opens sideways). Plans called for 120 units. S-23 damaged during tests and stricken 1981; S-21 damaged and stricken 1993. On Caspian.

Project: 1941 (TITAN)

NATO Class Name: KAPUSTA

Names:

SSV-33

Displacement: 32,780/34,640

Dimensions: 265 × 29.9 × 7.81

Armament: 4×8 launchers for Igla missiles (SAN-8)(32 missiles), 2×1 76 mm (AK-176), 4×6 30 mm (AK-630), 4×2 12.7 mm (UTES-M)

Machinery: 2 reactors of 171 MWT, 2 oil-burning boilers (VDRK-500), 2 geared steam turbines (GTZA-688, 27,000 HP each ahead, 6250 HP astern), 2 shafts, 21.6 kts; bow thruster. Endurance 180 days.

Complement: 923 (233 officers, 144 petty officers, 90 rated men)

Electronics: Radar: surface search MR-212/201 Vaigach-2, MR-750 Fre-

SSV-33 (U.S. Navy)

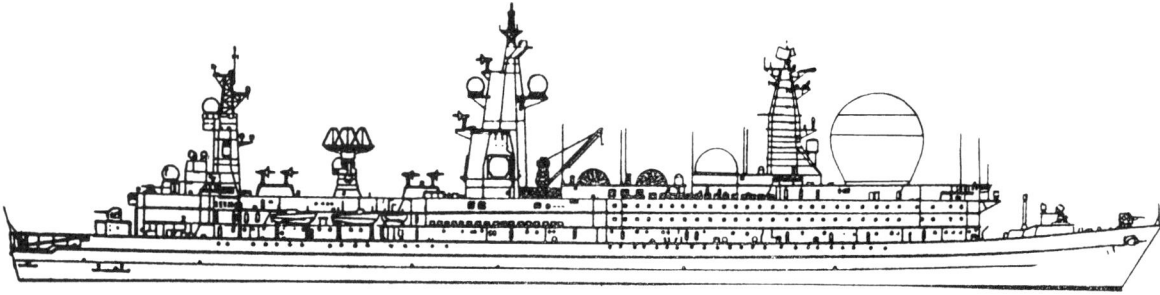

SSV-33 (U.S. Naval Institute Photographic Collection)

gat air search; Sonar: MGK-335 Platina, MG-747 Amulet; Communications system: Taifun; Space communications system: Tsunami; Navigation system: Andromeda-941

Pacific fleet command ship, built in Leningrad (Baltic yard). Now laid up.

Project: 864, 864B

NATO Class Name: VISHNIA

Names:

		completed
SSV-169	TAVRIYA	1986
SSV-175	ODOGRAF	
SSV-201	PRIAZOV'E	
SSV-520	MERIDIAN	
SSV-535	KARELIYA	5 June '86
SSV-208	KURIL'	16 Oct. '87
SSV-231	PELENGATOR	

Displacement: 2980/3396

Dimensions: 94.4 × 14.6 × 4.5

Armament: 2×8 launchers for Igla missiles (16 missiles), 2×6 30 mm (AK-630M)

Machinery: 2 diesels (12AB 25/30), 2 screws, 4400 HP = 16.5 kts, 7900 nm/12.5 kts, 2 auxiliary low-speed engines (300 HP), 7900 nm/12.5 kts. Endurance 45 days.

Complement: 151

Built in Poland (Gdansk) 1985–90. Medium data collecting ships of 2nd rank. SSV-175 and SSV-201 on the Black Sea.

SSV-169 (U.S. Navy)

Project: 1826

NATO Class Name: BALZAM

Names:

		completed
SSV-80	PRIBALTIKA	1983
SSV-493	AZIYA	3 Dec. '81
SSV-516	LIRA	1982
SSV-571	BELOMOR'E	1986

Displacement: 3100/4900

Dimensions: 105 × 15.5 × 5

Armament: 2×8 launchers for Strela missiles (16 missiles), 1×6 30 mm (AK-630 2000 rounds)

Machinery: 2 diesels, 8000 HP = 20 kts, 7000 nm/16 kts

Complement: 200

Built in Kaliningrad. SSV-516 and SSV-571 in Northern Fleet, rest in Pacific. *Lira* under repair.

SSV-516 (U.S. Naval Institute Photographic Collection)

SSV-493 (U.S. Navy)

Project: 394B

NATO Class Name: None

Names:

		completed
SSV-464	ZABAYKAL'YE	29 Mar. '71
SSV-465	PRIMOR'YE	
SSV-501	ZAPOZH'E	

SSV-502	ZAKARPAT'E
SSV-590	KRIM
SSV-591	KAVKAZ

Displacement: 2800/4100

Dimensions: $83.6 \times 13.7 \times 7$

Armament: 2×4 launchers for Strela missiles (16 missiles) in SSV-464, SSV-501, SSV-591; 1×4 launcher for Igla missiles (8 missiles) in SSV-590

SSV-501 (U.S. Naval Institute Photographic Collection)

Machinery: 2 diesels, 4000 HP = 12 kts, 10,000 nm/13 kts, 12,000 nm/10 kts

Complement: 110

Built 1960–71 in Nikolaev; based on *Mayakovskiy* class

large ocean-going fishing trawler. Large data collecting ships (BRZK). SSV-590 and SSV-591 on Black Sea. *Primor'ye* and *Zabaykal'ye* in Pacific, stricken 1992–94. SSV-464 and SSV-502 stricken 1993, SSV-465 in 1994.

SSV-501 (U.S. Naval Institute Photographic Collection)

SSV-501 (U.S. Naval Institute Photographic Collection)

Project: 10221, 1288.4*

NATO Class Name: BAMBUK

Names:

| SSV-391 | KAMCHATKA |
| SSV-189* | PRIDNEPROV'YE |

Displacement: 5500/8000

Dimensions: 107 × 18 × 6

Armament: 1 helicopter in hangar, 2×4 launchers for Igla missiles (16 missiles), 2×6 30 mm (AK-630M)

Machinery: 2 diesels, 2 screws, 8000 HP = 18 kts

Complement: 152

Built in Nikolaev 1988–92. *Pridneprov'ye* taken over by Ukraine, renamed *Slavootich*. Built to a simplified design (*) and completed 28 July '92 as flagship of Ukrainian Navy.

Kamchatka (U.S. Navy)

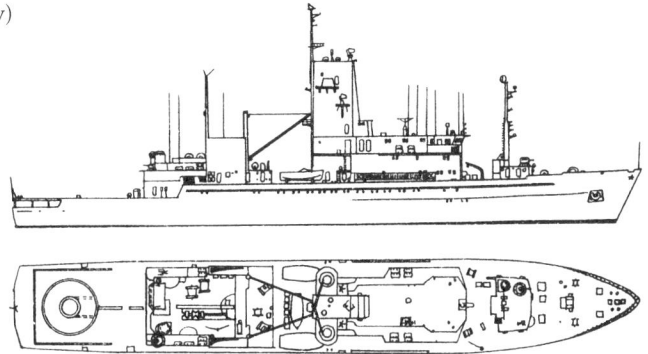

Project: 861M*, 861, 861P

NATO Class Name: MOMA

Names:

Data collection ships

EKVATOR

IUPITER*

KIL'DIN

SSV-472	IL'MEN'*
SSV-474	VEGA
SSV-506	NAKHODKA
SSV-509	PELORUS*
SSV-512	ARKHIPELAG*
SSV-514	SELIGER*
SSV-518	

Ocean survey ships

AL'TAIR

ANAL'R'

ANDROMEDA

ANTARES

ANTARKTIDA

ARTKTIKA

ASKOLD

BEREZHAN'

CHELEKEN

Moma class (U.S. Navy)

KOLGUEV
KRIL'ON
LIMAN
MARS
MORZHOVETS
OKEAN
RIBACHIY
SEVER
TAYMYR
ZAPOLYARE

Displacement: 1240/1600

Dimensions: 73.3 × 11.6 × 3.9

Armament: 2 launchers for Strela missiles (16 missiles) on SSV-472, AAV-514, *Iupiter*

Machinery: 2 Skoda diesels, 2 screws, 3500 HP = 17 kts, 9000 nm/11 kts

Complement: 85 (including 19 scientists)
   Built in Poland (Gdansk) 1967–72. Four laboratories. 7 t crane. Five units (*) modernized. Also built for navies of Bulgaria, Poland, and Yugoslavia. Ocean survey ships carry four large sea boats. SSVs are Large Intelligence Data Collection Ships.

Moma class (U.S. Naval Institute Photographic Collection)

Iupiter (Pavlov collection)

Project: 393R

NATO Class Name: MIRNY

Names:

LOTSMAN	KASATKA
BAKAN	BELUGA
VAL	
VERTIKAL'	

Displacement: 680/1250

Dimensions: 63.5 × 9.5 × 4.2

Armament: 2×8 launchers for Strela missiles

Machinery: 4 diesel generators (6-ChM-31, 8/33-1), 1 shaft, 1 motor, 4400 HP = 17.43 kts, 12.28 kts (on one generator), 8700 nm/11 kts; 2 DG-270, 1 DG-50 (230 V) generators; 217 t fuel, 100 t water. Endurance 12 days.

Complement: 80

Electronics: Radar: Don, Furumo; Echo-Sounder: NEL-5. Intelligence Data Collecting Ships. Built in Nikolaev (61 Kommunar yard); rebuilt in 1965 from whale hunting ships.

Intelligence collection ship (U.S. Navy)

Intelligence collection ship (U.S. Navy)

Project: 1914, 1914.1*

NATO Class Name: None

Names:

	completed
MARSHAL NEDELIN	1983
MARSHAL KRILOV*	23 Feb. '90

Displacement: 22,800/24,500

Dimensions: 211 × 27.5 × 8.5

Armament: 2–4 helicopters in hangars

Machinery: 4 diesels, 2 screws, 30,000 HP = 21 kts, 20,000 nm/18 kts. Endurance 120 days.

Complement: 450

Electronics: Radar: MR-320 Topaz (MR-750 Fregat*)

Built in Leningrad (Admiralty yard). Ships of Space System 1st Rank (Space Events ships), to observe and communicate with space craft; search for, salvage, and rescue crews from space capsules; also survey ships. Could be used as command ships. *Marshal Biryuzov* was stopped incomplete.

Marshal Krilov (J.M.S.D.F.)

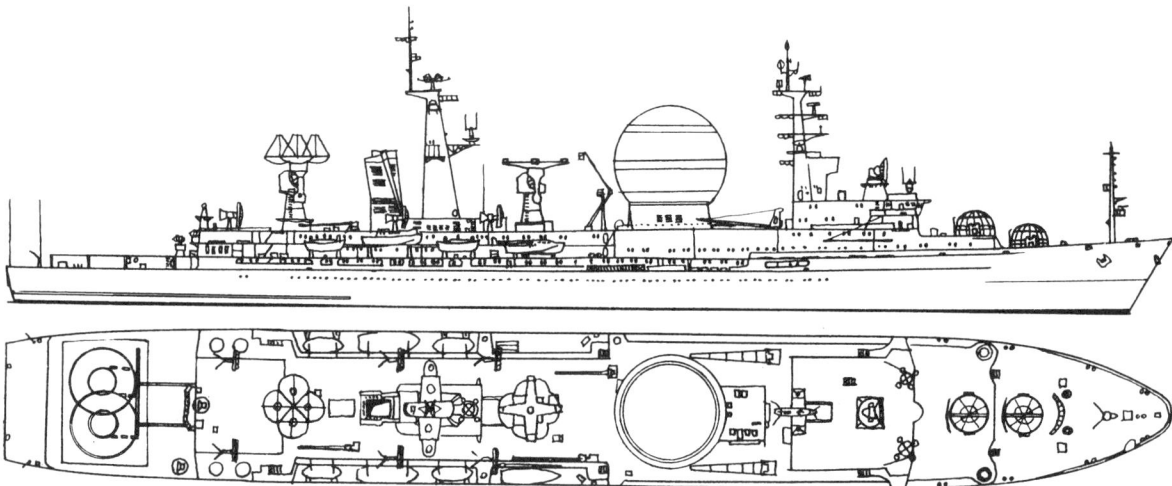

Project: 1886, 1886U*

NATO Class Name: UGRA

Names:

	laid down	launched	completed
PB-82	17 July '61	Sept. '62	27 Dec. '63
renamed *Vladimir Egorov* 1968			
PB-32	11 Oct. '61	28 Apr. '63	29 Dec. '64
renamed *Lena* 1970			
PB-20	4 Oct. '62	21 Sept. '63	25 Sept. '65
renamed *Tobol* 11 Feb. '67			
PB-6	10 May '63	28 Nov. '65	14 June '67
renamed *Ivan Kucherenko* 26 Sept. '68			
IVAN VAKHRAMEEV	23 Jan. '68	5 Nov. '68	30 Aug. '69
BORODINO*	30 Mar. '68	30 Jan. '70	16 Jan. '71
GANGUT*	28 Nov. '68	30 Dec. '70	10 Oct. '71
IVAN KOLISHKIN	9 Aug. '71	30 Mar. '72	27 Dec. '72

Displacement: 6780/7980

Dimensions: 144.8 × 18.1 × 5.8

Armament: Helicopter pad (hangar on *Ivan Kolishkin*), 2×8 launchers for Strela missiles (16 missiles), 4×2 57 mm (AK-725), 2 45 mm (K-21M)

Machinery: Diesel-electric, 4 DG (42 DD, 2000 HP each), 2 motors, 2 shafts, 6000 HP = 17 kts, 11,500 nm/9 kts, 6500 nm/17 kts; fuel 800 t, water 660 t; 4 DG-500 (400V, 50 HZ), 2 DG-300 generators. Endurance 45 days.

Complement: 220 (18 officers, 42 petty officers, 34 rated men, 126 seamen) plus 450 cadets as training ship

Electronics: Radars: MR-302, Don-3 and Tesla-1 navigational radar; IFF: Nikhrom-M, Nikel-KM; Sonars: MG-10, GS-572, MG-26 (communications); Gyrocompass: Kurs-5; Sounder: NEL-5 or -6

Built in Nikolaev (Nosenko yard) to supply two nuclear submarines each (forty-four torpedoes and provisions). *Borodino* (transferred from Baltic to Pacific 1973) and *Gangut* (Baltic) were Training Ships 1st Rank. *Tobol* was a command ship. *Volga* is on the Black Sea (under refit in Yugoslavia 1993). *Kucherenko* and *Vakhrameev* to breakers in India Dec. '94. An additional unit, *Amba,* was built for India in 1968 (laid down 5 Jan. '67, launched 18 Jan. '68, completed 31 Oct. '68).

Ugra class (U.S. Navy)

Project: 310

NATO Class Name: DON

Names:

	laid down	launched	completed
BATUR	6 Oct. '55	29 Nov. '56	28 Mar. '58

renamed PKZ-124 in 1966, then *Kamchatskiy Komsomolets* 12 Mar. '79–08 Apr. '92, then PB-9

	laid down	launched	completed
FYODOR VIDYAEV	24 Mar. '56	26 Apr. '57	30 Sept. '58
VIKTOR KOTELNIKOV	19 June '56	25 June '57	11 Dec. '59
MAGOMED GADZHIEV	10 Nov. '56	25 June '57	1 July '60
DMITRIY GALKIN	28 Apr. '59	31 Mar. '60	25 Dec. '60
NIKOLAIY KARTASHOV	18 Dec. '59	20 Dec. '60	31 May '62
PB-3	8 June '60	7 Oct. '61	30 Sept. '62

renamed *Magadanskiy Komsomolets* 16 Oct. '70–1991, then PB-27

Displacement: 6780/8900

Dimensions: 137.2 × 16.8 × 6.5

Armament: 4×1 100 mm (B-34 USM-A), 4×2 57 mm (ZiF-31B)

Machinery: Diesel-electric, 4 diesel generators, 2 motors, 2 shafts, 6000 HP = 17 kts, 21,000 nm/10 kts, 9500 nm/16 kts

Complement: 350 (28 officers)

Electronics: Radar: Ryf; Sonar: MG-26, Gyrocompass: Kurs-3

Built at Nikolaev 1957–62. PB for supplying four diesel submarines. *Viktor Kotelnikov* and PB-9 had a helicopter pad aft instead of after guns. Bow crane capacity is 100 t. In 1962 an additional unit, *Boris Kartashov* (Project 310M), was transferred to Indonesia *(Ratulangi)*. *Dmitriy Galkin, Gadzhiev, Kotelnikov* (Black Sea) were stricken 1993–95. PR-27 stricken in the Pacific, 1992.

Dmitriy Galkin (U.S. Navy)

Project: 11570 (SADKO)

NATO Class Name: None

Names:

	completed
ALEKSANDR BRIKIN	30 Aug. '85

Displacement: 16,000

Dimensions: 162 × 23.2 × 6.5

Armament: 2 launchers for Strela or Osa missiles, 4×6 AK-630M, 16 containers to transport RSM-52 missiles

Machinery: 2 diesel generators, 2 motors, 2 shafts, 9000 HP = 15 kts

Built in Leningrad (Admiralty yard) to carry reload missiles and torpedoes and to service Project 941 strategic missile submarines. Has 75 t and 15 t cranes.

Aleksandr Brikin (U.S. Naval Institute Photographic Collection)

Project: 304 and 304M*

NATO Class Name: AMUR

Names:

	completed
PM-5	
PM-9	
PM-10	
PM-15	
PM-30	
PM-34	
PM-37	
PM-40	
PM-49	1978
PM-52	

PM-56	
PM-59*	
PM-64	
PM-69*	
PM-73	
PM-75	
PM-81	
PM-82	
PM-86*	
PM-92*	
PM-94	
PM-97*	
PM-129	20 May '73
PM-138	

PM-139
PM-140
PM-156
PM-161
PM-163

Displacement: 5500

Dimensions: $122 \times 17 \times 5.1$

Armament: None

Machinery: 1 diesel, 1 shaft, 3000 HP = 12 kts, 13,000 nm/8 kts

Complement: 145

Built in Poland (Szeczin) 1968–83, 1983–85*. Northern Fleet: PM-34, PM-37, PM-64, PM-163 (stricken 1993).

PM-82 (French Navy)

Project: 2020

NATO Class Name: MALINA

Names:

PM-12

PM-63

PM-74

Displacement: 10,000/12,000

Dimensions: 136 × 22

Armament: None

Machinery: 4 gas turbines, 2 shafts, 60,000 HP = 17 kts

Complement: 260

Built in Nikolaev 1984–88. Floating Technical Base Ships (Repair Ships) of 2nd Rank. Cranes: 2 15 t PM-63 arrived in Northern Fleet Oct. '84. PM-74 to Pacific 1986. PM-16 was not completed.

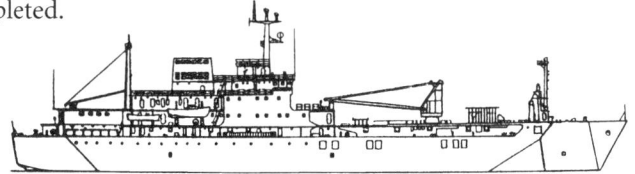

PM-74 (V. V. Kostrichenko)

Project: 301M

NATO Class Name: OSKOL

Names:

PM-2

PM-20

PM-21

PM-24

PM-26

PM-28

PM-51

PM-62

PM-68

PM-146

PM-147

PM-148

Displacement: 3000/3500

Dimensions: 88.6 × 13.7 × 3.66

Armament: 1×2 57 mm (ZiF-31B), 2×2 25 mm (2M-3M)

Machinery: 1 diesel (Skoda 6TAD-48), 1 shaft, 2200 HP = 14 kts

Complement: 100

Built in Poland (Szeczin) 1963–70. Some have no armament. PM-2 transferred to Shipbuilding Ministry. PM-21 to South Yemen 1988–91.

PM-24 (U.S. Navy)

Project: 323

NATO Class Name: LAMA

Names:

		completed
GENERAL RYABIKOV		
VORONEZH		
PRTB-15	PM-44*	ex-PM-93, ex-PRTB-93
PRTB-20	PM-131	
PRTB-43	PM-150	1 July '70
PRTB-13		
PRTB-33		

Displacement: 4100/5000

Dimensions: 112.8 × 15 × 4.4

Armament:

PTB-8: 2×2 57 mm (ZiF-31B)

PRTB-13: 2×2 57 mm (ZiF-31B), 2×2 25 mm (2M-3M)

PRTB-15: 2×4 57 mm (ZiF-75)

PRTB-20: 2×2 57 mm (ZiF-31B)

PRTB-33: 1×2 57 mm (ZiF-31B), 2×2 25 mm (2M-3M)

PRTB-43: 2×2 57 mm (ZiF-31B), 2×2 25 mm (2M-3M)

General Ryabikov, Voronezh:
1×24 missile launcher for Strela missiles, 1×2 57 mm AK-726

Machinery: 2 diesels, 2 shafts, 4000 HP = 14 kts, 6000 nm/10 kts

Lama class (U.S. Navy)

General Ryabikov (U.S. Naval Institute Photographic Collection)

Complement: 200

Built in Nikolaev 1963–72. Missile/torpedo transports (25 P-15 missiles) for submarines and surface craft. Project 323A ships carry P-6 and P-5D (18 missiles) or R-13 (12 missiles); Project 323B* carries R-21 missiles (12 missiles).

Ryabikov and *Vornonezh* are transports and repair ships. Cranes: 1 20 t or 2 10 t. *Ryabikov*, PRTB-13, PRTB-33 on Black Sea, rest in Pacific. PRTB-20 stricken June '93. Other PTBs were: Project 326 (PM-128), Project 771, and Project 1505 (non-self-propelled).

Project: 734

NATO Class Name: DNEPR-1, 2*

Names:

PM-17

PM-22

PM-30

PM-130*

PM-135*

Displacement: 4600/5250 (4900/5900*)

Dimensions: 113 × 16.5 × 4.4 (5.3*)

Armament: None

Machinery: 1 diesel, 1 shaft, 2500 HP = 12 kts, 6000 nm/8 kts

Complement: 50 plus 380 repair workers

Built in Nikolaev 1960–64. 1 30 t, 2 20 t, 1 or 2* 15 t cranes. PM-17 and 22 inactivated 1991.

Project: 1791, 1791M, 1791.2

NATO Class Name: None

Names:

	completed
AMGA	Dec. '72
DAUGAVA	1981
VETLUGA	1976

Displacement: 4800/5800

Dimensions: 102 × 17.8 × 4.5 (*Vetluga:* 108; *Daugava:* 112)

Armament: 2×2 25 mm (2M-3M)

Machinery: 2 diesels, 2 shafts, 9000 HP = 16 kts, 4500 nm/14 kts

Complement: 210

Transports and reload ships for RSM-40 strategic missiles. 50 t crane.

Project: V-30/1

NATO Class Name: SOLDEK

Names:

TAVDA

SMOLENSK

INZA   *(6. Novoshakhtinsk)*

VITEGRA

KALAR

ZANGEZUR

Displacement: 2900/3600

Dimensions: 87 × 12.5 × 4.9

Armament: 3×2 57 mm (ZiF-31B)

Machinery: 1 reciprocating steam engine, 1400 HP = 10.4 kts

Complement: 100

Built in Poland 1954–58 on a collier hull (Pervomaisk class). *Vitegra* may have been renamed PKZ-111 in 1966. Three were re-equipped as KS-2, KS-3, and KS-4. Stricken 1970–76.

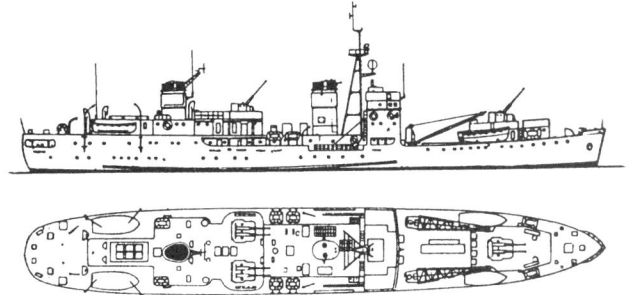

Project: 802

NATO Class Name: TOMBA

Names:

ENS-244

ENS-254

ENS-348

ENS-357

Displacement: 3500/5700

Dimensions: 107 × 17 × 5

Armament: None

Machinery: 1 diesel, 1 shaft, 5500 HP = 14 kts, 7000 nm/14 kts

Complement: 180

Built 1974–76 in Poland (Szeczin, Warskiy yard). Floating electric power stations to support *Kiev* class *Takr*. 3.5 t cranes.

ENS-357 (U.S. Naval Institute Photographic Collection)

Project: 233K

NATO Class Name: None

Names:

	completed
ATREK	30 Dec. '55
ANGARSK	31 Mar. '56
ARAT	3 Apr. '56
BRN-76	24 Aug. '56
BRN-77	30 Sept. '56
BRN-78	30 Nov. '56
BRN-79	31 Dec. '56
BRN-80	8 Oct. '57
BRN-81 EVGENIY OSIPOV	27 Nov. '57

AYAKHTA

BAKHMUT

Displacement: 3900/5500

Dimensions: 102.4 × 14.4 × 5.5

Armament: None

Machinery: 1 shaft reciprocating steam, 2800 IHP = 14 kts

Complement: 40

Built in East Germany (Neptun yard) as floating repair ships and accomodation ships for 400 men. In 1963 *Ayakhta* was transferred to Indonesia *(Tamrin)*. Lead ship *Atrek* was sunk in the Barents Sea, raised 1991, and sent for breaking up. Remainder were stricken 1980–93.

Project: 1833

NATO Class Name: None

Names:

	laid down	launched	completed
BEREZINA	18 Aug. '72	20 Apr. '75	20 Dec. '77

Displacement: 22,820/24,956

Dimensions: 209.7 × 29.1 × 8.23

Armament: 2×1 launchers for Osa missiles (20 missiles), 2×2 57 mm AK-725, 4×6 30 mm AK-630, 2×6 RBU-1000

Machinery: 4 diesels, 2 shafts, 60,000 HP = 21.8 kts, 15,000 nm/18.1 kts

Complement: 600

Built in Nikolaev (61 Kommunar yard); two units were planned. One-stop replenishment ship. In the Black Sea.

Berezina (U.S. Naval Institute Photographic Collection)

Project: DUBNA

NATO Class Name: None

Names:

	launched	completed
DUBNA		1974
IRKUT	Jan. '75	Dec. '75
PECHENGA		1978
SVENTA		Apr. '79

Displacement: 11,100

Dimensions: 130 × 20 × 7.2

Armament: None

Machinery: 1 diesel, 1 shaft, 6000 HP = 16 kts, 7000 nm/16 kts

Complement: 70

Built in Finland (Rauma-Repola). Load: 7000 t diesel fuel, 300 t water, 1500 t other cargo. *Dubna* and *Sventa* in Black Sea Fleet.

Irkut (U.S. Naval Institute Photographic Collection)

Project: 1559V, 1593*

NATO Class Name: None

Names:

BORIS CHILIKIN

BORIS BUSTOMA*

DNESTR

GENRIKH KASANOV

IVAN BUBNOV

VLADIMIR KOLECHITSKIY

Displacement: 22,000/24,450

Dimensions: 162.3 × 21.4 × 9.3

Armament: 2×2 57 mm AK-725

Machinery: 1 diesel, 1 shaft, 9000 HP = 16.7 kts; 2 DG-300, 1 TG-500, 1 DF-100 generators; 10,000 nm/16 kts

Complement: 75

Built in Leningrad (Baltic Yard) 1971–78 on a tanker hull (*Velikiy Oktyabr* type). Load: 13,000 t diesel fuel, 400 t ammunition, 400 t provisions, 500 t fresh water. Armament removed. Rated as Large Sea Tankers. *Bubnov* and *Chilikin* on Black Sea.

Dnestr (Pavlov collection)

Project: 1595

NATO Class Name: None

Names:

NEON ANTONOV

IRBIT

MIKHAIL KONOVALOV

IVAN LEDNEV

NIKOLAIY SIPYAGIN

NIKOLAI STARSHINOV

SERGEI SUDEISKIY

IVAN DENISOV

IVAN EVTEEV

DVINA

VASILIY SUNTSOV

Displacement: 3200/5100

Dimensions: $115 \times 15.7 \times 5$

Armament: 2×8 Strela launchers, 1×2 30 mm AK-230, 2×2 14.5 mm (UTES-M)

Machinery: 1 diesels, 2 shafts, 7000 HP = 17 kts, 8500 nm/13 kts

Complement: 40

Built in Pacific 1975–80. *Irbit* in Border Guards. Slavyanka type landing barge on board (Project 20150, 36/78.2 t, $21.9 \times 5.81 \times 1$ m, 470 HP = 9.8 kts).

Project: R-756

NATO Class Name: None

Names:

ANADYR

Displacement: 27,000

Dimensions: $226 \times 30 \times 6.5$

Armament: 2 helicopters

Machinery: 4 diesels (Wartsila-Vasa 16B-32D), 2 shafts, 33,042 HP = 20 kts

Complement: 70

Built in Finland 1988 (Wartsila); load 10,500 t. In Pacific from 1990 on.

Project: 577

NATO Class Name: UDA

Names:

	completed
TEREK	July '62
SHEKSNA	Dec. '62
DONETS	Aug. '64
DNEPR	Sept. '65
DUNAIY	Dec. '65
KOIDA	July '66
LENA	Dec. '66
VISHERA	June '67

Displacement: 5500/7200

Dimensions: $122.1 \times 15.8 \times 6.2$

Armament: None

Machinery: 2 diesels, 2 shafts, 9000 HP = 17 kts, 4000 nm/15 kts

Complement: 85

Built in Vyborg. *Dunaiy, Lena, Sheksna, Terek* modernized 1975 with foundations for 57 mm guns and a system for cargo transfer at sea. Carry 3000 t diesel fuel. In 1963–65 two sisters were sold to Indonesia. *Koida* is in the Black Sea, *Dunaiy* and *Vishera* in the Pacific.

Uda class (U.S. Naval Institute Photographic Collection)

Project: 437M

NATO Class Name: None

Names:

CHEREMSHAN

INDIGA

KHOBI

POVAT'

METAN

MOKSHA

ORSHA

SEIMA

SHACHA

SHELON'

SOS'BA

S'ISOLA

TARTU

TUNGUSKA

Displacement: 700/1500

Dimensions: 63 × 10.1 × 4.5

Armament: None

Machinery: 2 diesels, 2 shafts, 1600 HP = 13 kts, 2500 nm/12 kts

Complement: 35

   Tankers built 1957–59. In addition, two for Albania, one for Hungary, three for Indonesia; twenty-five units in all were built.

Indiga (Pavlov collection)

Project: 1481

NATO Class Name: None

Names:

BNS-180150

BNS-181150

Three others

Displacement: 600

Dimensions: 57,8 × 9.5 × 1.2

Armament: None

Machinery: 2 diesels (3D-12), 600 HP = 10 kts. Endurance 6 days.

Complement: 7

   Built 1974–76 at Kokuie (Sretenskiy yard). River tankers used as oilers by Border Guards. Double bottoms. Can be used as command ships.

Project: 1151

NATO Class Name: BELYANKA

Names:

	completed
AMUR	29 Nov. '84
PINEGA	17 July '87

Displacement: 6000/6500

Dimensions: 120 × 17.3 × 5.5

Armament: None

Machinery: 2 diesels, 1000 HP = 16 kts

Complement: 100

   Built in Vyborg 1986–87. Tankers to carry radioactive waste. A third unit is under construction in Severodvinsk. In the Pacific.

Project: 1541

NATO Class Name: LUZA

Names:

	completed
ALAMBAIY	
ARAGVI	
BARGUZIN	
DON	Sept. '63
KAMA	
OKA	
YENISEI	
SELENGA	

Displacement: 1900

Dimensions: 62.5 × 10.7 × 4.3

Armament: None

Machinery: 1 diesel, 1 shaft, 1000 HP = 12 kts, 2000 nm/11 kts

Complement: 60

Built Vyborg 1960–63 to transport missile fuel and special waste; load is 357 t oxidizer and 153 t missile fuel. One exploded. *Yenisei* stricken 1978.

Project: 1823, 1823V*, 1824B, 1824T

NATO Class Name: MUNA

Names:

	completed
VTR-48	
VTR-76	17 Dec. '85
VTR-77	
VTR-81	
VTR-82	
VTR-83	
VTR-84	
VTR-85	
VTR-86	
VTR-87	
VTR-89	
VTR-90	
VTR-91*	
VTR-92	
VTR-93	
VTR-94	
VTR-148	
GS-13	
GS-115	
UGLOMER	
OS-114	

Displacement: 800

Dimensions: 50 × 8 × 3

Armament: None

Machinery: 1 diesel, 300 HP = 10 kts

Complement: 40

Built in Nikolaev, Nakhodka, etc. 1970–76. Designed by TsKB Vympel (Gorkiy). To transport torpedoes. On the same hull were built survey ships (GS) and intelligence collectors. Four units on the Black Sea.

Project: 1783A

NATO Class Name: VALA

Names:

	completed
TNT-5	
TNT-11	
TNT-12	
TNT-17	
TNT-19	26 Dec. '71
TNT-22	
TNT-23	
TNT-25	25 June '69
TNT-27	
TNT-29	
TNT-42	

Displacement: 3100

Dimensions: 76.2 × 12.5 × 5

Armament: 2×2 12.7 mm UTES-M

Machinery: 1 diesel, 1 shaft, 1000 HP = 14 kts, 2000 nm/11 kts

Complement: 30

Built 1964–71 in Vladivostok and Vyborg, based on a non-self-propelled barge, to transport radioactive waste.

TNT-27 (G. G. Kiselev)

Project: 1549

NATO Class Name: None

Names:

MANITS

TAGIL

Displacement: 7700

Dimensions: $116 \times 15.7 \times 7$

Armament: 2×2 57 mm (removed 1981)

Machinery: 2 diesels, 2 shafts, 9000 HP = 18 kts, 7500 nm/16 kts

Complement: 90

Water tankers built 1972 and 1976 in Vyborg. Load: 4400 t.

Manits (U.S. Naval Institute Photographic Collection)

Project: 561

NATO Class Name: VODA

Names:

MVT-6	
MVT-9	
MVT-10	
ABAKAN	
MVT-16	
MVT-17	VODOLEI-17
MVT-18	
SURA	
MVT-20	
MVT-21	
MVT-23	
MVT-24	VODOLEI-3
MVT-134 after May '66	VODOLEI-10
MVT-135	VODOLEI-12
MVT-136	VODOLEI-21
MVT-138	
MVT-428	

Displacement: 3000

Dimensions: $81.5 \times 11.5 \times 4$

Armament: None

Machinery: 2 diesels, 2 shafts, 1600 HP = 12 kts, 3000 nm/10 kts

Complement: 40

Built 1955–60. Load: 1500 t. *Abakan* and *Sura* on the Black Sea. Stricken 1989–94.

Abakan (U.S. Navy)

Project: Unnamed

NATO Class Name: TOPLIVO-1

Names:

Thirty-six units

Displacement: 600

Dimensions: $33 \times 7 \times 3.1$

Armament: None

Machinery: 1 diesel (3D-12), 300 HP = 10 kts; 6 t fuel
   Built 1959–62 in Poland (Lenin yard in Gdansk). Used as tankers and oil bunkers. MNS-15250 used for ship repair work at Odessa as *Ye. Trofimov*.

Project: 1844, 1844D* (KAIR)

NATO Class Name: TOPLIVO-2

Names:

MVT-17

VTN-26

VTN-28

VTN-29

VTN-30

VTN-34

VTN-38–40

VTN-42–43*

VTN-45

VTN-46

VTN-48

VTN-50

VTN-53

VTN-58

VTN-60*

VTN-64

VTN-66

VTN-68

VTN-71

VTN-72

VTN-75

VTN-78

VTN-81

VTN-82*

Displacement: 466/1180

Dimensions: $54.3 \times 9.4 \times 3.4$

Armament: None

Machinery: 1 diesel (6-DR), 600 HP, 1500 nm/10 kts

Complement: 24

   Built from 1975 on in Kherson, Khabarovsk, and Alexandria (Egypt). Used as tankers and oil tank cleaning vessels. A later improved version was Project 1844.4 (lead ship MVT-17, built 1992 in Khabarovsk). Another fifty Toplivo-2 class tankers were built in the Soviet Union (1200 t, 53 m); two more were in the Egyptian Navy.

MVT-17 (Pavlov collection)

Project: 1818 (URAL)

NATO Class Name: None

Names:

VORKUTA   renamed BSS-169300 in 1988

Displacement: 2000/2900

Dimensions: 90 × 12 × 4.5

Armament: None

Machinery: 1 diesel, 880 HP = 12 kts, 2000 nm/10 kts

Complement: 42

Built in Vladivostok 1962–67 for Far East Military District to Navy 1969. Initially a missile transport, then became a transport, then (1990) a submarine tender. Has special crane usable in rough seas. A second unit was broken up on the slip.

Vorkuta (V. N. Muratov)

Project: 852

NATO Class Name: None

Names:

ADMIRAL VLADIMIRSKIY

AKADEMIK KRYLOV

IVAN KRUZENSHTERN

LEONID SOBOLEV

LEONID LEMIN

MIKHAIL KRUPSKIY

Displacement: 6600/9100

Dimensions: 147 × 18.5 × 6.26

Armament: None

Machinery: 4 diesels, 16,000 HP = 20.4 kts, 23,000 nm/15.3 kts

Complement: 90

Electronics: Navigational radar: Don

Built in Poland (Warskiy Yard, Szeczin) 1974–79. Twenty-six laboratories, air-conditioning, bow thrusters. Two small ocean survey ships. Expeditionary Ocean Survey Ships (EOS), rerated 1990 as Ocean Survey Scientific Ships, OE(I)S.

Mikhail Krupskiy (M.O.D Bonn)

Project: 976

NATO Class Name: None

Names:

ABKHAZIYA

ADZHARIYA

BASHKIRIYA

MOLDAVIYA

Displacement: 7500

Dimensions: 124.8 × 17.1 × 6.4

Armament: 1 helicopter in hangar

Machinery: 2 MAN diesels, 10,500 HP = 17 kts, 20,000 nm/16 kts

Complement: 105

Built in East Germany 1971–73 (Wismar, Matthias Tezen Werft). Bow thruster, air conditioning.

Project: 873

NATO Class Name: None

Names:

	completed
SIBIRYAKOV	Apr. '90
MUKLEVICH	1991

Displacement: 3500

Dimensions: 76 × 12 × 4

Armament: None

Machinery: 1 Skoda diesel, 1 shaft, 4200 HP = 15 kts

Complement: 30

Built in Poland (Gdansk). *Siriryakov* in Baltic, *Muklevic* in Northern Fleet.

Project: 1537.1

NATO Class Name: None

Names:

BAIKAL

BALKHASH

POLYUS

Displacement: 2400/6700

Dimensions: 106 × 14.4 × 6.3

Armament: None

Machinery: 2 diesels, 1 shaft (hydraulic/geared transmission), 3000 HP (POLYUS), 2500 HP (others) = 14 kts, 25,000 nm/12 kts

Complement: 120

Built in East Germany (Rostock) in 1962–63 as Andizhan class cargo ships, taken over 1966. To the Pacific 1967, stricken 1993–94. Load: 1195 t, deadweight 3897 t.

Polyus (U.S. Naval Institute Photographic Collection)

Project: 850 and 850M

NATO Class Name: None

Names:

ALEKSEI CHIRIKOV

ANDREI VIL'KITSKIY

BORIS LAV'DOV

VASILIY GOLOVNIN

GAVRIIL SAR'CHEV
  renamed SSV-468 LOSOS in 1965

SEMEN CHELYUSKIN
  renamed SSV-469 in 1965

FADDEIY BELLINSGAUZEN

FEDOR LITKE

KHARITON LAPTEV
  renamed SSV- 503 in 1966

NIKOLAI ZUBOV

SEMEN DEZHNEV

Displacement: 2674/3021

Dimensions: 89.7 × 13 × 4.6

Armament: None

Machinery: 2 diesels, 2 shafts, 5000 HP = 16.5 kts, 11,000 nm/14 kts. Endurance 60 days.

Complement: 68 including 26 scientists
  Built in Poland (Szeczin) 1964–68 with icebreaking bow and nine laboratories. *Vasiliy Golovnin* stricken Aug. '91. Two on the Black Sea.

Boris Lav'dov (U.S. Naval Institute Photographic Collection)

Project: 514

NATO Class Name: None

Names:

	laid down	launched	completed
NEVELSKOI	10 July '59	1961	18 Jan. '62

Displacement: 1700/2688

Dimensions: 88.28 × 12.98 × 3.5

Armament: None

Machinery: 2 diesels (8-DR), 2 shafts, 4000 HP = 18.5 kts, 5800 nm/18.5 kts, 6300 nm/15 kts, 9300 nm/12 kts

Complement: 65 (6 officers, 1 petty officer, 58 seamen)

Electronics: Don navigational radar, Kurs-4 gyrocompass, sonar Pegas-3M

Built in Sevastopol (Yard 497) in 1962. Five laboratories. First postwar-built Expeditionary Ocean Survey Ship. Pacific Fleet; laid up 1991, sold 1993 to a private firm.

Project: 862, 862.11, 08621, 08622*

NATO Class Name: YUG

Names:

	completed
BRIZ	
DONUZLAV	
GALS	
GIDROLOG	
GORIZONT	
MANG'SHLAK renamed SSV-704* in 1992	
MARSHAL GELOVANI	30 July '83
NIKOLAI MATUSEVICH	
PEGAS	
PERSEI	
PLUTON	
SENEZH	
STRELETS	
STVOR	
TAIGA	
VIZIR	
ZODIAK	
YUG renamed SSV-328 in 1990	

Displacement: 2000/2490

Dimensions: 82.5 × 13.5 × 3.9

Armament: 3×2 25 mm (2M-3M)

Machinery: 2 diesels (Skoda 6-TD48), 2 shafts, 4000 HP = 15 kts, 11,000 nm/12 kts. Endurance 45 days.

Complement: 66

Built in Poland (Gdansk) 1978–83; three in the Black Sea. In 1990–93 two were converted to intelligence collectors.

Stvor (V. V. Kostrichenko)

Project: 860

NATO Class Name: SAMARA

Names:

AZIMUT

ANADYR

VAIGACH

VOSTOK

DEVIATOR

GIDROMETR

GLUBOMER

GORIZONT

GRADUS

KOLESNIKOV

KOMPAS

PAMYAT'

MERKURIYA

RUMB

TROPIK

TURA

ZENIT

Displacement: 1000/1270

Dimensions: 59 × 10.5 × 3.8

Armament: None

Machinery: 2 Skoda diesels, 2 controllable-pitch propellers, 3000 HP = 15 kts, 6200 nm/10 kts

Complement: 45

Built in Poland (Gdansk) 1962–64. For installation, replacement, and servicing beacons (racks for four Large Sea Buoys were on the main deck). Crane: 1–5 t. *Anadyr'* stricken 1984 after grounding, *Rumb* (Pacific) stricken 1991. *Tura* equipped as a training ship (Project 860B).

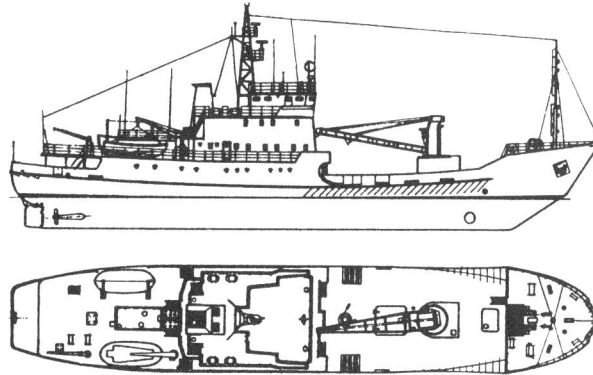

Gidrometr (U.S. Navy)

Project: 870

NATO Class Name: BIYA

Names:

GS-74
GS-182
GS-186
GS-193
GS-194
GS-198
GS-199
GS-200
GS-202
GS-204
GS-206
GS-208
GS-210
GS-212
GS-214
GS-271
GS-273
GS-275

    Total eighteen.

Displacement: 750

Dimensions: $55 \times 9.8 \times 2.6$

Armament: None

Machinery: 2 diesels, 2 controllable-pitch propellers, 1200 HP = 13 kts, 4700 nm/11 kts. Endurance 15 days.

Complement: 25

    Built in Poland 1972–76 for the navies of the Soviet Union, Cuba (GS-186 transferred Nov. '80), Cape Verde Islands (one in 1979), for Guinea-Bissau (one in June 1978). 5 t crane, four medium sea buoys, one laboratory. GS-212 and GS-273 in Black Sea, GS-202 in Caspian.

GS-214 (BMVg/MOD Bonn)

Project: 872 (Polish Project B-91)

NATO Class Name: FINIK

Names:

	completed
GS-44	
GS-47	
GS-84	16 July '83
GS-86	
GS-87	
GS-260	
OS-265	
GS-270	
GS-272	
GS-278	
GS-280	

GS-296
GS-297
GS-301
GS-388
GS-392
GS-397–405

Displacement: 850/1100

Dimensions: $61.5 \times 11.8 \times 3.3$

Armament: None

Machinery: 2 diesels, 2 shafts, 1500 HP = 13 kts, 3500 nm/12 kts

Complement: 30

    Built in Poland (Gdansk) in 1978–83 for navies of the Soviet Union, East Germany (one), and Poland (two). Improved version of the Biya class. 7 t crane. Bow thrusters. Four on the Black Sea.

Project: 871

NATO Class Name: KAMENKA

Names:

GS-66

GS-78

GS-82

GS-107

GS-108 (VERNIER)

GS-113 (BEL'BEK)

GS-118

GS-199

GS-207

GS-211

	laid down	launched	completed
GS-269			
ASTRONOM	1968	29 June '68	23 Dec. '68

Displacement: 654/760

Dimensions: $53.5 \times 9.1 \times 2.6$

Armament:

Machinery: 2 diesels (6 NVD-48), 2 controllable-pitch propellers, 1800 HP = 13.7 kts, 1720 nm/13 kt. Endurance 15 days.

Complement: 25

Built in Poland (Gdansk) 1968–72. One built for East Germany, one transferred to Vietnam. 5 t crane, four medium sea buoys. *Astronom* (Pacific) sold 1993 to a private firm.

Kamenka class (U.S. Navy)

Project: 1896, 1896U

NATO Class Name: NURYAT (GPB-480)

Names:

BGK-69

BGK-74

BGK-86

BGK-140

BGK-161

BGK-163

BGK-171

BGK-188

BGK-248

BGK-333

BGK-359

BGK-480

BGK-586

BGK-627

BGK-628

BGK-635

BGK-683

BGK-713

BGK-715

BGK-775

BGK-793

BGK-1631

Thirty-five others
 Total fifty-eight.

Displacement: 98/126

Nuryat class (U.S. Navy)

Dimensions: 28.6 × 5.4 × 1.7

Armament: None

Machinery: 1 diesel (3D-12, 300 HP or 6 ChSP 23/30, 450 HP) = 11.8 kts, 1600 nm/10 kts

Complement: 14

Built from 1955 on as roadstead survey launches (two cranes, 1 and 1½ t), patrol launches (for Border Guards), and other tasks.

Project: Unnamed

NATO Class Name: VINOGRAD

Names:

GS-525

GS-526

Displacement: 372/499

Dimensions: 32.9 × 10.4 × 2.8

Armament: None

Machinery: 2 diesels, 2 controllable-pitch propellers, 300 HP = 8.5 kts, 1000 nm/ 6 kts. Endurance 10 days.

Complement: 19

Built in Finland (Savonlinna, Rauma-Repola), completed Nov. and Dec. '85. Have two multi-channel sounders (side-looking sonars) on outboard legs to cover a 38 m wide swath; data are processed by computer. Baltic Fleet.

GS-525 (Rauma-Repola)

Project: 1403A (KAIRA)

NATO Class Name: None

Names:

MGK-710

MGK-749

MGK-751

MGK-753

MGK-760

MGK-771

MGK-1804

Twenty-three others
  Total thirty.

Displacement: 70

Dimensions: $11 \times 3 \times 0.7$

Armament: None

Machinery: 1 diesel, 1 shaft, 90 HP = 10 kts, 150 nm/10 kts

Complement: 6

Built beginning in 1969. Have fiberglass hulls. Ocean survey units also included launches of Projects 382-K, 727, 727A, and 16830.

Project: 537

NATO Class Name: None

Names:

EL'BRUS   20 Dec. '80

ALAGEZ   1982

AYUDAG   1993

Displacement: 14,300/20,500

Dimensions: $175 \times 24.5 \times 8.5$

Armament: 1 helicopter in hangar; 4×6 30 mm (AK-630)(none on *El'brus*)

Machinery: 4 diesels, 2 shafts, 20,000 HP = 20 kts, 5000 nm/20 kts, 15,000 nm/10 kts

Complement: 400

Built in Nikolaev. Two deep-diving vehicles (SPS), one for salvage (ARS), one (POHISK-2) to rescue crewmen from sunken submarines. Rescue chamber. TV system for underwater inspection. Systems are stabilized to work in rough seas. *Alagez* has Project 1855 salvage vehicle and *Pohisk-4*. *El'brus* on Black Sea, *Alagez* in Pacific, *Audag* in Ukrainian fleet.

Alagez (Ships of the World)

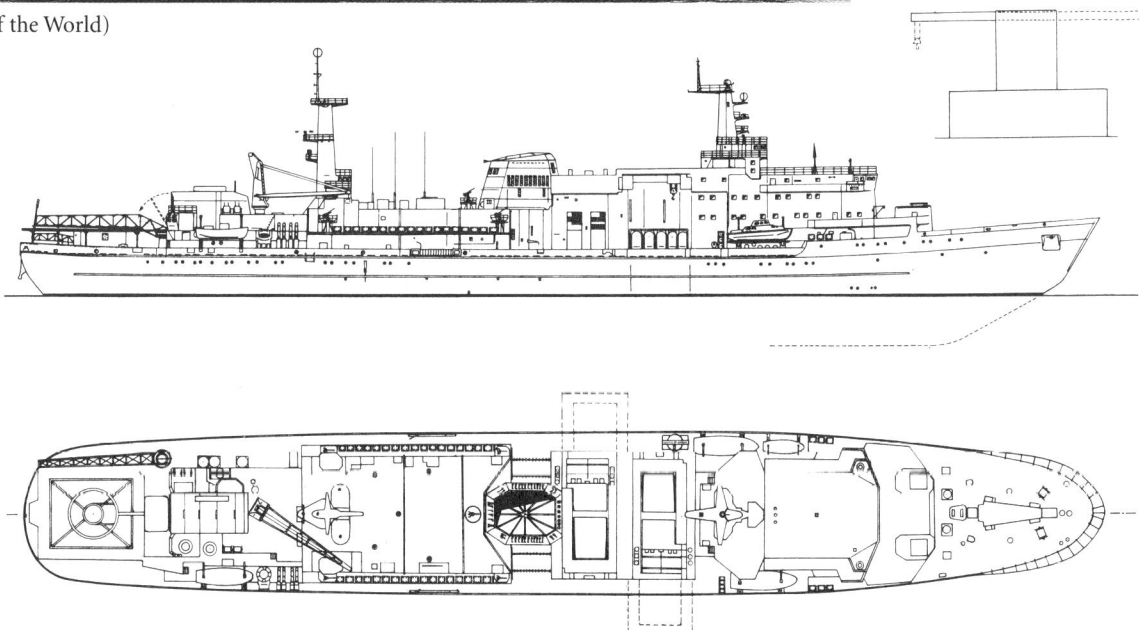

Project: 05360, 05361*

NATO Class Name: None

Names:

MIKHAIL RUDNITSKIY

GEORGEI KOZMIN

GEORGEI TITOV

SAYANY*

Displacement: 7600/10,700

Dimensions: 139.7 × 17.7 × 7.3

Armament: None

Machinery: 1 diesel (5 DKRN 62/140-3), 1 shaft, 6700 HP = 16 kts, 12,000 nm/15.5 kts. Endurance 45 days.

Complement: 72 (10 officers, 12 petty officers)

Electronics: Radar: Don, Okean; Sonar: MG-89*; Communications sonar: MGV-5N

Built in Vyborg 1979, 1980, 1983, and 1984, based on a timber-carrier hull (Pioner Moskvy class); 2 50t and 1 20t cranes, two salvage vehicles (ARS). Lifting system usable in Sea State 3 (with anti-roll system, in Sea State 5). In Navy's Search-Salvage Service.

Mikhail Rudnitskiy (V. V. Kostrichenko)

Project: 527, 527M, 05275*

NATO Class Name: PRUT

Names:

	completed
SS-21	1960
SS-22	1966 ALTAI [1965]
BESHTAU	27 Nov. '64
SS-87	1973 *Vladimir Trefolev* [1962]
ZHIGULI	1963
SS-23	1960
SS-44	1961
SS-26	1969 *Epron** [29 Oct. '59]
SS-83	1961

Displacement: 3000/3380

Dimensions: 89.7 × 14 × 6.57

Armament: 2×2 57 mm (ZiF-75)

Machinery: Diesel-electric; 3 DG-1250 generators; 2 motors, 2 shafts, 4200 HP = 20 kts, 2500 nm/16.5 kts, 4000 nm/10 kts; 260.2 t fuel. Endurance 35 days.

Complement: 35

Prut class (Siegfried Breyer)

Built in Nikolaev (61 Kommunar Yard). *Beshtau, Trefolev,* SS-83, *Epron,* SS-21 were modified 1969–74. They have cranes, compression chambers, diving bells. *Epron* on Black Sea. SS-21 (Black Sea) withdrawn from naval service 7 Jan. '92, offered for lease as *Podvodnik Marinesko.* SS-44 (Pacific) ran on the rocks during salvage of an SDK (amphibious craft) off Cape Koroviy, 1973. *Altai* burned 1969 while under repair at Murmansk (Sudo-Ryemontiy yard). *Zhiguli* (Pacific) sold to China 1993.

Project: 532, 532A

NATO Class Name: None

Names:

GIDROLOG

KHIBIN'

VALDAI

ZANGEZUR

KAZBEK

SS-30

SS-35

SS-38

SS-40

SS-47

SS-48

SS-50 SHAKHTER

SS-51

SS-53

Submarine rescue ship (U.S. Naval Institute Photographic Collection)

SS-35 (V. P. Zablotskiy)

Valdai (Siegfried Breyer)

Displacement: 725/930

Dimensions: 72 × 9.6 × 3.3

Armament: None

Machinery: 2 diesels (37-DR), 2 shafts, 4000 HP = 17 kts, 2500 nm/12 kts. Endurance 11 days.

Complement: 100

Electronics: Don radar, MG-11 sonar

Built 1961–62 in Leningrad (Yard 363) on hulls of Project 264 minesweepers. Stern crane 10 t, diving bell, decompression chamber, sick bay. In 1971 one of this class was transferred to India *(Nistar)*. *Gidrolog* (Pacific) was converted into an intelligence collection ship. SS-38 stricken 1991, SS-47 equipped as training ship. In 1991 *Kazbek* was sold to a private company. *Zangezur* and *Kazbek* were on the Black Sea.

Project: 530

NATO Class Name: NERA

Names:

	laid down	launched	completed
KARPATI	11 Sept. '63	24 Dec. '64	29 Mar. '67

Displacement: 5180/5776

Dimensions: 129.5 × 18.6 × 5.5

Armament: None

Machinery: Diesel-electric, 4 diesel generators, 2 motors, 2 shafts, 8000 HP = 16.5 kts, 8000 nm/12.2 kts

Complement: 270

Built in Nikolaev as submarine salvage ship. Working together, the two stern cranes can lift 750 t; there are also 100 t, 60 t, and 10 t cranes, a salvage bell, two deep water vehicles. First ship to have an underwater object location sonar system, underwater TV, echo-trawls, towed metal detectors (for depths down to 250 m). In June '69 this ship salvaged the missile submarine S-80, which was carrying two cruise missiles. She also worked on the wreck of the missile destroyer *Otavazhniy*. Refitted at Liepaya 1989–93. Based at Kronstadt.

Karpati (U.S. Navy)

Project: 706

NATO Class Name: NEPTUN

Names:

KILEKTORs 3

KILEKTORs 5

KILEKTORs 6

KILEKTORs 9

KILEKTORs 12

KILEKTORs 14

KILEKTORs 15

KILEKTORs 16

KILEKTORs 17

KILEKTORs 18

Displacement: 700/1230

Dimensions: 57.3 × 11.4 × 3.3

Armament: None

Machinery: 2 reciprocating steam engines, 1000 HP = 12 kts

Complement: 28

Built in East Germany (Neptun Werft, Rostock) 1957–60. Have 75 t bow crane.

Project: 145

NATO Class Name: SURA

Names:

KILEKTORs 1

KILEKTORs 2

KILEKTORs 21

KILEKTORs 22

KILEKTORs 25

KILEKTORs 27

KILEKTORs 29

KILEKTORs 31

KILEKTORs 32

KILEKTORs 33

Displacement: 2370/3150

Dimensions: 87 × 14.8 × 5

Armament: None

Machinery: Diesel-electric, 2240 HP = 12 kts, 2000 nm/11 kts

Complement: 40

Built in East Germany 1965–78. Cargo 900 t, 300 t diesel fuel (for transfer). Loading beams and 5 t crane. KIL-33 on Black Sea.

KIL-31 (U.S. Naval Institute Photographic Collection)

KIL-143 (BMVg/MOD Bonn)

Project: 141

NATO Class Name: KASHTAN

Names:

KIL-140

KIL-143

KIL-158

KIL-164

KIL-168

KIL-926

KIL-498

KIL-742

KIL-927

Displacement: 6000

Dimensions: 98 × 19.5 × 7.1

Armament: None

Machinery: 4 Wartsila-Vasa diesels, 2 shafts, 24,480 HP = 18 kts

Complement: 71

Built in GDR (Neptun-Werft) 1986–91. Stern crane: 5 t. 2 90 t gantries, 1 15 t crane. KIL-158 on Black Sea.

Project: 5757

NATO Class Name: BAKLAZAN

Names:

NIKOLAI CHIKER   SB-131

FOTII KRILOV   SB-135

Displacement: 5300

Dimensions: 99 × 19.45 × 7.2

Armament: Helicopter pad

Machinery: 4 diesels, 2 controllable-pitch propellers, 24,480 HP = 18 kts. Endurance 50 days.

Complement: 51 plus 20 survivors

Built in Finland (Rauma, Hollming). Lead ship completed 12 Apr. '89. Lifting power (when moored) 230 t. Diving equipment for 60 m depth, 2 8 t cranes. In 1992 *Krilov* was leased to a Greek company.

Nikolai Chiker (M.O.D. U.K.)

266

Project: 712

NATO Class Name: SLIVA

Names:

	completed
SB-406	20 Feb. '84
SB-408	5 June '84
SB-921	July '84
SHAKHTER	20 Dec. '85

was SB-922 until 1987

Displacement: 2600 (deadweight: 800)

Dimensions: 67.2 × 15.4 × 5.4

Armament: None

Machinery: 2 diesels (6PS 2.5L), 7800 HP = 16 kts

Complement: 43 (plus 10 in salvage party)

Built in Finland (Rauma-Repola).

SB-408 (J.M.S.D.F.)

Project: Unnamed

NATO Class Name: PAMIR

Names:

	completed
ARPAN	1957

renamed *Pamir* 1961,
renamed SSV-477 *Peleng* 1965

AGATAN	1960
ALDAN	1960

renamed *Gigrograf* 1970

Displacement: 1443/2050

Dimensions: 72.8 × 12.8 × 4.1

Armament: None

Machinery: 2 diesels (MAN 10 cylinder), 2 shafts, 4200 HP = 17 kts, 15,000 nm/17 kts. Endurance 30 days.

Complement: 77

Built in Sweden. *Agatan* underwent major repairs in Cuba 1990–91 after an accident. *Pamir* became a communications ship with 3 Strela AA missile launchers for self defense. *Peleng* was renamed UTS-253 and stricken 1988. *Gidrograf* was stricken 1984.

Aldan (U.S. Navy)

Project: 14611

NATO Class Name: IVA

Names:

PzhK-415

PzhK-900

PzhK-1514

PzhK-1515

PzhK-1544

PzhK-1547

PzhK-1859

Displacement: 320

Dimensions: $36.5 \times 7.8 \times 2.2$

Armament: None

Machinery: 2 diesels, 2 shafts, 1040 HP = 12.5 kts

Complement: 20

Built 1984–86 at Rybinsk. Fire-fighting launch, PZhK.

Project: 887

NATO Class Name: Unnamed

Names:

	completed
SMOLNIY'	1976
PEREKOP	1977
KHASAN	1978

Displacement: 5659/6956

Dimensions: $138 \times 17.2 \times 5.42$

Armament: 2×2 76 mm (AK-726, 1200 rounds), 2×2 30 mm (AK-230), 2 RBU-2500 (128 rounds), 2 saluting guns

Machinery: 2 diesels, 2 shafts, 16,000 HP = 21 kts, 10,870 nm/14 kt; 4 DG-640 (400 V, 50 Hz) generators; 1050 t fuel oil, 35 t lubricating oil, 396 t water, 61.2 t provisions. Endurance 40 days.

Complement: 132 (12 officers, 11 petty officers) plus 350 cadets

Built in Poland (Szeczin).

Project 887 (U.S. Naval Institute Photographic Collection)

Project: 888

NATO Class Name: VODNIK

Names:

LUGA

OKA

Displacement: 1698/1820

Dimensions: 71.4 × 11.6 × 3.95

Armament: 2×2 30 mm, 2×2 25 mm (removed)

Machinery: 2 diesels (Sulzer), 2 shafts, 3600 HP = 17 kts, 7800 nm/11 kts

Complement: 60 plus 100 cadets and instructors
Built in Poland (Gdansk) 1976–77 for navies of the Soviet Union, East Germany, and Poland.

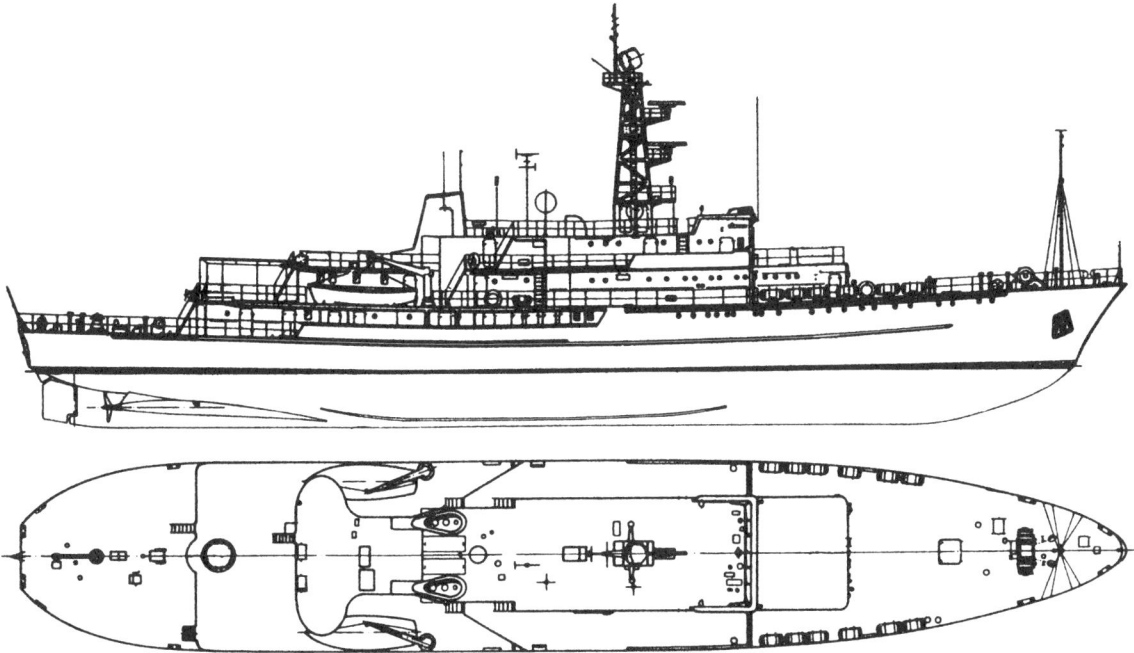

Vodnik class (U.S. Naval Institute Photographic Collection)

Project: 130

NATO Class Name: BEREZA

Names:

SR-23

SR-28

SR-59

SR-74

SR-120

SR-137

SR-216

SR-245

SR-370

SR-478

SR-479

SR-541

SR-548

SR-568

SR-569

SR-570

SR-936

SR-938

SR-939

Nineteen units.

Displacement: 2051/2700

Dimensions: 69.5 × 13.8 × 5.4

Armament: None

Machinery: 2 diesels (Skoda-Sulzer 8-TD 48), 2 shafts, 4400 HP = 13.8 kts; 2 DG-480, 1 DG-225, 2 DG-645, 1 DG-260 generators. Endurance 30 days.

Complement: 48

Electronics: Radar: Kivach

Built in Poland 1984–90; one built for Bulgaria. SR-137, SR-541, SR-548, SR-568 on the Black Sea.

SR-137 (U.S. Naval Institute Photographic Collection)

Project: 1799, 1799A

NATO Class Name: PELYM

Names:

SR-70	SR-180	SR-215	SR-280
SR-77	SR-188	SR-218	SR-281
SR-111	SR-191	SR-220	SR-334
SR-179	SR-203	SR-221	SR-344
	SR-241	SR-222	SR-370
	SR-407	SR-233	SR-455
	SR-409	SR-276	Total twenty-four units.

SR-203 (I. V. Borodulin)

Displacement: 1300

Dimensions: 65.5 × 11.6 × 4.3

Armament: None

Machinery: 2 diesels, 2 shafts, 4000 HP = 14 kts, 4500 nm/12 kts

Complement: 70

Built 1970–87 in Gorokhovets and Khabarovsk (fourteen units); one to Cuba Feb. '82. Three on the Black Sea, including SR-407. SR-191 was stricken in the Pacific in 1995.

Project: 220

NATO Class Name: SEKSTAN

Names:

VTR-3*

VTR-23*

VTR-24*

SR-9

SR-43

SR-127

SR-139

SR-140

SR-144

SR-150–154

SR-156

SR-160

SR-166

SR-171

SR-173

SR-174

SR-185

Total twenty-one units.

Displacement: 280/400

Dimensions: 40.8 × 9.3 × 4.3

Machinery: 1 diesel, 1 shaft, 400 HP = 11 kts

Complement: 24

Built in Finland (Laivateolissus yard) 1953–57 based on a seal-catcher hull (total seventy-two units built). Load 115 t, 1 3 t crane. Used as transports, ocean survey ships, and degaussing ships. Transfers: Albania (one), Egypt (one), Syria (one in 1983); SR-160 and SR-171 to Latvia Feb. '94.

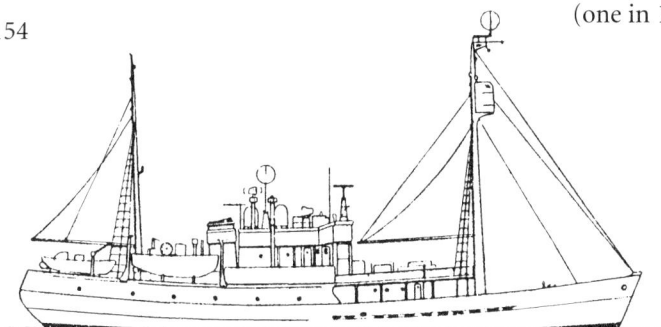

Project: 219R

NATO Class Name: KHABAROV

Names:

VTR-8

VTR-13

VTR-15

VTR-25

VTR-35

SR-2

SR-9

SR-43

SR-156

SR-158

SR-162–166

SR-911

Sixteen units

Displacement: 500/650

Dimensions: 46.5 × 8 × 2.8

Armament: 2 14.5 mm (2M-7)

Machinery: 1 diesel, 1 shaft, 400 HP = 10 kts, 1130 nm/10 kts

Complement: 40

Built 1952–56. Load 400 t, 4 1.5 t cranes. Border Guards transports, re-equipped as degaussing ships. Stricken: VTR-25 and VTR-162 in 1988, VTR-13 in 1991, SR-165 in 1993.

Project: 1806, 18061*

NATO Class Name: ONEGA

Names:

GKS-52

GKS-95

GKS-224

GKS-240

GKS-283

GKS-286

SFP-173*

SFP-177

SFP-288

SFP-295*

SFP-322

SFP-340

SFP-343

SFP-372

SFP-511

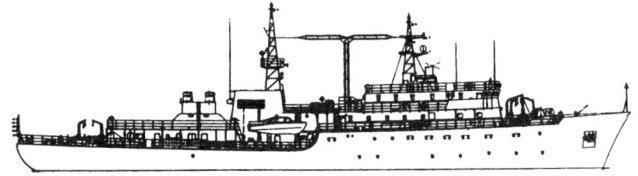

SFP-542

SFP-562

   Sixteen units

Displacement: 2100

Dimensions: 81 × 11 × 4.2

Armament: Helicopter pad

Machinery: Gas turbines, 2 shafts, 6000 HP = 20 kts

Complement: 45

   Built 1977–85 as Acoustic Measurement Ships (GKS, i.e., Hydro-Acoustic Control [Measurement] Ships) and as Ships of Physical Fields (SFP). SFP-177 on the Black Sea. SFP-340 (Pacific) stricken after a fire, 1990.

Project: 1236

NATO Class Name: POTOK

Names:

OS-100

OS-124

OS-138

OS-145

OS-149

OS-225

Displacement: 750/850

Dimensions: 2.1 × 9.4 × 2.5

Armament: 1×4 533 mm TT, 2×2 406 mm TT

Machinery: 2 diesels (40-D), 2 shafts, 4000 HP = 17 kts, 2500 nm/12 kts

Complement: 30

   Built 1977–79 on a minesweeper hull, to test new types of torpedoes and torpedo tubes, with torpedo retrieval equipment.

Potok class (U.S. Naval Institute Photographic Collection)

Project: 1388, 1388R*

NATO Class Name: SHELON

Names:

TL-288

TL-1127

TL-1302

TL-1478

TL-1717

TL-2021

TL-2023

TL-1128

TL-1536

TL-1616

TL-1551

TL-1596

completed

KRKh-1*

KRKh-321*

KRKh-528*   18 July '84

KRKh-579*

KRKh-1374*

Total thirty-two units

Displacement: 270

Dimensions: $46 \times 6 \times 2$

Armament: None

Machinery: 2 diesels, 2 shafts, 10,000 HP = 30 kts

Complement: 20

Built 1978–84; have torpedo retrieval ramp aft. On this hull were also built ships for radiation-chemical reconnaissance. Three units are on the Black Sea.

TL-1127 (A. N. Sokolov)

Shelon class (U.S. Naval Institute Photographic Collection)

273

Project: 368T, 368P, 368RS

NATO Class Name: POLUCHAT 1, 2, 3

Names:

TL-1

TL-140

TL-283

TL-301

TL-304

TL-308

TL-312

TL-540

TL-809

TL-811

TL-826

TL-827

TL-870

TL-980

TL-992

TL-996

TL-997

TL-998

AK-390–446

AK-470–491

Displacement: 84.7/92.8

Dimensions: 29.6 × 5.98 × 1.56

Armament: 1×2 14.5 mm (2M-7; 2352 rounds), BM-14-17 140 mm rocket launcher (85 rounds)

Machinery: 2 diesels (M-50F-4), 2 shafts, 2400 HP = 21.6 kts, 550 nm/14 kts, 250 nm/21.6 kts

Complement: 15 (1 officer, 2 petty officers, 2 rated men, 10 sailors—on AK)

Electronics: Radar: Donets-2; Sounder: NEL-3; Gyrocompass: Gira-KM; Log: LG-4; Radio transmitters R-657, R-609, R-619, R-607

Built in 1960–77 (Nikolaevsk-on-Amur and others) as torpedo retrievers (TL) and patrol launches (AK). A few had the BM-14-17 rocket launchers. Seven bulkheads. TL-1 (Pacific) was armed and reclassified as SK-29 in 1965. Thirteen on the Black Sea. In 1991 AK-394 transferred to KyuM (G Svobodniy). AK-487 to Vostok club, AK-401 to DOSAAF (Pacific)

Transfers: Algeria (3), Angola (3), Congo (3), Ethiopia (1), Guinea-Bissau (3), India (3), Indonesia (3), Iraq (2), Mozambique (6), Somalia (6), Syria (2), Tanzania (2), Vietnam (2), North Yemen (2), South Yemen (1).

[Ed.: According to Western sources, transfers amounted to: Albania (4), Algeria (1), Angola (2), Bangladesh (1), Congo (2), Cuba (1 or more), Egypt (2), Ethiopia (1), Ghana (4), Guinea (2), Guinea-Bissau (2), India (5), Iraq (2), Libya (1), Mozambique (1), Somalia (5), Tanzania (1), Vietnam (2), North Yemen (4), and South Yemen (1).]

Poluchat-1 class (U.S. Naval Institute Photographic Collection)

Project: 1392, 1392V (BURUNDUK)

NATO Class Name: None

Names:

KBM-332

KBM-702

Kts-543

KM-593

Kts-594

KM-731

Forty-three others

Displacement: 160/200

Dimensions: $39.6 \times 7.8 \times 1.5$

Armament: None

Machinery: 3 diesels, 3600 HP = 17 kts

Targets and target control boats built on missile boat hulls; stricken when worn out. Up to twenty are in service each year. [Ed.: Osa-class.]

Project: 1274

NATO Class Name: KLASMA

Names:

	laid down	launched	completed
INGUL	10 Oct. '61	14 Apr. '62	1962
DONETS	17 Dec. '68	1968	1968
INGURI	21 Oct. '76	7 Oct. '77	1977
KATUN'			
TAVDA	14 Apr. '76	21 Oct. '76	6 Oct. '77
TSNA	17 Dec. '68	1969	1969
YANA	4 May '61	1 Nov. '62	1963
ZEYA			1970

Displacement: 6000/6900

Dimensions: $130.5 \times 16 \times 5.8$

Armament: None

Machinery: Diesel-electric, 5 Wartsila-Sulzer diesel generators (4 in *Ingul* and *Yana*), 5000 HP, 2 motors, 2150 HP = 14 kts, 12,000 nm/14 kts

Complement: 85

Built in Finland (Wartsila, Helsinki); ice-strengthened cable-layers. *Yana* carries naval personnel and can be used as a minelayer. *Katun'* was stricken in the Pacific in 1995.

Klasma class (U.S. Naval Institute Photographic Collection)

Project: 1172

NATO Class Name: None

Names:

EMBA

NEPRYADVA

SETUN'

Displacement: 2050

Dimensions: $75.9 \times 12.6 \times 3$

Armament: None

Machinery: Diesel-electric, 2 Wartsila-Vasa diesel generators (6R-22), 2 shafts, 1360 HP = 11 kts

Complement: 40

    Built in Finland 1980–81.

Nepryadva (M.O.D. Bonn)

Project: 1275

NATO Class Name: EMBA-2

Names:

BIRYUSA

KEM'

Displacement: 2400

Dimensions: $86.1 \times 12.6 \times 3$

Armament: None

Machinery: Diesel-electric, 2 Wartsila-Vasa diesel generators (8R-22), 2 shafts, 2180 HP = 11.8 kts

Complement: 40

    Built in Finland (Wartsila); carry about 600 t of cable. In the Pacific Fleet from 24 Nov. '86.

Project: 1360

NATO Class Name: None

Names:

KRIM

KAVKAZ

Displacement: 158/220

Dimensions: $45.5 \times 8.7 \times 2.5$

Armament: None

Machinery: 2 diesels (M-503A), 8000 HP = 32 kts, 40 t oil, 500 nm/35 kts

Complement: 32

    Roll-stabilized. Presidential yachts under the flag of the Border Guards. On the Black Sea.

Project: 320/II

NATO Class Name: None

Names:

OB'

YENISEI

SVIR'

IRTYSH

Displacement: 9430/11,570

Dimensions: 152.8 × 19.4 × 6.3

Armament: 1 helicopter

Machinery: 2 diesels (Skoda 12 ZV 40/48), 2 shafts, 15,600 HP = 19 kts; 2125 t fuel; 20,000 nm/18 kts, 10,000 nm/14 kts. Endurance 40 days.

Electronics: Radar: MR-212, MR-250, MR-216; Gyrocompass: Kurs-10A-1; Echo sounder: M3-B; Log: KEL-1; Radio DR: Rumb.

Complement: 75 (+75 medical personnel)

Built in Poland (Szeczin) 1980–88. 200 beds for personnel, 100 hospital beds, seven operating rooms. Can evacuate up to 450 wounded. *Ob´* and *Irtysh* in the Pacific, *Yenisei* on the Black Sea.

Ob´ (G. G. Kiselev)

Project: SK-620 (DRAKON)

NATO Class Name: PETRUSHKA

Names:

SN-126

MK-391

MK-1277

MK-1407

MK-1408

MK-1409

MK-1410

MERNIK

Twenty-two others
 Total forty.

Displacement: 200/240

Dimensions: 32.7 × 7.4 × 2.8

Armament: None

Machinery: 2 diesels (31-AMN), 2 shafts, 620 HP = 12 kts, 1000 nm/10 kts

Complement: 14

  Built in Poland 1978–84. Seaworthiness: 7. One medical compartment: twelve beds; one isolation ward with two beds. Other launches of this type are used for personnel and for training boats.

SN-126 (V. V. Kostrichenko)

Part III
Transports and Cargo Vessels

Project: 502R, 502*

NATO Class Name: MAYAK

Names:

MPK-528

MPK-423

US-124

US-193

US-329

ANEROID*

KHERSONES*

KURS*

LADOGA*

GS-239*

GS-242*

GIRORULEVOIY*   GS-536

BUZULUK

ISHIM

LAMA

MIUS

RIONI

V'ITEGA

NEMAN

UL'MA

Displacement: 770/950

Dimensions: 54.2 × 9.3 × 3.6

Armament: On MPK and US: 1×2 25 mm (2M-3M,

Aneroid (U.S. Naval Institute Photographic Collection)

MPK-528 (V. N. Muratov)

130 rounds), 4×5 RBU-1200 (20 RGB-12), 2×1 406 mm (OTA-40-204, 4 SET-40 torpedoes), 2×6 depth charge throwers (BB-1). On intelligence data collectors: 2×8 Strela launchers (16 missiles). On *Aneroid*: 2×2 14.5 mm (2M-7).

Machinery: 1 diesel (8 NVD-48AU), 1 shaft, 800 HP = 12.1 kts, 8300 nm/9 kts, 6000 nm/11 kts; 3 DG-100 generators; 127 t fuel, 5.16 t oil, 75 t water, 4 t provisions. Endurance 30 days.

Complement: 75

Electronics: Radar: Don; Sonar: Paltus-M, MG-329, MI-110K

Built in Volgograd 1965–70 on the hull of a medium ocean-going trawler. Used as military transports and to train reservists. Small Intelligence-Gathering Ships of 3rd Rank, modernized 1972. MPK-528 was rebuilt from the trawler *Shimanovsk* (Pacific).

Project: 503, 503R, 05035*

NATO Class Name: ALPINIST

Names:

	completed
GS-7	
GS-8	26 Dec. '81
GS-19	
GS-20	
GS-39	3 Feb. '81
OS-104*	30 Dec. '84
MPK-300	
MPK-180	(ex-*Nayada*)

Total eight.

Displacement: 810/1140

Dimensions: 54 × 10.5 × 4

Armament: As MPK: 1×2 25 mm (2M-3M), 1×2 533 mm TT, 12 depth charges (BGB-1)

Machinery: 1 diesel (8 NVD-48), 1 VRSh, 1320 HP = 13 kts, 7000 nm/13 kts; 163 t fuel. Endurance 25 days.

Electronics: Radar: Don; Sonar: Paltus-MP; Sounder: Kalmar-P

Complement: 24

Built in Kiev (Leninskaya Kuznitsa yard) and in Volgograd on trawler hulls. Bow thrusters. GS-8 stricken in Black Sea 1994.

GS-39 (U.S. Naval Institute Photographic Collection)

GS-7 (U.S. Naval Institute Photographic Collection)

Project: 1332

Class Name: BARENTSEVO MORE

Names:

One unit

Displacement: 1320/1880

Dimensions: 59 × 13 × 4.87

Armament: 2×2 25 mm (2M-3M), 2×2 533 mm TT, 2 MRG-1

Machinery: 1 Skoda diesel (6L-525), 1 controllable-pitch propeller, 2200 HP = 13.7 kts, 2 DG-150 generators. Endurance 40 days.

Complement: 39

Built 1974 in Klaipeda (Baltiya Yard); in Northern Fleet.

Barentsevo More class (P. V. Veselov)

Project: 1128, 1129*
(Polish Project B-43)

NATO Class Name: None

Names:

CHUKOTKA*	ex-KIK-16	
SAKHALIN	ex-KIK-8	
SIBIR'	KIK-2	
SPASSK	ex-*Suchan*	ex-KIK-5

Displacement: 3820/7400

Dimensions: 108 × 15 × 6.1

Armament: 1 helicopter

Machinery: 2500 HP = 12 kts, 9800 nm/12 kts

Complement: 200

Electronics: Neptun radar, Khrom-K IFF, Kaktus communications antenna

Built in Poland 1957–59 (Donbass type), rebuilt 1959 (chief designer D. N. Zagaiykevich). Pacific, stricken 1991–93.

Sibir (U.S. Naval Institute Photographic Collection)

Project: 1130

NATO Class Name: DESNA

Names:

	completed
CHAZHMA	21 July '63
ex-*Dangara* or KIK-12	
CHUMIKAN	
ex-*Dolgoshchyel'ye* or KIK-11	

Displacement: 5300/13,600

Dimensions: 139.6 × 18 × 7.9

Armament: 1 helicopter

Machinery: 2 diesels, 5200 HP = 15 kts, 20,000 nm/13 kts

Complement: 300

Electronics: Communications stations: Tral, Arbat, Vympel-2, Angara; Radar: Don; ESM: Bizan'

Rebuilt 1963 from Dzhankoiy class colliers; chief designer Suderevskiy (TsKB-17); in Pacific Fleet. *Chazhma* stricken Oct. '92.

Project: Unnamed

NATO Class Name: OKEAN

Names:

ALIDADA

AMPERMETR

ANEROID   ex-*Kit*

BAROGRAF   ex-*Vitim*

BAROMETR

VOSTOK

DEFLEKTOR

EKHOLOG

FIDROFON   ex-*Gorbusha*

GIROSKOP

KRENOMETR

KURSOGRAF   ex-*Sudak*

LINZA

Linza (U.S. Navy)

LOTLIN'	GS-319
PELENG	ex-*Chavycha*
PELUKTOR	
PENITER	
TEODOLIT	
TRAVERZ	
ZOND	
EKHOLOT	

Displacement: 474/737

Dimensions: 50.8 × 8.8 × 3.6

Armament: 2×8 launchers for Strela missiles (16 missiles)

Machinery: 1 diesel (R8 DV-148), 1 shaft, 540 HP = 12 kts, 7900 nm/11 kts; fuel 100 t.

Complement: 70

Built in East Germany (Stralsund) 1965–69 and converted to intelligence collectors. Aluminum superstructures. *Alidada* stricken 1990. *Barograf* became target ship SM-346, *Deflektor* became SM-353. In 1990 *Kursograf* was given to the Vostok club as a base. *Ekolot* burnt out in Pacific.

Lotlin' (U.S. Naval Institute Photographic Collection)

Project: 650, 650RP*

NATO Class Name: TELNOVSK (TISSA)

Names:

ARAKS	
ANABAR	
AITODOR	
LOT*	
LAG*	
MANOMETR*	
SVIYAGA	
SIRENA	ex-*Porkhox*
UL'YANA GROMOVA	
BUREVESTNIK	
ISHIM	
STVOR	ex-*M. Krivonos*
VTR-73	ex-*E. Vil'de*

Displacement: 727/1900

Dimensions: 70.2 × 10 × 4

Machinery: 2 diesels (6-NVD 48), 2 shafts, 800 HP = 11 kts, 3000 nm/9.5 kts; 2 DG-57, 1 DG-50 generators

Complement: 50 (80 in *Ul. Gromova*)

Electronics: Radar: Neptun; Radio transmitter: Ersh; Radio receiver: Volna; Gyrocompass: Kurs-3; Sounder: NEL-3

Built in Hungary (Giorgiu-Dezh yard, Budapest) 1949–57 for the navy and merchant marine; three re-equipped as intelligence collectors (*). Load 1000 t, six bulkheads. *Burevestnik* and *Ishim* are military transports on the Black Sea. *Araks* and *Lot* (Pacific) and *Log* were stricken 1985–91. One unit was rebuilt as the communications ship KS-7 (stricken in the Pacific 1986). VTR-73 put on lease, renamed *Eduard Vilde*.

Project: Unnamed

Class Name: TUNTSELOV

Names:

IZMERITEL'   DNEPR

PROTRAKTOR   DNESTR

GS-236

Displacement: 750

Dimensions: $52.7 \times 9.2 \times 3.5$

Armament: 2 machine guns

Machinery: 1 diesel (Burmeister & Wain), 1000 HP = 15 kts

Built as tuna fishing boats during the 1960s in Japan (Ishikajima, Tokyo). There are also a few small Japanese schooners, seized by Border Guards and handed over to the ocean survey service in the Pacific (GPB-68 etc).

Project: 596P, 596M

NATO Class Name: VYTEGRALES

Names:

APSHERON	ex-*Vagales*
BASKUNCHAK	ex-*Kirishi*
DAURIYA	ex-*Viborges*
DIKSON	ex-*Vostok-3*
DONBASS	ex-*Vostok-4*

Project: 1282

Class Name: DALD'IN

Names:

– – –

Displacement: 315/360

Dimensions: $31.8 \times 7.2 \times 2.8$

Armament: None

Machinery: 1 diesel (8 NVD-36), 305 HP = 9.4 kts, 4300 nm; 33 t fuel, 2 DG-63 generators. Endurance 19 days.

Complement: 13

Built 1973 on a trawler (Karelia class) hull, to test a new type of mine. 1.5 t crane.

SEVAN	ex-*Severles*
TAMAN	ex-*Suzdal'*
YAMAL	ex-*Tosnoles*

Displacement: 3300/9920

Dimensions: $122.9 \times 16.7 \times 8.3$

Armament: Helicopter pad

Machinery: 1 diesel (Burmeister & Wain), 5200 HP; 3 DG-220 generators; 7350 nm/15 kts

Dauriya (U.S. Navy)

Dauriya (U.S. Navy)

Complement: 46

Electronics: Radar: Don; Sounder: NEL-5, Gyrocompass: Kurs-4

Rebuilt from timber carriers 1966–68. *Taman* and *Baskunchak* were military transports. *Apsheron* and *Sevan* are command ships of 2nd Rank. *Dikson* was rebuilt as a test ship (Project 1236?: 20 m beam, displacement 10,000 t). The remainder are search-salvage ships. Four are on the Black Sea.

Project: 391 (LOGGER)

NATO Class Name: LENTRA

Names:

KACHA	GS-4		GS-47	USACH
RUZA	GS-11		GS-48	
TIGIL'	GS-17		GS-50	
UFA	GS-34		GS-54	
UGRA	UNGO		GS-55	
VTR-1	GS-36	ATLAS	GS-56	
VTR-18	GS-41		GS-59	
VTR-20	GS-43	OKEANOGRAF	GS-60	
VTR-21	GS-46		GS-85	
VTR-22				
VTR-28				
VTR-31				
VTR-32				
VTR-75				
VTR-144				
VTR-145				
GS-1				
GS-2				
GS-3				

Lentra class (U.S. Naval Institute Photographic Collection)

GROT

TAIFUN

Displacement: 305/460

Dimensions: 39.2 × 7.5 × 2.8

Armament: None

Machinery: 1 diesel (8 NVD-36), 330 HP = 10 kts, 6900 nm/9 kts; fuel 41.7 t. Endurance 16 days.

Complement: 30

Built in Kiev and East Germany 1955–58 on a medium fishing trawler (SRT) hull. VTR-31 handed over to the gas industry ministry (Gazprom) and renamed *Geofizik*. GS-59 became a training barge *(Mechnikov)*. GS-1, GS-2, GS-4, GS-34, GS-47, GS-60, GS-85 became intelligence collectors; stricken 1980–87.

Project: 1850

NATO Class Name: ANDIZHAN

Names:

VENTA

VILYUIY

ONDA

POS'IET

Displacement: 2365/6800

Dimensions: 104.2 × 14.4 × 6.6

Armament: Helicopter pad

Machinery: 2 diesels (8-SV-55-UA), 1 shaft, 2500 HP = 13.5 kts; 3 DG-160 generators; 6000 nm/13 kts; fuel 238 t, oil 33.2 t, water 60 t

Complement: 100

Electronics: Radar: Don; Transmitter: Blesna; Sounder: NEL-5; Gyrocompass: Kurs-4

Built in East Germany 1959, transferred from merchant marine to navy. Rebuilt 1974–75. Six bulkheads. Military transports (VTR) with racks for 10 P-120 Malakhit missiles and 20 Volna missiles. *Vilyuiy* is on the Black Sea.

Onda (U.S. Naval Institute Photographic Collection)

Onda (U.S. Naval Institute Photographic Collection)

Project: 740/2V

Class Name: YUNYY PARTIZAN

Names:

PECHORA

VITSE-ADMIRAL FOMIN

TURGAY

UFA

Displacement: 2800/3096

Dimensions: $88.8 \times 12.9 \times 5$

Armament: None

Machinery: 1 diesel (Skoda-Sulzer), 1 shaft, 2080 HP = 13 kts, 4000 nm/12 kts

Complement: 35

Built in Romania (Turnu-Severin, Oltenitza) in 1975–76; total of 20 built. 2 20t and 1 10t cranes. *Turgay* on the Black Sea. *Vitse-Admiral Fomin* (Pacific) modernized as missile transport (Project 10680).

Turgay (V. V. Kostrichenko)

Turgay (U.S. Naval Institute Photographic Collection)

Project: 567

Class Name: LENINSKIY KOMSOMOL

Names:

SAMARA

KOLKHIDA

Displacement: 6190/23,000

Dimensions: 169.9 × 21.8 × 9.7

Armament: None

Machinery: 1 shaft, 13,500 HP = 19 kts, 2 KVG-25 boilers, 2 750 kW turbogenerators; 1 DG-340 generators; fuel 2370 t

Complement: 50

Chief designer K. I. Bokhanevich (TsKB-32). Built 1959–60 as commercial cargo ships, transferred to the navy 1980. Cranes: 2 60 t, 12 5 t. *Samara* went to the Pacific Fleet 16 Nov. '84, was stricken 19 Aug. '88.

Samara (U.S. Naval Institute Photographic Collection)

Samara (U.S. Naval Institute Photographic Collection)

Project: 550

NATO Class Name: AMGUEMA

Names:

YAUZA

MIKHAIL SOMOV

Displacement: 5118/14,470

Dimensions: 133 × 18.8 × 9

Armament: None

Machinery: Diesel-electric, 4 diesel generators (3D-100), 1 shaft, 7200 HP = 15 kts, 7000 nm/15 kts; 4 DG-220 generators; fuel 1000 t, oil 70 t, water 156 t

Electronics: Radar: Don; Transmitter: Blesna-SV; Receiver: Volna; Radio direction-finder: SRP-5; Sounder: NEL-5; Gyrocompass: Kurs-3

Built 1974 in Kherson as icebreaking transports. Load: 6500 t. Cranes: 2 60 t, 2 10 t, 6 5 t.

Project: V-53

NATO Class Name: MELITOPOL

Names:

MAYAK

INVELIR

PRIZMA

FORT SHEVCHENKO

INDIGIRKA

Displacement: 775/1200

Dimensions: 57.6 × 9 × 4.3

Armament: None

Machinery: 1 diesel, 600 HP = 11 kts, 2500 nm/10 kts

Complement: 50

Built in 1952–55; lead ship freighter *Melitopol* was built in Poland in 1952 (load 775 t).

Melitopol class (U.S. Navy)

Project: Unnamed

NATO Class Name: KEYLA

Names:

MEZEN'

ONEGA

PONOIY

RITSA

TERIBERKA

TULOMA

TVERTSA

UNZHA

USSURI

ERISLAN

Displacement: 900/2400

Dimensions: 78.8 × 10.8 × 4.6

Armament: None

Machinery: 1 diesel, 1 shaft, 1000 HP = 12 kts, 3000 nm/11 kts

Complement: 26

Built in Hungary (Budapest) 1958–61. Load 1200 t. Cranes: 1 15 t, 6 2.5 t. *Mezen'* on the Black Sea.

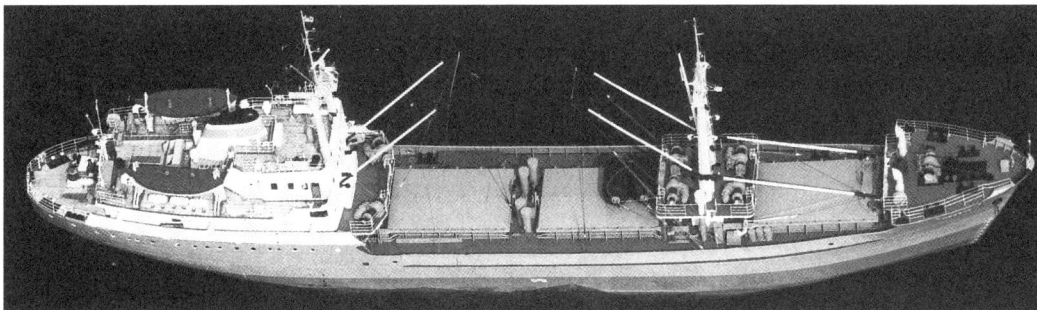

Mezen' (U.S. Navy)

Ritsa (U.S. Naval Institute Photographic Collection)

Project: Unnamed

Class Name: MIKHAIL KALININ

Names:

KUBAN' (ex-*N. Krupskaya*)

Displacement: 6400

Dimensions: 122.15 × 16 × 5.2

Armament: None

Machinery: 2 diesels (MAN 6 cylinder), 2 shafts, 8000 HP = 17 kts, 8200 nm/17 kts

Complement: 120

Built 1958 in East Germany (Matthias Tezen yard, Wismar) and transferred to the navy 1977(?) as a hospital ship; transferred to Bulgaria 1994. In all, twenty-four ships of this design were built. Carries 350 passengers, 1000 t of provisions.

Mikhail Kalinin class (U.S. Navy)

Project: Unnamed

NATO Class Name: None

Names:

	completed
BAIKAL	1954
renamed OS-30 in 1974	

Displacement: 10,000/12,600

Dimensions: 130.2 × 18.88 × 8.17

Armament: None

Machinery: 4 diesel generators (8-MN-42, 2050 HP each), 1 shaft, 6000 HP = 13.2 kts, 3 DG-225, 1 DG-100 generators

Complement: 63

Built in Holland (Vlissengen, de Schelde); Six units in all. Deadweight 7230 t, ten bulkheads, six holds. Ten cranes: 2 10t, 8 5t. As an OS this ship flooded at Novaya Zemlya.

Project: 233

Class Name: KOLOMNA

Names:

KUZNETSK

MEGRA

SVANETIYA   ex-*Krasnoarmeiysk*

Displacement: 6700

Dimensions: 102.4 × 14.4 × 6.6

Armament: None

Machinery: Reciprocating steam plant, 2800 HP = 14 kts, 6900 nm/13 kts

Complement: 44

Built in Germany (Neptun Werft), 1954–56.

Project: V-32

Class Name: TSYAL'IM

Names:

SEVERODONETSK

KAMCHATKA

INSAR

LENINSK-KUZNETSKIY

Displacement: 4500

Dimensions: 94.7 × 13.5 × 6

Armament: None

Machinery: 1650 HP = 12 kts, 8500 nm/11 kts

Complement: 40

Built in Poland (Szeczin) 1956. Load: 2300 t. *Insar* supports submarine missile firings.

Project: Unnamed

Class Name: ZABAYKAL'YE

Names:

ZAIBAIYKAL'E   PKZ-62

PRIAMUR'E   PKZ-63

Displacement: 5300/7100

Dimensions: 126 × 19.6 × 6

Machinery: 4 diesel generators, 2 shafts, 10,000 HP = 16 kts

Complement:

Built in Komsomolsk as ice-breaking railroad ferries 1958, rebuilt to liners (622 passengers), transferred to navy 1965, stricken 1977 (Pacific Fleet).

Priamure (U.S. Navy)

Project: 1552

NATO Class Name: SOFIA

Names:

AKHTUBA   ex-*Khanoiy*

Displacement: 13,230/62,600

Dimensions: 230.5 × 31 × 11.6

Armament: None

Machinery: 1 steam turbine (TS-2), 1 shaft, 21,000 HP = 17 kts, 2 750 kW turbogenerators; 1 DG-300 generator; 10,000 nm/17 kts; 4319 t oil fuel

Complement: 57

Designed by TsKB-32, built in Leningrad (Admiralty yard); twenty-one built in all. Transferred to the navy in 1971. Carries 45,000 t of diesel fuel (deadweight 49,370 t). Modernized 1992. Sold to Philippines to pay debts, 1994.

Akhtuba (V. N. Muratov)

Project: 160

NATO Class Name: ALTAY

Names:

EL'NYA

IZHORA

ILIM

KOLA

PRUT

EGORLIK

Displacement: 5500/7300

Dimensions: 106.2 × 15.4 × 6.75

Armament: None

Machinery: 1 diesel (Burmeister & Wain), 1 shaft, 3200 HP = 14 kts; 2 DG-260, 1 DG-22.4 generators; 1 96 kW steam generator, 8600 nm/12 kts, fuel 264 t, water 163 t

Complement: 40

Electronics: Radar: Don-3; Radios: Volkhov-M and Volna; Sounder: NEL-5; Gyrocompass: Kurs-4

Built in Finland (Rauma-Repola) in 1967–72, total of sixteen units for Ministry of Merchant Fleet. *Izhora* exploded in Vladivostok on 17 July '91. *Ilim* modernized in Singapore 1992.

Kola (V. P. Chernyshov)

Project: 563

NATO Class Name: KAZBECK

Names:

DESNA

VOLKHOV

ALAT'IR'

Displacement: 16,250

Dimensions: 145.5 × 19.2 × 8.2

Armament: None

Machinery: 2 diesels (8DR-43/61), 1 shaft, 3800 HP = 15 kts, 18,000 nm/12 kts; 3 DG-340, 1 DG-125 generators

Complement: 46

Designed by TsKB-32, built in Leningrad and Nikolaev 1961–64 in large numbers for Ministry of Merchant Fleet. Deadweight 12,000 t. *Desna* in Black Sea.

Desna (S. P. Davis)

Kazbek class (U.S. Naval Institute Photographic Collection)

Project: Unnamed

Class Name: PEVEK

Names:

OLEKMA

IMAN

ZOLOTOIY ROG

Displacement: 4000/6700

Dimensions: 105.4 × 14.8 × 6.7

Armament: None

Machinery: 1 diesel (Burmeister & Wain 550 VTBF-100), 1 shaft, 2900 HP = 14 kts, 8000 nm/14 kts

Complement: 40

Built in Finland (Rauma-Repola) with many sisters (thirty-four units) for the merchant marine. *Olekma* transferred to the navy in the mid-1970s. Equipped for underway replenishment. Deadweight 6482 t.

Iman (V. V. Kostrichenko)

Project: Unnamed

Class Name: KALININGRADNEFT'

Names:

ARGUN'

VYAZ'MA   ex-*Katun'*

Displacement: 4820/8600

Dimensions: 115.5 × 17 × 7

Machinery: 1 diesel (5-DKRN), 1 shaft, 3850 HP = 14.3 kts, 5000 nm/14 kts, fuel 432 t

Complement: 32

Built in Finland (Rauma-Repola) from 1978 on.

Vyaz'ma (U.S. Navy)

Vyaz'ma (Royal Netherlands Navy)

Project: Unnamed

Class Name: NERCHA

Names:

NARVA

NERCHA

KLYAZ'MA

Displacement: 1080/1080

Dimensions: $63.5 \times 10.1 \times 4.3$

Armament:

Machinery: 1 diesel (6 cylinder), 1 shaft, 1000 HP = 11 kts, 2000 nm/10 kts

Complement: 25

Built in Finland (Wartsila) 1952–55 (total five units). These ships were transferred to the navy in the 1970s.

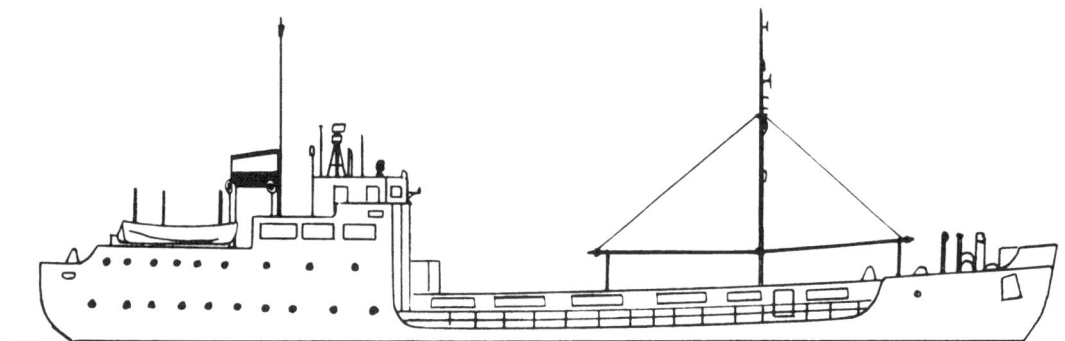

Project: Unnamed

Class Name: KONDA

Names:

KONDA

ROSSOSH'

SAYANY

YAKHROMA

Displacement: 1178/1980

Dimensions: 69 × 10.1 × 4.3

Armament: None

Machinery: 1 diesel, 1 shaft, 1600 HP = 12 kts, 2200 nm/11.5 kts

Complement: 36

Built in Finland 1955 on a tanker hull (ISKRA type). Ice-reinforced hull. *Rossosh'* (Pacific) stricken July '85.

Project: Unnamed

Class Name: IRTYSH

Names:

NARVA

Displacement: 1700

Dimensions: 68.5 × 10.4 × 3.7

Armament: None

Machinery: 1 diesel, 1 shaft, 880 HP = 12 kts, 2000 nm/10 kts

Complement: 40

Built in Sweden 1964. 1170 t of diesel fuel.

Project: 1545

Class Name: BASKUNCHAK

Names:

IVAN GOLUBETS

SOVETSKIY POGRANICHNIK

Displacement: 1260/2900

Dimensions: 83.1 × 12 × 3.8

Armament: None

Machinery: 1 diesel (8DR 43/61), 1 shaft, 2000 HP = 13 kts, 5000 nm/12 kts

Complement: 30

Built in Kerch (Zaliv yard) 1966, together with one unit for the East German navy and sixteen for the Soviet merchant fleet. Can transport four kinds of petroleum products simultaneously. 1500 t of diesel fuel. Thirteen bulkheads. For the Border Guards.

Ivan Golubets (V. V. Levchenko)

Project: 1452*, 1453

NATO Class Name: INGUL

Names:

PAMIR

MASHUK

ALATAU*

KARABAKH

Displacement: 3010/4050

Dimensions: 92.8 × 15.4 × 5.8

Armament: Foundations for 2 57 mm, 4 25 mm

Machinery: 2 diesels (16-cylinder 58 D-4R), 2 variable-pitch propellers, 9000 HP = 18.8 kts, 9000 nm/19 kts

Complement: 35 plus salvage party (18)

Built in Leningrad (Admiralty yard) 1975–87, plus *Bars* and *Yaguar* for merchant marine. Salvage pumps, fire monitors; can act as salvage tugs.

Mashuk (V. V. Levchenko, G. G. Kisyelov)

Project: 1124?

NATO Class Name: OREL

Names:

SB-38

SB-43

Displacement: 1750

Dimensions: 61.4 × 11.52 × 4.7

Armament: None

Machinery: 1 diesel (MAN), 1 shaft, 2500 HP = 13.5 kts, 14,000 nm/13.5 kts

Complement: 40

Built in Finland (Turku) 1961; are part of a class built for the Ministry of Fishing Fleet, transferred to the navy. Ice-reinforced hulls with six bulkheads. Have decompression chambers. SB-38 stricken 1990.

Project: V-99

NATO Class Name: IVA

Names:

VIKhR'-5

VIKhR'-6

VIKhR'-8

VIKhR'-9

Displacement: 3400

Dimensions: 72.3 × 14.36 × 4.6

Armament: None

Machinery: 2 diesels (2D-4T), 8000 HP = 16 kts, fuel 186 t; Built 1988–91. *Vikhr'-1* and *VIKhR'-4* in gas industry (Gazprom).

Project: 1893, 1993*

NATO Class Name: KATUN-1, 2

Names:

PzhS-64*

PzhS-92*

PzhS-95*

PzhS-96

PzhS-98

PzhS-123

PzhS-124

PzhS-209

PzhS-273

PzhS-279

PzhS-282

PZhS-551

Displacement: 920/1000

Dimensions: $62.6 \times 10.2 \times 3.5$

Armament: None

Machinery: 2 diesels (40 DM), 2 shafts, 4000 HP = 17 kts, 2000 nm/17 kts. Endurance 20 days.

Complement: 30

Built in Leningrad (Sr.-Nevskiy Yard) 1970–78. Project 1993* (Disbar-1): length 65 m, displacement 1200 t.

Project: 535M (KRAB)

NATO Class Name: YELVA

Names:

VM-143

VM-146

VM-152

VM-154

VM-266

VM-268

VM-270

VM-409

VM-413

VM-414

VM-415

VM-416

VM-420

VM-425

VM-807

VM-809

VM-917

Twenty units.

Displacement: 300

Dimensions: $40.9 \times 8.1 \times 2$

Armament: None

Machinery: 2 diesels (3D-12), 2 shafts, 600 HP = 12.5 kts

Complement: 30

Built 1971–83 in Gorokhovyets. Ice-reinforced hull, 1 t crane, diver's decompression chamber. Two such diving boats were built 1973 and 1978 for Cuba. VM-917 was transferred to Libya in Dec. '77.

VM-143 (M.O.D. Bonn)

Project: 364

NATO Class Name: POZHARNY-1

Names:

PzhK-1–55

PDK-70–89

PDK-179

PzhK-425–436
   Eighty-four units.

Displacement: 145.9/181

Dimensions: 34.9 × 6.2 × 1.8

Armament: 4 12.7 mm (UTES-M)

Machinery: 3 diesels (1 450 HP, 2 900 HP), 3 shafts, 2250 HP = 15.7 kts, 280 nm/15.7 kts, 1050 nm/10 kts, fuel 10 t

Complement: 26

   Built 1954–67 in Rybinsk (Volodarskogo yard) and Khabarovsk (Kirova yard) for USSR and for export: Iraq (1), South Yemen (1). Five were on the Black Sea. PZhK-4, PDK-15, PDK-71, PZhK-429, and PZhK-432 were transferred to various organizations. PDK-70 sunk in the Black Sea 1990. PDK-179 in the Caspian.

Project: 522

NATO Class Name: NYRYAT

Names:

VM-9

VM-11

VM-16

VM-18–22

VM-66

VM-70–77

VM-80

VM-82–93

VM-114–142

VM-147–151

VM-153

VM-155–189

VM-191–195

VM-201

VM-203

VM-260

VM-261
   112 units.

Displacement: 120

Dimensions: 28.4 × 5.5 × 1.7

Armament: None

Machinery: 1 diesel, 1 shaft, 450 HP = 12.5 kts, 1500 nm/10 kts

Complement: 15

   Built from 1955 on as patrol and divers' boats. Transfers: Albania, Cuba, Iraq, North Yemen.

Project: V-92/II

Class Name: NEFTEGAZ

Names:

ILGA

KALAR

NIKOLAEV

ALEKSEIY KORTUNOV

UMKA

RADON

Displacement: 2800

Dimensions: 81.2 × 16.3 × 4.9

Armament: None

Machinery: 2 diesels (Skoda-Sulzer), 7200 HP = 15 kts

Complement: 23 plus 12 passengers

Built in Poland (Szeczin) 1982–87 in large numbers (forty-three units). 600 t fuel. *Kalar* is a salvage ship.

Ilga (U.S. Navy)

Project: 714

NATO Class Name: GORYN

Names:

MB-15		
SB-931	BIRYUSINSK	MB-18
MB-32		
MB-35		
MB-36		
MB-38		
SB-521	MB-61	
SB-522		
BAIYKAL'SK	MB-105	
BILIBINO	MB-119	
SB-365	MB-62	
SB-523	MB-64	
SB-524	ex-MB-108	

Thirteen units.

Displacement: 2240/2600

Dimensions: 63.5 × 14 × 5.1

Armament: None

Machinery: 1 diesel, 3500 HP = 15 kts

Complement: 43

Built in Finland (Rauma-Repola) 1977–83. SB-524 and MB-36 on the Black Sea.

MB-105 (U.S. Naval Institute Photographic Collection)

MB-35 (U.S. Naval Institute Photographic Collection)

Project: 745, 07452*

NATO Class Name: SORUM

Names:

AMUR
BURYA
BREST
BUG
URAL
CHUKOTKA
KAMCHATKA
KARELIYA
LADOGA
NEMAN
PRIMORYE
MB-4
MB-6
MB-13
MB-19
MB-25
MB-26
MB-28
MB-30
MB-32
MB-37
MB-56
MB-58
MB-61
MB-76
MB-99
MB-100
MB-148
MB-175
MB-304
MB-307
MB-236
VERNIY
ENISEIY
VIKTOR KINGISEPP
YAN BERZIN
TAYMYR
OS-572*

Forty-one units.

MB-307 (U.S. Navy)

MB-61 (U.S. Naval Institute Photographic Collection)

Displacement: 1210/1620

Dimensions: 58.3 × 12.6 × 4.6

Armament: 2×2 30 mm (AK-230) on PSKR

  2×60 30 mm (AK-630) on *Sakhalin, V. Kingisepp*

Machinery: Diesel-electric, 2 diesel generators (Marki 25-DB 2), 1 shaft, 1 motor (2PG950), 2500 HP = 14 kts, 6750 nm/13 kts; 2 DG 950 generators.

Complement: 35

Built in Yaroslavl and Oktybr'skiy 1973–89. Seagoing tugs with fire-fighting system (3 monitors) and diving equipment. OS-572 re-equipped as ocean survey ship 1988. Four on the Black Sea, including MB-30 and MB-304. Pacific: MB-25, MB-32, MB-37, MB-61, MB-76, MB-99, MB-148, MB-175. *Taymyr* is in the Caspian.

Project: 733, 733S (Salvage)

NATO Class Name: OKHTENSKY

Names:

MB-5

MB-7

MB-8

MB-11

MB-12

MB-16

MB-21

MB-23

MB-24

MB-51

MB-52

MB-54

MB-85

MB-151

MB-152

MB-160

MB-162

MB-163

MB-164

MB-166

MB-170

MB-172

MB-173

MB-174

MB-175

MB-176

LOKSA

NEPTUN

ORION

SATURN

POCHETNIY

SB-3

SB-4

SB-5

SB-6

SB-9

SB-10

MB-166 (V. V. Levchenko)

SB-11
SB-15
SB-28
SB-36
Displacement: 930
Dimensions: 47.6 × 10.4 × 4.1

Armament: 1×2 57 mm in 5 Border Guards units

Machinery: Diesel-electric, 2 diesel generators, 1 shaft, 1500 HP = 13 kts, 8000 nm/7 kts, 6000 nm/13 kts, fuel 187 t

Chief designer Ye. S. Yasil'yev. Built in Leningrad (Petrozavod) 1958–66; sixty-two units in all. Ocean salvage tugs. Two (*Avacha* and *Ayanka,* Project 633P) were built as passenger ships. Five units were in Border Guards units. SB-15 (Black Sea) participated in the salvage of the large ASW ship *Otvazhniy*. Transfers: Cuba (1 in 1976), Egypt (4 in 1966), North Korea (2).

Project: Ch-1100
NATO Class Name: ZENIT
Names:
RB-112
RB-114
RB-119
Thirteen others

Displacement: 380/542

Dimensions: 48.5 × 9.32 × 2.3

Armor: None

Machinery: 2 diesels (Skoda L-275 PN), 2 shafts, 800 HP = 11 kts, 10,000 nm/8 kts; 2 DG-60 generators; fuel 145 t, oil 2.8 t. Endurance 10 days.

Complement: 23

Built in Czechoslovakia from 1951 on. Ice-reinforced hulls. Some were used as heating or steam-generating stations.

RB-122 (V. V. Levchenko)

Project: R-1234?

NATO Class Name: None

Names:

MB-330

MB-340

Displacement: 900

Dimensions: 45 × 10 × 4

Armament: None

Machinery: 2 diesels, 2 shafts, 2000 HP
   Built 1990 in Singapore (Yurong). Bow thrusters.

Project: A-202, AT-202

NATO Class Name: ROSLAVL

Names:

MB-45

MB-50

MB-69

MB-94

MB-95

MB-102

MB-125

MB-134

MB-136

MB-145

MB-146

MB-147

SB-41

SB-46

Displacement: 470/625

Dimensions: 44.5 × 9.5 × 3.3

Armament: None

Machinery: 2 diesels, 2 shafts, 1200 HP = 12 kts, 6000 nm/11 kts, fuel 86.8 t (for 16 days)

Complement: 30
   Built 1953–60 in Riga and in China (Dairen). Two in Romanian Navy.

Project: 730

NATO Class Name: TUGUR

Names:

MB-1–4

MB-6

MB-10

MB-14

MB-17–20

MB-26

MB-27

MB-33

MB-39

MB-40

MB-43

MB-44

MB-47

MB-48

MB-49

MB-55

MB-59

MB-60

MB-65

MB-66

MB-67

MB-70–75

MB-78–84

MB-86–93

MB-96

MB-97

MB-113/118

MB-158

MB-132

MB-423

POYARKOV
   Fifty-eight units.

Displacement: 725/923

Dimensions: 32.5 × 8 × 3

Armament: None

Machinery: 1 shaft reciprocating steam (PM-2), 500 IHP = 10 kts, fuel 50 t. Endurance 6 days.

Complement: 20
   Built in Finland in the 1950s. Steam-generating stations. MB-113 became heat-generator OT-463. MB-423, transferred to the Ministry of Fishing, became *Smelyy*. MB-75 (Pacific) stricken 1984.

Project: N-3291

NATO Class Name: None

Names:

RB-346–348

Displacement: 725/923

Dimensions: 51.5 × 12 × 2.3

Armament: None

Machinery: 2 diesels (G-70), 2 shafts, 2400 HP = 13 kts. Endurance 13 days.

Built in Budapest (Obuda yard) 1988. Roadstead tugs for Baltic.

Project: 498, 04983*, 64985**

NATO Class Name: None

Names:

RB-7

RB-179

RB-217**

RB-239*

RB-265

RB-308

RB-360

RB-362

Eight others

Displacement: 360

Dimensions: 29.3 × 8.3 × 3.4

Armament: None

Machinery: 2 diesels, 2 shafts, 1600 HP = 11 kts

Complement: 3 (watch)

Lead ship built in Gorokhovyets Oct. '83.

Project: 192, 192A*

NATO Class Name: MB-70

Names:

RB-22*

RB-325

RB-326

RB-167

RB-136

RB-280*

Four others

Displacement: 350

Dimensions: 34.8 × 8.5 × 2.8

Armament: None

Machinery: 2 diesels, 1200 HP = 11 kts

Built in Germany (Magdeburg) from 1970. Bow thrusters.

Project: 9.8057, 8059

NATO Class Name: SHOLLE

Names:

Seven units

Displacement: 190/247

Dimensions: 28.9 × 6.8 × 3

Armament: None

Machinery: 1 diesel (R-6 DB 148), 400 HP = 12 kts. Endurance 10 days.

Complement: 13

Built in East Germany from 1962 on at Magdeburg in several versions.

Project: 376U, G-376*, R-376

NATO Class Name: YAROSLAVETS (PO-2)

Names:

P-120–180

MGK-511–726*

RVK-220–500

RVK-780–790

RVK-850–900

UK-190–210

ARMEETS

VNEZAPNIY

BESSTRASHNIY

RK-45

RK-162

MK-300–310

AK-601–634

KTSR-1239

KTSh-1351

Total 640.

Displacement: 32.2/38.2

Dimensions: 21 × 3.9 × 1.4

Armament: Reinforced for installation of two 2M-1 or 2M-7 (AK and PSK were armed)

Machinery: 1 diesel (3D-6), 1 shaft, 150 HP = 10 kts, 1600 nm/8 kts. Endurance 5 days.

Complement: 6

Designed by TsKMB Almaz. Built from 1958 on at Rybinsk, Yaroslavl, as patrol, personnel, ocean survey, and divers' boats. Twenty-six served the Ministry of Internal Affairs of Russia.

Project: 737K, 737M*

NATO Class Name: SIDEHOLE

Names:

RB-1–5

RB-20

RB-23–50

RB-168

RB-193

RB-199

RB-232

RB-233

RB-237

RB-240

RB-244

RB-246

RB-247

RB-256

RB-310

RB-311

Total fifty-six.

Displacement: 183/206

Dimensions: 24.2 × 7.3 × 2.2

Armament: None

Machinery: 2 diesels (6 ChN-25/34), 600 HP = 10 kts

Complement: 12

Built at Leningrad (Petrozavod) 1970–83. Twenty-six tugboats have 900 HP engines, vertical-axis propellers (type DKK-20/5).

Project: 1496

NATO Class Name: None

Names:

RB-63

MB-301

MB-315

MB-317

MB-322

P-303

Six others

Displacement: 91.3/108.5

Dimensions: 23.4 × 5.87 × 1.87

Armament: None

Machinery: 1 diesel, 315 HP = 10.5 kts

Complement: 8

Built from 1966 at Sovgavan and Azov. Tugboats and PSKR for Border Guards.

Project: 286 (NAKHIMOVETS)

NATO Class Name: None

Names:

PSK-1–19

PSK-1993

MK-40–60

Total 40.

Displacement: 85/105

Dimensions: 26.9 × 5.3 × 1.85

Armament: None

Machinery: 1 diesel (3-D12), 300 HP = 11.2 kts

Built from 1954 on in USSR and in China. Ice-reinforced hulls, 123 passengers. PK-10 transferred to fisheries control, renamed *Bryusov.*

Project: 772 and 772U*

NATO Class Name: BRIZA

Names:

MK-40–55

MK-1997

MK-214

PSK-225–236

MK-320–336

MK-501–545

Total eighty-six.

Displacement: 135/144.5 (142*)

Dimensions: 28.8 × 6.3 (6.6*) × 2 (1.86*)

Armament: None

Machinery: 2 diesels (3D-6 or DM-150), 2 shafts, 300 HP = 10 kts, 1100 nm/10 kts. Endurance 5 days.

Complement: 11

Built in Poland (Visla yard, fifty-nine units) and USSR 1967–79 for training and personnel transport. PSK-20-52 on Caspian by Neftyegaz.

Project: 688, 688A

NATO Class Name: BOLVA

Names:

PKZ-32

PKZ-56

PKZ-145

AKHTUBA

ANEROID

VEKSA

PAUGAVA

GAUYA

IMATRA

IRBIT

IG'ICH

ISHIM

KOTLAS
MIASS
MICHURINSK
MOLOGA
NARIN
OLENEK
OLONKA
SAIDA
SAMIR
SAMARGA
SAIMA
SEVERNAYA
TAGIL
TOSNA
TURA
VENGA
VIGA
VORKUTA
VIKSA
ZAPOLYAR'E
TULOMA
PM-80
Twenty-five others
    Total fifty-nine.

Displacement: 6500

Dimensions: $112 \times 13.8 \times 2.8$

Armament: Helicopter pad on 40 units

Machinery: 3 diesel generators of 300 kW

Complement: 350–400 beds

    Built 1960–74 in Finland (at Helsinki, Valmet) as accomodation barges. Accomodations: 30 single bed cabins, 37 doubles, 74 four bed cabins, 60 t provisions (60 days), 120 t diesel fuel (60 days); deadweight 1000 t. *Viksa* became a floating restaurant on the Moskva River in 1991.

Project: 351, 73, etc.

NATO Class Name: None

Names:

RK-126

K-512

RK-1007

    Total ninety.

Displacement:

Dimensions:

Armament:

Machinery: 1 diesel (3D-6) 150 HP

Tugboats and auxiliary launches for lakes, rivers, and calm waters.

    The Ministry of Internal Affairs also operated launches of Projects 371-bis (26 units), 1398 (19 units), KS-100 (7 units), T-63 (2 units), and other craft.

Project: 1415

NATO Class Name: TANJA

Names:

P-1–17

FLAMINGO

PELIKAN

RVK-615

RK-340

RVK-187

RVK-1200

RVK-1200–1254

RVK-1390–1405   Total seventy-nine.

Displacement: 54

Dimensions: $21.2 \times 3.93 \times 1.4$

Armament: Border Patrol boats (18 units, Project PV-1415): 1 MRG-1 grenade launcher; 4 have 1 57 mm gun each

Machinery: 1 diesel (3-D12), 1 shaft, 300 HP = 11 kts

    Built from 1976 on in Rybinsk, Yaroslavl, and on Vyatka Rive (Sosnovskaya Yard) for various roles.

Project: V-99

NATO Class Name: IVA

Names:

VIKhR'-5

VIKhR'-6

VIKhR'-8

VIKhR'-9

Displacement: 3400

Dimensions: $72.3 \times 14.36 \times 4.6$

Machinery: 2 diesels (2D-4T), 8000 HP = 16 kts, 186 t fuel

Complement: 16

    Built 1988–91, *Vikhr-1–4* to gas ministry.

Index

The **Naval Institute Press** is the book-publishing arm of the U.S. Naval Institute, a private, nonprofit, membership society for sea service professionals and others who share an interest in naval and maritime affairs. Established in 1873 at the U.S. Naval Academy in Annapolis, Maryland, where its offices remain today, the Naval Institute has members worldwide.

Members of the Naval Institute support the education programs of the society and receive the influential monthly magazine *Proceedings* and discounts on fine nautical prints and on ship and aircraft photos. They also have access to the transcripts of the Institute's Oral History Program and get discounted admission to any of the Institute-sponsored seminars offered around the country. Discounts are also available to the colorful bimonthly magazine *Naval History.*

The Naval Institute's book-publishing program, begun in 1898 with basic guides to naval practices, has broadened its scope in recent years to include books of more general interest. Now the Naval Institute Press publishes about 100 titles each year, ranging from how-to books on boating and navigation to battle histories, biographies, ship and aircraft guides, and novels. Institute members receive discounts of 20 to 50 percent on the Press's nearly 600 books in print.

Full-time students are eligible for special half-price membership rates. Life memberships are also available.

For a free catalog describing Naval Institute Press books currently available, and for further information about joining the U.S. Naval Institute, please write to:

Membership Department
U.S. Naval Institute
118 Maryland Avenue
Annapolis, MD 21402-5035
Telephone: (800) 233-8764
Fax: (410) 269-7940
Web address: www.usni.org